P9-EMG-723

The
Well-Tempered
Keyboard
Teacher

The
Well-Tempered
Keyboard
Teacher

MARIENNE USZLER
STEWART GORDON
ELYSE MACH

Foreword by André Watts

SCHIRMER BOOKS
A Division of Macmillan, Inc.
NEW YORK

Collier Macmillan Canada
TORONTO

Maxwell Macmillan International
NEW YORK   OXFORD   SINGAPORE   SYDNEY

786.07
Us9w

Barton College Library
Wilson, N.C. 27893

Copyright © 1991 by Schirmer Books
A Division of Macmillan, Inc.

All rights reserved. No part of this book may be reproduced or transmitted
in any form or by any means, electronic or mechanical, including
photocopying, recording, or by any information storage and retrieval system,
without permission in writing from the Publisher.

Schirmer Books
A Division of Macmillan, Inc.
866 Third Avenue, New York, N. Y. 10022

Collier Macmillan Canada, Inc.
1200 Eglinton Avenue East, Suite 200
Don Mills, Ontario M3C 3N1

Library of Congress Catalog Card Number: 90-32083

Printed in the United States of America

printing number
1   2   3   4   5   6   7   8   9   10

Library of Congress Cataloging-in-Publication Data

Uszler, Marienne.
    The well-tempered keyboard teacher / Marienne Uszler, Stewart
Gordon, Elyse Mach ; foreword by André Watts.
        p.   cm.
    ISBN 0-02-871780-5
    1. Piano—Instruction and study.   I. Gordon, Stewart.   II. Mach,
Elyse.   III. Title.
MT220.U9   1990
786'.07—dc20   90-32083
                                                                     CIP
                                                                     MN

CONTENTS

v

FEB 17 1991

FOREWORD

It is more than a little daunting to write an introduction for such a huge collection of historical information and erudition as contained in *The Well-Tempered Keyboard Teacher*. (The witty title does nothing to simplify this task!)

After thinking at length about learning and teaching, I wanted to reexamine the precise definitions of three words: "teach," "learn," and "know."

"Teach" means to cause to know.

"Learn" means to gain knowledge, understanding, and skill.

"Know" means to have understanding and direct cognition of something.

There is a wonderful cycle inherent in the process of learning and teaching. The more we learn, the more we know, the more we can teach—*and*—the more we teach, the more we learn. This book addresses that cycle because it is not a "how-to" volume, but a source of information about many aspects of keyboard pedagogy.

When we listen to a concertizing musician we become aware not only of relative strengths and weaknesses in execution but, over a period of years, we are made conscious of the presence or absence of ongoing musical development. This development is nothing more than the ability to learn. In the case of many performers, this translates into the ability to teach oneself and learn from one's own teaching—in other words, having the learn/know/teach/learn cycle inside oneself. This never-ending process is what occurs in performers we cherish. We cherish them precisely because they teach us something every time they recreate a musical composition.

This continuing acquisition and dissemination of knowledge is also the teacher's joy and responsibility. A quote from Jean-Jacques Rousseau points very nicely to the responsibility: "The apparent ease with which children learn is their ruin." I find this sweeping generalization slightly annoying but very thought-provoking. Although Rousseau was, for the most part, referring to the "monkey see, monkey do" abilities of children, I also believe that his statement speaks strongly to the student-teacher relationship. Lack of knowledge coupled with the desire to learn likens a person of any age to a child in its innocence. With intelligent, informed, and responsible teaching, we would all wish for the "ease with which children learn" because our results would be far from our ruin indeed. I like to think Rousseau would be pleased that those of his intellectual children involved with the keyboard can avoid their ruin by reading this book.

André Watts

PREFACE

"Well-tempered" certainly has historical overtones. To some the allusion seems hallowed, implying reference to a landmark work. To others the adjective is somewhat nebulous, if not awkward. (Consider the usual explanation, by teacher to student, of the exact meaning of *Das wohltemperierte Clavier*.) It is one of those taken-for-granted definitions that every pianist assumes other pianists fully grasp. Why, then, should "well-tempered" be used in the title of this book?

A first analogy relates to use. The famous "48" are not meant to be read or performed as a set, from beginning to end. One selects what one needs or desires. *The Well-Tempered Clavier* is a resource upon which to draw both intermittently and over a period of time. So with this book. It is, first of all, intended as a resource. Its aim is to present material and information not always easily gathered between two covers.

In *The Well-Tempered Keyboard Teacher* there is information relating to everyday studio needs—surveys of educational print material on a number of levels, advice about business concerns, suggestions for teaching the transfer student. There is information not available elsewhere—a historical look at the growth and development of educational print materials and the sources from which particular "schools" or "movements" have arisen. There is information not condensed elsewhere—salient facts concerning the history of keyboard pedagogy in general, and specific innovators in particular.

There is a suggested point of reference for the pianist considering a career as a keyboard teacher and practical information weighing the advantages and disadvantages of several routes such a career might take. There is provocative material—honest discussion of competitions, exposure to the thoughts of great contemporary pianists regarding technique, memorization, nervousness, and teaching. There is "new direction" information—an overview of electronic technology, a survey of twentieth-century learning theories, a discussion of the keyboard pedagogy major. What is offered is a compendium of information, not a handbook of "how-to" techniques.

A second reason to borrow the adjective "well-tempered" relates to format. The WTC was a practical work, one that sought to prove a point. The preludes and fugues were sequenced chromatically to epitomize the useful value of a particular tuning system. This book also is meant to be practical. While the overall style is narrative, there are a considerable number of comparison charts, repertoire lists, and methods descriptions. In most cases comparative points of view offer the reader the chance to draw individual conclusions rather than to react to the personal perspective of the writer. The repertoire lists are selective and annotated as objectively as possible. Care has been taken to provide a serviceable bibliography both in the footnotes to most chapters and in the appendixes.

A third analogy is more sensitive. That the WTC was a pedagogical work Bach made clear in the original title: "For the Use and Profit of the Musical Youth Desirous of Learning." It is considered by most a kind of touchstone, a work by which keyboard performers of more than two and one-half centuries have measured themselves as well as others. As such, it has contributed to the setting of standards. While this book makes no claim to setting standards, its aim is to encourage readers to be aware of living up to their own. One way in which to do so, of course, is to acquire or develop a broad range of knowledge about one's own field. At times this a matter of supplementing an existing information base. It may also mean expanding one's scope of interest in entirely new directions or challenging oneself to look beyond comfortable and accustomed surfaces. It seems reasonable to believe that a keyboard teacher with curiosity and discrimination will necessarily be "tempered" by further, or deeper, inquiry.

Thus the "well-tempered keyboard teacher" is one who will use this book in several ways and for different purposes.

A number of authors have collaborated in the writing of this book. Although each may express ideas in a different voice, there is commonality in their desire to provide substantial information without representing a specific, much less a united, view or position. In that sense, this is not a "personal" book. There is no wish to express or represent a particular performance or pedagogical philosophy. Singleness of purpose is found, instead, in an effort to be helpful—by furnishing data that may enable others to save time, make better-informed judgments and choices, access a wide range of materials, become acquainted with a more extensive bibliography, uncover new interests, and—ultimately—to integrate the conglomerate in a uniquely "tempered" approach to keyboard teaching.

ACKNOWLEDGMENTS

The Well-Tempered Keyboard Teacher owes much to the ideas and efforts of many in addition to those listed as authors and contributors. The book began to take shape quite by accident, growing out of conversations between Ken Stuart, then Schirmer's editor-in-chief, and Elyse Mach. In planning for a book with such wide scope, it seemed wise to involve several individuals, each contributing his or her expertise. And so the project grew and grew . . . and grew. Maribeth Anderson Payne, Schirmer's current editor-in-chief, came on board very early in the book's history and has served through the long gestation process as sounding-board, counselor, and friend.

As each author joined the task force, outlines shifted and expanded to accommodate differing opinions and special concerns. The book's ultimate formation as a resource volume rather than a practical handbook evolved from discussions at national conferences, in hotel rooms and restaurants, over the phone, and during long plane rides.

There are many individuals each author and contributor would want to cite as helpful and significant. While not all can be noted here, some must be recognized as uniquely valuable. Gratitude then: to Nancy Bricard and Sherwyn Woods who took time to react to so many ideas in crucial chapters and who shared special insights and pertinent references; to Dean Elder and Homer Ulrich whose collegiality and guidance have been long-standing and generous; to Ann and David Pope and Christopher Pavlakis for innumerable helpful suggestions and staunch support; to Richard Clark, colleague in USC's Department of Education, whose careful reading of the learning theories chapter allowed its author to publish it with some degree of equanimity; to Jim Bonn who, flying between concerts, sifted through the ideas relating to technique and offered both perspective and helpful argument; to Maurice Hinson, whose special insights were so much a part of the early planning; to Bob Silverman who, as friend of all the authors, spent hours reading a very long manuscript at a critical time in the editing stages; to the official reviewers all of whose observations were noted and appreciated; to André Watts whose foreword is as gracious as it is instructive; to Ralph Pierce who cheerfully provided publication information whenever asked; and to the review board members of the USC Faculty Research and Innovation Fund who saw fit to make an extended library tour for one of the authors a reality.

Schirmer's editorial staff has shepherded the entire project with adroitness and patience. Special thanks are due Gretchen Gordon, an eagle-eyed copy editor; Robert Axelrod, who held things together amid changes and fluctuations; and Michael Sander, whose production savvy guided this book through the final stages.

Beyond any doubt, those with whom the authors and contributors have worked and lived are owed loving thanks for a thousand big and little things— for furnishing quiet, information, food, phone time, interest, trips to mailboxes and federal express offices, affection, and support. It is largely they who kept these writers reasonably "well-tempered."

AUTHORS AND CONTRIBUTORS

AUTHORS

Marienne Uszler is a professor in the Department of Keyboard Studies at the University of Southern California. She is editor for articles for *American Music Teacher,* and review and contributing editor for *The Piano Quarterly.* She co-authored *Piano Pedagogy in the College Curriculum* and published numerous articles and reviews in keyboard periodicals. She chairs the Committee on Historical Research for the National Conference on Piano Pedagogy and is national coordinator of Music Learning and Research for the Music Teachers National Association.

Stewart Gordon is a professor in the Department of Keyboard Studies at the University of Southern California. He has served as music department chair at the University of Maryland (College Park) and as Provost and Vice President for Academic Affairs at Queens College of the City University of New York. He established and for over a decade directed the University of Maryland International Piano Festival and Competition (now the William Kapell Competition) and is current artistic director of Savannah Onstage, an annual music festival in Savannah, Georgia.

Elyse Mach is a professor in the Department of Music at Northeastern Illinois University. She is author of *Great Pianists Speak for Themselves* Vols. 1 and 2, *Contemporary Class Piano,* and editor of *The Liszt Studies* and *Franz Liszt-Rare and Familiar-28 Pieces for Piano.* She has been an American Liszt Society member from its inception and published numerous articles on Liszt pedagogy. She has served as Chicago *Sun-Times* music critic and has three times been recipient of the Presidential Merit Award at Northeastern Illinois University.

CONTRIBUTORS

Gayle Kowalchyk is a keyboard editor for Alfred Publishing Company and editor for *Keys* piano music magazine. Together with her husband, E. L. Lancaster, she operates a large independent piano studio that combines both group and private instruction. She is the author of instructional materials for beginning and intermediate pianists.

E. L. Lancaster is a professor of music and Associate Dean of the College of Fine Arts at the University of Oklahoma. He serves in national leadership capacities for the Music Teachers National Association and the National Conference on Piano Pedagogy. He is the author of over twenty instructional books for beginning and intermediate pianists.

Louise Lepley chairs the Piano Department at the Colburn School of Performing Arts in Los Angeles. She is an experienced competition adjudicator and her students have distinguished themselves as festival and competition winners. Her published articles focus on the development of the precollege professional student.

Thomas J. Lymenstull is an assistant professor in the Department of Keyboard Studies at the University of Southern California. As a Fulbright Fellow he studied at the Vienna Hochschule. He began using electronic instruments and computers in his private and institutional teaching to explore possibilities for developing the creative potential of his students.

Barbara English Maris is a professor of music at The Catholic University of America. A recipient of research grants from the National Endowment for the Humanities, she has a special interest in performance practices of the eighteenth century and piano repertoire of the twentieth century. She is published extensively in professional music journals.

PART ONE

Keyboard Teaching as a Profession

CHAPTER I

Career Possibilities

Many things said about the piano-teaching profession twenty years ago are no longer true. The title of this book is itself indicative of change. "Keyboard" has, once again, the many meanings it had two centuries ago. Whereas then keyboard might have meant harpsichord, organ, spinet, clavichord, virginal, or fortepiano, the word "keyboard" may now be used with reference to a grand piano, a studio upright, a pipe organ, an electronic organ, an electronic piano, a digital piano, a synthesizer, or any number of other electronic keyboard instruments. The eighty-eight key acoustic piano is no longer "everyman's" keyboard.[1]

What does this mean to the young pianist contemplating a career as a teacher and who expects to be actively pursuing that career into the twenty-first century? First, it means that playing the acoustic piano itself will become a choice. The prospective student will not only have selected the acoustic piano as one among many types of instruments, but these other instruments will also include other kinds of keyboards. That was not the case during most of the nineteenth and twentieth centuries.

Second, manufacturers of musical instruments are already producing a wide selection of keyboards that are less expensive than acoustic pianos. These keyboards have advantages. They are easily portable, occupy less space, may be practiced without disturbing others, may not need tuning, and often provide enhanced backgrounds and special effects. Parents who are considering a musical education for their children will have increasing reason to gravitate toward the purchase of the less expensive high-tech keyboard rather than the eighty-eight-key (even secondhand) acoustic piano while they wait to see whether the child will enjoy lessons or show promise. Adults beginning keyboard instruction may find these electronic instruments more enjoyable as well as more accessible.

The teacher of beginners who is knowledgeable, even if not entirely enthusiastic, about electronic keyboards will more likely be making a living than will the teacher whose only teaching instrument is the acoustic piano.

> A studio with both acoustic and electronic instruments can offer an inducement to students who otherwise would resist piano lessons. The synthesizer and its electronic relatives can be a Siren on the rocks to lure these reluctant keyboardists into our studios. Once in the studio their interest in the piano will grow along with their discriminatory powers.[2]

Further, the availability of high-tech accessory equipment (e.g., the computer, sequencer, drum machine) that may be used in teaching even the eighty-eight key acoustic piano will give the advantage to the teacher who knows how to employ such equipment in the studio or college classroom.

Another element of change can be seen in the types of student keyboard instruction is attracting. The range of those who currently take keyboard lessons has widened considerably within the past few decades. Whereas the usual independent studio used to be populated almost entirely by students aged six to eighteen, all of whom took individual lessons on an acoustic piano, it now often includes groups of preschool students, adult beginners (studying in small groups or otherwise), leisure pianists returning after an absence of playing and/ or studying, and students of all ages in some type of group instruction (perhaps musicianship or ensemble classes)—this in addition to elementary and high school–aged students, many of whom still study piano individually.

Piano instruction at the college level is likewise more diversified. Keyboard majors still take individual lessons and play in master/studio classes, juries, recitals, and competitions. But members of the keyboard faculty also provide group instruction to non-keyboard music majors and non-music majors (frequently in electronic piano laboratories), teach other specialized classes (e.g., keyboard harmony, functional piano classes for elementary school teachers, sight-reading, accompanying, ensemble classes, and so on), offer individual or small group instruction to music and non-music majors, teach classes in piano literature (both general and specialized), organize piano pedagogy courses and programs and, increasingly, supervise student teaching in many of the preceding teaching situations.

It would be encouraging if the piano-teacher-to-be might be able to regard these varied possibilities as so many different hats to wear, with only the necessity of choosing the one that fits or looks most attractive. The simple truth, however, is that piano teachers will need to wear at least several hats in order to run a financially, as well as musically, successful independent studio. There will always be a few outstanding specialists, of course, who will be able to teach only the most gifted students, at the same time pursuing active playing careers, and realizing significant incomes as a result. But these artist-teacher "stars" have never truly been numerous.

A look backward provides evidence that the independent piano teacher has been—probably for more than a century—the core of the music profession. Many practicing music professionals owe something to a local piano teacher who provided encouragement as well as instruction. This is true even for those who have become professionals on instruments other than the piano or who are now singing, conducting, composing, doing music research, or writing music criticism. However, those piano teachers—most of them female—generally were not the sole breadwinners of families nor were they individuals expecting to make mortgage payments on single-person homes or condominiums. Today's piano teacher *is* often a person in such a position and must, therefore, look to make a living wage as a piano teacher that is considerably higher than what would have passed for such even two decades ago.

> In order to make a good living [the piano teacher] will have to recruit and teach a large number of students. This may mean giving up evening and weekend time, paying 100 percent of his health insurance and retirement and, at the same time, charging less for a lesson than what he has to pay per hour to a mechanic to fix his car.[3]

The independent studio teacher must now also be a business person as well as a musician and educator.

How does one develop from a sixteen-year-old piano-playing contest winner into a musically prepared and professionally savvy—a "well-tempered"—keyboard teacher?

THE PROFESSIONAL EDUCATION OF THE PIANO TEACHER

No one ever makes a decision very early on to become a piano teacher. One first becomes aware that playing the piano is something that one can do very well and that it is a most important part of one's own life. Therefore, the first step is to become an excellent pianist or, at least, the very best pianist that one can be. That goal is never fully satisfied. Throughout one's professional life there will always be the search for still better technique, still greater musical assurance, a still richer repertoire. Although most young people are not very highly developed pianists by their mid-teens, identity as a pianist and a desire to have a career as such becomes clear at about this time. Having a pianistic career is a generalized dream involving nearly equal parts of playing and feeling good about oneself.

The first major career step is usually enrollment in a professional music school, whether college or conservatory. There "career" takes on new (at times quite unexpected) dimensions. The first of these is likely to be the element of competition. Second, the piano faculty seems insistent that one be able to sight-read, accompany, transpose, learn repertoire rapidly and on one's own, attend to a technical regimen without much supervision or encouragement, and (above all) find time to practice. Third, many other musical areas require one's attention. Harmonic study, ear training, analysis, detailed knowledge of music history, learning how to read an orchestral score—all of these become components of one's education in addition to those studies required by one's major. The pursuance of a "career" is then more clearly understood.

A later aspect of professional development involves preparing the student to become a teacher as well as a performer. (This, in itself, is a phenomenon that has burgeoned only recently.) For the pianist, pedagogical training—although it differs from school to school—is usually more extensive, more complex, and more well-organized than the pedagogical preparation provided for any other instrumentalist.[4] At this point the young professional pianist is, at least, made aware of the extent of methodological literature, is given some working knowledge of teaching strategies, and may be introduced to the idea of developing a teaching philosophy. In some professional schools, there is also an opportunity to do student teaching under supervision.

The young pianist, even at this point, may not yet wish to become a teacher. The desire to make music is stronger than the desire to teach someone else to do the same. For many pianists, becoming a teacher is a decision made more by necessity than by true ambition. Often one begins to teach because one has already come so far and has no great desire to pursue a different professional career. Although this seeming backing into place is the route traveled by many pianists in the process of becoming teachers, a large number of them discover a new part of themselves when they begin to teach. They learn that interest in the development of others feeds the self. Examining and choosing ways to direct others' playing illumines the knowledge of one's own technique and musicality. Thus a professional self begins to emerge as the result of making *and* teaching music. The career as a pianist is more multi-faceted, by necessity and by choice, than what was dimly envisioned years earlier.

PROFESSIONAL TEACHING POSSIBILITIES

This overview assumes that the career of the keyboard teacher will include continued performance at whatever levels or in whichever situations the teacher may have opportunities to play. Although these performing opportunities are satisfying, important, and necessary to the teacher, they are seldom financially very rewarding. There are, of course, a small number of pianists who are good jazz/pop musicians/improvisers who may play professionally in commercial situations such as restaurants, clubs, and the like. Such positions (if one can find them, and if one is willing to work the hours required) may afford moderately good, to very good, financial support. Yet, making one's living as a pianist and teacher usually centers around one of the following roles and often includes functioning in several:

The independent piano teacher

The piano teacher working in a cooperative partnership

The piano teacher in a precollege or community school

The college/university piano teacher

The first category includes the majority of pianists. There are many **advantages to running an independent piano studio.** The independent studio may be part of one's home or it may be outside the home (e.g., in a shopping center, neighborhood church, or community center). The independent teacher:

Answers to no one other than the self

Earns 100 percent of the profits

Sets one's own schedule—daily, weekly, and yearly

Arranges one's own working environment

Establishes one's own studio policies and teaching preferences

Often does not have to travel, or travel very far, to work

Is bound only by personal talent, energy, and ambition

There are, of course, some **disadvantages to teaching independently:**

One usually cannot begin as a fully employed person, but needs to build a studio gradually.

Income can almost never be determined in advance.

It is difficult to offer scholarships for needy, deserving students.

Working hours are likely to be concentrated in the late afternoons, early to late evenings, and weekends.

One must arrange carefully for summer employment.

One must provide one's own insurance, retirement plan, and "paid" vacations.

One must do one's own billing and bookkeeping and keep accurate account of professional expenses for tax records.

One may feel isolated from musical colleagues unless one is an active participant in professional organizations.

Homogeneity in the studio is unlikely. One will usually need to teach students of disparate ages and advancement levels.

Teaching in one's home may "de-professionalize" the environment and may be disruptive to the family at large.

The **cooperative partnership involves** the establishment of a teaching studio or music center together with one, or several, colleagues who share all financial and musical risks, responsibilities, and profits. Here the **advantages** seem to include "best of both worlds" aspects:

Joint financing may allow for a more professional-looking teaching environment and better professional equipment than one could afford to provide for oneself.

All facets of recruitment (e.g., publicity and contacts) are shared. What promotes one, promotes all. This is especially beneficial to the teacher just starting out, or new in the area.

One works with (a) colleague(s), thereby stimulating professional growth and challenge.

One's students have greater opportunity to hear and see other students, participate in more varied recital and/or group activities, and develop a sense of musical community.

Tax benefits may be greater since business aspects of running the studio are more visible.

Billing and bookkeeping may be more complicated, but there is greater likelihood that these duties would be performed by the "business-inclined" partner, a part-time paid professional, or a competent family member.

The **partnership arrangement has some built-in difficulties.**

Finding the right partner(s) with whom one is willing and able to share both financial/musical concerns and interests is not at all simple.

A joint financial investment generally presupposes that the teachers undertaking such are relatively stable in their own careers as well as in their intentions to reside in a particular area. Teachers beginning a career may want, or may have, to regard themselves as more mobile.

A joint partnership becomes a legal as well as a professional and musical venture.

In many respects, disadvantages in the cooperative partnership arrangement mirror those of the teacher in the independent studio: income is never predictable; the working hours are similar; there must be self-provision for insurance, retirement, and vacations; summer employment must be anticipated.

There are other types of independent studio organization than those summarized here.[5] The case can be made for the itinerant teacher, the cooperative multi-teacher studio (business expenses are shared, but the teachers are otherwise self-employed), and the teacher in the community arts center. Varied styles of studio organization underscore the possibility of diversity as well as the entrepreneurship with which individual teachers may develop unique teaching situations in specific locations.

Some pianists teach as **faculty members in varied types of music institution** where they are able to secure full-time, or substantial part-time, employment teaching in a precollege (preparatory) department or in a community (private or public) performing arts school. The following **advantages** are typical of such situations:

Teachers share in, and benefit from, association with the name and reputation of the school.

Teachers generally do not have to recruit students. In some instances, they do not even audition students. (This may not always be an advantage.)

Professionalism of the school environment may attract more serious students.

If teachers are full-time faculty, they have a guaranteed (or, at least, a reasonably predictable) income. They may receive retirement, medical, or insurance benefits.

Teachers are provided with a studio and instrument(s), and usually have access to other types of audiovisual equipment.

Teachers are not responsible for billing, bookkeeping, or collecting tuition and fees.

The faculty shares the services of a support staff (receptionist, secretary, building maintenance, and so on).

The teacher may enjoy the stimulation of working with musical colleagues in both teaching and performing situations.

Financial aid may be available to students without the teacher's needing to sacrifice personal income.

The school may pay for membership in professional organizations for its faculty.

Homogeneity within a studio is possible. One may sometimes work with students of a specific age group or advancement level.

These advantages have **offsetting features**:

Lesson fees and teaching salaries are often much lower than those commanded by independent studio teachers of equal experience and background.

Teachers may have little or no choice in the selection of students for their own studios. Early "typecasting" of a teacher may limit the kind of students assigned to that teacher.

An instructor may be required to teach a certain number of beginners (or students in other categories) as part of the school policy or in order to equalize the teaching load.

Teachers may be expected to serve on jury and audition committees, or offer occasional workshops and clinics for no extra fee.

Faculty is sometimes expected to use specific teaching materials.

Teachers may feel caught in a situation where there is little hope of advancement either in prestige, fringe benefits, or teaching fees.

Teachers may be deluded into hoping that teaching at the precollege level is a likely prelude to college teaching.

The number of precollege teaching positions available in the United States is limited. In addition, it is difficult to find out about vacancies that do, or might, arise in such schools since these positions are not regularly advertised in any public, specific places (as are university and college positions). The positions often go to graduates of the university or professional school to which the pre-college school is attached (if that is the case), or they are filled by means of personal recommendations and other professional contacts of those already on the faculty. Some of these positions are also filled by persons who have joint appointments with a college school of music (often in conjunction with a piano pedagogy program).

The pianist who teaches on the **keyboard faculty of a university or college has a different set of advantages**:

The prestige of being associated with a professional school of music and/or an institution of higher learning

A fixed yearly income

Retirement, insurance, and medical benefits; family of faculty are (reasonably) assured of obtaining a college education

Granting of tenure assures continued employment

Possibilities for promotion, advancement, and upward (or lateral) moves to other institutions

Possibly having the summer months to pursue professional interests; most faculty teach summer programs or give clinics, workshops, and master classes to supplement their income

Association with colleagues in both performing and teaching situations

Working with higher-level students on repertoire that is substantial and musically satisfying

There are notable disadvantages:

Salaries in university and college schools of music, as in arts faculties generally, often are among the lowest salaries paid to higher-education professionals. Relative to comparable professionals outside the academic world, music faculty salaries are very low indeed.

Requisites for advancement and promotion, and the complexities of pursuing such, are more demanding than ever before.

Tenure decisions are granted with greater care. Many institutions find it more financially expedient to employ several part-time faculty than to grant tenure to one individual. Many positions are advertised as non-tenure-track positions.

Music faculty teaching loads are frequently heavy, almost always heavier than teaching loads of faculty in other disciplines.

Full-time faculty are expected to participate in much committee, recruitment, and administrative work in addition to serving on jury and audition committees.

Advancement and promotion are determined by the quantity and quality of professional work one does that is in addition to one's teaching responsibilities.

Securing a college teaching position is difficult because so many pianists
are adequately qualified to teach at the college level. "From the time a freshman
piano major begins his college or university studies to the time he receives his
degree, somewhere between 28,000 and 32,000 other piano majors will also
have graduated!"[6] Admittedly, these numbers represent pianists graduating with
the bachelor, not the doctoral, degree. But many students pursue higher degrees just because there seems to be little they can "do" with degree(s) they
have. College administrators, on the other hand, currently are speaking about
going through a period of retrenchment. No longer are schools multiplying (as
in mid-nineteenth-century America), and many that are in existence are worri-
edly seeking students. Course loads of the tenured piano faculty now include
many teaching hours devoted to students who are not keyboard majors. Junior
faculty positions are disappearing. The college teaching scene will not change
appreciably for the better in the relatively near future (except, perhaps, in some
specialized fields as the market dictates). The young professional pianist seeking
a college teaching position is between a rock and a hard place.

Conclusion

The keyboard-teacher-to-be needs to look at the current and near-future scene
for pianists in this country without wearing rose-colored glasses. An analysis of
the 1985 marketplace offers a realistic perspective.

> Economic fluctuations have made dramatic changes in the job market for piano
> teachers in the last decade. The demand for private teachers has increased in many
> areas because of cutbacks in public school programs. At the same time a decrease
> in the number of music majors has caused a declining demand for college piano
> faculty.[7]

All piano teacher "roles" should be examined, noting that each has pros, each
has cons. It is often the case that the person ready, willing, and able to do several
things will likely be successful in finding a teaching position somewhere or
will know how to create something in a given situation or circumstance. Few
professionals are handed "plums" at the outset of their careers. Most work his-
tories involve seizing the opportunity at hand, making a success of it, using that
experience to open new doors, once again utilizing what is then at hand to
progress in yet further, or other, directions. Moving in this way through one's
professional life requires energy and demands risk, but it is ultimately fulfilling
because one is always an active ingredient in establishing one's own professional identity.

CHAPTER 2

Functioning as a Professional

Although keyboard instructors may pursue that profession in a variety of settings, the greatest number operate independent studios and/or offer keyboard instruction in music institutions. This chapter will examine practicalities relating to each of these situations and then briefly discuss alternative, or auxiliary, careers.

THE INDEPENDENT KEYBOARD TEACHER

Equipping the Independent Studio

It must be stressed at the outset that the only matter of real importance in the establishment or maintenance of a successful piano studio is the quality of the teaching. No quantity of equipment, no particular method, no magic scheduling formula, no specified amount of space can be equated with, or ensure, excellent instruction. Many young pianists, when contemplating the establishment of an independent teaching career, are frustrated or discouraged when they see diagrams of elaborate private studios or read of the value and importance of audiovisual equipment in the operation of the successful professional studio. Therefore the following outline distinguishes between "must-haves" and "if-you-cans." Note also that the "if-you-cans" are presented in order of day-to-day practicality, with the least expensive items listed first.

TYPE OF INSTRUCTION OFFERED IN THE STUDIO	MUST-HAVES	IF-YOU-CANS
Individual lessons	Acoustic piano(s) or Electronic or digital keyboard	Chalkboard Cassette recorder/player Music file Computer + software Rhythm machine Sequencer
Small groups (2–4) + partner or individual lessons	Acoustic piano(s) or Electronic or digital keyboard	Chalkboard Cassette recorder/player Music file Plastic (dummy) keyboards Tables, chairs Computer + software Rhythm machine Sequencer
Preschool children	Acoustic piano(s) or Electronic or digital keyboard Large, free space	Chalkboard; flannel board Rhythm instruments Cassette recorder/player Plastic (dummy) keyboards Tables, chairs (small) Music file
Large groups (5–8) + partner or individual lessons	2–4 acoustic pianos (or) Acoustic piano + 2–4 electronic or digital keyboards	Chalkboard Cassette recorder/player Music file Ensemble, multiple-piano music library Computer + software Rhythm machine Sequencer

N.B. For further information about electronic equipment, see Chap. 24.

Scheduling

The times of the day and week that the independent teacher will work are not entirely a matter of choice. If the studio roster is composed almost entirely of children, one will usually teach during mid- and late afternoon hours, early evenings, and on the weekends. Some teachers also offer lessons very early in the morning, before children go to school. If the studio roster includes a percentage of adult (college-age and above) students, there will be considerable concentration of teaching in the early and late evenings if most of the adults work, or teaching may occur in the mornings or early afternoons if most of the adults are not (fully) employed. Preschool classes may also be scheduled in the mornings or early afternoons.

An independent teacher who teaches varied student age-groups therefore may find it possible to fill a day's schedule in the following manner: early morning individual lessons; preschool morning classes; early afternoon adult lessons (group sessions); late afternoon and early evening lessons (group sessions). With such scheduling, it may be feasible to leave a weekday free without jeopardizing one's income. One might also look into the possibility of using released-time from school for teaching students who could obtain such. Allowance for this depends upon the school system.

The matter of scheduling is personal. Some teachers prefer to plan large blocks of tightly scheduled teaching time, thus allowing different blocks of time to be used to maximum advantage. Some teachers, however, need breathing spells in order to sustain their teaching and physical energies. For yet other teachers, arranging a varied schedule (e.g., adult small groups in the early afternoon, small groups plus partner lessons in the late afternoon, individual lessons in the early evening) allows them to teach almost steadily yet maintain some resilience in their energy level because the teaching situations change.

Group sessions (whether regularly scheduled or occasional musicianship, ensemble, or studio class sessions) may also help a teacher sustain personal teaching concentration and energy since the group dynamic in such situations allows for interaction among group members and does not always demand direct interaction between the student(s) and teacher. Although time spent in preparing for and leading a group session is, in some ways, more challenging and time-consuming for the teacher, it should be remembered that loss of energy and interest is not necessarily linked with the actual amount of hours spent in teaching. It is obvious that the teacher who is capable of teaching in many different teaching situations is in the position of creating a more flexible schedule.

Scheduling Example 1: Small Group Plus Partner Lessons

3:00–3:30   Students A, B

3:30–4:15   Students A, B, C, D

4:15–4:45   Students C, D

Partner lessons: Work at technique, individual repertoire

Group sessions: Presentation of concepts/skills; ear training, rhythm, improvisation activities; ensemble; mini-performance sessions

Scheduling Example 2: Small Group Plus Individual Lessons

Monday: 3:00–3:30   Student A

               3:30–4:15   Students A, B, C, D

	4:15–4:45	Student B
	4:45–5:15	Student E
	5:15–6:00	Students E, F, G, H
	6:00–6:30	Student F
Wednesday:	3:00–3:30	Student C
	3:30–4:00	Student D
	4:00–4:30	Student G
	4:30–5:00	Student H

Purposes of each session type: As in Scheduling Example 1, above

Lesson Fees

There can be no formula for determining appropriate lesson fees. To some extent, keyboard teachers are subject to what the market bears. Ideally, personal experience and background would be the major determining factor in the setting of lesson fees. Sometimes that is not the case. The beginning teacher is likely to feel this disparity most keenly. The diploma from "the best" school, the M.M., the D.M.A., or the competition prize no longer guarantee employment, let alone richly rewarded employment.

Which conditions must be examined to determine what a teacher's market can bear?

> To establish a fair and appropriate fee for your services you should consider five important factors: the prevailing rates of other music teachers in the community; the economic status of the families you expect to reach; the demands for lessons locally; the overall costs of operating an independent studio; and your own background, experience, and level of musical and pedagogical expertise.[1]

Although inclusion of the last factor, one's personal credentials, suggests that these do influence the setting of the fee to some degree, the other four factors are equally influential.

In many cases, the location of the studio may be the dominant determinant. While it may be tempting to locate one's studio in a more affluent area (hoping thereby to command a higher lesson fee), bear in mind that children of affluent parents are also likely to be involved in many activities (computer clubs; tennis, swimming, or dancing lessons; and so on) that will compete for music study time. If one expects or hopes to teach many children, the studio must be located in a family neighborhood, near a school (with curtailment of many school music programs there is greater reliance on the independent teacher to provide music instruction and performance opportunities), or near a church (perhaps one that has a strong interest in music activities or that sponsors Head Start sessions or after-school programs for "latchkey" children).[2] If one expects or hopes to teach many adults, beginners and otherwise, the studio should be proximate to places where adults work (such as shopping malls and downtown areas) and live (such as condo developments and retirement communities). There are many ways to access this information, including writing "the city hall's urban planning department and [requesting] maps showing population density and neighborhood make-up. This information will be most productive if [studied] in conjunction with a map showing the location of schools and churches."[3] Before setting up a studio, it is important to check city zoning laws and regulations. These differ considerably in terms of both scope and enforcement. This may be an especially sensitive consideration for a teacher intending to establish a home studio.

Although the majority of independent teachers probably use part of the home as the studio, there is increasing interest in establishing studios or renting teaching space outside of the home—in a church, school, community center, music store, small shopping mall, and so forth. The costs incurred in operating an outside studio often require an initial outlay of funds that may be greater than expenses attached to teaching at home, but the feasibility of reaching more and/or certain types of students may be worth the investment in the long run. Establishing a joint studio or music school with other teachers may be a way of gaining access to this kind of teaching space.

Professional Billing

Tuition costs are best presented to students (or parents) as term or yearly rates, rather than as weekly or monthly payments. Longer-term billing encourages the student to think in terms of commitment and perseverance. Music lessons should not be thought of as something that one considers on a contingency basis (if things get hectic or become less fun, lessons are discontinued). Term billing also encourages regular attendance. Payment should be made in advance. Some reduction may be offered to those who pay in advance for the year or for the term. Payments might also be scheduled in installments—for instance, two or three times a term. If installment payments are made more frequently (e.g., the first or last lesson of the month), it must be understood that these are installment payments, not payments merely to extend instruction through the next month. This is difficult to enforce in practice, however. The teacher may also wish to consider assessing a late charge to encourage prompt payment. Additional consideration may be extended to families with several children enrolled.

A teacher able to offer different types of instruction, in varied teaching situations, will find that flexibility may increase financial returns. Tuition rates, of course, will vary dependent upon the type of instruction arranged, and the length of contact time with the instructor. Tuition rates might, and probably should, include some of the following (as appropriate): a yearly registration fee to help defray billing, phoning, mailing expenses; recital fee(s); fees for musicianship or ensemble classes (if these are not already included in the type of instruction for which the student is registered); a library fee (whereby the teacher may accumulate a sight-reading or ensemble library, or a library of standard books and pieces to be used in lieu of "forgotten" music); a computer fee (for weekly computer time either before or after the lesson).

The billing form should clearly explain what the fee covers, the length of each term or semester, the policy regarding missed lessons, late charges, possible considerations for advance payment or instruction for additional family members, and other relevant information.

Bookkeeping

The business aspect of operating an independent studio includes record keeping. Not only is this necessary for tax preparation, but it is also important in order to apprehend one's real income. Especially when setting up a studio—for the first time, or in a new situation—expenses, as well as income, must be anticipated. Care in projecting expenses, while not always easy to do, may make the difference between financial success or failure.

Professional expenses also become tax deductions, but only if piano teaching is one's primary career. The keeping of accurate records, together with accompanying receipts and cancelled checks, is crucial. The best and easiest way to do this is to: (1) keep one's books up to date weekly (a small nuisance every week offsets a yearly major headache); (2) create a filing system wherein one can immediately place receipts, invoices, and other bookkeeping information into separate, appropriate categories; (3) total one's expenses and income at the end of each month (which, again, makes the yearly job much simpler and also keeps one apprised of one's financial status). A computer used as a teaching aid also can serve one's business by being the depository of bookkeeping records, student information, repertoire files, and music/record/cassette library inventory.

It is always best to seek advice from a tax consultant concerning one's individual tax situation. "Tax laws have recently been the subject of such dramatic revision that only the sophisticated professional can be aware of all the ramifications."[4] The determination of legal deductions as applied to the operation of an independent studio within the home is more problematic than ascertaining deductions concerning studio operation outside the home. The home studio deductions may be calculated in a number of ways and it is safest to seek professional advice in trying to understand these in the light of one's own circumstances. It may also be prudent to seek this advice before making physical changes in the home that are costly and/or require construction.

The same words of caution about seeking professional advice may also be applied to the determination of deductions concerning business-related transportation (including automobile maintenance), insurance (relating to liability for accidents in or near the studio), and retirement plans. Many teaching-related expenses, however, are fairly predictable. Accurate records and receipts should be kept for instrument purchase and maintenance; purchase and maintenance of miscellaneous teaching equipment (e.g., files, cupboards, desks, lamps, recorders, metronomes, computer hardware used solely for teaching or business purposes); bookkeeping, mailing, and telephone expenses; recital, advertising, and reception expenses; professional memberships and periodicals; music library purchases (books, music, records, cassettes, computer software); professional education or involvement (tuition, transportation and housing expenses incurred while at school, conventions, master classes); and fees related to concert, audition, competition attendance. Determination of just which of these expenses is deductible, and to what extent, should be worked out with the tax accountant.

Several manuals[5] provide commentary on tax-related concerns for the independent piano teacher, as well as on all other practical aspects of operating the independent piano studio. Keyboard periodicals also include articles pertinent to studio management and business practice. These may alert piano teachers to general guidelines, or may call attention to unique procedures or ideas. (For further information, see Appendix 1.)

Setting and Stating Studio Policy

A hallmark of the professional teacher is a statement of the studio policy. This lets students and parents know what to expect and serves the purpose of setting forth in print what may be more difficult and time-consuming to do in person. The preparation of the studio policy should be a matter of careful concern and planning since it represents the teacher's regard for his or her own professional responsbilities. At the same time, it affirms that the student also has responsibilities and it states clearly what these are. The policy statement need not be expensively reproduced, nor need it be lengthy.

The statement should include:

Instructional schedule: when terms (or semesters) begin, end; when (if) summer instruction is offered; which holidays (and holiday times) will be observed

Tuition rates for varied instructional arrangements

Billing/payment procedures and regulations

Telephone times/number(s) when teacher is available for conference or question

Policy regarding missed or late lessons

Recital (or, where appropriate, audition) policies

Importance of having, and caring for, an instrument in the home

Practice expectations and recommendations

Importance and value of parental involvement and specifics as to what this involvement should be: e.g., attendance at lessons (or not), control of the practice environment

Importance and value of support for music in the home, concert attendance, and music appreciation generally

Teacher's professional background and current professional affiliations

In some cases, a teacher may use the policy statement to indicate a particular or personal teaching philosophy (e.g., the educational value of group instruction; the importance of musicianship classes; the necessity for many performance experiences). Such a declaration allows a teacher to give students and their families an idea of the teacher's musical and educational priorities.

Auditioning and Interviewing Students

It is wise to interview and/or audition students before accepting them into one's studio. This is true even if they have had no previous musical instruction or even if they are very young children. An actual meeting between teacher and student is helpful to each. The student has met a person (not just a teacher), knows what the studio environment is like, and has some sense of what might be expected at the lesson or class by the way the teacher speaks, moves, and interacts with the student. Especially in the case of a small child, all these things are very important because (to the child) such factors represent big unknowns. A personal meeting is also beneficial to the teacher. The perceptive teacher not only listens to what is said or played, but observes the student's body language and social adaptation. Further, the teacher has the opportunity to see how the student responds both to verbal suggestions and to musical stimuli. When the meeting is with a young child whose parent is also present, it is very important that the teacher interview the child, not the parent. Finding out directly from the child such things as his or her address, phone number, birthday, grade, school, and so forth, alerts the teacher not only to the child's knowledge, but also to the child's independence.

Each interview/audition should include some activities that allow the teacher to assess the prospective student's rhythmic response, pitch perception, physical coordination, and ability to follow instructions. "Prepare all of your materials ... before the prospective student arrives. Do not improvise. This is probably the first time the student will see you in action, and he will form many of his attitudes toward you and your teaching during the audition. Be organized, direct, and efficient."[6]

Auditions might incorporate activities such as the following:

Preschool Children (4–6 Years Old)

Hold a group orientation session, perhaps 30 minutes in length.

Give children and parents a preview of what the class will be like.

Note: how the group works; the relative maturity of individuals; which children can follow directions, know numbers/letters, are physically coordinated, and other developmental indicators.

After the session, tell parents what is to be accomplished in the class, the nature of parental involvement, and answer questions they might have.

Beginner (5–7 Years Old)

Teach and test (by means of games) perception of low/high sounds.

Using clapping, tapping, or drumming: see if child can imitate simple rhythm patterns, keep steady beat to accompaniment.

Sing and play a simple song; ask the child to join in singing.

Teach an easy rote piece (probably using only a few black keys).

Beginner (8–12 Years Old)

By rote, teach a well-known tune playable on the black keys.

Using clapping, tapping, or drumming: see if child can imitate simple rhythm patterns, keep steady beat to accompaniment.

Using groups of 2 or 3 black keys, do some play-back dictation involving simple rhythms combined with pitch movement.

Have brief conversation about your expectations regarding the music lesson, student's expectations regarding same.

Beginner (12 and Older)

Quickly teach black key ostinato using fifths, simple rhythm. Have student play ostinato as you improvise simple black key melodies. Reverse roles.

Using small group of black or white keys, do some play-back dictation involving rhythms combined with pitch movement.

Find out if student can read any music or has other background musical knowledge (e.g., chords, scales, playing by ear).

Have brief conversation about your expectations regarding the music lesson, student's expectations regarding same.

Transfer Student

Invite student to play whatever (s)he would like. Never criticize or re-teach piece(s). Compliment what you can, but be honest.

As you listen, try to determine student's "real" level, especially if you feel it differs from level of piece(s) played.

Ask student to sight-read short examples. It is best to use several varied examples that allow you to observe:

> how student approaches pitch/rhythmic reading
>
> student's knowledge of clefs
>
> what student sees on the page (e.g., tempo, slurs)
>
> if student hears what (s)he reads

Use dictation playbacks suited to the student's level.

Use ostinato/melody improvisation suited to student's level.

Ask many questions.

(For further detailed discussion about the transfer student, see Chap. 11.)

To function as an independent piano teacher is to be at once a musician, an educator, and a business person. As a musician, one loves and makes music, is knowledgeable about it, and regards it as a primary force in one's life. As an educator, one is concerned about the development of others, seeks to communicate information, ideas, and attitudes, and recognizes the extreme importance of education in the preservation and refinement of society. As a business person, one is looking to provide for one's own daily needs (and perhaps those of others), to use efficiency and organization as a means to convenience and security, and to remain abreast of whatever information, trends, and procedures are at the cutting edge of one's profession.

THE INSTITUTIONAL KEYBOARD TEACHER

Although little exists in print about the institutional keyboard teacher, this subject is a matter of interest to many keyboard majors, particularly those in graduate degree programs. They regard a college teaching career as a viable goal. They want to know how to get there.

The Résumé

Preparing a professional résumé may be the first practical step toward such a career. It gives the possible future employer an overview of a candidate's background and qualifications. It also affords the candidate an opportunity for self-evaluation. Assembling one's résumé is a type of stocktaking. It is wise to begin assembling a résumé as one nears completion of undergraduate study. Thereafter, the résumé can be readily updated and/or altered.

Marketing specialists place great stress on how the résumé looks. They advise that the résumé that makes a graphic "statement" is the one that gets attention. If by "graphics," one means clean page format, organization, and clarity of presentation, the observation is accurate. If, however, "graphics" means eye-catching visuals, the advice may be misleading. In academic circles, the résumé is taken quite seriously. One that is overtly trendy, clever, or individual may elicit suspicion or amusement rather than careful scrutiny. Marketing specialists also often recommend follow-up phone calls, not only to confirm the arrival of the résumé but to keep the candidate's name in the employer's awareness. This is seldom effective. During most university faculty searches applications are screened by a committee and that process is time-consuming. The wheels of academic bureaucracy grind quite slowly. Calls placed to serve as reminders of a candidate's interest in a position, or calls to "psych out" a particular candidate's chances, may be considered obtrusive.

Some general guidelines may aid in preparing the résumé.

Introductory Information

Name, address, phone number(s)

Not recommended: Disclosure of age, state of health, marital status, citizenship

It may help to offer a brief statement of professional goals—for example:

To obtain a position at a university or college where I may be able to teach in a class piano program and to function as accompanist for school/faculty recitals. I also have an interest in teaching children and would welcome the opportunity to teach in, or to develop, a preparatory program.

Educational Background

List most recent first

Institution(s); degree/major; month, year of (expected) completion

Teachers in major (or other important) fields

List study in independent studios prior to college only if:

B.M. is the most current education completed

Such study has been with a well-known teacher

Participation in significant master classes/workshops

Teaching Experience

List current first

Institution(s)/title(s)/years

List classes/levels taught. Summarize—for instance:

Group piano classes for piano secondaries

Studio lessons, non-music majors

List auxiliary experiences done as part of the position—for instance.

Organized recitals and performance forums

Established new classes/curricula

When listing independent teaching, give:

Size of class or number of students weekly

General age level of the students

Student teaching experiences may be included if the scope of such is clear—for instance:

> I taught two children weekly (studio lessons) as part of my undergraduate pedagogy class.

> I taught segments of a group piano class for adults (non-music majors) as part of my graduate pedagogy course.

Other Professional Experience

List most recent first

Workshops/lectures given

Adjudications

Related professional employment—for instance:

> Organist/choir director (list church name, years)

> Music camp counselor (list camp, place, dates)

Publications, if few; if many publications, list as a separate category

Other Employment Experiences

List such only if they:

> Explain what you were doing during a particular period—for instance, year(s) between official study

> Relate to your current profession—for instance: Office manager in community school of performing arts

> Offer insight into an otherwise non-apparent skill area—for instance: worked as a computer programmer, Bank of America

Performance Experience

> List most recent first

> Recital performance: Place, date, concerto, and conductor (if appropriate)

> List summary of recital content only if it offers evidence of special expertise—for example: all-Chopin recital; concerts of music by women composers

> Recordings/television appearances

> Delineate among performances if there is reason to do so—for instance, solo recitals, chamber music recitals, orchestral appearances

> Accompanist at competitions, festivals, or similar experience

Awards/Prizes

Competitions; scholarships/fellowships; grants

Recording contracts

Membership in Professional Organizations

List memberships, offices held (years, levels)

References

Indicate if/ where you have a placement file

Best to list a small (4–6) select group of people as references

List individual's name, position (if appropriate), address, phone number

Be sure to obtain permission from those whose names you include

If possible, list people who may speak to different abilities: performance teacher(s), pedagogy teacher(s), conductors, supervisor(s)

Organization of Résumé

List introductory information and educational background first

Lists that follow depend upon the type of position you are seeking:

If teaching, list teaching experience first

If performing, list performance experience first

If you play another instrument or have another area of expertise (e.g., church organist, writer of educational materials), list as a separate category

Desirable

Professionally printed, word-processed, or neatly typed format; clear page layout

Grouping and highlighting that enables reader to fix quickly on salient points

Complete, but succinct, statements and descriptions

Accompanying letter that offers pertinent information as to which position you are applying for and why you have interest in that particular position

Avoid

Undue length, long lists (especially of repertoire, performances)

Ambiguous or overinflated statements

Appending programs, tapes, pictures (unless requested or pertinent to position)

The Interview

A great number of résumés, perhaps as many as a hundred or more, might be submitted in response to a single faculty vacancy. From these, a search committee selects a few candidates—usually two or three—and invites them for an in-person interview. The interview is a time of mutual assessment: It enables the institution to assess a candidate's ability to teach, play, and interact in situations that would constitute his or her working milieu, and it affords a candidate the opportunity to gain a picture of possible future students, colleagues, administrators, and physical surroundings.

What constitutes an interview differs considerably, depending upon both the position to be filled and the institution. Most interviews are spread over a period of two days, although some may be briefer and less intense. A candidate is usually observed in three types of activities: performance, instruction, and discussion. The length and circumstances of the performance relate to the nature of the position. A candidate for a major studio position may be asked to perform a full-length recital before a general, or faculty, audience. A candidate for a keyboard position requiring specific skills will be asked to demonstrate that expertise—perhaps to perform as a chamber musician, or to give a lecture-demonstration. Performance by a candidate for a position that does not involve studio teaching of instrumental majors may be shorter, or played for a smaller audience (e.g., the department or search committee).

The candidate is usually asked to teach. If the interview takes place between terms, or when students are not readily available, that aspect of the interview may be omitted or abbreviated. Normally the candidate is asked to teach in situations required by the position—perhaps in a piano literature class, a group piano class, or a pedagogy class—as well as to give a studio lesson. Members of the search committee and/or the department are likely to be present for some, or all, of the teaching segments of the interview.

There are meetings (with the department, the search committee, or an ad hoc group) at which the candidate may be expected to respond to questions or comments concerning his or her interest in the position, qualifications, professional career plans, teaching philosophy or performance expectations, and the like. Frequently these meetings are in somewhat social situations—over lunch or dinner, perhaps—where, although the setting may seem casual, the purpose is entirely clear. It is important for the candidate to understand that these discussions often furnish significant indications of a particular individual's ability to fit in with future colleagues. Interpersonal relationships are part of the working condition and collegiality is a sensitive factor. Conversation with a candidate for a junior position may also be a vehicle whereby a department, a search committee, or a chairperson seeks to ascertain to what extent the candidate, once hired, may be promotable. Questions may be directed to discover the professional ambitions of a candidate and to evaluate the likelihood of that candidates being able to achieve those goals, or to do so as a member of a particular faculty.

The meeting with the major administrator is generally formal and straight-forward. While he or she is also looking for the appropriate faculty person, there are additional concerns. It is the administrator who discusses rank, salary, employment benefits and, sometimes, cost of living considerations. The candidate, on the other hand, may have questions to raise about these matters and the administrator is in the best position to offer information or to propose realistic

Barton College Library
Wilson, N.C. 27893

solutions. Since the meeting with the administrator usually comes later in the interview process, the candidate may also have concerns arising from interactions with students and faculty, or as a result of firsthand experience with equipment and space limitations or contingencies. The meeting with the administrator is the forum in which such matters should surface.

An interview occasionally may terminate in a job offer, usually tendered at the meeting with the administrator. But this is not generally the case. More often the candidate returns home and awaits notification of the decision. This, too, takes time—especially if one is the first of several candidates interviewed. Regardless of the outcome, the opportunity to interview is always professionally valuable. It affirms one's viability as a (potential) candidate for a faculty position, it serves as an introduction to other professionals with whom one may interact in future associations, it affords a personal glimpse of the workings and personnel of a particular institution, and—not least—it may serve as leverage in the "back-home" situation to enhance one's reputation and income.

The Faculty Position

The faculty member, new or otherwise, may find that a problematic aspect of institutional teaching is the matter of prioritizing one's time. To the outsider it appears that the college teacher has an enviable schedule, with ample vacation and weekends free. While teaching contact hours may sometimes be blocked conveniently (within the week or term), unseen requisites of filling a faculty appointment create other demands. There is, first of all, the need to practice and perform. The stakes are higher, the performances more "public," and the scrutiny intense (one's students are often the most critical audience). There are recitals and concerts—by students, colleagues, and visiting artists—to attend. In larger institutions, the recital agenda itself may be formidable. If one is teaching classes, preparation for them may take considerable time, as may the grading of separate exams or juries associated with various class projects or assignments. Arrangment of contact teaching hours may not be a matter of personal preference but rather a schedule dictated by the availability of rooms, equipment, rehearsal space, and the complexities of a master schedule.

There is, further, the matter of multiple duties. Providing instructional time is only one aspect of a faculty load. Meetings, forums, committee work, auditions, juries, registration, advising, and similar involvements are more demanding at some times than others, but these responsibilities are ongoing. Quite often a junior faculty position or a position with a particular focus (e.g., group piano, pedagogy, functional skills, chamber music, or literature instruction) requires scheduling one's time around priorities that may not be immediately obvious (rehearsal scheduling, class hours at which instrumental [other than keyboard] majors are available, times at which student teaching may occur, and so on). Many of these ancillary activities may also involve travel time. The most unfulfilling obligation of the institutional instructor is the amount of paperwork that must receive attention.

The faculty member is also expected to develop a professional career, the musical version of "publish or perish," without which one cannot expect to be promoted, be granted tenure, earn merit consideration, or maintain the respect of one's colleagues. Absorbing and, perhaps, personally enriching as these activities may be, they are seldom rewarded financially—at least not in any way commensurate with the amount of time one spends on them. Thus a large portion of one's life is devoted to performing, writing, researching, editing, or planning that contribute to one's overall betterment, but often not immediately. The successful faculty member is self-initiating and self-sustaining and able to conserve these energies over a long period of time despite criticism, absence of interest or acknowledgment (on the part of others), and/or competition.

To serve as a member of a keyboard faculty is to be at once a musician, a specialist, and a politician. As a musician, one loves and makes music, is knowledgeable about it, and regards it as a primary force in one's life. As a specialist, one has achieved distinctive professional expertise, is contributing to the development and scope of that field, and is considered a noteworthy exponent of particular techniques and ideas. As a politician, one has learned the importance of cooperative effort, understands both the power and vulnerability of leadership, and values circumspection and discretion.

AUGMENTING ONE'S INCOME/ALTERNATIVE CAREERS

The majority of pianists, whether working independently or in an institution, fuse a career out of playing and teaching. Some perform as soloists or ensemble partners on the concert circuit. Others play as free-lance accompanists, in church-related positions, or as entertainers. Increasingly, however, pianists are becoming more inventive about ways in which to augment their incomes while remaining within the music profession. Sometimes what begins as a supplementary job grows into the primary professional activity or leads in an altogether new direction such as music administration or arts management.

Current periodicals as well as convention presentations and panels are focusing more and more on these alternative, or supplementary, career possibilities. Some ancillary jobs are "naturals" for pianists and have always represented other, or extra, routes. Many musicians who began as pianists have become piano technicians and music store owners, for example. But pianists are also working as instrument builders (largely as a reuslt of increased interest in the harpischord and fortepiano); electronic technicians; touring staff performers (for keyboard manufacturers); writers of educational keyboard materials; dance studio pianists; music journalists, broadcasters, and critics; electronic keyboardists (playing with professional and semiprofessional entertainment groups and/or for commercial recordings); music publishers and editors; and even "circuit rider teachers"[7] (bringing a whole new dimension to the concept and clientele of the itinerant piano teacher).

This diversification, within pianists as a group as well as in the working life of an individual pianist, certainly reflects economic necessity. Perhaps it also represents facets of the current "multi-career person" who relates to divergent social groups and expects to change jobs or even professions in the course of a lifetime. The "well-tempered" keyboardist will have not only multiple keyboards from which to choose, but a perspective that will accomodate change and welcome variety. Multi-careers and multi-keyboards are likely to be a twenty-first-century tandem. (For further reading related to the contents of this chapter, see Appendix 1.)

PART TWO

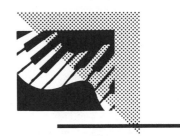

How Learning Takes Place

CHAPTER 3

A Survey of Learning Theories

One way to approach the subject of teaching is to consider what it means to learn. Everyone has learned something. Much learning, in fact, happens not in formal learning situations (e.g., schools, churches, psychiatrists' offices, sit-down talks with Mom/Dad) but during life's daily experiences and social interactions. It is often the most valuable learning that each of us does. In that sense, one must agree with Gilbert Highet's observation that "we are all pupils and we are all teachers."[1]

What are the conditions in which learning takes place? In which state is the learner best suited to learn? How is the learner stimulated both externally and internally? Answers to these questions are not simple, of course. Neither is it possible to compile a list of responses to these questions with which everyone would be completely comfortable. Educational psychologists are not always in agreement about the conditions associated with successful learning. The following survey examines these differences. It may also serve as an introduction to a study of the learning process in light of both historical and recent research.

THE PURPOSE OF THE SURVEY

The extent of a survey of learning theories depends on where one chooses to begin and on how inclusive a range one intends to cover. Some would begin with Socrates, others with Rousseau and Tolstoy, a few with Comenius and Pestalozzi. Contributions to ideas about learning might be drawn from the writings of philosophers, psychologists, novelists, physiologists, humanists, educational psychologists, and a host of others whose ruminations and diagnoses have bearing on the learning process. Because this survey seeks to connect ideas about learning to the study of piano performance, one might also examine the opinions of music educators.

This survey will briefly describe some major theories about the learning process; it seeks only to sketch an outline of various (chiefly twentieth-century) premises relating to learning theories, to provide a short compendium of important names and works connected with psychology (educational and otherwise), and to provoke a general inquisitiveness on the part of the reader to consult these and other authors directly.

Readings in psychology are replete with multi-syllabic jargon and terminology special to the field. The following survey aims to express concepts simply, to make viewpoints and theories reasonably clear if only at very basic levels. Some terms common to psychology must be used, of course, to allow readers to identify ideas about which they wish to do further research on their own.

INTRODUCTION TO THE SURVEY

John Dewey (1859–1952) provides a valuable platform from which to begin an examination of learning theories: "The history of educational theory is marked by opposition between the ideas that education is development from within and that it is formation from without."[2] One may agree either with John Locke (1632–1704)—that the newborn infant is a tabula rasa, essentially passive and reacting only when stimulated—or with Gottfried Leibniz (1646–1716)—that the human intellect is self-propelling, manipulating its environment according to its nature. Locke holds that what is external and visible is more fundamental than what is not. According to Leibniz, what is internal is of primary importance. These are strikingly different viewpoints: A person is either a *collection* of acts (activity seen as the result of stimulation) or a person is a *source* of acts (activity seen as purposive).[3]

Locke's position is reflected in the theories of behaviorists such as John B. Watson, Edward Thorndike, and B. F. Skinner. Leibniz's point of view is the same as that espoused by cognitivists like Jerome Bruner and Jean Piaget and humanists like Abraham Maslow and Carl Rogers. The ideas of these twentieth-century psychologists follow in more detail.

THE ASSOCIATIONISTS: FORMATION FROM WITHOUT

The theorists called associationists have certain things in common. They:

Apply methods of the natural and physical sciences to the study of human behavior.

Believe that only directly observable behavior is proper to scientific study.

Refer to the link between a stimulus (something outside the learner) and a response (reaction of the learner to the stimulus) as an "association," or series of associations.

Rely on laboratory experiments with animals as the source and test of theories.

Maintain that learning must be controlled in order for it to be efficient.

The experiments of the Russian physiologist Ivan Pavlov (1849–1936), who conditioned a dog to salivate at the sound of a bell rather than at the sight of food, were championed in America by some psychologists. The dog in Pavlov's experiment was passive; no action or movement on the dog's part was required. The response (salivation) was elicited by the experimenter. Such conditioning is referred to as "classical conditioning." Pavlov's principle of classical conditioning led to the emergence of the doctrine of behaviorism, so named by John B. Watson (1878–1958). Watson was influential in establishing the importance of objectivity in psychological studies, since he considered psychology to be the science of observable behavior.

> The position of a Watsonian behaviorist can be illustrated amusingly in a morning conversation. Ordinarily, a conventional greeting would go as follows: "Good morning, how are you?" "I'm fine, and yourself?" "Just fine." But such a greeting implies introspection. Each person is "looking into himself" in order to decide what kind of shape he [or she] is in. Presumably [according to a behaviorist], this is scientifically impossible. Instead the two persons would need to inspect each other. The proper salutation of a behaviorist would be, "Good morning, you appear to be fine; how am I?"[4]

Although he is regarded as the founder of behaviorism, Watson did not develop learning theories based on that idea.

Edward Thorndike (1874–1949), a protégé of the great American psychologist William James (1842–1910), was another pioneer who researched animal learning and whose research also influenced the ideas of behaviorists. Thorndike's experiments (cats, dogs, and chickens learning to escape from problem boxes) convinced him that trial-and-error learning was influenced by rewards (the animal was fed) for effective responses (the animal "learned" to escape from the box). Trial-and-error repetition was an essential factor in causing the learning of the connections (associations) between stimulus and response. Thorndike sought to establish laws of learning that were patterned after the laws of physical science. His lifetime of search in this direction has led many to view Thorndike as the first American learning theorist.[5]

One of Thorndike's laws—he called it the "law of effect"—is often referred to as the pleasure-pain principle. Although Thorndike's experiments involved only animals, the law of effect was also regarded as influential in conditioning human learning. This law stated that if a response is rewarded with something pleasurable (e.g., gold star, praise), the tendency to respond in that particular manner is strengthened. If, however, the response is followed by displeasure (e.g., criticism, scolding) or no reward (e.g., the response is ignored), the tendency to respond is weakened. Psychologists (especially behaviorists like Skinner) have since used the term "reinforcement" to describe events that Thorndike called the law of effect. It is apparent that, in many cases, the use of positive reinforcement (rewards) may prove effective in a learning situation. It continues to be questioned, however, whether positive reinforcement is sufficient to motivate and sustain human behavior in complex learning situations.

The work and opinions of B. F. Skinner (1904–1990) have received a great deal of attention since the publication of *The Technology of Teaching* (1968) and, especially, of *Beyond Freedom and Dignity* (1971). As a behaviorist, Skinner endorses the scientific study of observable behavior and derives his theories from animal experiments involving stimulus-response (S-R) conditioning. Skinner's conclusion is that teachers and textbooks should condition students by means of S-R associations, thereby shaping student response by carefully controlled step-by-step presentation and reinforcement. The clearest example of the application of this theory to the teaching situation is the use of programmed instruction with or without the use of teaching machines.

Although his theories built upon earlier behaviorist experiments and postulates, Skinner's views on conditioning and reinforcement are somewhat different from those of his predecessors. For Skinner, reinforcement is not necessarily dependent on a reward, but "is the name for a particular arrangement of stimulus and response conditions that bring about the learning of a new association."[6] The learner must *do* something, must *operate* in some way, to bring about the response. Hence Skinner refers to "operant conditioning." Moreover, the manner in which the learner operates is controlled, so that only a *particular* response is reinforced. In programmed instruction, for example, the response must be correct in order for the learner to proceed in the program.

Programmed instruction also involves taking the learner through the program in a large number of very small steps. Since the learner's progress is dependent on correct responses, and since the attainment of these correct responses is itself reinforcing, Skinner argues that such a mode of instruction maximizes positive reinforcement and minimizes possible negative feelings and attitudes resulting from incorrect responses. Each learning block is small, and the blocks are carefully graduated to lead the learner through the program content methodically, logically, and consistently. Although this procedure appears to benefit the slow learner, Skinner points out that programmed instruction allows each student to proceed at his/her own pace. Thus very quick learners may move rapidly; at the same time, use of the program ensures that the quick learner does not skip over important details or connections. Computer-assisted instruction is an obvious use of the principles of operant conditioning.

To many Skinner's ideas are provocative. To some they are unacceptable, if not dangerous. Yet Skinner's influence is widespread. Individuals and groups use techniques derived from, or related to, a stimulus-response theory often without knowing they are doing so. Skinner has been criticized and denounced, especially by those who fear or reject the rigorous control at the core of operant conditioning.[7] Yet in some situations, or in certain types of learning, the ideals and practices of programmed instruction seem both practical and beneficial. Gagné summarizes what might be an appropriate stance regarding the persuasiveness of the stimulus-response association theory:

> It is now generally recognized by those who conduct scientific investigations of learning that even the most deliberately simplified learning situation cannot be adequately accounted for as an association between an S and an R. . . . Nevertheless, the idea persists, with considerable justification, that association is one of the processes that occurs in learning [and] with such frequency that it deserves to be called a *basic* process.[8]

COGNITIVE THEORISTS: DEVELOPMENT FROM WITHIN

Cognitive theorists hold different, sometimes opposing, viewpoints from associationists. They:

Regard learning as a thought process (cognition) of a person in an individual situation, subject to the influences of that particular environment.

Believe that psychologists should concern themselves with underlying mental processes (which cause behavior) rather than with the study of observable behavior only.

Maintain that learning is a result of the rearrangement of thought patterns leading to new patterns, or insights.

Rely on experiments with higher-order animals and man, often in more natural situations than laboratories.

Feel that learning can be encouraged, but not controlled, by arrangement of environment.

Suggest that cognition and environmental factors interact in influencing behavior.

The German gestalt psychologists, among them Max Wertheimer (1880–1943), Kurt Koffka (1886–1941), and Wolfgang Köhler (1887–1967), proposed that learning be defined as an "insight," or "a suddenly occurring reorganization of the field of experience."[9] They stressed the importance of the perception of a pattern or configuration (gestalt), pointing out that the understanding of a whole is a stronger determinant of successful learning than the accumulation of understandings about separate contingent parts. Since patterns of ideas are, or lead to, perception of structure, the concept of structure is of primary importance.

Köhler's experiments with an ape named Sultan (who "figured out" how to combine the use of two sticks, which he used as rakes, to reach a banana) demonstrated the significance of the making of relationships to the process of learning. Sultan's environment was arranged, but he made his own "connections" by discerning the relationship among three objects. Kurt Lewin (1890–1947), another gestaltist, established that in behavioral situations the environment as perceived by an individual is not the same as the environment looked at objectively. Lewin spoke of this as the lifespace concept, which allows that "people do not behave solely because of the external forces to which they are exposed. People behave as they do as a consequence of how things seem to them."[10]

Jerome Bruner (b. 1915), one of the most widely read and influential of the cognitive theorists, believes that learning "serves the future."[11] One way it does so is by *specific* transfer of training—the application of a learned concept or skill to a new, but highly similar, concept or skill. Specific transfer, admittedly, is a part of operant conditioning. There is, however, also a *nonspecific* transfer which Bruner regards as the more important. In nonspecific transfer, what is used (transferred) to serve the future is the understanding of a general idea, a principle, or an attitude. Bruner calls this type of transfer "the heart of the educational process."[12] Such transfer can only be accomplished by comprehending the structure of a subject so as to view subsequent information or events as related (or not) to a whole. The so-called spiral curriculum is one in which general principles are presented at the outset and specific applications of these basic ideas occur (or "spiral") in ever-increasing complexity and subtlety.

Bruner also contends that learning is a process, not an end. A learning environment in which the learner solves problems, discovering for the self how general principles may be used in seeking solutions, is also one in which the learner sharpens learning strategies—the how-to-do-it-by-myself skills that serve the learner in ways far beyond the grasp of certain ideas or the arrival at specific solutions. Problem solving also fosters the development of intuition whereby the learner may choose to take risks that may (or may not) pay off. It is in seeking the "payoff"—finding the clue that beats the system by uncovering the underlying principles that organize the system—that a learner moves rapidly toward an understanding of how learning really *does* serve the self. Thus the teacher who is a believer in cognitive theories is a question asker rather than an information font, a fellow prober with the learner in the process of arriving at ideas.

Cognitive theorists claim that although they organize circumstances or events in which learning is to take place, they do not wish to *control* the learning process. Here the difference between the views of Skinner and Bruner is seen most clearly.

> Skinner suggests that [the teacher] first explicitly state terminal behavior and then arrange learning experiences so that ... students are led to achieve it—step by step. The early experiments by Gestalt psychologists led to Bruner's suggestion that teachers arrange learning situations so that students will make their own discoveries.[13]

Just as programmed instruction is the hallmark of teaching strategy employed by S-R theorists, so the discovery method is at the core of teaching strategy suggested by early cognitive theorists.

Bruner also places great emphasis on the importance of teaching the structure of whatever is to be learned. He suggests that the presentation of fundamental principles, if done at the outset of the learning process, makes a subject easier to comprehend and remember. The close link between the understanding of structure and long-term memory is demonstrated in many cognitive theorists' experiments. To those who would contend that such a method of teaching is best suited only to the bright student, Bruner rejoins that "good teaching [which] emphasizes the structure of a subject is probably even more valuable for the less able student than for the gifted one, for it is the former rather than the latter who is most easily thrown off the track by poor teaching."[14]

Bruner's theories, while not as controversial as those of Skinner, are attacked by those who are uncomfortable with open-endedness or who desire immediate results and neatly defined feedback. *The Process of Education* (1960), nonetheless, has become a classic in the writings of its kind and, together with Bruner's other books on the subject of education,[15] has served as both catechism and cudgel for those who defend the principles of learner-oriented, rather than teacher-oriented, education.

In forming a personal assessment of the cognitive theory, one must admit there is a dilemma. Learning environments that excite discovery, challenge intuition, and stimulate participation are desirable. However, it may not always be possible to achieve the balance between risk and control in each learning situation.

> Is it better to surround children with stimuli and partly structured experiences and allow them considerable freedom to choose *what* they find meaningful *when* they find it meaningful? Or is it better to note what appear to be characteristic, progressive patterns, or stages, in child development and then systematically lead all children through this sequence?[16]

At this point in the survey, it may be helpful to summarize the positions taken by associationists and cognitive theorists by placing pertinent ideas about each in a comparative context. The second outline also notes some usual criticisms of both positions.

FORMATION FROM WITHOUT	DEVELOPMENT FROM WITHIN
LOCKE:	LEIBNIZ:
Tabula rasa: Human beings are essentially passive and react only when stimulated.	The human intellect is self-propelled, manipulating its environment according to nature.
What is external is more fundamental than what is not.	What is internal is of primary importance.
A person is a collection of acts.	A person is a source of acts.
PAVLOV: Conditioning.	GESTALT PSYCHOLOGISTS: Pattern.
WATSON: Behaviorism.	KÖHLER: Relationships.
THORNDIKE: Trial and error.	LEWIN: Lifespace concept.

SKINNER:	BRUNER:
Use of methods of physical and natural science to be as objective as possible.	Reliance on more natural experimental situations.
Only overt behavior is measurable or is appropriate to scientific study.	Underlying mental processes cause behavior and thus must be of concern.
Learning is the accumulation of associations between stimulus and response.	Learning is the rearrangement of thought patterns. Knowing is a process, not a product.
Teacher controls both ends and means in the learning situation.	Teacher arranges the environment; students make own discoveries.

STIMULUS RESPONSE ASSOCIATION	COGNITIVE THEORY
Operant Conditioning *Programmed Learning*	*Structure/Intuition* *Discovery Process*

TENETS	TENETS
Eliminate mistakes to produce utmost in positive reinforcement.	Making mistakes is essential to learning.
Students work with teaching machines, computers, at own pace.	Students work in groups, by means of discussion, participation in activities.
Learning is efficient since teacher or program has clear ends in mind and clear goals to reach these ends.	Problem solving is a vital educative tool because it promotes transfer of learning (insight) and fosters intuitive thinking.

CRITICISMS	CRITICISMS
Glorified version of animal-training techniques.	Great thinkers build on the past; they do not rediscover it.
Students must go through program.	Process is time consuming, inefficient.
Allowance is not made for those who synthesize quickly, surmise easily.	Not all discussions are productive or produce closure.
Machines will replace teachers.	Teacher's position is ambiguous. Students may resent that teacher will not tell what he/she knows.
Produces regimentation. Limits creativity. *What* is to be learned is totally controlled by teacher or program.	Absolves teacher from sense of failure by making instruction unnecessary.
Protects lowest common denominator. Students can answer almost every question correctly. Fails to develop skills to do harder work on one's own.	May work best only with bright, self-confident students or with students at a certain age or development level.

DEVELOPMENTAL THEORISTS

One of the touchiest of current debates on the educational scene involves the structuring of educational programs in relationship to various theories concerned with readiness. Readiness describes that optimum moment at which the learner is prepared to do certain things or comprehend certain concepts. Traditionally, children (and other learners) have been grouped by age levels, and educational goals have been planned accordingly. Since individuals of all ages vary so greatly, some educators feel that learners ought to be allowed to learn at their own pace. These educators favor respect for natural readiness and would allow considerable freedom, for example, in setting the time at which a child might be exposed to formal instruction. Others feel that this procedure is inefficient and, therefore, choose to prime readiness in children by exposing them to concepts (e.g., reading and number experiences) at very early ages, nearly from infancy on. These latter are the proponents of the "superbaby." More about this debate, and its implications for music education, will be found in chapter 5.

A number of theories concerning readiness are based on various criteria for determining critical accomplishments and adjustments that must be made by each human being. These may be referred to as developmental theories since, in each theory, progress to the next level or stage cannot be made until the individual has satisfactorily resolved the particular challenges of the preceding level. Most of these theories are not learning theories, nor do they attempt to relate life-learning tasks to specific educational premises. However, since each learner may be viewed as moving through varied life cycles, no educational program can afford to overlook the implications of what these theories demonstrate.

The work of Jean Piaget (1896–1980), which is concerned entirely with the intellectual development of children, has had considerable influence on certain educational psychologists because the theory deals with the growth of cognition in the very young. One of Piaget's theses is that children think in different ways than adults. Piaget claims that each child has two basic, and inherent, tendencies—to organize and to adapt. The child needs to achieve a state of balance in dealing with intellectual processes just as (s)he does in developing biologically. The child does this by adapting "schemes"—organized thought or behavioral patterns. (Ball throwing, for example, is a behavioral scheme; learning that there are different kinds of balls is a cognitive scheme.) There are two ways to adapt: (1) reorganize a new experience so that it fits an existing scheme (assimilation); (2) change an already learned scheme so that it includes the new experience (accommodation).

One of Piaget's most famous experiments involved a child's comprehension of amounts of liquids in containers of various sizes. The child is first shown the same amount of liquid in two identical glasses; the child sees this and agrees that the amount of liquid is the same. Next, the liquid from one glass is poured into a very tall, thin glass and the child is asked if the tall glass then contains more liquid. Piaget observed that most children younger than six answer that the tall glass has more liquid in it. They are unable to retain the invariant properties of something if its appearance is changed in some way—a principle that Piaget refers to as "conservation." Young children also have difficulty in imagining the reversal of a mental action (e.g., mentally pouring the water from the tall glass back into the small glass in order to judge the sameness). For Piaget, this is the concept of "operation," and it is the way by which the understanding of conservation is achieved. Many of Piaget's experiments, most of which employ an interview method with the child, could be used by anyone wishing to gain personal insight into the thinking process of the very young.[17]

Piaget describes four developmental stages through which each child must pass:

Sensorimotor stage (birth–2 years): the building up of schemes through direct physical contact and manipulation of things.

Preoperational stage (2–7 years): the extension of schemes to include language, but not the capability of reversing mental actions.

Concrete operational stage (7–11 years): capable of reversing mental actions, but only as applied to things which are concrete, actually present.

Formal operational stage (11 years and older): ability to generalize and deal with hypotheses by way of grasping the form, or structure, of things.

Piaget's postulates about development clearly put him in the cognitive theorists' camp. The attention paid to inner thought process rather than just observable behavior, the stress on the importance of the perception of patterns and structure, the value placed on discovery through activity and direct experience—all are cognitivist concerns. Like other cognitive theorists, Piaget believes that intrinsic motivation is the most effective; the achieving of the state of intellectual balance is the strongest and most natural reinforcement.

While ideas about developmental theories are most often used with reference to the developmental stages of infancy and childhood, there is growing interest in the process of adult development. Freud's developmental categories are based on the resolution of psychosexual adjustments, although Freud himself did not focus great attention on the adult years as developmental stages.

> Where Freud centered development around the psycho*sexual* stages of the infant and child, [Erik] Erikson was interested in the psycho*social* stages throughout the life cycle. Erikson emphasized that the psychosexual stages of development expressed not only a biological need but also cultural and interpersonal needs of the developing individual. He described a "life cycle" of stages, each of which presented the organism with tasks to be achieved and a developmental "crisis" during its attempted achievement.[18]

Greater awareness currently exists regarding the relationship between a particular developmental stage and the learning propensities of someone in that particular stage. Three issues may affect learning. The first is the learner's unconscious self. "There are important feelings, thoughts, and desires that remain out of awareness and cannot be brought to awareness by an ordinary effort of will and yet serve as major sources of motivation and determinants of behavior."[19] Such "feelings, thoughts, and desires" affect, if they do not altogether determine, what and why the learner learns. Second are the multiple defenses that each person uses to protect the self, which may hinder learning at any given moment. Teaching may become, in some cases, a matter of being able to work through the learner's resistances. Finally, there is the matter of the individual's self-esteem, which has enormous impact on what that individual perceives him/herself capable of learning. The psychoanalyst would say that, in the matter of learning, while the present (or the environment) *is* important, the learner in the present environment may be distracted by past, or unconscious, experiences.[20]

Some psychoanalysts are examining the viewpoints of learning theories with reference to the doctor-client as a kind of teacher-learner relationship.

> The fundamental problem with which we are faced in psychoanalytic therapy is that of how we can enable or cause the patient to give up certain acquired patterns of thought, feeling, or behavior in favor of others which are considered more "mature," "adaptive," "productive," or "self-realizing." The learning theorist, if he is a member of the stimulus-response school, structures this as an effort to teach the patient new habit patterns; or, if he belongs to the cognitive school, as an effort to teach the patient new patterns of perceptions and new cognitive "insights."[21]

*H*UMANISTS

For some thinkers, no learning theory is adequate if it does not take into consideration how the learner *feels* while learning. They believe that a more holistic approach to the understanding of learning must also regard the affective field of forces that are part of each learning situation. "Third force" psychologists (neither associationists nor cognitive theorists) look at learning as a preeminently human activity and are, therefore; often referred to as humanistic psychologists. For them, the idea of education is very broad, including much more than what is, or might be, learned in formal learning circumstances. Interest in third force psychology as applied to education was ignited by several reactionary books[22] that decried excessive teacher control and championed open education. The tenets of humanistic psychology became new rallying points around which gathered many cognitive theorists who recognized in this appraoch the furthest extension of learning by discovery.

Abraham Maslow (1908–1970), a psychologist and an antibehaviorist (even though, earlier, he had been a research assistant to Thorndike), "approaches psychology from a Gestalt point of view."[23] His humanistic theory of psychology is an outgrowth of his lifelong study of mentally healthy and, particularly, creative people. Maslow considers need gratification as "the most important single principle underlying all development."[24] Thus an awareness of the framework of Maslow's hierarchy of needs may be enlightening when reflecting on, or dealing with, motivation. He distinguishes between "deficiency" needs (primary needs, such as physical comfort, safety, love and belonging, esteem) and "being" needs (higher needs, such as self-actualization, the fulfillment of one's desire to know and understand, aesthetic needs). A person works to get rid of deficiency needs, thereby attaining relief or satisfaction. One *seeks* the pleasure of attending to being (or growth) needs since these activities lead to the fully realized, completely human, person.

While Maslow's is not a learning theory, ideas about education are shot through much of his writing. For him, the function of education is to encourage each person to become self-actualized, not to impart facts or skills. In *The Farther Reaches of Human Nature* (1971), Maslow includes a section on education in which he draws a clear picture of ways each learner must interact with the self that craves safety and ease, and with the self that must stretch and risk.

Like Maslow, Carl Rogers (1902–1987) is a humanistic psychologist. He advocates the use of his psychotherapy techniques as teaching strategies. Such techniques are learner-centered, involving both teacher and student in intensive group experiences by means of which both teacher and student may change, adapt, and develop. Such learner-centered teaching "is essentially an 'ultimate' version of the discovery approach."[25]

In *Freedom to Learn* (originally published in 1969, completely revised in 1983), Rogers details his opinions on the educational process. Learning is of two general types: (1) learning which is "from the neck up" (without involvement of personal meanings or feelings) and (2) experiential learning (involving the whole person, both feeling and cognition). He maintains that education has, for the most part, been left-brain oriented. It has proceeded only logically and in a straight line—step by step, with careful attention to details, ideas, concepts. Rogers proposes that learning, and therefore also education, involves right-brain activities. Growth of the whole person can be brought about only if there is allowance for, and development of, intuition, creativity, feeling, and imagination. "Significant learning combines the logical *and* the intuitive, the intellect *and* the feelings, the concept *and* the experience, the idea *and* the meaning. When we learn in that way, we are whole."[26]

Both Rogers and Maslow make frequent reference to the value and importance of making choices and of learning to do so. Each of them is a supporter of learning situations that allow the student options. When a student chooses what may have personal appeal or value, the self-chosen activity often becomes its own reward. Reinforcement, then, arises from within the learner rather than from the teacher or other outside source.

Third force psychology, although not offering a distinct theory of learning, has nonetheless changed the perspective in which education is viewed. The focus on the learner as a feeling as well as thinking person, together with the inclusion of the feeling-thinking teacher as an active ingredient in the educative process, has had ramifications in the areas of curriculum planning and teacher education quite different from those reevaluations suggested by attention to the theories of associationists or cognitive theorists. A consideration of the learner as a cooperator in determining what is to be learned and how goals may be reached places fresh emphasis on the importance of active participation and motivational urgency. Humanistic psychology has also led to the making of contracts between students and teachers, to more relevant testing procedures (sometimes student-chosen), and to the practice of competency-based education (wherein a commitment made by the student to develop a competency is judged by noncompetitive evaluation). Teaching strategies predicated on humanistic tenets reflect greater awareness of the learner's individuality and stress the value of empathy, on the part of the teacher, for the learner's viewpoints, attitudes, and problems. Humanistic psychology as a separate focus with reference to learning, however, is no longer much discussed. Cognitive theories now represent and include most issues that have been identified with humanism.

INFORMATION PROCESSING

Some current psychologists are attempting to formulate a theory of learning in ways that derive from Skinner and Bruner yet result in different, although related, hypotheses. Noting the limitations of operant conditioning with regard to the development of problem-solving skills, and unsatisfied with the practical use of discovery-method techniques in many learning situations, these psychologists are working toward an explanation of learning based on the principles of what has come to be known as "information processing." The impetus for this new direction arose post–World War II. Research psychologists moved from activities directed to military personnel training to interest in electronic information transmission, referred to in the 1950s and 1960s as "information theory." Such research was primarily concerned with effective and efficient communication. Communications research, in turn, began to examine learning as human information processing.

The emergence of the computer, and the proliferation of its use in nearly every aspect of daily life, was further cause for interest in the processing of information. The comparison of the human mind with the computer was inevitable. A key factor in studies concerned with this comparison is the function of human memory and how information comes to be selected, processed (encoded), and recalled. Although such studies have "triggered a veritable landslide of research,"[27] there is, as yet, no single theory (or theorist) connected to information processing that can be considered dominant. What seems clear is that theories connected to information processing have fused with theories related to cognitive psychology. Today's learning theorists speak of "cognitive information-processing psychology."[28]

In the language of these theorists, computer terminology is ubiquitous. Reference to storage, retrieval, encoding, input/output, and routines is characteristic. Many theories are diagrammed in flow charts that identify each segment of information processing and indicate how these segments "interface." Despite the mechanistic and scientific language common to these studies (making it seem as if close parallels might be drawn to behavioral theories) information-processing models "propose an elaborate set of internal processes to account for the events of learning and retention."[29] Thus these models are more closely allied to cognitive theory, even though attention here has shifted from discovery to memory techniques.

At the heart of these theories and models is the contention that learning is a set of processes. Information is transformed (processed) in a number of ways and in different phases (routines). Ultimately learning completes a loop. The stimulus received from the environment at the outset of the cycle is internalized and reflected back into the environment by way of a response. Although the words "stimulus" and "response" are used in this context, attention here is focused entirely on the inner "processing."

At the outset, information is received by means of selective attention and transformed into neural information. This information then enters the short-term memory, which is very limited (some claim that only seven bits of information can be held from two to five seconds). The information may be rehearsed for immediate use (e.g., quickly memorizing a telephone number for as long as it takes one to dial the number). Because of its limited capacity, the short-term memory may choose to "chunk" the information to reduce the number of stored parts (memorizing the last four digits of the phone number as a year—1986—rather than 1-9-8-6). From the short-term memory the information moves to the long-term memory, a process referred to as "encoding." This is the critical point at which the information becomes meaningfully organized, often by means of relating the new information to information already stored. The capacity of the long-term memory is enormous (some theorists would claim both unlimited and permanent).

Proof of learning is the retrieval from long-term memory. Retrieval may be triggered by "cues"—signals that allow the long-term memory to search for the information desired or required. Certain theorists believe that such information is returned to the short-term memory—which they call "conscious memory"—from whence it may be acted upon or used. If what is recalled needs to be applied to new situations or problems, "transfer of learning" takes place. Continued transformation of the information requires a response. The response generator determines whether the outcome will be directed to muscles involving, for instance, speech or movement. "Telling" or "doing" (something that can be externally observed) follows. The last link of the loop is the feedback provided by the learner's awareness of the telling or doing.

An information-processing model may resemble the following:

Input	Environment; Stimuli
Sensory Register	Attention; Selection
Short-Term Memory	Possible rehearsal
Long-Term Memory	Organization; Encoding
Retrieval Strategies	Cues; Search
Response Generator	Neurons; Muscles
Output	Telling, doing, etc.
Feedback	Reinforcement

Although this flow chart of routines looks (and is) complicated, information-processing theorists further point out that the entire cycle may be governed by "control processes." Executive control—the learner's capability to fix attention on *which* stimuli are to be perceived, determining how information is to be encoded, responding to *this* rather than *that* signal in the retrieval of information, choosing the means to demonstrate that learning has occurred—may influence this routine or any series of routines. Beyond that, expectancy—what learners intend to accomplish or assume will be accomplished—further influences all phases, or any phase, of the information-processing cycle.

Awareness of control processes is referred to as "metacognition" (from the Greek *meta,* transcending, and "cognition," thought). Thus metacognition, a term coined by the information-processing theorists and not in vogue until the mid 1970s, describes "knowing *that* I'm knowing" and "knowing *what* I'm knowing." Such an awareness allows one to observe oneself learning. The experience, of course, is not new. But recognition of that experience as influencing the manner and outcome of learning is of more recent interest.

The most fertile research emerging from the information-processing theorists concerns the functions and capabilities of the human memory and the part that memory plays in the process of learning. Instruction that enhances or supports rehearsal techniques may be instruction that assists the learner in grouping or "chunking" separate bits of information into more unified wholes. The use of rhymes (*i* before *e* except after *c*), acronyms (*HOMES* as a way to remember the names of the Great Lakes), acrostics (*every good boy does fine* to remember the lines of the treble staff), and similar mnemonic (memory-aiding) devices may facilitate storage in short- and long-term memory by reducing the information "wholes" that must be retained.

For the information-processing theorist, the most important aspect of instruction is that it supports, directs, and cues the learner throughout the various phases of learning. Studies tend to demonstrate that the younger the learner, the greater the need for specific cueing at each phase. Instruction is not simply a matter of presenting information, or of providing feedback to a response that indicates learning has taken place. The best type of instruction guides the learner in honing the executive control processes—it directs or challenges the learner to choose, focus, solve, anticipate, and relate. In this manner the learner finds the way to self-instruction.

SUMMARY AND SUGGESTED READINGS

Knowledge of learning theories is not necessary in order to be a good teacher. Many inspiring and excellent teachers possess seemingly innate instincts to do, say, and demonstrate what helps others to learn. It is always tempting to agree that teachers are born, not made. Yet if that were the total truth, if effective teachers did not themselves learn from outside sources (whatever these might be) how to increase diagnostic acumen, develop communicative skills, or succinctly structure a presentation, they would likely not be regarded as remarkable educators. Successful teachers are always quick—and good—learners. They unerringly perceive and utilize any information, device, or technique that increases their own capacity to understand the entire learning-teaching process.

It seems logical, therefore, that the more one knows about how learning takes place, the more one is able to increase one's own capacity to learn. Information about various learning theories may furnish insight as one observes oneself learning (the metacognition process). Whether the increased awareness is only for one's own benefit or, in turn, is used in helping others to become successful learners, the time and effort spent is practical and may be enlightening.

The following list is offered as an aid in choosing reading background for a general study of learning theories or in researching areas of special interest. The list is annotated so that the evaluation may serve as an introduction to book and/or author.

GENERAL BOOKS

BIEHLER, ROBERT F., WITH JACK SNOWMAN. *Psychology Applied to Teaching.* 5th ed. Boston: Houghton Mifflin, 1986 (available in paperback).

An excellent overview of all theories of learning. Editions vary considerably; the 1986 edition contains a separate, updated chapter on information processing. The book is designed as a textbook. Each chapter opens with lists of key points covered. Wide margins with high-lighted summary statements make it easy to locate main ideas. Each chapter also contains suggestions for teaching that are substantial and practical. A separate glossary defines "ed-psych" words and phrases.

The writing style is simple and direct. Attractive pictures, homely analogies, and useful examples add to the book's effectiveness.

BIGGE, MORRIS L. *Learning Theories for Teachers.* 4th ed. New York: Harper & Row, 1982. Available in paperback. (This is a slightly revised version of a larger book by Bigge and Maurice P. Hunt, *Psychological Foundations of Education.* 2d ed. New York: Harper & Row, 1968.)

Emphasizes the nature of contrasting psychologies of learning and places them in semihistoric context. Each learning theory is presented as if the author were an adherent; criticism is only occasional. Bigge defines "two major families" of learning theory, but devotes separate chapters to Gagné, Bandura, and the lifespace concept as well as to Skinner and Bruner. There is no attention paid to Piaget, Maslow, Rogers, or information-processing theories.

The book reads easily and attempts to be both practical and brief. The style is that of an extensive catechism since all, even subordinate, headings are phrased as questions to which the text provides answers.

GAGNÉ, ROBERT M. *The Conditions of Learning.* 3d ed. New York: Holt, Rinehart, & Winston, 1977.

Describes learning in terms of different learning outcomes: intellectual skills, cognitive strategies, verbal information, motor skills, attitudes. Specific learning theories are discussed in relationship to those capabilities in which they figure most prominently. The book is designed as a textbook, primarily for students of educational psychology. Each chapter concludes with a section on the educational implications of the chapter's content.

Although all learning theories are treated in the book, the third edition emphasizes an interpretation of learning events in terms of information processing. The first chapter is an especially fine, and objective, treatment of the history of learning theories.

OPERANT CONDITIONING

SKINNER, B. F. *The Technology of Teaching.* New York: Appleton-Century-Crofts, 1968.

Skinner's most practical and concise book. Chapter 3 details Skinner's ideas on programmed instruction; it also explains (and illustrates) the use of teaching machines. In chapter 5 Skinner points out why he feels that teachers fail. His views on personal freedom and determinism are discussed in chapter 8, which deals with the creative student.

NYE, ROBERT D. *What is Skinner Really Saying?* Englewood Cliffs, NJ: Prentice-Hall, 1979.

Nye is not a disciple of Skinner but is friendly towards his views; this book provides a relatively quick and easy explanation of Skinner's theory. Interesting chapters also discuss why Skinner's ideas are controversial, compare Skinner to Freud, and offer Skinner's criticisms of Rogers (*both* disparage the current educational system). The final chapter is a down-to-earth examination of the uses and effects of Skinnerian theory in everyday life, including reference to *Walden Two*.

The book is a good introduction to Skinner's views, or a helpful summary and analysis after having read Skinner's original writings.

COGNITIVE THEORY

The best way to gain an overview of Bruner's ideas is to read selected chapters from three of his original works.

BRUNER, JEROME. *The Process of Education.* New York: Random House, Vintage Books, 1960 (paperback).

This short book actually reports themes and tentative conclusions of a 1959 conference of natural scientists, psychologists, and educators that Bruner chaired, but the book has become identified with Bruner's own views. It is frequently quoted not only in reference to Bruner, but also in reference to cognitive theories in general. Chapter 1 is an introduction to Bruner's overall perspective on education. Chapter 2 reveals Bruner's thoughts about the importance of understanding and teaching structure. Chapter 4, on intuitive and analytic thinking, is perhaps the most interesting, even though it does not offer pat conclusions or direct advice.

BRUNER, JEROME. *Toward a Theory of Instruction.* Cambridge, MA: Harvard University Press, Belknap Press, 1966 (paperback).
Contains Bruner's most practical suggestions for implementing discovery-method teaching. In chapter 3, Bruner defines the major features of any theory of instruction; the chapter offers further insight into Bruner's attention to the importance of teaching structure and contains interesting sections on reinforcement and problem solving.

BRUNER, JEROME. *On Knowing: Essays for the Left Hand.* Cambridge, MA: Harvard University Press, Belknap Press, 1962; paperback, 1979.
The "left hand" in the title refers to Bruner's more intuitive, creative side. Thus this book is more personal than the others, less didactic or "logical." The three chapters in part 2 relate to education. "On Learning Mathematics" contains a clear description of the teaching-learning process in terms of discovery, intuition, translation, and readiness. "After John Dewey, What?" is a discussion of education as it applies to social consciousness. The book is actually an expansion of essays derived from various papers, articles, and addresses.

BIGGE, MORRIS L. *Learning Theories for Teachers* (as in General Books above).
Chapter 10 presents a compact and practical explanation of how Bruner's theory of learning is applied to the teaching situation. Bigge summarizes Bruner's thinking on the cognitive process, the purpose of education, and experiences that predispose learners to learn. The last portion of the chapter defines the "spiral curriculum" and suggests procedures that stimulate thought in the school setting.

DEVELOPMENTAL THEORY

PIAGET, JEAN, AND BARBEL INHELDER. *The Psychology of the Child.* Translated by Helen Weaver. New York: Basic Books, 1969.
The number of Piaget's books and articles is extensive; he published consistently during a very long life. This short book, written by Piaget and his associate, is a summary of several volumes. Each developmental level is described, together with some supporting documentation of experiments.

A helpful summary, "Factors in Mental Development," gives some idea of the link between Piagetian developmental theory and the process of education. To Piaget, learning theories are too much concerned with teaching and not enough concerned with children.

The writing is clear and effective, concise yet thorough. It affords an opportunity to read Piaget in his own terms.

PULASKI, MARY ANN. *Understanding Piaget.* Rev., exp. ed. New York: Harper & Row, 1980.

A practical guide to Piaget's research. It presents basic Piagetian principles, provides an overview of developmental stages, and discusses the work of Piaget's associates. At the end is a chronological list of Piaget's works and a list of English translations. Pulaski shows how Piaget's ideas are affecting parenting as well as education.

The book is highly readable, intended for a more general audience than psychologists and educationists. Pulaski succeeds in avoiding Piaget's frequently multi-syllabic terminology. The last section on education discusses Piaget's ideas about, and criticisms of, education.

HUMANISTIC PSYCHOLOGY

MASLOW, ABRAHAM. *The Farther Reaches of Human Nature.* New York: Viking Penguin, 1971; paperback, 1976.

A compilation of articles published after Maslow's death and largely unedited. Maslow's philosophy of self-actualization is here explored as relating to health and pathology, values and society. Part 2, "Creativeness," demonstrates Maslow's interest in the observation of productive and creative people and offers advice—in down-to-earth language—on how to release creativity within the self. Part 4, "Education," presents Maslow's view of humanistic education. His discussion of peak experiences contains pertinent reference to works of art, literature, and music.

ROGERS, CARL R. *Freedom to Learn for the 80's.* Columbus, OH: Charles E. Merrill; paperback, 1983.

A revision of the book that first appeared in 1969. In the early version, Rogers stated his ideas about learner-centered education, but offered little hard evidence of such in practice. The 1983 revision is substantially bolstered by ample (and lengthy) descriptions of schools and/or classrooms in which Rogerian theory can be seen in action. The most valuable chapters to read for an explanation of Rogers' views on learning are "The Challenge of Present-day Teaching" and "Researching Person-centered Issues in Education." Although the latter is replete with data and tables, it helps to clarify some of the processes used in learner-centered teaching.

An early chapter, "As a Teacher, Can I Be Myself?" and a section of five chapters, called "For the Teacher," provide direction and encouragement for those interested in trying the Rogerian approach to teaching in their own situations. While this is by no means a how-to-do-it book, the examples (often in the words of teachers or students themselves) are effective, and affecting, models of learner-centered teaching.

Kohut, Daniel L. *Musical Performance: Learning Theory and Pedagogy.* Englewood Cliffs, NJ: Prentice-Hall, 1985.
Kohut is a music educator whose book is directed to teachers of singers and instrumentalists. While some of his ideas are immediately applicable to piano performance, most of the practical suggestions relate to breathing, embouchure, tone production, and similar skills.

In parts 1 and 2, Kohut bases his exposition of learning theories as they relate to perceptual-motor learning and teaching psychology on three sources: Gallwey's "Inner Game" philosophy; Suzuki's "Mother Tongue Approach"; and Maltz's ideas about "Psycho-Cybernetics." While the book does not espouse humanistic psychology per se, the general thrust of its theses and arguments is closer to the position associated with current popular humanistic themes than it is to any other learning theory category.

INFORMATION-PROCESSING THEORY

Wingfield, Arthur. *Human Learning and Memory: An Introduction.* New York: Harper & Row, 1979.
Wingfield consolidates views on learning theory with studies of human memory, an examination of cognitive processes, and a discussion of the conceptual development of children. In that sense this book is useful, since most other books concentrate on only one of these areas. The book is textlike, however, and requires fairly intense reading. Of special value is the way Wingfield makes pertinent reference to the theories of Skinner, Bruner, Maslow, and others as these relate to information processing in general, or one of its "phases" in particular.

Wingfield, Arthur, and Dennis Byrnes. *The Psychology of Human Memory.* New York: Academic Press, 1981 (paperback).
This text is intended for undergraduates with little background in psychology. Each chapter begins with an outline and topic questions, and concludes with a summary of chapter contents. Overall, the book shows how memory is interdependent with learning, perception, language, problem solving, and reasoning.

Chapter 1 provides an excellent orientation to information processing in the light of earlier learning and psychological theories. Chapter 9 discusses memory research as applied to practical problems. In a presentation of "metamemory" (knowledge about one's own memory), there is valuable reference to what children know about knowing, especially as related to structure, rehearsal, and cueing techniques. The chapter concludes with interesting insights into aging and memory, as well as the associations between sleep or biological rhythms and memory.

CHAPTER 4

The Keyboard Teacher and the Process of Teaching

Playing the piano is a complicated act. Learning to play the piano is the result of acquiring and perfecting many different but interdependent skills. Teaching someone to play the piano, therefore, is neither simple nor undemanding. The teacher must know which skills relate and how they do so, and be able to communicate that understanding so others are led to achieve their own synthesis of interdependent skills. The process of becoming a teacher is the process of developing a rich accumulation of insights and the means to share them. Becoming a teacher should be as personally enriching as it is an expression of altruism.

Any teacher, but certainly the beginning teacher, needs to examine each learning skill in order to grasp its individual components as well as to be able to place that skill in the larger context of the piano-playing, music-making act. Such an examination must attend to each skill separately, even though the understanding of the interdependence of skills is the desired and necessary outcome. This chapter, therefore, will discuss individual skills used in making music at the piano. Each discussion will address both the learning and the teaching of the skill.[1]

*P*LAYING: *MOTOR SKILLS*

The entire body participates in the act of playing the piano, and a great deal of piano teaching and learning is directed to the goal of guiding and controlling movements. The multitude of movements required in the performance of even a short, simple piece is staggering if one considers how many separate limbs, muscles, and neurons must cooperate in the skillful execution of piano-playing gestures. Such skill is often referred to as "technique." Although technique is much more than the control of movements, the word is, nonetheless, commonly used to apply to the general category of motor skills.

All motor skills depend on the precision and timing of muscular movement. The learning of a motor task generally moves through certain stages:

1. *Early phase:* The learner must grasp the general idea of the skill to be acquired.
2. *Intermediate phase:* The learner must apply previously learned motor skills to the acquisition of the new skill. This is the practice stage wherein assimilation and/or adjustment of multiple motor skills must take place.
3. *Final phase:* The learner is able to perform the motor skill "without thinking," that is, without concentrated attention on the movement or series of movements.

Interaction between the teacher and learner throughout these stages also generally follows a pattern. The amount of direction and guidance from the teacher decreases from the early through the final phase. At the same time, the learner's reliance on personal, internal cueing and feedback must grow to the point of independence as the teacher's role changes. The teacher-learner interaction throughout these stages may be described as:

1. *Instruction phase:* The teacher provides verbal instruction coupled with visual and aural demonstration. The learner must absorb these external cues in order to translate them into a personal, internal cueing system.
2. *Association phase:* The learner practices the skill, attempting to improve its precision and timing. Feedback from the teacher supports this process, yet teacher feedback must become less necessary as the learner strives to internalize the skill. Ultimately, the learner develops an internal cueing and feedback system to initiate, control, and judge the performance of the skill.
3. *Independence phase:* The direction and support of the teacher are no longer necessary. The learner also has no further need to rehearse the internal cueing system, that is, the learner no longer needs to "think what to do" while performing the motor act. This phase, while final, is not static. As long as the learner continues to perform the motor act, smoothness and precision are further perfected and/or confirmed.

While the activities in all phases are important, the association stage is critical. Accidentally succeeding in the performance of the motor act is no indication that the motor act has been learned. (There is a *New Yorker* cartoon that depicts a golfer, having just made a hole-in-one, remarking "I wish I knew what I did right!"[2]) The crucial factor during the association phase of motor-skill learning is the learner's transference of external direction and modeling to an internal system of rehearsal and feedback. This internal awareness must guide the learner, while he or she repeats the motor act, by "reporting" to the learner to what extent the necessary accuracy has been acquired.

> By repeating the essential movements in successive trials of practice, the learner [must discover] the kinesthetic cues which signal the difference between error and error-free performance. . . . Internal cues [must] come to control and regulate the performance, [thus leading] to increasing degrees of precision and timing accuracy. Practice is necessary, then, because only by repeating the essential movements can the learner be provided with the cues that regulate the motor performance.[3]

For almost every learner, the *learning* (not the accidental successful performance) of a motor skill is a gradual process. *Occasionally* one comes across a learner whose internal processing and cueing is transferred so quickly from an external stimulus that the acquisition of the motor skill seems instantaneous. Yet even the extremely quick learner goes on to perfect and confirm the motor skill through repeated use of that act. In all cases, the speed of learning depends upon the speed at which the learner acquires the ability to correct and adjust the movement on the basis of internal feedback. A nonlearner is one who does not, or cannot, translate external cueing and feedback into internal cueing and feedback. The slower learner either takes longer to make this transference or needs more time to learn to trust internal cueing and feedback in judging observable results.

Guiding the learner to and through the association stage is the teacher's most important role in the teaching of technical motor skills. Too often the teacher regards the telling and showing ("this is how you do it") stage as the essential feature of instruction. This first stage is not without significance, of course. Inaccurate or disorganized telling and showing frustrates the entire learning process at the outset. But even when the teacher's verbal advice and visual and aural demonstration are superbly presented, motor-skill learning will not take place unless the learner is also guided to establish and trust correct internal cueing and feedback.

The ability of the teacher to see the learner through the association stage is dependent upon the teacher's diagnostic, rather than presentational, skills. Perceiving what is going wrong is only one part of the diagnosis. Understanding (or even second-guessing) *why* the learner is not making, or cannot make, the transference to internal cueing and feedback is the real crux of the matter. The teacher able to do so is then in the position of providing auxiliary external stimuli either to aid the learner's internal processing, or to motivate the learner to activate an inner correcting and reporting system.

Much of the time a piano-playing gesture is not a single act or a single motor skill. It is actually a series of consecutive motor acts that form a "routine" or "procedure." Making a two-note slur, for example, requires movement of the arm to the correct place on the keyboard, selection of the finger that will play the first note of the slur, descent of that finger to the keyboard, depression of the key, transference of weight from the finger that played the first note to the finger that depresses the second key, release of the second key, and a movement of the hand and arm upwards from the key. The mere description of what most pianists would regard as a single gesture points up the true complexity of that gesture and helps to underscore the many steps along the way that require discrimination and/or adjustment if the entire routine is to be smooth, precise, and musical.

How the mover learns to discriminate among the many movements that are possible (and either selected or not) is, itself, a matter of some sophistication. In drawing a letter, for example, it is the eye that informs the moving parts whether to adjust or not, since the eye "reports" whether the letter is being formed accurately. In the making of a piano-playing gesture, however, both eye and ear may furnish evidence which can assist the moving parts to complete their task successfully. For most learners, acquisition of a playing skill requires considerable attention to visual cues—both in relationship to the model as well as to the self—in the instruction and association stages of motor-skill learning. Ultimately, however, it should be the *ear* rather than the eye that is the final judge of the success, or nonsuccess, of a movement or gesture. For the musician, "in the long run technique, like everything else, is a matter of ear-training."[4]

At later stages of technical development, kinesthetic muscle response provides a cueing and feedback system of its own, reporting pain or tension or the sensation of freedom and ease. Movements made early during the process of technical training, however, will seldom be of sufficient or prolonged intensity to produce pain or discomfort. Kinesthetic cueing and feedback, therefore, may go "unreported" for many years. Thus, bad technical habits acquired at the beginning of study may result in pain, tension, or stiffness at a later stage, when the pianist is performing more advanced repertoire or is playing for longer periods of time.

There is an abundance of how-to-do-it or how-to-teach-it technical books available, some of which are very good. Almost all of them, however, concentrate completely on the instruction phase of technical teaching. While they do, of course, recommend particular practice regimens, they have paid little if any attention to suggesting ways in which the learner may be led to the establishment of internal cueing and feedback systems.[5] Recently, however, interest in biofeedback techniques, information-processing theories, and holistic experiences as applied to teaching has generated the emergence of both written and visual aids that either concentrate on or include aspects of developing inner control and awareness.[6] Such aids offer teachers and learners practical advice about getting in touch with the inner self that develops the personal cueing and feedback system.

READING AND COUNTING: INTELLECTUAL SKILLS

Learning to play the piano need not involve learning how to read music. People who only "play by ear" are proof of this truism. In most cases, these are also people who have not had a teacher. They have learned to play by watching others and by trial-and-error. They are frequently said to have "good ears," enabling them to bypass reading a score and to play directly from an aural impression. Pianists who *have* learned to read (whether with great success or not) are assumed to be those who have taken lessons. Thus, "teacher" and "learning to read" seem to relate as cause and effect. In fact, many people do not seek a teacher until they wish to receive, or have their children receive, instruction in reading and counting. They may also acknowledge the need for technical guidance, but this is probably not the primary reason for beginning piano instruction.

Most piano teaching of beginners validates that impression. The greatest amount of lesson time *is* spent in learning to read and count. Since this extensive activity has not produced (in the main) generations of confident and efficient readers, one must question the use of that time in terms of the results. Is it that learning to read music is more difficult than learning to read other sets of written symbols (like language and numbers)? Are the materials used to teach music reading inadequate or poorly organized? Could it be that music teachers are largely unaware of how to teach reading effectively? Are students not truly motivated to succeed in the reading of musical symbolism? No simple answers here, certainly—although one is tempted to admit that each question probably deserves an affirmative response.

Some of the difficulty lies in the fact that learning to play the piano and learning to read music at the piano are two separate skills. Because both teacher and student are eager to direct their efforts to the playing of pieces, insufficient attention may be given to the acquisition of *both* playing and reading as *separate* skills. It is the teacher who must be aware "that the process of making an able executant is quite distinct from that of making a good reader."[7]

Learning to read is *conceptual* learning, even though the proof of reading music at the keyboard results in a motor activity. Conceptual learning begins with discrimination. One must be able to tell the difference between one thing and another: for example, the difference between a note on a line and one in a space. Only thus can noteheads in two different places be understood as symbols for two different pitches. Perceiving further differences having to do with the direction and distance of one notehead from another is also the result of making discriminations. While all of this is true even if no pitch is played, the learner will grasp these concepts more surely if they become something concrete, something the learner can physically experience. The more sense experiences brought to bear in helping to establish the concept concretely, the more certainly and quickly will the concept be recognized and remembered. While it is primarily the young learner who profits most from sense experiences (especially multiple sense experiences) in the establishment of concepts, learners of all ages are influenced in this way.

The importance of concrete experience in establishing a concept is sometimes overlooked. This is especially true when the teacher is trying to get across an idea—like intervallic distance—and becomes heavily reliant on verbal cues and explanations. At times this may mean that the learner seems to understand the concept but cannot really use the information in actual context.

> The great value of concepts as means for thinking and communicating is that they have *concrete references*. The importance of this characteristic cannot be overemphasized. But since concepts are learned by the human being via language, there is often a danger of losing sight of this concreteness. Learning can become ototoverbalized.[8]

Another aspect of the importance of concrete experience is its role in the natural order of learning as demonstated, for example, in the developmental levels described by Piaget. The young child first encounters the environment, then learns names for objects seen and touched, actions observed or experienced. Traditionally formal education (especially before the twentieth century) has reversed that process, presenting first the definition, then the thing defined. Many teachers still teach that way. Even teachers who are cognizant of developmental theories sometimes find themselves *telling* the learner *about* something the learner has never experienced—and becoming frustrated when the learner does not learn. The thing before the sign, the experience before the definition—that is the natural learning route. Even adults, who are accustomed to dealing with conceptual definitions and are sometimes more comfortable talking about a thing than doing it, learn more quickly and securely when working from the experience to the symbol.

A concrete experience, however, does not necessarily lead to a conceptual grasp of the thing experienced. Learning about pitch, for example, is not primarily an intellectual activity. Awareness of pitch is not the same thing as knowing names for pitches or understanding how pitches may relate to one another in conceptual groupings such as scales or chords. Pitch perception is an aural experience even when this relates to the sound of scales or chords, wherein the ear recognizes a sense of association. It is not until the pitches are named or the relationships are defined and perceived *as* scales or chords that intellectual skills are involved.

Reading musical notation is further complicated by the fact that a note represents both a pitch name and a rhythmic value. Discrimination, therefore, includes distinguishing between or among those parts of the note that designate its time value as well as between those aspects of the note that specify pitch names and relationships. Initial rhythmic discrimination is between sounds that are long or short, proceeding thereafter to the gradual perception of an infinite variety of long/short combinations. Here, too, the perception of rhythm is an aural experience, having no necessary linkage between just hearing rhythm (as all people do daily, whenever they hear music on TV and cassettes, in supermarkets, in elevators) and being aware of relationships among the long/short combinations along with a perception of those relationships as groups or patterns.

It is important to distinguish, however, between learning the name for something (or learning a fact about something) and learning the *concept* of the thing named (or of the fact to be remembered). Learning that "quarter-note" is the name for a particular graphic symbol is not the same as understanding the concept of a quarter-note in the scheme of notational rhythmic relativity. Learning that in a 4/4 meter a quarter-note receives one count may only be the learning of a fact, not an indication that the process of metric counting is understood or that it can be translated into experience.

Learning names and facts is "verbal information learning." It is important because it is useful.[9] Verbal information learning enables someone to talk about—*verbalize*—things, facts, or ideas. Some teachers disparage such learning, claiming that the real aim of education is the fostering of the processes of understanding and creative thinking. These latter processes, however, are more efficiently accomplished if the learner has a storehouse of readily available information to be used in higher-order cognitive processes. As long as a teacher distinguishes between the student's learning of a name and learning of a concept, or does not accept the former as an indication of the latter, teaching that includes verbal information learning will be helpful in the overall process of establishing concepts.

The influence of gestalt psychology permeates many explanations of pitch and rhythmic perception, and likewise it permeates many contemporary presentations of teaching pitch and rhythmic reading. Often this is not the result of the writer's or teacher's deliberate choice of a particular learning theory as much as it is an outcome of that individual's own experience in learning. Teachers, for example, whose focus in the teaching of music reading is on the perception of the interval as the smallest building block, and on the establishment of the reading process as the perception of ongoing intervallic relationships, have already accepted the fact that an interval itself is a gestalt.

The apprehension of rhythm as the experience of relating to patterns (rather than duration values for individual notes) is also based on the acceptance of grouping as a primary building block.

> As a piece of music unfolds, its rhythmic structure is perceived not as a series of discrete independent units strung together in a mechanical, additive way like beads, but as an organic process in which smaller rhythmic motives, while possessing a shape and structure of their own, also function as integral parts of a larger rhythmic organization.[10]

Growth in rhythmic perception is the reorganization of smaller patterns into larger groupings. This kind of awareness fosters, and is fostered by, attention to structure. Larger rhythmic form evolves from the organized grouping of smaller sub-units.

Ultimately, the aural/physical perception of pitches or rhythms must be coupled with conceptual understanding of a *process* of reading pitch and rhythmic symbols before the interaction of these two modes of knowing can result in a performance of what is read. Most learners also go through phases of learning in arriving at the "ownership" of a concept.

1. Initial phase: The learner has a concrete aural/physical experience. The teacher is either the stimulus for the experience or arranges the learning situation to cause the occurrence of the experience.

2. Conceptual phase: The learner acquires a name for the experience or a definition that explains a relationship or procedure involving the experience. The teacher provides the name or definition or chooses a teaching tool that does so.
3. Reinforcement phase: The learner incorporates the defined experience or procedure into already established routines and also develops an internal cueing and rehearsal system. The teacher may provide occasional external cues and may arrange activities wherein the learner continues to use the newly defined concept.
4. Ownership phase: The learner no longer needs to refer to the internal cueing and rehearsal system in applying the defined concept. The teacher is no longer "in the picture."

Difficulties for the learner may occur if the initial phase, that of concrete experience, is overlooked entirely or if it follows the definition. It is not enough that the learner has experienced the concept to be defined *sometime* in the past, although that, at least, may be a remote aid. It is much more effective if the experience immediately, or almost immediately, precedes the definition. Thus, the experience of hearing and playing regularly recurring pulses should come before the exposure to the concept of notes as symbols for pulses. Likewise, experience with whole and half steps should occur prior to their presentation as the constructive elements of a major scale.

A definition should be accurate but is most truly effective when presented simply, without exceptions and tangential references. The teacher, who has an abundance of knowledge about the concept being defined, often cannot refrain from including information that is not necessary to the learner's momentary requirements in dealing with the concept. A satisfactory definition is one that distills the essence of a concept to its simplest components. The definer must not only grasp the structure of the concept in order to know what the essence is, but must be able to relate that essence in words that can be understood by the learner.

Sometimes this is a matter of using an appropriate vocabulary, one the learner can relate to past experience. It is not helpful to define "3/4 meter" as a meter in which there are three beats to a measure, with the quarter-note receiving one count, if the learner has not already experienced and understood the concepts of meter, measure and quarter-note. A definition may fail to make its point because it is ordered awkwardly: "When you have a quarter-note and there are three of them in a measure, or some amount of notes equal to three beats, you have what is called a 3/4 measure." Definitions may be inaccurate even when the immediate context makes them seem true. Such is the case when a dotted half-note is defined as a note that receives three counts. Since that is only true when the quarter-note is the unit beat, the definition is ultimately misleading. An accurate definition is one in which the relativity of the dotted half-note to the quarter-note is clear regardless of the metric context. It is more accurate to state that a dotted half-note lasts as long as three quarter-notes. That will always be true. The effective definition is one that anticipates future exceptions but does not prematurely attempt to include them.

The third phase of conceptual learning may be the most misunderstood. Although a concept may be grasped completely in a general sense, through both experience and definition, it is often not secure until it has been applied in contexts similar to its original presentation and then tested in more-challenging contexts. Use of the concept in similar circumstances allows the learner to begin the development of the internal cueing/rehearsal system with reasonable ease. Occasional external cueing by the teacher may be necessary, but such cueing should always attempt also to guide the learner toward being responsible for the concept independently. The greatest role the teacher plays in this phase is in supplying supportive materials or organizing reinforcing activities. Next the learner needs to encounter the concept in contexts that require greater differentiation between the newly acquired concept and a larger assortment of already learned concepts. At this stage, the learner is moving toward reliance on the internal cueing/rehearsal system in recognizing the concept readily with new appreciation of its place in the scheme of things. External cueing from the teacher should be largely unnecessary. The teacher, however, is once again the probable source of most, if not all, of the materials and activities that will provide more challenging contexts.

Teachers should keep in mind that sheer repetition of a concept is only minimally reinforcing. Repeating the use of the concept in exactly the same context tends to dull the internal cueing/rehearsal system, since attention is neither provoked nor stimulated. This is quite unlike the repetition necessary in the evolution of motor skills, where the movement itself is not really learned until after many attempts. In conceptual learning, the concept is generally there in its complete form in the early stages. What is needed is not so much practice in developing a concept to a perfect state, but practice in differentiating the new concept from all other concepts.

When the internal cueing/rehearsal system no longer needs to operate in order to use or recognize a concept in any context, the concept is "owned." The cueing/rehearsal system is not discarded and may be retrieved and activated whenever a new situation requires reexamination of the concept. This may be the case whenever a concept needs to be expanded or raised to a higher or more complex level. A fundamental understanding of the relationship between tonic and dominant, for instance, may remain essentially unchanged for a considerable period of time. At the point where the use of secondary dominants is introduced, the tonic-dominant concept may need to be reinspected for the new concept to be understood in its turn. The cueing/rehearsal techniques used in the establishment of the tonic-dominant concept are then retrievable to assist in the fixing of the new concept. If the learning of the original tonic-dominant concept had not advanced to the point of ownership, or had not generated any internal cueing/rehearsal system (instead relying completely on external cues and teacher support), then the concept of the secondary dominant would not be grasped until *both* levels of understanding have been achieved. Because cueing/rehearsal systems are retrievable and reusable, intact or with minimal adaptation, educators who teach their students to internalize the learning process regard this teaching strategy as productive and efficient. Moreover, any teaching technique that stimulates students to "know how they know" also promotes independent learning.

PROBLEM SOLVING: COGNITIVE STRATEGIES

The application of problem-solving skills in learning to play the piano, or in learning about music as it relates to piano performance, is not a frequently used teaching strategy. Some teachers believe that they are using problem-solving teaching techniques because they ask many questions or use more open-ended, awareness-provoking directives. Using a discovery-method approach is not necessarily the same thing as using problem-solving techniques. Discovery-method teaching strategies may include accentuation of contrast, emphasis on structure, stimulation of informed guessing, arousal of awareness, and encouragement of participation—as well as the solution of problems. The search for a solution, however, may lead to a specific kind of learning, and that is why it is is regarded separately in this chapter.

"Problem solving," as a cognitive task, involves more than simply finding answers to conventional mathematical problems or providing answers to organized questions. Such cases are "solved" by the application of previously learned rules. The use of a rule in arriving at an answer proves that the rule is understood and has been selected and applied correctly. Actual "problem solving" is an *extension* of rule learning.

> It is a process by which the learner discovers a combination of previously learned rules which can be applied to achieve a solution for a novel situation.... When [the learner] finds a particular combination of rules that fit the situation, [the learner has] not only "solved the problem" but has also learned something new.[11]

What is newly learned may be either a higher-order rule or a fresh way to solve problems. The learning of a higher-order rule enables the learner to use that rule to solve similar problems. The learning of the new way to solve problems, however, also teaches the learner something about his/her own cognitive strategies. The learner has gained insight into how (s)he can respond in other, general, problem-solving situations. Something individual has happened which is not merely an awareness of another rule.

Problem solving follows a general pattern. Psychologists often refer to this as *heuristics,* or the techniques of problem solving.

1. Presentation:	The learner becomes aware that there is a problem. This may be a discovery on the part of the learner. The teacher may present the problem.
2. Definition:	The learner defines for him/herself what the situation reveals and what the problem is.

	The teacher may offer further cues to enable the learner tó grasp the problem.
3. **Experimentation:**	The learner forms and considers hypotheses that may resolvė the problem or lead to a solution. The teacher may furnish cues, but the cues may not contain the solution.
4. **Verification:**	The learner determines which hypothesis is successful, by trial and error if necessary. The teacher is no longer "in the picture."

In order to solve problems, the learner must have acquired a fund of verbal information, concepts, and rules on which hypotheses for solving the problem can be based. Therefore teaching strategies involving problem solving are more appropriate for use with learners who are older or who have, at least, a sufficient depository of prerequisite knowledge to solve a specific problem. Occasionally, however, a learner without the necessary preknowledge to solve a problem, or without all aspects of that knowledge, may be challenged to arrive at an original solution in a situation requiring one. In such an instance, the learner must fill in the gaps and "teach the self" those concepts or rules needed to solve the problem. While this may be stimulating and exciting for certain students at certain times, a teaching plan or method based on frequent use of such challenges may frustrate the learner or create a learning atmosphere suffused with tension or fear.

Suggesting that a student work out original fingering solutions for a new piece of music is one example of how problem-solving techniques can be used as part of piano instruction. If the new piece is a classic sonatina (e.g., Beethoven's Sonatina in G Major), the technical and fingering prerequisites would include the ability to extend the range by means of thumb crossings (in upward as well as downward passages), an understanding of fingering patterns associated with the performance of two-note slurs, an awareness of the efficacy of a fingering change on repeated notes, and the experience of fingering chordal patterns in both five-finger and extended positions. The *presentation* of the problem is the assignment of the piece with instructions to work out the fingering, possibly penciling in special fingerings where changes, shifts, or slurs do not lie under the hand. The *definition* of the problem by the student occurs when the student actually begins to play and finger the piece, at that time becoming aware of exactly which situations might require fingering adjustments. *Experimentation* takes place as the student tries out fingering combinations in various places, eventually selecting those that seem to suit the piece and the hand. Performing the piece, noting that the selected fingerings work, is the *verification* to the student that the choices are practical and wise.

The value of the learning involved in fingering the sonatina is not the accomplishment of having fingered any particular passage, although in some cases specific fingering solutions may serve the learner in future pieces where similar passages occur. The significance of this experience is that it teaches the learner, in a concrete and personal way, *why* successful piano performance requires employment of efficient fingering and, further, *how* fingering choices are determined and notated for personal remembrance or for communication to others. Although the student needed to play the passages in order to arrive at fingering solutions, the analytical, critical, and judgmental processes that controlled the entire experience were internal. The student was learning, in a general way, why and how all pieces are fingered. In addition, the student was aware of the *self* as the controller of these internal processes achieving thereby not only the exhilaration of solving the problem but also the ego-supporting reinforcement of learning to trust the self.

One might question the efficacy of using this type of teaching strategy. Can problem solving truly be taught? Aren't some individuals born problem solvers, curiously sifting, measuring, and choosing information and ideas that they reshape in original ways? From the opposite perspective, one might question why educators don't spend *all* their time involving students in problem solving so that time spent in formal education would be concentrated on the highest goals instead of on the accumulation of facts, skills, concepts, and rules.

Evidence indicates that the better the learner's foundation (the storehouse of facts, skills, concepts, and rules), the more likely it is that the learner will be able to solve problems and arrive at original solutions. It also seems reasonable to hold that unless some students are challenged or encouraged to solve problems, they may never discover within themselves the power to think and judge independently. The teacher's responsibility, then, with regard to the use of problem-solving techniques is twofold. The first task is to determine when the time is right, when there are enough appropriate materials in the student's information stockpile to provide multiple and workable hypotheses that may be used in particular acts of problem solving. The teacher's second charge is to select and arrange an appropriate problem that will develop the learner's capacity to arrive at original conclusions.

Some psychologists have noted, and most people have experienced, that in solving certain problems there is a period of seeming inattention (at times quite long) during which the problem, perhaps together with several hypotheses, just sits there. The incubation period may end abruptly with an "Aha! experience"— sudden awareness of what the solution is. Both teacher and learner must respect this ruminating time. The teacher cannot always cue; the learner cannot always jump to the right conclusions. The silent minute (or week, or month) is necessary so that quiet sifting may occur. Teachers who forever insist upon immediate results risk the elimination of efforts (on the part of both learner *and* teacher) that might lead to valuable insights or unusual interpretations.

Problem solving is a route to independent thinking.

> When students practice solving novel problems, they presumably learn not only rules applicable to those problems, but also general ways of accomplishing problem solving. That is to say, they learn ways of exercising control over their own thought processes: how to seek relevant features of the problem, how to keep

in mind what has been tried previously, how to weigh the probabilities of their hypotheses, and so on. These capabilities of self-control are the *cognitive strategies* of thinking.[12]

MOTIVATING: ATTITUDES

Most people do not attend to the fact that they learn attitudes just as surely as they learn information, motor skills, concepts, and ideas. The learning of attitudes usually takes place less consciously than the learning of other capabilities, and happens, for the most part, outside of formal learning situations. Family, friends, the immediate environment, advertising, movies, religious groups, written communication—all are teachers of attitudes. Some of these influences—advertising, religious groups, certain kinds of writing—deliberately seek to shape attitudes, while others—parents, family, friends—may affect attitude formation either willfully or not.

Attitude learning is also an element of musical learning. While it may sometimes be a factor in formal instruction time, at the lesson or in the class, the acquisition of attitudes toward music and toward piano playing is generally a result of exposure to many people and situations only some of whom (or which) are consciously trying to shape or affect a particular learner's attitude toward music or piano performance. Because the sphere of influence is wide, the teacher who would deliberately seek to influence a learner's attitudes must be aware of how and why attitudes are adopted and expressed.

An attitude is "an internal state that influences (moderates) the choices of personal action made by the individual."[13] An attitude does not necessarily result in action, of course, but many actions are the direct consequence of attitudes. It is true that whenever someone acts, they are choosing to do one thing rather than another, although these choices are often not made consciously. Yet there are certain times when one is more aware of "choosing"—for instance, selecting which movie one will attend, or deciding which pieces to program on a recital. The making of such choices is affected by one's attitudes. Psychologists are not at all in agreement about whether attitudes originate in ideas or beliefs (and are therefore outgrowths of cognition) or if they arise from emotional states (and therefore stem from affective sources). Personal experience would seem to corroborate that attitudes have both cognitive and affective components, but that it is not always possible to tell which of these is primary in a given situation.

People's attitudes may be deduced from their actions. But usually people express, or are asked to express, their attitudes verbally. Quite often an individual describes an attitude in a very general way—for example, "I don't really like piano lessons." This may mean many things: I don't like the pieces I'm playing; I don't like the long bus ride to the lesson; I don't like the teacher because he is impatient, and so on. Until the person (or the person who would change the attitude) can get at the heart of the matter, nothing can be done to affect the attitude. It is sometimes difficult for a person to express an attitude adequately or honestly—or even to express it at all—for fear of reprisal or loss of face. So determining the true attitude, much less its source, may be complicated if not occasionally impossible.

Attitudes may be acquired quickly, on the basis of a single experience, or they may be formed gradually, sometimes over a period of many years. The attitude acquired quickly is often negative, the result of a sudden fright, painful sensation, or confusing circumstance. The attitude acquired gradually draws its substance from a sequence of continued successes or pleasures (positive attitude) or a succession of failures and frustrations (negative attitude). As the successes or failures accumulate and deepen, so does the positive or negative quality of the attitude become established and strengthened.

Attitudes and motivation are intrinsically linked, although one is not the other. Since the concern here is attitudes toward learning (or the motivation to learn), a consideration of learning situations that are attitude producing (or motivating) is in order. Operant conditioning—immediate reinforcement to the response—can be effective in activating the learner to attain short-term goals. The perception of success—which may be reported to the learner via grades, applause, trophies, diplomas, or other reinforcement, or which might also derive from a personal awareness of growth and competency—supports the achievement of longer-term goals. The role model—whom the learner imitates, or from whom the learner looks for approval—is the strongest and most effective influence.

Types of motivation are distinguishable:

1. Extrinsic motivation: Reinforcement in the form of rewards, payment, acceptance by peers, approval from the model or superiors.
2. Intrinsic motivation: Realization of growth and development, sense of self-confidence and power, awareness of likeness to the model, appreciation of independence.
3. Achievement motivation: Attainment of goals, feeling of completion, excitement of competition.

It is tempting to suggest that all human behavior should be the result of intrinsic motivation since it is the most deeply satisfying and noble. But the truth is that people use and need extrinsic motivation throughout their lives, depending on rewards and payments of many kinds to get them through each day. The passion to achieve, stronger in some people than others, may be perceived either as totally self-aggrandizing or as an appropriate challenge to the human potential. A balance among these three types of motivation must be found. That balance may be affected by age, personality, and culture. Ideally an adult should be intrinsically motivated in relation to the primary goals of life, using immediate, tangible rewards to push small pieces of business through to completion. A child, whose experience thus far in life is based on the immediate and tangible, should develop the capacity to sustain effort for abstract and psychic reasons, and learn to enjoy the inner payoff.

In the piano lesson, as elsewhere, extrinsic motivation may be powerfully effective. Stickers, treats, praise, a hug—these, or variations of them—are necessary when dealing with the young child. Even a child with enormous talent relishes immediate, tangible approval. A concert pianist, speaking of her first teacher and earliest lessons, remembers the rewards fondly: [She] carried a big basket of Hershey bars and gold stars for the music and I was crazy about this lady. All I had to do was play the right notes in the right rhythm and I got a Hershey bar."[14]

The materials themselves may be motivators—an attractive book, a special, exciting piece of sheet music, use of ensembles, taped accompaniment or background. Motivators contained in the materials, even though they are extrinsic, are a step up on the way to learning for its own sake. The older student continues to be interested in external rewards—grades, an audition report, the teacher's praise, admiration of piano-playing peers, a trophy, a scholarship—but these come at the end of a much longer period of effort (during which multiple immediate "payments" might have been a sustaining factor).

Effective though they are, extrinsic rewards have limitations. There is, first of all, the possibility that the student may begin to feel manipulated, perhaps irritated and demeaned by the necessity of earning approval by striving for rewards. Self-worth may become equated only with achievement, or "winning." Second, the external reward is by nature temporary. If external reinforcement is used as the only, or chief motivator, what has been learned may be "trashed" as soon as the prize has been won. Last, the carrot-before-the-horse routine may create a dependence difficult to shed if and when the carrot disappears.

Movement, on the part of the student, from reliance on external motivators to greater awareness of the pleasure and value of internal satisfaction may happen somewhat naturally. The development is usually gradual and is the result of enjoying successes as well as learning to overcome setbacks. The student may find technical practice a chore (or a bore), yet may be performing certain pieces very well or improvising with great ingenuity. Intrinsic satisfaction may develop in response to the success of playing and improvising even though more tangible motivators are still needed to keep up the technical regimen.

It may be worthwhile to stimulate greater reliance on the student's own self-teaching abilities by arranging appropriate problem-solving activities, helping the student to move from dependence on the teacher for all instruction, correction, and approval. Assigning a piece to be worked on independently—perhaps discussed with the teacher after it has been prepared but not necessarily polished and reworked by the teacher, even if some things have not been totally suitable—is one technique to awaken the awareness and trust of self necessary to the appreciation of inner rewards. The most important reason to provoke the student's reliance on internal motivation is that what the student learns in this manner has the greatest potential for "transfer of learning."

Teaching so that students begin to appreciate self-directed learning even as they continue to need some external supports and crutches in the form of tangible payoffs is not without problems. Chief among these is the probability that some, possibly many, students are not that easily stimulated to seek their own answers or solve their own problems. This is especially true if the problem-solving tasks they are given require extensive detailed work or challenge skills that are not yet firmly fixed. In such cases, the fault lies with the teacher in the choice of the problem-solving task. However, if the assignment is appropriate but the student does not rise to the bait, there may not be much to do until, or unless, the student can be brought to a point of stimulation by the achievement of some notable success.

> Frequently, the best way of teaching an unmotivated student is to ignore his motivational state for the time being, and to concentrate on teaching him as effectively as possible. Some degree of learning will ensue in any case, despite the lack of motivation; and from the initial satisfaction of learning he will, hopefully, develop the motivation to learn more. In some circumstances, therefore, the most appropriate way of arousing motivation to learn is to focus on the cognitive rather than on the motivational aspects of learning, and to rely on the motivation that is developed from successful educational achievement to energize further learning.[15]

It is often thought that students need to be motivated to reach goals. Sometimes it is the reaching of the goal itself that is the motivator. While this is particularly true with regard to the attainment of short-term goals, it is equally accurate that students may be energized to perform in order to reach long-term goals. A student's realization that what looks like an extended piece is really only sixteen measures long (because of repetitions or, perhaps, transpositions) may be motivation enough to work on the piece with enthusiasm. The student knows that (s)he can learn sixteen measures without much trouble, so expectations for success are enhanced by virtue of the short-term goal. Preparing a piece for performance at a monthly group session or informal recital may be another effective short-term goal. Auditions, recitals, and competitions are all examples of long-term goals that may be positive motivation for some students. The completion of some task, or the arrival at some state of closure, may here mingle (as motivation) with the expectation of the superior rating, the round of applause and pride of parents, or the the first-place prize. It is, of course, the satisfaction of doing well, finishing the job, or bringing a piece to a state of relative perfection that the teacher wishes to inculcate as the important true result of the audition, recital, or contest. Self-completion, rather than peer competition, has the greatest lasting value and is not subject to the vicissitudes of others' opinions. Ultimately, "cooperative or individualized learning situations are generally preferable to competitive situations. If only a few students can earn high grades by 'defeating' classmates, the many 'losers' will have little incentive to learn and may feel inferior or inadequate."[16]

Often overlooked as a motivating influence is the difference that *choice* makes. Because the teacher has plans for a particular student (or, perhaps, for each student) and knows so much better than the student what it will take to fulfill these expectations, the teacher may make all the decisions about everything—which pieces to play, how each is to be played, how to practice, the chronological events at each lesson, and so on. All of this is generally done in the name of benefit to the student and efficient use of time. It is valuable not only to allow the student some choice in the use of his/her time and energies, but actually to create situations in which the student can learn to choose, and can learn by choosing.

The long-range repertoire design usually includes performance of pieces in Baroque style. It is more interesting to both teacher and student, and certainly more motivating to the student, if the teacher prepares and performs four pieces of comparable pianistic difficulty from which the student may choose the single piece on which (s)he will work. This procedure has several benefits. The student is pleased to choose and often acquires a sense of responsibility to that particular piece just because it has been a personal choice. The student also hears more than just the one piece that has been selected for study and thereby increases his/her awareness of a larger repertoire. In addition, it is possible that the student may be attracted to two of the pieces and decide to play them both.

Although this kind of presentation takes greater time for the teacher to prepare, the teacher also profits by the experience. The search for comparable pieces may reawaken the teacher's own interest in some forgotten teaching material. In playing for the student the teacher not only has the pleasure of performance but increases his/her credibility as a performer in the eyes of the student. The teacher also learns something about the student's proclivities and viewpoints by the student's choice, or by the way in which the student makes the choice.

Investigators of motivational attitudes differ considerably on many points of emphasis, but they are all in striking agreement about one notable conclusion. "One of the most dependable sets of events that has been found to produce changes in attitudes is the phenomenon of *human modeling*.[17] The person who serves as the model may be in the learner's real world, or may seem real from afar (e.g., a sports hero or TV star). For older learners, the model may also be fictional or entirely imagined. The model's actions or expressed attitudes are imitated by the learner since, to the learner, the model is admired and respected or viewed as having particular credibility. The learner, when imitating the model, is sometimes rewarded for his/her behavior and the attitude, and action resulting from it, is reinforced. The reinforcement is especially effective if approval, or other positive notice, comes directly from the model. Most often, however, the learner observes the rewards that accrue to the model (fame, power, popularity, success, salary, prestige, adulation) and the reinforcement is vicarious.

Psychologists call attention to the importance of the development of the superego in the id-ego-superego division of the psyche. The superego is the self-critic that enforces standards. These internalized standards form the "ego ideal," which most often develops as the result of the observation and the influence of role models. In the development of the performing artist, however, "the ego ideal is limited to and patterned after the two significant adults [the parent, the teacher] in the lives of [the developing artist]. It [therefore] suffers in growth and scope because of the lack of value systems incorporated from different significant adults. The self-rewarding system is constricted and limited to achievement.[18] It is, nonetheless, precisely the emergence of a strong superego that enables the young developing performer to survive the discipline and deprivations required to achieve notable performing success. "The teacher's presence alone motivated, inspired, and instructed.... First and foremost the teachers provided role models of the highest order.... The pianists learned attitudes and habits and ways of working that they often were not even conscious of learning, simply by being in the presence of the master."[19]

The forceful effect of role modeling on motivation is underscored when one heeds the results of the many studies conducted to measure the influence of advice, admonition, or other such communication. While these studies also examined the effects of different kinds of messages (e.g., messages which aroused fear, appealed to reason, drew conclusions, or evoked emotional responses), evidence was overwhelming that it was not so much the content of the message that mattered, but the *source* of the message. Sometimes communication is heeded because the source is powerful and controls the receiver of the communication in some way. (Teachers often trade in on this kind of communication.) Occasionally the source is regarded as someone with whom the receiver identifies and the communication is absorbed and acted upon with eagerness. The older one gets, the more important it is that the source be credible. Little or no attention is paid to communication from a source that is not deemed trustworthy and believable or that cannot be seen as having some kind of expertise or experience.

Modeling as part of the piano lesson or class may be used to good effect in several ways. First, it is important that the teacher be a model pianist. The student must *hear* beautiful sounds, lucid phrasing, nuance, and sensitivity. The student must also *see* how a pianist looks, how gestures are made, how motor skills are negotiated. The student must sometimes *feel* what is happening in the teacher's arm or wrist, or feel what his/her own body is experiencing when the teacher demonstrates a particular sensation on the student's hand or arm. The teacher who is forever sitting to the right of and slightly behind the student—pointing, tapping, manipulating the metronome, and writing in the assignment book—does not serve as a model pianist. One of the values of group experiences is the availability of more models to observe even though not all of these models may be admirable at all times. Recitals are modeling times as well. Less-experienced pianists hear the performances of those with greater skill and experience. Attending the concerts of artists is extremely important. These are the superstars of piano playing and serve as models for teacher and student alike.

The teacher also models the *world* of music to the student. The teacher who is enthusiastic and vital when playing or speaking about music, who can be perceived as leading a rich and fulfilling life, who reflects sensitivity and respect for students and colleagues, who is observed to be disciplined and highly motivated in the pursuit of professional aims, who is encouraging and thoughtful when guiding and correcting—this teacher is also the model musician. While no one should actively seek to be another's role model, the awareness of how one's own actions and attitudes affect others—especially those for whom one is responsible—should be a matter of concern and watchfulness.

The catholic sense in which the teacher represents the status of model musician recalls the humanistic view of learning. Maslow's theory of need gratification underpins the concept of the teacher as the "self-actualizing model" and the learner as moving through the stages of attending to "deficiency" needs while observing the teacher as the exemplar of one who is gratifying "growth" needs.

> All self-actualized people have a cause they believe in, a vocation they are devoted to. When they say, "my work," they mean their mission in life.... Self-actualizing people ... seem to do what they do for the sake of ultimate, final values, which is for the sake of principles which seem *intrinsically worthwhile*.... These values are not abstract to the self-actualizing person; they are as much a part of them as their bones and arteries. Self-actualizing people are motivated by the eternal verities.[20]

THE PRACTICAL USE OF LEARNING THEORIES

Having investigated the teaching of piano performance with reference to several theories of learning, it may be useful to ask the question posed by educational psychologist Edward L. Walker: Do learning theories have anything to offer the educator? His answer is not only revealing, but also practical and sensible.

> I think learning theories should be seen as a source of possibly useful concepts. Concepts are useful if they provide intellectual handles that permit the educator to analyze and understand the problems being faced. They are useful if, and only if, they suggest something useful and effective to do in motivating and guiding the student.... You should not confine your attention to any single theory. Rather you should examine all available theories ... for any concept that fits well into your head, and you should find as many such concepts as possible.[21]

Using whatever "fits well into one's head" is also a good way to deal with ideas connected to the examination of individual learning capabilities. No teacher, experienced or inexperienced, works at improving teaching strategies by hoping for, or looking for, a formula or system that will make it possible to attend to the development of all teaching skills at once. Integration takes place as the teacher attends to certain things at certain times but keeps the information pool about varied learning theories as large as possible. That is the advantage of having examined all available theories.

One area in which an awareness of learning theories might prove particularly helpful to the piano teacher is in examination of materials used for instruction. A teacher need not be overly pedantic or analytical in looking at method books this way. A general, informed awareness is often enough to grasp the underlying psychology in any textual presentation. The teacher is then in a much stronger position to use materials in such a way that the educational approach taken by the author(s) may be more effectively supported or wisely complemented. It is also illuminating to notice that sometimes method books deliver mixed messages; the knowledgeable teacher is better able to compensate for what is missing or out of place. Attempting to use discovery-method techniques with material designed in an associationist format is frustrating to both teacher and learner. Awareness that in a particular method concepts are presented in wholes before being shown as separate parts enables a teacher to utilize this cognitive teaching strategy as intended. Piano methods do not usually come with how-to teaching manuals. And even when a teacher's handbook is available, it cannot begin to provide sufficient psychological background to support and explain the teaching techniques it suggests. A broad knowledge of learning theories, then, may at least give the teacher clues as to where to seek supportive background.

The teacher may likewise draw on a pool of information to evaluate the many kinds of teaching strategies applicable to the piano lesson or class. Perhaps more open-ended, problem-solving activities (such as improvisation or independent learning of pieces) need to be incorporated into a teacher's overall learning plan in order to teach more holistically. It may be that the teacher's attention to skill areas (such as the presentation of technique) has resulted in the overuse of "telling" and "showing" instructions and neglected the application of "awareness" instruction to assist the learner in forming internal cueing and feedback systems. Knowledge and application of varied learning theories enrich one's teaching perspective, which in turn engenders the emergence of both a more diversified and enthusiastic teacher and a more interested and wholly developed student. Because so many skills (psychomotor, cognitive, behavioral, affective) must be integrated in the piano lesson, ideas from many learning theories may "fit well in the head" and be used to advantage.

PART THREE

The Elementary
Student

CHAPTER 5

The Preschool Student

The preschooler who begins music instruction is usually between four and six years old. Some children, of course, may begin instruction earlier (at three, perhaps) but this is dependent upon particular circumstances, such as unusual talent on the part of the child, or special interest or expertise on the part of the teacher in working with children at that age. Although certain children have always begun music study at ages four, five, or six, it is only in the latter decades of the twentieth century that many children are doing so. Two major reasons appear to be influencing this trend. On the one hand, medical science and educational psychology are providing an abundance of information and opinion about the abilities and developmental characteristics of the young child. Awareness of these factors as they relate to the perception of music—for example, the preschooler's acute aural sensitivity—has aroused music educators to recognize and develop such propensities by providing more extensive, and more varied, preschool musical instruction. Parents, on the other hand, are becoming increasingly concerned—largely as a result of this information explosion—that the early years of their children's development are not wasted. They therefore seek to involve their children in enrichment activities, not necessarily to discover possible latent talents as much as to stimulate awareness (on the part of the children) of many modes of communication and expression.

At the crux of the concerns of both medical and educational professionals and parents is the matter of readiness. At which point is a child ideally suited to do certain things, appreciate certain experiences? Should the parent seek evidence of the child's interest (for example, in making music) or attempt to arouse such an interest? Can instruction at an early age prime a particular readiness or should it rather encourage and support development of whichever readiness manifests itself?

Now more than ever one sees examples of parents and educators who believe in the priming of readiness. Day-care centers, "gymborees," movements like the Better Baby Program,[1] and classes such as those for very young swimmers and skiers are much on the increase.

> Thousands of mothers and fathers are caught up in a phenomenon that educational psychologists call 'hot-housing,' trying to jump-start tiny students toward success. Since 1970, enrollment in early programs, both private and public, has surged from 4,104,000 to more than 6 million. Judging by the parental push, the trend will accelerate.[2]

Music educators are providing a variety of musical experiences for this early age group and one hears and sees a growing number of tiny violinists, pianists, and players of drums, tuned bars, and tonettes.

This proliferation of organized and/or highly visibile activities available to the preschool child is not, however, based entirely on physical and psychological premises or observations. This is the age of the two-income family and the single parent. The importance of these preschool activities is very real. Day-care centers and nursery schools are, for many parents, necessities, not merely enticing extras. While no one would claim that all nursery schools and day-care centers are places in which enrichment experiences are the order of the day, the possibility for incorporating such experiences into the daily routine of these institutions is immeasurablely increased by virtue of their number and influence.

INFLUENCES ON PRESCHOOL MUSICAL INSTRUCTION

Many of the forces influencing the nature and direction of preschool musical instruction, especially as this relates to instrumental (in addition to vocal) music-making, arise from sources outside the United States. The educational ideals and teaching strategies associated with Émile Jaques-Dalcroze (1865–1950), Carl Orff (1895–1982), Zoltán Kodály (1882–1967), Shinichi Suzuki (b. 1898), and the educators (among them Eizo Itoh) who developed the Yamaha Music Education Ssytem have all had bearing on the musical training of very young children as currently practiced in this country. Some of these musicians and educators work(ed) directly with preschool children; others do (did) not. Yet vestiges of what they taught, or are teaching, surface repeatedly in much preschool musical instruction. These influences are not always consciously adopted or acknowledged. Nonetheless, they are traceable by those whose own background has included exposure to the teaching of these music educators. A brief description of the ideals and practices of each educator follows in order that these influences may be more easily recognized and genuinely appreciated.

Émile Jacques-Dalcroze

Dalcroze was a professor of harmony in the Geneva Conservatory of Music when, in 1892, he devised an approach to the teaching of ear training and keyboard improvisation that sought to sensitize the listening and creative abilities of his students. Since he felt that "musical sensations of a rhythmic nature call for the muscular and nervous response of the whole organism,"[3] Dalcroze exercises called for rhythmic responses involving the use of the whole body. These exercises sought to stimulate awareness of the body's own natural movements and rhythms (e.g., breathing, or the balance involved in walking) as well as to develop the ability to express various aspects of music (metric patterns, melodic progression, dynamic change) by means of physical movement. Gradually, the term "eurhythmics" (good rhythm) came to be applied to the Dalcroze method in particular, but also, in a more general sense, to any system teaching rhythm through movement.[4]

Formal Dalcroze training involved more than just the use and development of rhythmic movements. It also encompassed training in solfège, ear training, and keyboard improvisation. The Dalcroze teacher improvised as the student interpreted the music's rhythmic, melodic, and dynamic patterns, thus awakening within the student awareness of these factors as they developed and interacted. The student, by means of this direct contact with, and expression of, music as experienced, was thus encouraged in the art of improvisation, learning to express at the keyboard what had already been expressed through bodily movement. "One of the basic principles of Jaques-Dalcroze's teaching is that sound can be translated into motion and motion can be translated into sound."[5] Further, such training aided in the refinement of rhythmic precision as well as in the development of musical memory.

Dalcroze also worked with children, allowing and encouraging them to respond physically in natural and unrestricted ways. Since most movement activities used with children were, at the time, principally regimented movements, Dalcroze techniques were freeing as well as stimulating. "The student does not imitate the movements of the teacher.... The student must bring powers of imagination to the process of solving the problem of the exercise."[6]

Dalcroze techniques were introduced in some American public schools during the first two decades of the twentieth century. Educators like Carl Gehrkens "strongly supported a program of eurhythmics, believing that the music teachers of his day neglected, or approached merely through mathematical concepts, the rhythmic side of music teaching."[7] Despite the urgings of such progressive educators, however, music teachers were generally slow to use eurhythmic practices in any extended or organized way. Teachers who did often adapted certain Dalcroze techniques—almost entirely those having to do with rhythmic movements—to suit their own purposes. Actual Dalcroze practice would have required the teacher to be a person of great creativity and resourcefulness (particularly in the areas of improvisation and ear training), and most American music teachers had not been prepared, by their own educations, to function effectively in other than strictly re-creative ways. In the process, eurhythmic practice became many things to many people. "Terms of contemporary movement activities such as 'rhythmic movement,' 'child rhythms,' and 'rhythmic education' all originate basically in Dalcroze's teaching, [yet] many represent in practice a digression from his methods."[8]

Carl Orff

Orff was himself influenced by the ideas and ideals of Jaques-Dalcroze. Like the Swiss educator, Orff believed in the primacy of rhythm. Early in his career, Orff became associated with Dorothee Günther, a teacher of natural movement. During the 1920s some German teachers of physical education (Günther among them) were interested in the development of movement programs which combined the use of free movements, gymnastics, music, and dance. These teachers formed the Deutscher Gymnastik-Bund, which comprised private schools espousing the new approach to the teaching of gymnastics. One of these *Bundesschules* was an institution founded in Munich in 1924 by Günther and Orff. Working at this school, Orff developed an approach to the teaching of rhythm and melody which grew out of the use of basic (some would say primitive) speech, singing, and movement patterns. This method, which became known as the Orff *Schulwerk,* was published between 1930 and 1933 and was a result of Orff's teaching experiences.

The Orff *Schulwerk,* like the Dalcroze method, believed in full-body expression of rhythm and melody. Orff's method, however, totally avoided the use of the piano, concentrating instead on giving children extended experiences on mallet-playing instruments. In his concern that children be exposed not to toys but to instruments of real musical quality, Orff produced (for use in his teaching program) a number of drums (some tunable), percussion accessories, and other metallophones which have since come to be known as Orff instruments. By using these instruments, children could express rhythm and melody in a most direct and physical manner.

Orff's development of the child's singing response was carefully planned. Beginning with what he regarded as the most natural interval, the falling minor third, Orff gradually expanded the intervallic vocabulary. Because of his belief in the importance and value of folk song—many of which melodies have limited ranges and non-Western tonal implications—all early melodic experiences were pentatonic. At the same time, the use of speech patterns (familiar through nursery rhymes and singing games) was used to develop the child's understanding of meters and rhythms. The combination of melodic and speech/rhythm patterns was the foundation of the Orff approach. Because these patterns were frequently used as ostinatos, the child began to "own" them and could, therefore, use them as a means of personal, improvised expression. As in the Dalcroze method, creativity through improvising was both a means and a goal. The Orff method brought together "natural rhythmic activity (clapping, running, skipping, stamping, snapping fingers, swaying, chanting), instrumental techniques, movement, aural training, and solo and choral singing."[9]

Although well-developed and influential, the new-gymnastics movement was not acceptable to the Nazi regime and the *Bundesschules* (among them the one founded by Günther and Orff, which, since 1931, had become known as the Güntherschule) was disbanded. After World War II Orff reestablished the *Schulwerk* in the form we know it today. *Music for Children,* a five-volume work of Orff's own composition for use in the teaching of the *Schulwerk,* was an outgrowth of Orff's efforts at this time. All volume 1 melodies are pentatonic. The use of the major scale appears in volumes 2 and 3, the minor in 4 and 5.

> Functional harmony appeared only after the introduction of melodies in major, but the commonplace dominant-tonic relationships were carefully avoided. Consistent with the composer's feeling toward twentieth-century harmonic practices, the introduction of supertonic and submediant chords in parallel motion took precedence over the more traditional dominant relationships.[10]

Orff's teaching philosophy was that music making was for everyone and should be begun as early as possible. Since all beginning melodic and rhythmic experiences were simple and frequently repeated, this approach to music education was reasonable as well as practical. Many teachers, however, including some in the United States, felt that the delayed introduction to major sounds and basic Western harmony was unnecessarily exaggerated and out of keeping with the child's day-to-day experiences. As happened with the Dalcroze method, teachers began to adapt ideas and activities from the Orff *Schulwerk* into more general approaches to the teaching of music. To offset this misuse of the Orff system, the Orff Institute was established to provide training in the use of the *Schulwerk*. The organized training of teachers then became in itself an object of criticism to some who argued that Orff's "pedagogical music seemed unduly complex in spite of his concern with improvisation, and the written material required rehearsal and discussion by the children."[11]

Orff's impact on music education, nonetheless, is recognized internationally as having provided an important example of "teaching music through creative play."[12] Orff instruments have enriched the instrumental world available to the young child, affording a unique means of combining instrumental performance with the ideas of personal expression. The attention focused by Orff and others on the perception of rhythm as a fundamental musical experience has influenced rhythmic training in most places where music is taught—whether as part of school music programs in general, or as part of specific instrumental instruction.

Zoltán Kodály

Like Orff, Kodály was a composer intensely concerned with the musical development of his own people, and he devoted a major portion of his life to the establishment of a music education system for the children of his native Hungary. Kodály also resembled Orff in the way

> he likened the historical development of music from primitive folk song to art music to the development of the child from infant to adult. In addition, he considered the simple short forms, the basically pentatonic scale, and the simplicity of the language all characteristics which would contribute to good pedagogical use of such music with children.[13]

His abiding interest in the collection and preservation of Hungarian folk song—a project in which he collaborated with his fellow countryman Béla Bartók—

was another aspect of Kodály's contribution to music and one that in turn, influenced the use of Hungarian folk materials in his own music and in the content of his teaching method.

Kodály sought to provide a musical education that would pervade the entire time the child spent in school—which, for the majority of most children in Hungary, began at age three when they entered nursery schools or day-care centers. Music literacy, not just enjoyment or enrichment, was the ultimate goal of Kodály's plan. The choice of materials for this educational system and the sequencing of their use was based on a child-developmental, rather than on a purely logical, cognitive approach. Thus melodic and rhythmic perception grew out of the use of melodic and rhythmic patterns that were part of singing games and nursery rhymes. Intervallic recognition derived from frequently repeated chants, not from the presentation of patterns connected to an understanding of scale formation. The perception of rhythmic figures, likewise, evolved from the use of simple speech rhythms, not from a mathematical explanation of rhythmic note values or metric organization.

The content and sequencing of Kodály teaching materials developed gradually as teachers associated with Kodály used these materials in the curricula of various state and private schools. Books appearing in 1938 and 1940[14] were collections to be used with children at the intermediate level. The first volume of materials for younger children, *Iskolai Énekegyüjtemény (A School Collection of Songs)* by Kodály and Gyorgy Kerényi, was published in 1943. Various works (by Jenö Adam, Vera Irsai, Márta Nemesszeghy, and Erzsébet Szönyi[15] continued to be produced throughout the next decades, each developing certain aspects of the Kodály approach (e.g., sol-fa teaching), and each exemplifying a surer and slower presentational pacing.

Several teaching techniques are basic to the Kodály method. The first of these is the use of movable *do* and solmization as the foundation of the singing approach and the means by which vocal sight reading is taught. To reinforce understanding of solmization—particularly as this relates to the awareness of tonal distance (intervals) and tendencies—a second teaching device, the use of hand signals, is employed. These specific hand shapes visually identify each tonal degree in a way that also describes that degree's characteristics (e.g., the closed fist, signifying the stability of *do;* the straightened, upward-pointing hand and fingers, signifying the rising tendency of *re,* and so forth).[16] A third important technique is use of rhythm-duration syllables for vocally expressing rhythms and rhythmic figures (e.g., a quarter note would be vocalized as *ta;* an eighth note as *ti;* four sixteenth notes as *ti-ri-ti-ri*). At the earliest levels, children express rhythms and melodic shapes by full-body movements. Movements are gradually reduced to the use of hand signals, then notation.

Although the Kodály method concentrates heavily on singing, and considers the voice to be the most natural instrument, the use of instruments is included, although not until after children have learned to read and write music as a result of vocal experiences. The use of the piano—either as a functional tool on which to teach musical concepts such as intervals, scales and chords, or as an instrument to accompany singing—is avoided. Kodály believed in the importance of the untempered scale. His intention is that the first harmony experiences should also derive from singing (2- and 3-part singing is introduced very early in the method). The first instruments the child plays are xylophones with removable bars. Thus the child's playing range can be controlled to develop no further and no faster than the child's singing range. The use of string instruments is introduced at the third-grade level, wind instruments at the fifth.[17]

Although Kodály had begun his efforts to improve music education in Hungary in the 1920s, the Kodály approach did not take hold until the 1950s. The method was introduced to the world at large at the 1958 (Vienna) and 1963 (Tokyo) Conferences of the International Society for Music Education. At the 1964 I.S.M.E. Conference in Budapest, the results of Kodály's efforts were both demonstrable and impressive. As the method began to be adapted in other countries (its use has spread to many European countries, North and South America, Japan, and Australia), music educators in each country needed to locate and select indigenous folk and children songs from which the basic melodic and rhythmic patterns were to be drawn. Thus the Kodály method also continues to undergo adaptation.

In 1966, Kodály and Szönyi—through their appearances at the I.S.M.E. Interlochen Conference and other symposia throughout the country—gave United States music educators the first in-person contact with the Kodály system, even though the writings of Mary Helen Richards had already introduced the method and many of its concepts to American music teachers. Compared with the teaching techniques of Dalcroze and Orff the Kodály method has had less direct impact on the teaching of instrumental music in this country, but it has, nonetheless, underscored the importance and value of music education for the very young child. Kodály's method has increased awareness on the part of both teachers and parents of the readiness of preschool children not only to perceive melodic and rhythmic fundamentals, but to learn to read and write musical symbols at the same time, and in much the same way, as they learn to read and write their native language.

Shinichi Suzuki

The Suzuki method is distinct from the methods developed by Dalcroze, Orff, Kodály, or the Yamaha Music Education System because it is designed to teach instrumental *performance,* even at the very youngest ages. Also, unlike the aforementioned music-teaching programs in which instruction is group-oriented, the Suzuki approach concentrates on the teaching of a single child, although the parent (and perhaps other children) may also be present at the lesson. The group performance, which is perhaps the most recognizable public form of the Suzuki approach, is an important part of the Suzuki program, but it is meant to serve as an opportunity for repertoire and performance reinforcement and is not group activity in the usual sense of that term.

Rote teaching is the heart of the Suzuki method. Much is made of this fact both by proponents of the method (who point to the importance of musical training that concentrates on development of the ear) and by the method's opponents (who claim that Suzuki students do not learn to read music, or do so only with reluctance and difficulty). The roots of the method's teaching strategies and the foundation of Suzuki's own teaching philosophy rest on what Suzuki refers to as the "mother tongue approach." Impressed by the way in which children learn their native language—first listening, then using the language by means of repetitive copying, and only then learning to read and write the language by means of graphic symbols—Suzuki sought to teach music in the same manner and sequence.

The origin of Suzuki's teaching approach came as the result of his attempts in the 1930s to teach a four-year-old to play the violin. His keen observation of the young child's natural learning processes, coupled with his own (largely German) musical education, which had developed in him a sensitivity to beauty and fullness of sound, stimulated Suzuki to devise an approach to instrumental study that acknowledged and developed the acute hearing capacity of the child at that early age. Suzuki noted not only the child's reliance on imitative repetition to learn new skills and concepts, but also the child's delight in the repetitive process itself. Further, Suzuki sought to provide encouragement and support to the child in the process of learning to play a musical instrument, just as the child received encouragement and support in the process of learning to speak. Since this process of encouragement happened largely in the home, as the child interacted with parents and siblings, Suzuki's teaching approach involved the training of a parent in tandem with the training of the child. Thus the parent learned to continue the methods of the lesson in daily activities and in the natural surroundings of the home.

Although Suzuki's approach began and developed as a string- (principally violin) teaching method, its successful use stimulated the teachers of other instruments to examine the possibilities of adapting Suzuki's teaching strategies. For approximately fifteen years before the appearance of the *Suzuki Piano School* in Japan in 1970, Suzuki, together with Shizuko Suzuki (his sister-in-law) and Haruko Kataoka, worked to transfer the principles and techniques of Suzuki instruction to performance study at the piano. The first English edition appeared in 1972.[18] The Suzuki teaching method has also been applied to the teaching of the cello, viola, flute, and harp.

There are six volumes of the *Suzuki Piano School*. "Because Suzuki's method of learning music depends heavily on training the ear, recorded performances supplement most of the printed materials. Actually, if teachers utilize the *Suzuki Schools* the way he intended, it is the music books (print materials) that supplement the recordings (non-print materials)."[19] Teachers usually begin to teach music reading after the student has completed the first volume. Various books may be, and are, used to teach reading. One of these, the *Méthode Rose*[20] by Ernest Van de Velde, is a volume that seems to have been of some influence on Suzuki, for it contains pieces and written directions that have found their way (with some slight alterations) into the *Suzuki Piano School*. "Japanese teachers do not instruct American teachers and parents how to teach the reading of notation. . . . Many American Suzuki teachers use other Western reading methods as well" as the Rose Method.[21] When the process of teaching music reading begins in earnest, "there is a 'drop back' to reading music easier than that which the student is currently performing. It is equivalent to what a child experiences when learning to read the letters, words, and sentences that make up his native tongue."[22]

Although the Suzuki piano books are easily available and may be used by anyone choosing to do so, the printed materials themselves offer no clues or suggestions as to what constitutes the Suzuki *method*. In order to learn the Suzuki approach to the teaching of piano, aspiring teachers work with a training teacher in a situation much like an apprentice program in addition to attending summer workshops and teacher training courses (often given in this country by Kataoka herself). Since 1980 the Suzuki Association of the Americas registers teacher-trainers who, in turn, assume responsibility for those whom they train.[23]

Suzuki's name has certainly become synonomous with successful performance training for the very young. In some ways, the playing skills attained by young Suzuki performers challenge positions taken by many observers of, and commentators on, child behavior. Statements that four-year-olds are unable, or less able, to control small muscle activities must be, at least, reexamined as one sees Suzuki-trained four-year-olds playing their instruments with considerable precision and finesse. The Suzuki teaching approach has attained noteworthy attention in the United States, even though many teachers and parents do not yet truly understand all that Suzuki training implies. There are those who claim, however, that it is a method peculiarly rooted in certain cultural expectations and does not transplant easily or successfully to other (especially non-Oriental) countries. Others make opposite claims—that the Suzuki approach has indeed transplanted well in the musical mainstream of other cultures and is, in fact, not nearly as influential in Japan as in the countries to which it has been exported. What "Suzuki" represents, however—whether one applauds and espouses this type of training or whether one questions its philosophy and teaching strategies—is the presence of a method that seems to be making a significant difference in the way instrumental music is taught to young children.

The Yamaha Music Education System

The Yamaha Music Education System, in the context of this discussion of non-American teaching methods that have influenced musical training of the preschool child, has its own unique characteristics. It is the only program that did not emerge as the result of a single musician's pedagogical vision and ideals; in fact, the program developed as the educational division of a manufacturing organization, Nippon Gakki/Yamaha Motors. Further, its training program concerns itself with the development and encouragement of popular, as well as classical, music. Only the *Primary Course,* which does not differentiate among musical styles, will be considered in this chapter.

The Yamaha Music Education System began as a desire on the part of Genichi Kawakami, chairman of the board of directors of both the Nippon Gakki and Yamaha companies, to encourage and develop what he refers to as "music popularization." There are "four basic areas of activity: (1) research and development on music and music education methods (preschool children through adults) for use in Yamaha Music Schools; (2) the training of music leaders for the popularization of music on a diverse scale throughout society; (3) the execution, development and promotion of music popularization activities among the public through music festivals, contests, and concerts; (4) the popularization of music education and music through the publication of teaching materials and other documents."[24] From the beginning, Kawakami placed great importance on the development of creativity—not just directing attention to those who exhibit special talent in this area, but also encouraging creativity as a means of stimulating the pleasure and understanding of all who begin, and continue, the study of music.

In the 1950s, Kawakami assembled a group of Japanese music teachers, charging them to develop an original course that could be used to teach music effectively and attractively to very young children. The piano methods then currently known to these teachers seemed to be limited to standard European methods such as the beginning book of Beyer and the etudes of Burgmueller. These educators sought to resist the influence of "foreign scholars" (presumably traditional pedagogues such as Beyer and Burgmueller) and to work directly with children, discovering not only what children were capable of doing but also what was attractive and communicative to them. Kawakami describes the development of the Yamaha textbooks as "a story full of hardships and unceasing effort."[25] The resultant books and the Yamaha method are worlds away from Beyer and Burgmueller and embody a teaching philosophy that regards the study of music as a training in basic musicianship rather than the study of performance on a particular instrument. The Yamaha course is *not* a piano method.

Since the Yamaha materials offer a unique contribution to the world of music education, it seems regrettable that those educators responsible for the design and development of this program do not receive public recognition. This group of educators is described as "an eclectic team supervised by founder, Genichi Kawakami. . . . Anonymous authorship is consistent with Yamaha's typical R & D [research and development] procedures."[26] It is true, of course, that the Yamaha Education System has benefited from the contributions of a number of educational professionals, some of whom have been associated with Yamaha for only a limited period of time. However, Eizo Itoh, the Yamaha music education director in Japan, has been with Yamaha since the inception of its educational program and must, therefore, have played a significant role in the Yamaha philosophy as embodied in its curriculum and teaching strategies.

The four volumes of the Yamaha *Primary Course* are designed as a two-year basic musicianship program for children ages four to six. Although the American editions of these books bear 1978 and 1979 publication dates, the course had undergone development (in Japan as well as in the United States) during the two preceding decades. The Yamaha books, like the Suzuki materials, contain no information (within the student's volumes) of how the course is structured or taught. Insight into the teaching philosophy, and knowledge of the teaching strategies used as a result of this philosophy, can only be gained by observing Yamaha classes or by enrolling in a Yamaha teacher-training program. Yamaha materials, in fact, cannot be purchased except through Yamaha schools. The Yamaha *Teacher Reference and Primary Planning Guides* (which are the only sources that would give any indication of how the program really functions) are not available to any but Yamaha teachers.

The Yamaha teaching philosophy emphasizes the primacy of experience, particularly that of the ear. The beginning student learns to express rhythmic and melodic patterns through whole-body activities and singing. "The basic technique is to give patterns by imitation (Yamaha calls this process *by-copy*) and the basic goal is *by-ear* accomplishment."[27] Fixed *do,* rather than movable *do,* is the basis of solfège singing, since one of the goals of the ear-training experiences is to establish an exact sense of pitch. Since C is *do,* transference of solfège recognition to the keyboard (the Yamaha *Primary Course* uses organs rather than pianos) results in a reading approach centered on middle C. Rhythms are verbalized syllabically (e.g., a quarter note is *tahn;* a half note, *ta-ahn;* two eighth notes, *tuh, tuh,* and so on), but also referred to by name.

The *Primary Course* is a prereading course, but one that is in no hurry to urge the child away from aural and oral experiences as visual recognition, and dependence upon it, becomes stronger. An introduction to the keyboard is part of the primary program, but there is no attempt to teach piano playing, and therefore no attention to technique or tone production. Yamaha refers instead to "keyboard learning" as knowledge of keyboard mechanics, geography, and fingering patterns learned "by-copy." These activities constitute "a process which combines ear training with sense of touch and memory of intervallic distances, [and this process is] considered by Yamaha as basic to the functional harmony training ahead in [the Yamaha] Extension Course."[28]

At the primary level, all Yamaha instruction is group instruction. Average class size is eight to twelve children. A parent is required to attend each class, participating in all activities so that these activities are continued at home. The ideal is that the parent and child work together to accomplish the goals and enjoy the pleasures of musical instruction. The United States Yamaha research division has also developed the Parent Education Project, "an attempt to guide American parents to understand and respond to the learning opportunities in the *Primary Course.* [The] underlying goal [of this project] is to prevent dropouts. . . . [Yamaha believes] that the major cause of dropouts is misconception on the part of parents as to what and how the child should be learning."[29]

The Yamaha Music Education System has expanded rapidly. Since its inception in Japan (in 1954) and its introduction in the United States (in 1965), its courses (there are several others beside the *Primary Course*) and materials have been put into use in more than 33 countries. Yamaha claims to have reached over 750,000 students worldwide, of whom approximately 15,000 are in the United States.[30] Since the Yamaha Music Education System is a closed program (its materials and teaching techniques available only to teachers officially associated with Yamaha), its educational goals are frequently misunderstood or misrepresented because of lack of information.

The Yamaha Music Foundation recently has begun a more intensive public exposition of its program and teaching philosophy. Through Yamaha demonstrations at local, national, and international conventions and conferences, the world of music education is gradually learning what Yamaha training involves. Development of musical understanding through improvisatory and creative activities clearly is among Yamaha's major contributions to the music education process. It is equally clear that many Yamaha teaching techniques are outgrowths and developments of programs begun earlier in the century, notably those of Dalcroze and Orff. Since the Yamaha Music Education System has a heavy commitment to preschool music instruction, and is best known by the outstandingly creative young performers/composers it showcases, it seems likely that many other (non-Yamaha) educators will seek, and appreciate, further information about its educators and educational programs.

PRESCHOOL PIANO (MUSIC) METHODS IN THE UNITED STATES

Since the preschool period is short, and since preschool music students have minimal need for books or reading materials, the number of music books written for preschool children is more limited than those designed for any other category. Occasionally the preschool method is presented in a single book, often as a preliminary or introductory volume to a more extended course of instruction. In some cases, a book (or perhaps a pair of books) stands alone, anticipating that subsequent instruction may be provided by any method or teacher. Some educators have become especially identified with preschool approaches, having presented no other type of material. More often the preschool method is part of a larger music curriculum. Only sometimes is the preschool volume the first book published for the series. More frequently the preschool material develops later, as the author(s) discover(s) the need to precede already published books (often for the average-age beginner) with books designed for the much younger learner.

In the United States, developments in preschool music education have corresponded to periods of intense interest in early childhood education. These research periods have had focal points in each half of the twentieth century. The 1930s witnessed particular attention paid to early childhood education by progressive educators who regarded the school as a social force and education as contributing to the formation of the productive citizen. In the second half of the century, research sought to examine quantifiable rather than social objectives. "In the late 1960s and 1970s, many American women joined the workforce causing the day-care system in America to begin to grow rapidly. In addition to expanded day-care, research revealing the importance of cognitive growth before the age of five became an impetus for creating early intervention programmes such as Project Head Start."[31]

Preschool materials for piano students emerged at the same time as more general preschool music programs. In the 1930s, there was widespread interest in the development of keyboard courses whose aim was to provide a basic introduction to music via instrumental study. This resulted in the production of methods less performance-oriented than the piano-teaching materials then in current use. Focus began to shift from methods stressing the development of technique and repertoire to methods using teaching strategies that regarded the piano as an instrument on which to chord along and experiment. Although this movement had the greatest effect on the development of piano methods for the average-age student (see chapter 6, especially "The Teaching of Musicianship"), it was also evident in the publication of piano methods for the preschool child.

Louise Robyn's *Teaching Musical Notation with Picture Symbols* (1932)[32] was a teacher's manual that contained elaborate explanations of how to use "rote cards" (materials for the children) presenting prereading and early technical fundamentals. Children who studied with Robyn at the American Conservatory of Music in Chicago were also enrolled in classes in Dalcroze eurhythmics at the same time that they were beginning their piano instruction via the "rote cards." These experiences prepared the child for Robyn's *Keyboard Town* (1934),[33] a book whose subtitle bears the remarkable message, "For Beginners from Pre-school to Adult Age." Robyn's detailed prefatory commentary proves that she was serious in declaring that a book "especially designed to develop fluent note-reading habits in the work of the pre-school child, aged three to six" could and ought to be used in giving beginning lessons to adults. "Adult beginners are very often able to read completely through *Keyboard Town* in one or two lessons . . . and are having too much fun playing the piano to even notice that *Keyboard Town* contains childish pictures and titles."[34]

Ada Richter's *Kindergarten Class Book* (1937)[35] was designed for group instruction (approximately ten children) of four- to six-year-olds. The method was woven around the story of Goldilocks and the three bears. The bears personified the three Cs and directional reading was established from these guide notes. The tonic chord and the two-note V$_7$ were introduced about midway in the text. The format of the books contained specific lesson plans to enable the teacher to use these books as intended.

The *Kindergarten Piano Method* (1939)[36] by May B. Kelly Kirby and John Kirby, a Canadian publication, was used in many (particularly northern) states. The four books comprising this method are all in card/flashcard format. The student receives a new card as appropriate, generally one a week. The method places high priority on ear training, rote learning, physical movement, and the principle of the sound before the sign. The middle-C approach to reading is presented in very small increments. A detailed teacher's manual, *The Key to Music Teaching,* appeared in 1963. The manual offers precise lesson plans for teaching each unit of the four books, and states the educational philosophy on which the method is based.

Another, slightly larger, spurt of preschool piano books emerged in the 1940s and 1950s: The *Music Readiness Books* (1946) by Sister M. Xaveria, Zepp and Montague's *Musical Kindergarten Course* (1953), Richter's *Preschool and*

Kindergarten Book (1954), Frisch's *The Play-Way to Music* (beginning in 1954), and Frances Clark's *Time to Begin* (1955).

The books by Sister M. Xaveria present and develop off-staff directional reading after the child has experienced music making via rote pieces. Letter names are learned in groups, with letter names appearing on noteheads. This leads to grand-staff reading, but only of notes a fifth up and down from middle C.

The Zepp-Montague books present an introduction to music in which playing the piano represents only a small part of the instruction. The course was intended for use in large group settings. Although the student learns letter names for keys, high and low (as related to the keyboard), and the playing of five-finger legato (through rote pieces), instruction in note reading is not attempted.

Richter's 1954 book, like the 1937 *Kindergarten Class Book,* is based on three-C reading, preceded by rote pieces on black (played with the fist) and white keys. The Frisch books were essentially a multi-key preschool method. Clark's *Time to Begin* was the most highly developed of the off-staff reading approaches, one that advocated the use of two-, three-, and four-line before the introduction to five-line and grand-staff reading. The specifics of this book are covered in detail in chapter 6.

As a corollary to the flurry of interest in early childhood education in the 1970s, the number of preschool piano (or general introduction to music) books grew considerably. It should be recalled that it was not until the late 1960s and early 1970s that the methods of Orff, Kodály, and Suzuki were becoming more widely known in the United States. These same decades saw the rise of great interest in the educational theories of developmentalists like Piaget, cognitive theorists like Bruner, and rekindled interest in the child-oriented learning theory of Montessori.[37]

Some American methods developed at this time—for instance, Madeleine Carabo-Cone's *A Sensory Motor Approach to Music Learning* (1969)[38]—used the piano as a teaching tool but were not methods designed specifically to ready children for playing that instrument. Other methods—for instance, Jane Bastien's *The Very Young Pianist* series (1973)[39]—represented approaches to piano instruction that could be used with preschool children. The 1970s and 1980s saw a continual increase in preschool music-teaching methods that reflect this duality of purpose.

SOME PRESCHOOL PIANO (MUSIC) METHODS

The following brief descriptions group preschool methods into two categories: (1) methods that provide a general introduction to music but use the keyboard as a teaching tool, and (2) methods that are readiness courses for piano playing per se. Courses that present an introduction to music fundamentals but do so *primarily* as a result of singing and movement experiences are not included.

Introduction to Music: The Keyboard as a Teaching Tool

CARABO-CONE, MADELEINE. *A Sensory-Motor Approach to Music Learning.* **New York: MCA Music, a division of MCA Inc.**

Book 1: *Primary Concepts*	(1969)
Book 2: *Materials: Pupil's Edition*	(1971)
Book 2: *Teacher's Edition*	(1971)
Book 3: *Identification Activities*	(1973)
Book 4: *Identification Activities: Growth and Development*	(1974)

BOOK 1

For the teacher only. *Primary Concepts* presents the teaching philosophy on which the method is based. Ten chapters offer psychological background, comparison of this with other (Montessori, Dalcroze, Orff, Suzuki) methods, explanations of the room environment, the use of the child's body as a learning aid, and other important specifics.

The heart of this method is the creation of a "grand staff environment" that the child explores. The entire room images the grand staff. The child also uses the body to represent the staff (feet, bottom line; knees, second line, and so on) as well as the hand (with thumb pointing down, each finger becomes a line, spaces between fingers represent spaces on the staff).

In each class, students "become" and "own" a specific pitch and rhythmic value which they "wear" (as hats, notes looped over the shoulder, and similar representations). Rhythmic note values are experienced with full body movements, and in many ways. Each child uses a one-syllable name (or nickname) that becomes his/her equivalent of the one-pulse symbol/word.

BOOK 2

Pupil's Edition contains piano key, staff, clef, note-name cut-outs, which child uses in the class. *Teacher's Edition* explains how materials in the pupil's edition are used.

BOOK 3

A teacher's manual that provides a detailed description of what is needed for each activity and exactly how to teach it. Although not offering actual class plans, teaching suggestions are highly specific.

BOOK 4

A continuation of the activities and format of book 3.

All books include many photographs of Carabo-Cone working with children. These pictures are the best clue to understanding how this approach is to be taught. All materials and equipment can be made simply and inexpensively. Use of this method requires only a sufficiently large space in which a group of children may move, lie on the floor, and perform other activities called for in the method.

The use of the piano keyboard is an important link in the process of equating note identification staff placement. A large picture of the grand staff is placed on its side, between the keys and the fallboard, so that the F line matches F below middle C, the A line matches A a third higher, and so on, and the spaces on the staff correspond to the piano keys between the line notes so that the child may "see" how the staff "works."

Carabo-Cone claims that the method may be used by nonmusic specialists as well as by musicians. The books are replete with imaginative and helpful suggestions to use in the presentation of reading readiness symbols and experiences. What is less clear is what music the child actually hears, sings, and (eventually) plays.

These books would be a worthwhile resource for any music teacher who works with children of preschool age whether in the general classroom, the music classroom, nursery schools, or day-care centers.

YAMAHA MUSIC EDUCATION SYSTEM. *Primary Course* (English edition). Tokyo (Primary Course Books) and Buena Park, CA (accompanying guides): Yamaha Music Foundation.

Book 1	(1978)
Books 2, 3, 4	(1979)
Yamaha Education System Teacher Reference Guide	(n.d.)
Yamaha Education System Primary Planning Guide	(1984)
Teacher Accompaniment Books 1–4	(n.d.)

The review is included so that readers may know what the Yamaha method contains. These materials are not available on the open market.

In each student book there are three types of pieces:

SONGS:	To extend the child's aural abilities. Sung, not played. Identified by a picture of a singing face. Score (of melody) in child's book, smaller notes.
REPERTOIRE:	To develop motor skills. These are played. Identified by picture of a small organ. N.B. Some pieces are sung and played. Until end of book 2, all pieces played are in C major. Other keys for songs.
KEYBOARD HARMONY:	To accompany melodies. Single pitches (tonic, dominant); dyads; triads.
READING	Book 1: C-major 5-finger pattern; treble, bass staff; pattern not identified. Book 2: Notes within 3-C range; C, G major. 5-finger pattern melodies. Book 3: Extension to sixth; C, G, F major; D-natural minor. Accidentals. Book 4: Upper ledger lines; LH in treble clef; C, G, F major; d, a minor.
RHYTHM	Book 1: Quarter, half, dotted half notes. 2/4, 4/4. Book 2: All basic note values, meters. Book 3: Eighth notes; dotted quarter. Book 4: Eighth-note upbeat; tie.
HARMONY	Book 1: Accompany with single pitches. Book 2: Accompany with 2-note intervals, I V7 (close position). Book 3: I IV V7 (close position) C, G, F. I V7 (close position) d. Book 4: I IV V7 (close position) C, G, F, d, a. C, G, major scales, 1 octave; regular fingering.
PRIMARY PLANNING GUIDE	Without reference to this guide, it is impossible to grasp the focus of this method or to understand the teaching strategies used in the course.

There are seven basic activities: (1) singing with words; (2) learning rhythms by imitation; (3) learning solfège by imitation; (4) learning keyboard playing by imitation; (5) preparing for music reading; (6) reading music; (7) experiencing movement, ensemble playing.

"Layering" these activities is the most important factor in bringing about the desired results. Each piece goes through each of the "activity" stages (generally in sequential weeks). As one piece is in the singing stage, another will be in the rhythm by imitation stage, another in the solfège by imitation stage, and so forth.

The primary focus is on ear training and learning by rote (imitation). Rote learning prepares for learning to read, and music reading is taught gradually.

Solfège (fixed *do*) is used from the beginning and throughout. The purpose of using fixed *do* is to develop pitch memory. *Do* is middle C on the keyboard. Thus the method uses the middle-C approach, although it does not teach reading by introducing single notes up and down from middle C.

Rhythms are verbalized syllabically. There is continual use of full-body movement to experience both rhythms and melodic direction. Singing and playing rhythm instruments in ensemble is an important part of each class.

All lessons are large group lessons (8–12 children). A parent must attend all lessons, participating with the child in group activities. It is expected that the parent continue the class activities at home. Early keyboard instruction generally takes place on small Yamaha organs, not pianos. There is no attention to keyboard technique beyond some help with, and allowance for, coordination difficulties.

The Yamaha teacher must be able to play the piano well, improvise, sing while playing, and have a solid foundation in keyboard harmony. There are intensive, usually one-week training sessions. Updating sessions continue as the teacher moves on to teaching at higher levels, or as Yamaha research and development introduces new ideas. Master teachers regularly visit Yamaha schools.

Readiness Courses for Piano Playing

BASTIEN, JANE SMISOR. *The Very Young Pianist.* San Diego: Kjos West.

Book 1; oversize	(1970)
Books 2, 3; oversize	(1973)
Listens and Creates, Books 1, 2, 3	(1975)
Workbooks A, B (to correlate with *The Very Young Pianist* books 2 and 3)	(1973)

	Pre-reading Solos	(1971)
	Solos for the Very Young Pianist, Book 1	(1975)
	Solos for the Very Young Pianist, Book 2	(1976)

Supplementary sheet solos. Flashcards.

BOOK 1 — 11 units. Introduces hands, numbers, letters, fingers. Student plays, colors, writes, matches. 2/3 black keys. Names of white keys. Up/down; high/low. 3-note positions (C-D-E; E-F-G). 5-note positions: C (much), G. Entire book: Off-staff notation. Triad (I), 2-note V$_7$ introduced. Rhythms: Basic; eighth notes; dotted quarter; 3 eighth notes, grouped. Nominative counting. Measure bars, but no time signatures. Pages 66–72: Excellent, practical notes and directions to teacher. Discusses readiness, advantages of early lessons, practice advice.

BOOK 2 — Comes with page of stick-on notes. 8 units. Leads to elementary stages of note reading. Units 1–3: off-staff notation. Unit 4: Grand staff. From unit 5: Stresses reading by skips; lines, then spaces. Student sticks letter names on noteheads for most drills, pieces. Student plays in C, F, G 5-finger pattern (by picture). Student reads in G (many pieces); F (1 piece). Key signature, but no time signature. Continuation of all rhythms from book 1. Nominative counting. Teaches 2-note V$_7$ very early. Uses figured bass below notes. Only LH.

BOOK 3 — Comes with page of stick-on notes. 10 units. Units 1–3: Keys of C, F, G, middle-C position; keys of D, A, E. Unit 4: D-flat, A-flat, E-flat introduced. Unit 6: G-flat, B-flat introduced. Stick-on letter names used on all notes when keys are new to students. Key signatures used, not explained. Keys are always named. Continued use of I- and 2-note V$_7$. Continuation of all rhythms from book 1. Nominative counting. Introduces idea of warm-ups that involve playing, reading, writing.

LISTENS AND CREATES BOOKS — All books correlate, by unit, with *The Very Young Pianist* books. They could also be used (1) alone as an introduction to music and the keyboard; (2) as supplementary to other preschool piano books. At the back of each book, complete directions and music are given for the use of the book.

All books contain (principally) ear-training and (some) creative activities. Student responds verbally and by coloring and writing, to what the teacher plays. Students also play some "pieces," improvising melodies to given words and rhythms. In book 2, rudimentary rhythmic dictation begins as student "fills in" the rhythm that is heard. Rudimentary harmonization is also begun. Books 2 and 3 reinforce reading, playing writing knowledge of intervals.

WORKBOOK A AND B

Books correlate, by unit, with *The Very Young Pianist* books 2 and 3
All activities within the books are writing, drawing, coloring.

SOLOS BOOKS

Pre-reading: 12 pieces; off-staff notation; includes use of hands-together, intervals, chords, 5-note clusters. Rhythmic values given, but no meters, bar lines. Includes basic note values; eighth notes; 6/8. Pieces written out (for teacher) at end of book. Books 1 and 2: 8 pieces each; staff reading. Keys: C, F, G, D, and a (book 2). No ledger lines. All pieces have words. Many big, sometimes full-page, pictures to color. Time signatures used.

FEATURES

A preschool course with its own supplementary books. Prepares student for a multi-key reading approach. Very early, and continued, use of hands-together and chord playing. Use of stick-on letter names when grand staff is presented might, if teacher is not alert, encourage student to read by letter names only. Student reads many rhythmic note values, even at the beginning, but does so only by using nominative counting. Bar lines are used, but none of the books (except *Solos* books 1 and 2) use time signatures. Meter is not taught, although student plays in all simple meters and in compound time. The *Listens and Creates* books are imaginative and well suited to the abilities and interests of the preschool child. The directions to the teacher (at the back of each book) make these volumes easy to use. The general considerations and suggestions (to the teacher) at the back of *The Very Young Pianist: Book 1* offer practical, and very helpful, advice to the teacher who may have little or no experience in teaching piano to children of this age group.

COLLINS, ANN, AND LINDA CLARY. Champaign, IL: Stipes Publishing Co.

Sing and Play, Books 1, 2, 3	(1981)
Sing and Play, Teacher's Manual	(1981)
Write and Listen, Books 1, 2, 3	(1984)
Mother Goose	(1984)
Partners	(1984)

All *Sing and Play* books are organized into concept blocks. Each concept block includes keyboard, ear training, reading, writing, technique, rhythm/movement, and improvisation activities as well as songs to sing and play.

BOOK 1

Concept blocks 1–4. Introduces low/middle/high, up/down, slow/fast, long/short, letters. Stress on knowing letters forward/backward. 2/3 black keys. C, D, E, F, G. White key pitches isolated and in groups.
Entire book: Off-staff notation. All pieces taught by rote, but some rhythms/technical exercises are read. G clef; identify middle C, D.
Rhythms: Quarter, half, and dotted half notes. Count individual values of each note; no bar lines, meters.
Technique: All keyboard playing: closed hand, fingers 1 and 2 braced.
Ear training: Same/different pitches/rhythms.
Flashcards (to cut out) at back of student book.

BOOK 2

Concept blocks 5–8. F and G clefs; reading range F-clef F to G-clef G. First 25 pages are all G-clef reading. Directional reading advocated but pitch reading is more a matter of remembering small groups of pitches, as in middle-C approach. Flats introduced.
New rhythm: whole note. Measure bars, but no meters. Count value of each note. Movement activities in march, gallop, waltz, jazz styles.
Technique: Most of book, closed-hand. Legato, fingers 1, 2, and 3 introduced.
Ear training: Same/different melodic and rhythmic patterns; some orchestral instruments (recordings); fugal (round); march styles; major, minor.
Improvisation: Question/answer on 3 black keys; "play a picture."
Flashcards (to cut out) at back of student book: Both isolated pitches and one-measure "flashes," which can be variously grouped and regrouped.

BOOK 3

Concept blocks 9–12. Range extended to bottom line G (F clef) and top line F (G clef). Flat used in pieces. Sharp introduced, but not used in pieces. No key signatures.
New rhythms: Quarter rest; rit.
Technique: Extends to 5-finger legato; dynamic control (including crescendo and descrescendo).
Ear training: Skips; major, minor; rhythmic dictation. More orchestral instruments (Peter and the Wolf).

Improvisation: Pentatonic melodies; question/answer on varied white-key groups (including 5-note pattern).
Flashcards: As in book 2.

TEACHER'S MANUAL	Necessary to teach books as intended, particularly as this applies to the variety and extent of rhythmic, ear-training, and improvisatory activities. Organization of all concept blocks, with suggestions for implementation and correlation.
WRITE AND LISTEN	Ear-training and writing activities books that correlate with *Sing and Play* books. Many printing and coloring activities. Responses to ear training activities are often responses to same/different or choice of two printed representations. Easy to use even without manual.
MOTHER GOOSE	Pianistic settings (by Collins) of Mother Goose rhymes. May be used during or after *Sing and Play* book 3. Rhythm is largely a matter of reciting the rhyme. Several pieces use hands-together material that is musical but not always easy.
PARTNERS	Folk-song arrangements (by Collins) intended as duets for parents and preschool children. Parents must be able to read music (frequently using two F clefs). Children read from unstaffed letters and traditional notation. May be used throughout the study of *Sing and Play* books 1, 2, and 3.
FEATURES	Provides an example of how to organize and use a well-integrated musical/keyboard approach in teaching music to the preschool child.

Teaches music reading gradually, using a middle-C approach. By the end of book 3, the reading range includes all pitches on the grand staff. Approach, however, does emphasize directional reading with special attention to steps and skips (thirds).
Singing, movement, rhythm, and ear-training activities are well coordinated and, if used as intended, will provide a broad and solid musical development. Other books and materials (including orchestral recordings) are needed to complete the teacher's resources. These are listed at the back of the teacher's manual.
The student *Sing and Play* books contain explanatory pages, opposite each picture/reading

page, that may be used by both teacher and parent to direct the child's learning and practicing. Although the pages include notation of many rote pieces the child plays, the pieces are written simply. There are no teacher accompaniments. Even a parent unable to read music could probably grasp this notation.
The technical approach moves from use of whole arm/hand playing (all of book 1, most of book 2) to use of individual finger legato (with 2, then 3, 4, and 5 fingers) beginning with the thumb.
The format of the books, while readable and uncluttered, looks like printed manuscript copy.

GLOVER, DAVID CARR, BETTY GLASSCOCK, AND JAY STEWART. Miami: CPP/Belwin.

My First Music Book	(1984)
My Piano Book A	(1985)
My Color and Play Book A	(1985)
My Piano Book B	(1985)
My Color and Play Book B	(1985)
Songs for Singing	(1985)

Cassette recordings to accompany all books.

MY FIRST MUSIC BOOK

The presentation of concepts and skills is divided into nine "programs" (units). The presentation of each program is likely to require several lessons, dependent upon the age, maturity, and abilities of each child or group. The student is introduced to the concepts of high/low, loud/soft, 2/3 black-key groups, finger numbers, and unit counting (quarter and half notes only). Although clefs are presented in program two (associated chiefly with the use of RH/LH) and the grand staff presented in program five, grand-staff reading is not taught. By the book's end, the student identifies (isolated) notes as these relate to the line or space the note is on. Most pages consist of large illustrations (to color) that teach or drill concepts or skills. The black-key groups are played with the fist.

The primary activities are singing, movement, storytelling, ear training. Activity songs are included (melodic lines with lead-sheet symbols) in the lesson plans for each program, at the back of the book. They are also available in a separate book *(Songs for Singing)* with teacher piano accompaniments.

The last 20 pages offer specific teaching guidelines for each program. These guidelines are in the nature of outlined lesson plans (for the teacher) and home assignments to guide the parent (also encouraged to be present at the lesson). All activity songs are recorded on cassette, available as supplementary material.

MY PIANO BOOK A
MY COLOR AND
PLAY BOOK A

These books (correlated by page number) present a middle-C approach to reading in seven "programs" (units). Introduction is by single note, related to a child's name (e.g., [C]harlie, [D]anka, [E]llen). Each note is identified by picture placement and a one-note piece. Notes are then combined, as learned, leading to establishment of a 5-finger position up and down from middle-C. The student first learns and plays all 5 right-hand notes (written on a single staff), then all left-hand notes (also on a single staff). Grand-staff reading occurs in the last program.

Bar lines are used, but not time signatures. Unit counting is continued throughout. "Counting numbers" are placed above/below every piece. Initial finger numbers are separated from the counting numbers. The book uses only quarter, half, and whole notes.

The *Color and Play* book suggests many additional activities (motor, rhythm, and ear training) in addition to presenting opportunities for note drawing, rhythm reviews, and clapping/playing. The back of the book contains a scope and sequence chart for teaching the programs and correlating all activities. There is a guide to lesson-plan elements and a sample lesson plan. Activity songs are also presented (melodic lines with lead-sheet symbols) at the back of the book.

MY PIANO BOOK B
MY COLOR AND
PLAY BOOK B

These books present the concepts of time signature (the dotted half note is introduced together with 3/4 meter), quarter rest, sharps, flats, and staccato. The reading range remains the same as in the *A* books, but all music is read on the grand staff. There is more extensive use of alternating hands.

Unit counting is continued throughout both books although the counting numbers are no longer present in the pieces. The material is grouped into nine programs. Flats (presented first) and sharps are taught uniquely. Five flats (G-flat, A-flat, B-flat, D-flat, E-flat) and five sharps (F-sharp, G-sharp, A-sharp,

C-sharp, D-sharp) are presented at once, enabling the student to play and read black-key pieces.

In the *Color and Play* book the unit counting numbers continue to appear in all the rhythm drills and games. The book presents some pieces (connected to notes in the *Piano Book,* rhythm games, and "stories with sound." There is a scope and sequence chart and melodies with (lead-sheet symbols) for the activity songs.

FEATURES

These books present an approach to preschool piano instruction that mixes singing games, ear training, and middle-C reading.

My First Music Book is a reading-readiness book that prepares the student by means of keyboard orientation (high/low, black-key groups, LH/RH, etc.) and experiences with finger numbers, basic rhythms, and listening experiences.

The *A* books teach note reading by presenting a pitch at a time, first completing a RH, then a LH 5-finger group from middle-C. Quarter, half, whole notes and measure bars (but no time signatures) are used in the context of unit counting.

The *B* books do not extend the reading range, but increase grand-staff reading experiences in which the hands alternate rather than play individually. The concept of time signature is introduced.

Rhythmic activities using whole-body, large-muscle movements are an element of the activity songs.

The activity songs (nursery rhymes, folk tunes, or original music written for the series) are contained in student books (with melody lines and lead-sheet symbols). A separate book *(Songs for Singing)* includes activity songs for all books, with teacher accompaniment.

There are several teaching aids: guidelines and lesson plans in *My First Music Book;* scope and sequence charts at the back of the *A* and *B* books; cassette recordings for all activity songs which assist the teacher (in class) and the parent (at home) to use these materials to develop and reinforce musical/ motor concepts.

Ear-training development combining pitch movement with rhythmic patterns is outlined at the back of *Piano Books A and B.* The books are ideally suited to group teaching, especially if activity and rhythm experiences are to be used to fullest advantage.

The books are colorful, the printing is clear, and notation is larger than usual. Activity pages often look crowded and over-busy. Several pages can be cut and made into flashcards.

PACE, HELEN AND ROBERT PACE. Milwaukee: Lee Roberts/Hal Leonard.

Music for Moppets, Child's Book	(1971)
Music for Moppets, Teacher's Manual	(1972)
Moppets' Rhythms and Rhymes, Child's Book	(1974)
Moppets' Rhythms and Rhymes, Teacher's Book	(1974)
Flash cards.	
Kinder-Keyboard, Child's Book	(1977)
Kinder-Keyboard, Teacher's Manual	(1974)

Kinder-Keyboard is a preschool book designed to precede *Music for Piano* 1 (discussed in chapter 6). It moves more quickly than *Music for Moppets* to introduce pitch and rhythmic reading, and to identify multi-key 5-finger patterns. Because *Music for Moppets* is more extensively developed at the preschool level, it is the only set of books reviewed here.

MUSIC FOR MOPPETS, CHILD'S BOOK

This text is colorful yet still has opportunities for the child to do meaningful coloring (e.g., certain black-key groups). The book presents illustrations for the pieces as well as pictures of which piano keys to use for performing the pieces. Students play on both black and white keys. Attention is drawn to directional reading, yet the method does not stress identification of individual pitches. Some pieces are notated (using large notes); some are not. All pieces are taught by rote or rote-note.

Although rhythmic perception and feeling are carefully developed, and while notated pieces use regular rhythmic notation, the student is not yet asked to identify notes by name (i.e., quarter, whole note), nor expected to count.

Several pages are play-a-story pages which encourage and direct creativity and free expression of musical ideas. Other listening-game and question-and-answer pages foster ear-hand experiences first by having the student imitate, then vary, what the teacher plays. By the book's end the student is able to tune up in several 3-finger and 5-finger positions (although 5-finger patterns are played with two hands, using fingers 3-2-1, 2-3).

MUSIC FOR MOPPETS, TEACHER'S MANUAL

The manual offers a clear explanation of the method's teaching psychology and educational goals. Pieces and activities are grouped into 16 units (this is not apparent in the child's book), each of which combines the development of already learned skills and concepts with the presentation of new information and experiences. Each unit is outlined very practically, noting what needs to be prepared for each class (e.g., art work, musical examples, equipment) as well as presenting a narrative lesson plan. Music that the teacher will play for rhythmic activities, music stories, and listening games is supplied exactly where needed, together with ideas of ways in which the teacher may continue to vary and improvise on the written examples.

The method is designed for group instruction (6–12 children recommended) in 45-minute classes twice a week, along with 45-minute orientation sessions for the parents twice a month. The parents are not present during the children's classes, but are strongly encouraged to participate in the child's home practice. The orientation sessions are designed to aid this process. An evaluation test for helping to assess (and therefore group) the preschool child is presented at the outset along with a sample class-reservation form to aid the teacher in establishing and communicating professional studio policy.

MOPPET'S RHYTHMS AND RHYMES, CHILD'S BOOK

This book may supplement *Music for Moppets,* or be used alone following completion of that text. It presents a collection of rhythmic game-songs, some based on nursery rhymes or folk tunes, some original. Although materials are chosen because they have obvious educational function, they are meant to provide fun as well as reinforcement.

The child's book combines "piece" pages with activity pages (coloring, copying, play-a-story). Note reading on lines and spaces, clefs, letter names for keys, letters placed directly on the staff, and sharps and flats are concepts introduced in this book.

Although regular rhythmic notation is used, note names are not defined.

MOPPETS'
RHYTHMS AND
RHYMES,
TEACHER'S BOOK

The teaching tips offered in this manual explain the educational purpose of each game-song, present the melody and accompaniment that the teacher will play in its use, suggest ideas for the play-a-story, listening, and "copy-cat" pages, and outline the teaching strategies used in working with the game-songs. A practical and unique teaching device is the careful listing of activities that can accompany going through the book a first time, with another list of further-developed activities that could be the focus of a second, or continued, use of the book.

FEATURES

Books combine a presentation of reading and playing concepts with ear training and improvisational activities useable in group teaching. Pitch reading is taught by direction and pattern recognition rather than by stressing equation of letter names with certain keys or guide notes. Rhythms are learned in patterns, by rote and through extensive drill. Rhythmic note values are not defined or taught. These books prepare the preschool child for multi-key reading, but the child is not asked to play 5-finger patterns with a single hand. The technical approach uses combinations of braced fingers, pointer fingers, and fingers 1, 2, and 3. From the outset the child is exposed to contemporary sounds and encouraged to use these while creating musical ideas for the play-a-story experiences. A high priority is placed on allowing the child to experiment at the keyboard by providing well-sequenced "small bits" of improvisational suggestions. Both teacher's manuals are practical and helpful. Not only do they offer a clear exposition of how to teach this method, but they could serve as models of class plans for teaching at the preschool level.

SUZUKI, SHINICHI. *Suzuki Piano School* **(English edition).** Tokyo: Zen-On Music Company, Ltd.; available through Summy-Birchard/Warner Bros., Secaucus, NJ

Volume 1	(1978)
LP recordings/audio cassettes (Meiko	(n.d.)
Miyazawa) of all music in Suzuki volumes 1	
and 2, 3 and 4	

Kataoka Performs Suzuki, with all pieces   (1984)
from volume 1, each piece 5 times in
succession
Only Volume 1 of the 6-volume *Suzuki Piano School*
series is considered here as it is the only Suzuki piano
book that might be regarded as preschool.

VOLUME 1

Studies for RH, LH; staccato repetitions on each note
of 5-finger pattern; hands alone; hands together.
    "Twinkle, Twinkle" Variations (A, B, C, D); same
in both hands. Variations are rhythmic, not melodic.
Each hand plays melody. Folk songs, two-hand
arrangements: Most LH parts are Alberti bass or
blocked chord style; I IV V_6 V_7 (close position.) Two
pieces have independent (single-voiced) LH parts.
One piece uses both hands parallel, 1 octave apart.
In one piece LH plays fifths, broken octaves.
"Tonalizations" and short "Studies" interspersed
throughout.

    Of the 20 pieces (counting the "Twinkle"
Variations), all are in C except for 2 in G, 1 each in
a, d minor. In 8 of the pieces, the LH plays pitches
above/around middle-C. International import of book
is obvious. All directions are in four languages:
English, French, German, Spanish (Japanese
subtitles).
Looking at the student volume(s), there is no way that
a teacher could tell what the Suzuki method involves
or intends. Nor is there a teacher-training manual or
guidebook available (as part of the Suzuki series itself)
to suggest how the Suzuki method is to be put into
practice. Several books, however, written by American
Suzuki specialists do offer insight into the method as
well as teaching directives and suggestions. These
include: *Introducing Suzuki Piano* and *Teaching
Suzuki Piano: A Guidebook for Teachers*, volumes 1
and 2, by Doris Koppelman; and *More Than Music* by
Carole L. Bigler and Valery Lloyd-Watts. Several
periodicals also provide teaching aids and guidance:
American Suzuki Journal; *Suzuki World*; and *Talent
Education Journal*.
    The entire volume 1 is taught by rote. The Suzuki
piano student is introduced to note reading after its
completion. The music read is always easier than that
which the student is currently performing.

Specialists stress that:
1. The "Twinkle" Variations are the foundation of Suzuki literature.
2. Study of one, or part of one, "Twinkle" Variation is to be part of every lesson and practice session while student is working in volume 1.
3. "Twinkle" Variations are to be played hands separately, not hands-together, as printed.
4. All pieces in volume 1 are to be memorized with right hand alone before playing any pieces hands-together.
5. All pieces in volume 1 should be learned by repeatedly listening to recorded music rather than by "rote gimmicks."[40]

There is careful attention to technique from the outset of instruction. The teaching of technique is also aurally based. Listening experience concentrates on achievement of a legato, singing quality ("tonalization").

Suzuki instruction is always individual instruction (with parent present). Other children, however, may be present at Suzuki lessons as observers. Group meetings are for group performance of repertoire. Some American Suzuki teachers also use group activities (stressing pre-reading or reading training and games) to supplement the individual lesson.

The Suzuki Association of the Americas registers Suzuki teacher-trainers in the United States who, in turn, offer teacher-training courses (often half-week sessions) in various locales. Haruko Kataoka (see page 82, this chapter) frequently tours the U.S. in a teacher-training capacity.

CHAPTER 6

The Average-Age Student

The "average-age" piano student is seven or eight years old. This arbitrary demarcation is shop-worn, if not suspect, but most piano teachers would have no trouble understanding the rationale behind the age choice. The second grader (the seven-year-old) is generally regarded as having achieved a number of things: a transference of trust from total parent authority to parent/teacher authority; an awareness and acceptance of a societal place outside the home (school and classmates); the ability to read and deal with numbers somewhat independently; and a physical readiness for the use of some finer muscle movement. The majority of piano courses are designed with such a student in mind.

Second and third graders have also become more comfortable with the responsibilities that going to school entails. They are not yet at the age when peer-group activities tend to dominate the social and school life. Therefore they presumably are at a receptive age for extraschool involvements such as piano lessons. Although many American children are adjusting to learning environments earlier than the first grade—by attendance at preschools, nursery schools, Head Start groups, day-care centers, and so on—many teachers still believe that the seven-year-old is the ideal beginner, and they suggest that music lessons be started at this time unless particular talent or unusual interest warrants otherwise. The many books designed to be appropriate for this age group, therefore, still find a large and stable market.

THE TEACHING OF READING

The teaching of reading, counting, and technical skills is often assumed to be the sole responsibility of the instructor, not of method books or print materials.

Nevertheless, books on keyboard instruction, whether called method books or not, generally provide technical guidance in the form of exercises, études, and/or commentary. It was not until early in the twentieth century, however, that authors of piano method books began to direct attention to the development of reading and rhythmic skills as essential components of their texts.

Some American methods written toward the end of the nineteenth century and during the first quarter of the twentieth (Mathews's *Standard Graded Course of Studies,* 1892–1894[1] Williams's *Very First Piano Book,* 1925[2]) presented initial pages of fundamentals: names of notes, rhythmic values of notes, metrical divisions, and so on. Other books published in the early twentieth century (Blake's *Melody Book,* 1916;[3] the Diller-Quaile *First Solo Book,* 1918[4]) began with the presentation of simple melodies, divided between the hands and based on middle-C reading. Although all such material provided implicit assistance to the teacher in presenting reading and rhythmic fundamentals, these books offered no explanation of the reading process or illustrations linking notes on the staff to keys on the piano.

In the 1920s and 1930s, however, method books began to appear that dealt in greater detail with the process of teaching music reading. Robyn in *Teaching Musical Notation with Picture Symbols* (1932) developed a preschool approach in which extended knowledge of the keyboard (five-C range), concepts of directional reading, and recognition of intervals were taught by means of rote cards plus a coordinating text, *Keyboard Town* (1934).[5] The group of educators who produced the *Oxford Piano Course* (1928)[6] taught children to play by imitating what they could already sing. This approach needed to consider the range of the child's singing voice. Thus playing in many keys (G, F, A, B-flat) at the very beginning of study was a prominent feature of this piano course designed for the public-school classroom.

Throughout the following decades, instructional techniques important to the Robyn and Oxford methods were expanded and developed. Burrows and Ahearn's *The Young Explorer at the Piano* (1941) made reference, in the preface, to a "psychological approach to reading."[7] The authors stressed four phases: rote, rote-note, guided reading, and independent reading. Their materials reflected continued attention to multiple-key presentation combined with emphasis on keyboard exploration. At the same time, other courses continued the approach used by earlier method books—reading of melodic lines divided between the hands with thumbs on middle C. The most popular of these, Thompson's *Teaching Little Fingers to Play* (1936),[8] combined the same presentation of fundamentals as that used by Mathews and Williams, but also provided graphics linking notes (and pitch names) on the staff with keys on the piano.

With the publication of Clark's *Time to Begin* and *Write and Play Time* (1955),[9] a method appeared that clearly advocated the use of an intervallic reading approach. In this method, a considerable amount of reading from off-staff notation leads to extensive experiences of reading from partial staves. Grand-staff reading evolves as a development of all preceding reading activities.

Three Reading Approaches

By the 1960s, piano methods began to be classified by their approaches to the teaching of reading. There were three: (1) the middle-C approach, (2) the multi-key approach, and (3) the intervallic approach. By far, the middle-C approach was the one used by most method books published since the 1930s. Everyone understood this approach and, presumably, how to teach it. The multi-key approach, with its roots in the realm of group (class) teaching, was supported and developed by teachers with interest in using the piano functionally, as a tool on which to harmonize and improvise as well as perform. The intervallic approach stressed the development of spatial-directional reading habits connected with the formation of hand-shapes and movements that follow from intervallic recognition.

Characterizing a piano method only by identifying it with one of these three reading approaches was, and is, simplistic. Continuing to apply these classifications to methods published quite recently is further complicated by the fact that some of these methods attempt to combine the best features of each reading approach. Nonetheless the use of such classifications persists, and teachers still form many opinions about an entire method based on the reading approach used within it.

Proponents of each reading approach defend what they see as advantages of that particular approach, even as critics claim that these same features are weaknesses. A list of claims and counterclaims associated with each approach is offered in a comparative summary.

Modified and Eclectic Approaches

Although some methods clearly represent only one of the three reading approaches described above, recently published courses may combine features of different approaches in order to offer more reading advantages. A method that utilizes aspects of both middle-C and multi-key reading might well be regarded as using a modified middle-C approach (if the method begins with middle-C orientation but incorporates transposition and harmonization) or a modified multi-key approach (if directional reading within five-finger patterns leads to eventual concentration on the middle-C position as one of the patterns).

Some methods are more eclectic. Pre-staff or partial-staff reading experiences may prepare for intervallic reading beginning with middle-C orientation, but the method may then branch out quickly to three-C, or other multiple guide-note, reading. Yet again, attention may be called to intervallic reading at the time when vertical, or chordal, reading appears in an otherwise middle-C method.

Labeling reading approaches is less important than being aware of the use and sequencing of whatever reading approach(es) any method presents. Teachers who are alert to the underlying principles of each reading approach are in

---

Middle-C Reading Approach

ADVANTAGES	DISADVANTAGES
Middle C, on staff and piano, is an easy, because visually obvious, guide.	One guide note is unduly limiting. It is equally easy to establish association with two or more.
Fixing and confirming a limited amount of pitch names and piano key locations is easy.	Limitation of pitch and key recognition to those around middle C forces students to play with hands close to the body at the beginning of study.
Developing a sense of the key of C (before moving into other keys) fosters ear/hand security.	Variety of sound stimulates the student's ear and imagination more than the recognition of just one key color.
In the beginning, it is helpful to associate certain fingers with certain keys and pitch names.	Students read from finger numbers rather than from knowledge of pitch names or directional sense.
Playing from thumb to outside of hand is required in keyboard literature. Moreover, this kind of technical beginning in one hand reinforces the same development in the other (mirror playing).	The thumb is an awkward finger at the keyboard. The fingers move more easily from the weak side of the hand to the strong.
Students learn best by absorbing small increments of information. Adding one pitch at a time is a logical, time-tested teaching technique.	Add-on learning delays transfer of knowledge based on recognition of patterns and groupings.

---

the best position to judge whether a particular combination of reading directives or activities forms a successfully unified method of instruction.

---

*T*HE TEACHING OF RHYTHM

The experience of rhythm is at the core of listening to music as well as making it. Rhythm is a physical sensation, easier to feel than to describe. Rhythm cannot be taught by either teacher or book. Basic to the experience of rhythm is the realization of pulse and the grouping of pulses. It is only against the background

Multi-Key Reading Approach

ADVANTAGES	DISADVANTAGES
The concept of the 5-finger pattern, both on staff and keyboard, is a single idea repeated in different contexts.	Students become locked into the 5-finger pattern. Changing fingering and hand shapes later on is more difficult to achieve.
Melodic lines are best read directionally and by comparison of same and different groupings.	Students read from finger numbers or positions since the type of music played is similar for a long time.
Early chord playing is satisfying and is the basis of harmonic understanding.	Students' hands are not technically ready for chord playing at the earliest stage.
Playing in varied locations and ranges fosters technical freedom (principally of the arm and shoulder).	Simultaneous 5-finger playing is difficult even though arms may be free of the body. Use of thumb on black keys is unpianistic.
The piano should be an instrument on which to explore and create as well as on which to perform; this fosters the development of the ear and personal individuality.	Early stress on variation may undermine accurate reading of literature. Interest in improvising may supersede attention to authentic performance technique.
Much keyboard literature is homophonic—melody in one hand, accompaniment in the other. Learning to read (play) this way at the beginning prepares student for both classical and popular literature and sounds.	Melody playing accompanied by blocked or broken chords is the only kind of music played in the early stages.

of pulse and grouping that rhythm becomes clearly defined. Teaching someone to count may be a way to assist that person to feel rhythm. Yet, too frequently, teaching someone to count becomes the only teaching strategy used in helping a student develop a sense of rhythm and an understanding of the principles of rhythmic notation. Of course, no one can completely bypass the use of a counting system. Nonetheless, *what* one counts, or *that* one counts, is much less important than what one *is aware of* while counting and/or playing.

What sort of counting systems teachers (and, perhaps, students) used during the first half of the twentieth century is difficult to determine with certainty. Who can know what actually happened in practice? It *is* certain, however, that no

Intervallic Reading Approach

ADVANTAGES	DISADVANTAGES
Off-staff directional notation allows student to read all over the keyboard from the start.	Student never gains a secure sense of location; too much freedom causes confusion.
Early intervallic recognition on a staff of less than 5 lines assures directional reading even before student need remember certain fixed guide notes.	Building up to reading on the grand staff is a slow process. Students can grasp the concept of pitch placement on the grand staff without this gradual procedure.
Since early reading is not based on recognition of patterns (other than intervals), students must look to the score for information about placement and fingering.	Bright, talented students may be able to work on their own, seeking information from the page, but average students need more direct repetition.
Off-staff, or limited-staff, reading done on black keys tends to use fingers 2 and 3 or 2, 3, and 4. These fingers are most natural to use at the outset.	Delayed use of thumb and fifth fingers is unnecessary. Correct hand position must be developed with the whole hand from the beginning.
From the start, music is played in many keys and ranges without use of 5-finger patterns or key signatures. There is variety of sound and effect.	Few folk or popular tunes are apt to be included in beginning music. Students (and parents) would rather hear familiar melodies.
Harmonic reading is intervallic also. Blocked fifths, sixths, thirds, and so on prepare for reading and playing of 3-note chords.	Harmonic reading and playing is often delayed. Single-line (thin-textured) music is less satisfying to the student.

suggestion for anything other than metric counting is found in method books published during these decades.[10]

Different emphases with regard to rhythmic training were advocated by Robyn (1932) and the *Oxford Piano Course* authors (1928). All of these educators urged total-body involvement in the experience and expression of rhythm. Robyn's students at the American Conservatory of Music (Chicago) took classes in Dalcroze eurhythmics[11] at the same time that they studied in classes using Robyn's rote cards. The Oxford authors, in the *Teacher's First Manual* (1929), called attention to the importance of "swinging the arms, swaying the body, marching, dancing, rhythmic games."[12] Both Robyn and the Oxford authors stressed the value of presentations of rhythmic values through rote teaching before rote-note, or note, teaching.[13] Student materials in each course, at beginning levels, were without instructions or graphics explaining the basic principles of rhythmic notation.

New Ways to Count

From midcentury on, beginning method books and demonstrations of these materials began to incorporate the use of other counting systems. Nominative counting (chanting the name of the note value) was often included before, or alongside, metric counting (counting the number of pulses in each measure, according to the time signature). Some methods began to advocate the use of unit counting (counting one for each quarter note, one-two for each half note, and so on, regardless of meter or the placement of notes within the measure). A few methods established a system of syllabic counting (the use of neutral syllables such as *ta, na, na-ah, tah-tay,* in the same manner as unit counting, without regard to meter or metric placement). Recently published piano methods are likely to suggest the use of several (or all) of these counting systems, enabling the teacher either to choose whichever (s)he prefers or to substitute and interchange these systems to reinforce the rhythmic experience.

Metric	1	2	3	4	1 and	2	3	4
Unit	1	2	3	1	1 = *na*	1	1	2
Syllabic	*Ta* = *ah*	= *ah*		*Ta*	*Ta* = *tay*	*Ta*	*Ta* = *ah*	
Nominative	Half-note	dot		quar-ter	two-eighths	quar-ter	half-note	

As with the approaches to the teaching of reading, advantages may be claimed for each system of counting. Nominative counting "defines, as it accompanies, the succession of note values." Unit counting reinforces "the relationship of notes to one another and relates them to a basic pulse." Syllabic counting eliminates "the confusion between 'counting numbers' and 'finger numbers'" and provides "extended, continual sounds for longer note values."[14] The use of systems other than that of metric counting makes it possible for students to experience meter and read rhythmic patterns before needing to understand the concept of meter. Every method book, of course, presents metric counting at some point. It is the preparation for metric counting that may differ.

Unit and syllabic counting systems also make it possible for students to play pieces using less common, or irregular, meters from the beginning of study. Methods that advocate these systems often include meters of 5/4 or 6/4, as well as changing meters, in very early pieces. Methods that present metric counting at the outset of study are less likely to use meters other than 2/4, 3/4 and 4/4.

Other Rhythmic Supports

Rhythmic activities involving large-muscle, or total-body, movement are also suggested in many methods appearing after midcentury. Instructions to swing, sway, walk, or conduct are found in some student books, most teacher's manuals or teaching aids, and are regularly practiced and promoted in teaching demonstrations. Special attention is frequently paid to the development of rhythmic performance by the inclusion of separate rhythmic drills (without pitch notation) to promote rhythmic security and physical coordination (often between hands). These drills may be found in the core text, in supplementary books (such as project, theory, or musicianship books), and/or in other teaching aids such as flash cards or computer programs.

Ensemble playing not only stimulates musical interest, but provides rhythmic impetus and support. Piano methods published after the 1950s show a markedly increased inclusion of teacher-student duets, student-student duets (or music for multiple pianos), and teacher accompaniments to pieces, rhythmic drills, and improvisatory activities. Supplementary music in these various categories is also on the increase.

Methods published later than midcentury generally provide significantly greater amounts of reinforcement material than methods published earlier. Supplementary pieces and books, of course, have always been used by teachers for purposes of reinforcement. It is the inclusion of extended repertoire and drills *within* the method, or core text, that is noticeably different not only from American methods published in the late nineteenth and first half of the twentieth century but also from piano methods appearing at any other time and from any other country.

One reason for this is the growing awareness, on the part of keyboard teachers as well as method authors, of the need for more reinforcement material between presentations of new concepts and skills, allowing for greater internalization of these concepts and skills on the part of the student. In no area is this more true than in the area of rhythmic development. A second reason may be an extension of the first. Learning psychologies generally agree that reinforcement activities (including homework or practice) that cause the student to rework concepts and skills in slightly different contexts are more productive than activities that require mere repetition.[15] Home practice, therefore, that demands the reapplication of learning skills to a variety of similar pieces or activities rather than the perfection of just a few, is desirable. Methods that include ample learn-on-your-own practice pieces make it easy for teachers to assign new music without risking the possibility that students may encounter unknown situations.

Expanding the Teaching of Rhythm

Since the 1960s, an increasing number of writers[16] have directed attention to aspects of rhythmic performance and the teaching of rhythm that go far beyond systems of counting and reinforcement by means of drill, reapplication, and/ or repertoire. In discussing rhythm in relationship to tension and relaxation, structure, awareness, or the perception and communication of groupings, they are providing greater insight into rhythm as a universal, as well as a musical, experience. The rhythms of harmonic change, larger phrase groupings, and rhythm as related to structural growth are only a few areas that teachers (and all musicians) need to examine more closely.

The Teaching of Technique

The piano methods and tutors of the nineteenth century were, in large part, books on technique. They contained various combinations of technical commentary, exercises, and études. The word "method" itself was (and perhaps still is) interpreted as a method of playing, a "school" of technique. Late nineteenth- and early twentieth-century American piano methods dealt with the matter of technique by offering advice and commentary (usually in a preface, occasionally in a teacher's manual), by interspersing short exercises among the pieces, or by providing little études contained either within the text or grouped in supplementary books. These method books did not generally regard repertoire as essential in the development of technique. Rather, technique already practiced was applied to the playing of pieces.

The preface to Mathews's grade 1 book in his *Standard Graded Course of Studies* (1892–1894)[17] presented the rudiments of technique as well as other fundamentals. However, Mathews urged the use of William Mason's *Touch and Technic* (1890–1892)[18] in conjunction with the use of his own method. The preface to the grade 2 book is a very careful and lengthy discussion of Mason's principles. John Williams not only offered basic technical advice in the preface of *First Year at the Piano* (1924)[19] but continued to do so throughout the book. Blake's *Melody Book* was supplemented by *Keyboard Secrets* (1927) and also by *First Steps in the Use of the Pedal* (1925).[20]

Robyn's *Technic Tales,* book 1 (1927) and book 2 (1930)[21] complemented the "rote cards" and *Keyboard Town.* The technical presentation was most explicit. Single gestures—the movement of the hand from lap to keyboard and back, the placement of other fingers while each individual finger is depressing a key, the exact position of the thumb—are differentiated and sequenced. A teacher's manual contained fuller explanations and pictures.

The concern of the *Oxford Piano Course* was to ensure that technical demands developed from the music itself. The teacher's manual "strongly recommends" that technical drill, in the early stages, be confined to the class period and not given as home practice.[22] Many of the "technic games" suggested by the manual for use during the first year of study are drawn from Robyn's *Technic Tales* and similar materials.[23]

Throughout the next decades (1930–1950), books dealing with technique were published either as supplementary to a series (Thompson's *Keyboard At-*

tacks, [1936] and *First Grade Etudes* [1939],[24] Schaum's *Hanon-Schaum* [1946] and *Technic Tricks* [1950][25]) or as separate books or series (Hirschberg's *Technic Is Fun,*[26] beginning in 1941; Weybright's *Technic for Pianists* [1947][27]; Burnam's *Dozen a Day,*[28] beginning in 1950; Maier and Bradshaw's *Thinking Fingers* [1954][29]).

Beginning on the Black Keys

From mid century on, approaches to the teaching of pitch reading made greater use of black keys at the beginning of study. Some methods required an extended use of the black keys before students explored the entire keyboard. A technical approach beginning with the placement of thumbs and proceeding to adjacent fingers—either note-by-note or as an entire five-finger pattern—is awkward on the black keys. Attention therefore was shifted to the use of the longer, middle fingers. The black-key groupings usually determined the fingerings: 2 and 3 on the two-blacks; 2, 3, and 4 on the three-blacks. Some books also included the use of the thumb and fifth finger if the music required a single hand to play five adjacent black keys.

Methods advocating this technical approach to the keyboard stressed additional reasons for using the middle fingers first. The positioning of the third finger puts the hand in balance. If the fingers drop onto the keys from above, the third finger, because it is the longest, reaches the key first. As the wrist is lowered, the other fingers assume their places in a somewhat semicircular curve in relationship to the third finger. Another reason for introducing individual finger movements from the weak side of the hand to the strong (4-3-2 rather than 2-3-4) is that this action is more natural. When drumming one's fingers on a table, for example, one notices that the fingers move easily from the fifth to the second rather than in the opposite direction; the thumb is seldom a part of the "drumming" process.

Beginning with the Non-Legato Approach

Sometimes early black-key pieces were to be played with a group, or cluster, of fingers (1, 2, 3 with tips touching; the second finger braced with the thumb), with the hand in a fist (playing either on the knuckles or on the side), or with only the middle finger of each hand. The use of any of these positions dictates a non-legato touch as the first keyboard attack. Advocates of whole-hand use at the beginning of study point out that this technical approach causes the student to move the hand in conjunction with the forearm and/or causes the hand to be directed from the shoulder. Use of larger movements, in turn, encourages and fosters the feeling of arm-weight (and arm-weight release), which is the basis of rich tonal production.

Such technical approaches are very different from immediate attention to the playing of adjacent finger, or five-finger, legato—which has been, and continues to be, the technical method of most other books and teachers. There is no method, of course, that does not deal with the process of playing legato, whether at the beginning of study or at some point in the early stages. The introduction of this technique, however, varies greatly both in manner and purpose. Initial legato movements required in methods range from the performance of a two-note slur to the projection of a two- (or more) measure phrase.

Presenting Scales

The presentation of scale forms, complete with fingerings, has long been a staple inclusion in beginning piano books. In most methods, certainly in most published prior to the mid twentieth century, the performance of a scale (frequently a one-octave scale) and the introduction of the thumb crossing occur simultaneously, the former being the reason for teaching the latter. In these same books, the thumb motion is first a matter of tucking the thumb under the third finger, or fourth. Individual scales are taught and practiced in this manner. Scale charts and diagrams depict parallel scales in which the fingering groupings rarely coincide. Both the scale form and the fingering for it must, therefore, be memorized.

Recent pedagogy is more careful to distinguish that learning to build a scale and learning to play a scale are two different experiences. Some recently published methods introduce the *concept* of scale well before the playing of a scale becomes a technical goal.

In some methods, motions involving the use of the thumb are included throughout the early stages of technical training in ways that prepare the hand for the extended and continual thumb adjustments needed in the playing of multi-octave scales. Experiences of the hand crossing over the thumb precede the teaching of the thumb-under approach. In some methods, also, scale playing is introduced in the descending right hand/ascending left hand forms so that the crossing over the thumb movement is the first motion practiced. The cooperation of the arm and wrist in the making of such crossings is a more natural probability in the cross-over technique. The arm-wrist-finger cooperation can then be applied to thumb-under motions.

Recently published methods are more likely to emphasize the *concept* of scale fingering than to teach fingerings for individual scales in turn. A student's awareness that all scale fingerings comprise alternate groupings of three and four, and that many scales have identical fingerings, makes it possible to teach (and practice) several scales at a time, or to expect a student to work out a fingering for a new scale based on past examples and expectations.

Technique in the Core Text

A few methods integrate technical training into the core text rather than offer supplementary books to provide that training. The inclusion of short, specific exercises throughout the book, or a collection of such at the back of the book, may underscore the importance of these technical routines and demonstrate their relevance to the repertoire. In most cases, these are methods in which the technical approach is least like the standard, so awareness and application of the technical curriculum is necessary if the use of the method is to achieve the results intended by the author(s)/composer(s).

*T*HE TEACHING OF MUSICIANSHIP

The nature of the keyboard instrument itself makes it possible for piano teachers to combine the teaching of instrumental competence, music literacy, and functional skills. However, using the keyboard as an instrument on which to study *music,* not just the playing of pieces, is a fairly recent concern for most teachers. Certainly there have always been keyboard teachers who inspired and directed study of deeper consequence than merely the performance of repertoire or the perfection of technique. But since the majority of teachers taught from books, and since piano tutors and methods were largely compendiums of technical exercises and repertoire, it is difficult to imagine that much musicianship instruction was part of the keyboard curriculum during the nineteenth century.

In the first decades of the twentieth century, the growth and popularity of piano instruction in American public-school classrooms created a new focus for keyboard training. These classes sought to introduce children to the fundamentals of music and, at the same time, regarded the making of music as another means of personal expression. Such classes directed little attention to technique. Greater care was taken to associate instructional pieces to the child's immediate life and surroundings, and to use teaching language that deemphasized technical jargon and foreignness. Since method books did not exist for this kind of instruction, class piano teachers and music educators wrote them.

Expanding Horizons in Early Methods

Such books began appearing early in the century.[30] The *Oxford Piano Course,* in particular, was to have significant influence. Its advocacy of singing before, and while, playing; its immediate attention to the establishment of the five-finger position in many keys; its notation of music in phrases;[31] its early introduction of the primary triads as resources for harmonization; its inclusion of unfinished musical phrases and pieces; its directions for the "varying" of pieces and "creative practice"—all of these emphases were an indication that performing was not the only goal of piano study.

The decades of the 1930s through the 1950s saw the publication of several types of books. Burrows and Ahearn's *The Young Explorer at the Piano* (1941) and *Young America at the Piano* (1945, 1946, 1948)[32] revealed many of the same interests as those of the authors of the *Oxford Piano Course.* On the other hand,

Thompson's *Modern Graded Piano Course* (1936–1942)[33] continued the middle-C tradition but called some attention to the structure of music by allusion to the use of same and different motives and phrases. Thompson's course also introduced scales via tetrachords.

Separate theory books began to make their way into print at the same time that supplemental technique and etude books were becoming more common. Fletcher's *Theory Papers* (1943, 1945, 1947),[34] Schaum's *Theory Lessons* (1946) and *Harmony Lessons* (1949),[35] Thompson's *Note Speller* (1946) and *Scale Speller* (1947),[36] and, somewhat later, Kahn's *Theory Papers* (1955, 1958) and *Note-Speller and Ear-Training Book* (1959)[37] were examples of books used by independent piano teachers becoming aware of the value of providing broader and more functional musical activities for students.

The Unified Course

In the 1950s and 1960s, methods began to emerge that encouraged closer alliance of performance, functional, and musicianship skills.[38] Although material dealing with these aspects of keyboard instruction was published in separate books, it was clearly the pedagogical intention of these methods that the materials were most productively used in conjunction with one another. An increasing number of methods since the 1960s have begun to offer a more extensive program of instruction:

1. Music/activities for use in developing reading/rhythmic skills.
2. Repertoire (recital, solo, and ensemble music).
3. Music and activities to develop skills in harmonization, transposition, and improvisation (creativity).
4. Exercises and/or etudes to guide the development of technique.

Change of emphases with regard to the teaching of keyboard musicianship skills is observable particularly in three areas:

1. The presentation of the concepts of scale, key, and key signature.
2. The development of harmonic understanding and function.
3. The type and sequencing of improvisational and creative activities.

Scale, Key, and Key Signature

In most early (as well as some current) methods, sharps and flats are introduced in conjunction with the first presentation of the major scale. Almost at the same time, reference is made to the meaning and use of key signature. At that point, the playing of pieces in keys (usually G and F) begins. An increasing number of methods published since midcentury, however, present accidentals apart from their necessary presence in the formation of scales. In such methods, repertoire makes frequent and early use of accidentals by writing in sharps and flats as needed, without the inclusion of a key signature or reference to one. Consequently, students will have experienced playing in a key before needing to understand tonality or the visual symbols connected to its notation. When key signature is presented, it is understood as shorthand notation for a concept already encountered.

Understanding the concept of scale building requires the knowledge of intervals, or at least the recognition of major and minor seconds. Some methods introduce the minor second at the same time as the presentation of sharps and flats. In many methods, intervallic pattern building commences with the explanation and use of the major five-finger pattern (pentascale, pentachord). In multi-key methods, this concept is taught very early. Continued and varied use of five-finger patterns forms the basis of the repertoire and of technical and improvisatory activities. In methods in which the approach to reading is intervallic, the introduction of the major five-finger pattern often occurs just after the development of the reading range to the interval of the fifth. More recently published middle-C methods also present this pattern sometime during the first months of study, although students may play the five-finger pattern in exercises and repertoire before it is identified.

The introduction of major scale patterns may take various forms.

The tetrachord approach to scale presentation allows a student to construct the entire scale as a unit. The teacher may have the student play all the notes simultaneously (somewhat like a very large cluster). This helps a student to "see" the scale formation. It also provides a basis for building the next scale (in the circle of fifths) by equating the bottom tetrachord of the new scale to the upper tetrachord of the scale just built.

Where the identification and use of the major 5-finger pattern has been an essential component from the beginning (as in multi-key methods), the formation of the major scale may be presented as an extension of the pattern already known—the pentascale plus whole, whole, half (steps).

In yet other scale presentations, the sixth and seventh degrees of the major scale are first demonstrated as extensions of the five-finger pattern, the sixth degree as a whole step above the highest pitch, the seventh as a half step down from the lowest. This procedure is especially practical when used in conjunction with accompaniments involving IV_6 and V_6.

Reading Vertically

Vertical, or harmonic, reading is introduced in different ways. In some methods, especially earlier courses using the middle-C reading approach, triads are defined and drilled as combinations of alternating letter names (C-E-G, F-A-C, and so on) and referred to by the letter name of the root (C chord, F chord). There is little or no harmonization of melodies or experimentation with accompaniment styles. The repertoire includes pieces in which blocked and broken triads are used to create big sounds, often in conjunction with the first use of the pedal.

In some (particularly multi-key) methods, attention is drawn to the line-line-line or space-space-space staff formation of triads and the use of alternating fingers in playing these. The triads are identified by their functional names (I, IV, V_7). The hand-shapes for each Roman numeral become a harmonic "habit." Reading (especially left-hand reading) is sometimes from Roman numerals only. An important component of such methods is the use of these harmonies both to provide accompaniments and to serve as the basis for an understanding of harmonic and formal structure when improvising and creating.

Methods that stress intervallic reading often begin the development of harmonic reading with the introduction of two-note combinations (dyads). Reference is made to the harmonic function plus the interval number (tonic fifth, dominant sixth, and so on). Three-note chords (triads) result from the addition of another interval to the dyad. These chords are read, and referred to, in figured bass terminology (tonic $\frac{5}{3}$, dominant $\frac{6}{3}$) because the intervallic orientation of the reading approach has made this seem natural. The repertoire in such methods provides examples of pieces in which intervals and interval-shapes are prominent features of the music's construction. The harmonization of melodies also begins with the use of dyads in varied styles/ranges.

Experimenting at the Keyboard

The encouragement of experimentation at the keyboard, whether in the form of harmonizing melodies, improvising, or creating, has been included in many post-midcentury methods. The number and type of experimental activities suggested in these methods varies considerably. In general multi-key methods place a high priority on harmonic knowledge, which, in turn, supports and guides the improvisation of accompaniments, melodic phrases, and ostinato-based pieces. Intervallic methods also provide incentives to accompany, but are equally likely to include specific directives for using intervals to create short pieces. Middle-C methods have been slower to include experimental or improvisatory activities, although many of them recommend supplementary theory or harmony books. The format of these supplementary books is mainly expository and student response is often only in written form. Recently, however, middle-C methods have begun to incorporate materials aimed at stimulating keyboard, in addition to written, response.

Since there is considerable variety in the type and scope of improvisatory and creative activities suggested in available methods, a teacher looking for stimulation or guidance in this area will likely find something with which (s)he can be comfortable. Some teachers prefer to incorporate such activities into group sessions or into monthly musicianship classes. Others find ways to involve students in keyboard exploration at every lesson. Certain instructors see creative experiments as being more appropriate for some students than others. Teacher's manuals or workshop handouts often give very helpful and specific suggestions regarding the how-to of guiding improvisation. Teachers with less confidence in their own abilities to improvise may find these teaching aids practical as well as stimulating.

Jazz and Pop in the Piano Method

In some teachers' opinions, the encouragement and guidance of improvisation is linked chiefly to jazz, pop, rock, and blues styles. Teaching materials to direct such improvisation were, at first, available only as separate jazz/pop series. These books contained mostly charts of progressions. They did not include supportive repertoire, nor did they concern themselves overmuch with pedagogical sequencing. By the 1960s and 1970s, however, jazz/pop/rock/blues books were published as supplementary material to many piano courses.[39] These courses also often included repertoire in the core text(s) that used jazz/pop/rock/blues sounds and forms. With the aid of these books—and workshops in which these books were demonstrated—teachers, most of whom had no jazz/pop playing skills themselves, learned to experiment in such styles even as they taught them to their students. Only very recently have experienced jazz/pop players begun to produce jazz/pop methods that are pedagogically sound.[40]

The Computer as a Theory and Musicianship Teacher

During the 1980s, some teachers began examining the possibilities and rewards of using the computer as a teaching aid. Computer software has principally provided instructional programming that presents music theory information, although there are programs that offer history or "appreciation" education. In addition to programs presenting conceptual approaches to the understanding of music, other programs are designed as ear-training (pitch) and rhythm-training packages. Very recently, piano methods have begun to include computer software that is to be used in conjunction with particular courses. The supplementary theory "book" is actually theory software. The next decades will undoubtedly see an increase in the development and use of computer programs (as well as other electronic resources) as adjuncts to the teaching of piano. See chapter 24 for a more detailed discussion of keyboard teaching and new technology.

THE ELEMENTARY METHOD: IS IT NECESSARY?

For most piano teachers, the first two years of a student's instruction are approached as a general preparation for the teaching of the classics. "Classics" include music from the *Anna Magdalena Bach Notebook;* the dances and other easy pieces of Beethoven, Mozart, Haydn, Schubert, and Schumann; Clementi (and other) sonatinas; or Bartók's *Mikrokosmos* (volumes 1–3). Two preparatory years, of course, must not be interpreted strictly. Some students are ready for the classics in a much shorter time; others may take somewhat longer. Although it is not axiomatic that all students must eventually learn to play the classics, the majority of piano teachers base their instructional planning (or at least their hopes) on that assumption.

The rationale for this preparatory period is that the reading of pitch and rhythmic notation, basic technical skills, and general dynamic, agogic, and harmonic principles should be taught *before* the student is exposed to classical literature. In other words, the student should not be struggling to read, count, or negotiate the performance of legato and staccato while learning a Bach minuet or a Beethoven ecossaise. This is by no means a universal opinion, but it is one held by many American piano teachers.

An opposite viewpoint is one in which the necessity of some preliminary reading and technical instruction is admitted, but such preparation is either not expected to occupy a very long time or is attended to while the learning of classics is begun. While this is commonly regarded as the European approach to beginning piano instruction, many American piano teachers believe that the use of method books encouraging a preparatory period of almost two years postpones, rather than stimulates, advancement. Such teachers also are likely to feel that too much of the "teaching material" music used during this period is of questionable quality.

The descriptive summaries of beginning piano methods immediately following this section will include books representing both former and latter viewpoints. However, since the majority of books published (and hence reviewed) advocate the elementary period of almost two years, it may be helpful to catalog the concepts and skills that are regarded as essential components of such courses.

*T*HE ELEMENTARY PIANO COURSE: CONCEPTS AND SKILLS COVERED

Every concept and skill included in the following list will not, of course, be found in every preparatory course book.[41] It is also true that while some concepts and skills on the list *are* presented in each course, the sequencing of the activities related to the teaching of a particular concept or skill may differ significantly from method to method.[42] The list therefore suggests skills and concepts generally covered as part of preparatory training without wishing to imply that presentation of each single item is either desirable or necessary in every individual course.

Beyond cataloging the content of preparatory books in order to evaluate a method, questions should be raised regarding sequencing, choice of language and texts, cultural and ethnic assumptions (for instance, what is the nature of folk tunes used?), pertinence and clarity of graphics, format, and—above all—the quality of the music the method contains.

The Presentation of Reading Skills and Concepts

PITCH NOTATION

Preparatory Activities May be:

Pre-reading (rote) experience.

Unstaffed notation: finger numbers, letter names, notes.

Gradual staff notation: 2-line, 3-line.

Grand-Staff Reading/Reading Approach May be:

Middle-C.

Multi-key.

Intervallic.

Modified middle-C.

Modified multi-key.

Eclectic.

Reading Reinforcement May be:

Extensive repertoire in core text.

Written activities.

Flash cards.

Supplementary book(s).

RHYTHMIC NOTATION

Note Values and Rhythmic Symbols

Basic note values (quarter, half, dotted half, whole); eighth notes; dotted quarter; triplets, sixteenths, dotted sixteenth.

Equivalent rests.

Ties.

Systems of counting used: nominative, unit, syllabic, metric.

Meters

2/4, 3/4, 4/4; possibly 6/4, 6/8.

2/2 or alla breve.

Irregular or changing meters (possibly).

Rhythmic Reinforcement May be:

Repertoire in core text.

Ensemble playing: teacher-student, student-student, multiple piano.

Separate rhythmic drills.

Eurhythmic suggestions: swing, step, sway, conduct.

Written drills in core text, in supplementary book(s).

REVIEWS OF SELECTED METHODS

In the following reviews please note:

All books that complete the main texts in any library are listed. Supplementary books are generally listed only as such, not by separate title, except where they form an integral part of the method's teaching viewpoint.

The Presentation of Technical Skills and Concepts

Touches/Articulations
  First playing technique: whole hand/arm, single/braced finger, 5-finger legato.
  First legato experience: 5-finger, 2- or 3-note slur (N.B., fingers used).
  Staccato, phrasing, tenuto.
Movements
  Lateral movements or change of position.
  Coordination: alternating hands, hands-together, parallel/contrary motion.
  Extensions/contractions within hand.
  Thumb crossings.
Fingerings
  Fingerings as related to 5-finger patterns and extensions.
  Scale fingerings.
  Chord, inversion, and arpeggio fingerings.
Nuance/Sound
  Dynamics.
  Agogics: rit., a tempo, accel., fermata.
  Pedaling: for effect; syncopated; rhythmic.
Technical Reinforcement May be:
  Exercises in core text, in supplementary book(s).
  Etudes in core text, in supplementary book(s).
  Built into core text repertoire.

Only books that comprise texts for the *elementary years* are *reviewed*. In some cases, there may be unavoidable overlap where higher books in a series present repertoire that might be viewed as intermediate, but the series has not yet completed presentation of some concepts and skills that are usually part of elementary training.

Counting systems are described as nominative, unit, syllabic, and metric. Although these terms are not in general use, they may conveniently describe a method of counting. For the reviewer's definition of these terms, and the importance they may have to a method's presentation of rhythm, please refer to pages 109–111 in this chapter.

BASTIEN, JAMES, AND JANE SMISOR BASTIEN. *Bastien Piano Basics.* San Diego: Kjos West.

PIANO: Primer and *Levels 1–4*	(1985)
THEORY: Primer and *Levels 1–4*	(1985)
PERFORMANCE: Primer and *Levels 1–4*	(1985)
TECHNIC: Primer and *Levels 1–4*	(1986)

Supplements: Christmas, duet books, others.

The Presentation of Theory and Musicianship Skills and Concepts

Keyboard Patterns
Major/minor 5-finger pattern.
Major scales.
Parallel (or relative) minor scales.
Chords and Inversions: chord names, Roman numerals, figured bass.
Cadences.

Understanding of Key
Key signature.
Reading/playing in keys: few? many? all?
Major/minor changes.
Modes: Dorian, Phrygian.

Improvisation/Creativity May be:
Suggestions and directions in core text, in supplementary book(s).
Approach using question/answer, ostinato, accompaniment, variation, original pieces.
Written work in core test, in supplementary book(s).

Signs/Symbols
Tempo terms.
Shorthand signs: repeat, ottava, 1st/2nd endings.
Glossary/dictionary.

Theory/Musicianship Reinforcement May be:
Presented in core text, or in supplementary book(s).
Activities that require playing and/or written response.
Suggestions for ear-training activities.

Pitch/Rhythm Reading

PRE-READING	Off-staff reading (black keys) by finger numbers; (white keys) by combined letter names and finger numbers.
GRAND STAFF	*Piano Primer:* C, G positions; middle-C position (both thumbs, middle-C); by picture placement, letter names, interval reading.
COUNTING	Nominative; then metric.
RHYTHMS	*Piano Primer:* Basic note values, rests, meters; eighth notes. *Piano 1:* Dotted quarter. *Piano 2:* 6/8. *Piano 3:* Triplets. *Piano 4:* Sixteenths; syncopation.

Technique

BEGINNING	Legato on black keys.
FIRST LEGATO FINGERINGS	2-3-4; 1-2-3; both hands.

CROSSINGS

Piano 2: Thumb under, with major scale.
Technic books are correlated with *Piano* books, by page. Mix exercises and short etudes.

Theory

SCALE

Piano 2: 1 octave; regular fingering; C, G, F, D, A, E.

HARMONIZATION

Theory 1 on: Playing from Roman numerals; transposing; harmonizing lead lines; accompaniment styles.

CREATIVE

All *Theory* books: Limited amount; question and answer.

Repertoire

COMPOSERS

James Bastien and Jane Smisor Bastien. *Piano 4:* 1 piece by J. C. Bach.

FAMILIAR TUNES

Some use of folk and well-known tunes throughout. Higher level books: arrangements of classical music.

ENSEMBLE

Teacher accompaniments to many *Piano Primer,* some *Performance Primer* pieces.
   The music offers a good mix of well-known tunes, pop and blues sounds, and original compositions throughout the course. All pieces at the *Piano and Performance* primer level have words. At higher levels, words are often included with folk songs. Although repertoire from level 2 on tends to focus on specific keys, there is greater stylistic variety than is often found in multi-key courses. Many pieces are imaginative in mood and texture and spiced with some harmonic and formal surprises.

Teaching Aids

Flash cards; student assignment notebook; teacher's record book; erasable slates; stickers.

Features

This multi-key method seems written for the student who needs time to become acquainted with basic piano positions before exploring the full range of reading and playing in many keys. Books at early levels provide a firm grounding in the keys of C, G, and F. Books thereafter introduce new keys in groups: level 2 (D, A, E); level 3 (D-flat, A-flat, E-flat; level 4 (G-flat, B, B-flat). While similar to earlier Bastien methods, this course has maximum visual appeal with multi-color illustrations, laminated covers, and very contemporary references (computers, UFOs, jeans; "This Old Man" wears mod roller skates!). The repertoire shows greater variety in style and texture than many multi-key methods. The *Theory* books offer reinforcing playing, as well as writing, experiences. The harmonizing that is so much a part of multi-key courses is concentrated more in the *Theory* than in the *Piano* books. The books at level 1 could also be beginning books since they recap the conceptual presentations with which the *Primer* books ended.

CHRONISTER, RICHARD, AND DAVID KRAEHENBUEHL. *The Keyboard Arts Method.* Los Angeles: National Keyboard Arts Associates.

> *The Basic Music Study Program: Books 1–40*
> (1980). Each 8 pages; 39 supplementary pieces of
> sheet music.
>
> *The Intermediate Music Study Program: Books 41–*
> *60* (1980). Each 12 pages.

Pitch/Rhythm Reading

PRE-READING	Books 1–4: Reading first from single 5-line staff, then double 5-line staves; letter clefs. Directional reading.
GRAND STAFF	Books 5–12: Gradual introduction of G, F clefs (one at a time) coupled with continued use of letter clefs. Book 13: Grand-staff reading. Guide notes: treble B, bass D, middle C. Reading by direction, interval. From book 31: High and low ledger lines.
COUNTING	Syllabic. From book 3 on: Unit counting.
RHYTHMS	Books 1–15: Basic note values, rests. Books 13–15: Top number of time signature. Book 16: Eighth notes. Book 24: Three eighth notes and dotted quarter in compound meter. Book 31: Triplets in simple meter. Book 33: Dotted quarter; eighth. Book 35: Sixteenths. Irregular meters from the beginning. Each book has 3 "miniflashes" (student cuts these out), that drill combined reading and rhythmic concepts pertinent to each book. Miniflashes are also cumulative. Each flash counted and played twice, slow tempo; immediately counted and played twice as fast.

Technique

BEGINNING	Whole hand/arm. Second finger braced by thumb (closed hand). Book 5: Blocked fifths.
FIRST LEGATO FINGERINGS	Book 9: 1–5; 5–1; both hands.

CROSSINGS   Book 42.

Theory

SCALE   Book 25: M 5-finger pattern. Book 29; m 5-finger
                        pattern. Book 43: Major scale.

HARMONIZATION   Book 27: Harmonizing with tonic fifth. Book 32:
                        Harmonizing with tonic fifth, IV_6. Book 36:
                        Harmonizing with tonic fifth, V_6.

CREATIVE   Composition in each book. Written (staves
                        provided). Pieces are played.

EAR TRAINING   One-measure written dictation drawn from current
                        repertoire included in each book.

Repertoire

COMPOSERS   Almost entirely by Kraehenbuehl (including
                        supplementary pieces).

FAMILIAR TUNES   Each book contains a "mystery tune," that student
                        must either complete or accompany. These are all
                        folk and well-known tunes. Supplementary sheet
                        music includes arrangements of symphonic themes.

ENSEMBLE   Most pieces (except mystery tunes and including
                        sheet music) have imaginative and colorful teacher
                        accompaniments.
                            Repertoire provides reinforcement of concepts
                        studied. The supplementary sheet music is more
                        appealing since it incorporates fresh sound-
                        combinations and metric vitality.

Teaching Aids

Teacher Reference Book. Explains authors' teaching philosophy, offers scope
and sequence charts, and provides reading-practice tests. "Miniflashes" are included in each student book.

Features

This course is well-organized and sequenced. Nothing has been left to chance.
Preparation for new concepts is always provided in advance. The authors regard
preparation for home practice as the key ingredient to learning success. Student
materials contain explicit (albeit repetitive) practice steps for everything, in ev-

ery book. The approach to the understanding of pitch notation sequences a development of intervallic reading in which materials at times interweave reading from single staves (using picture or letter-clef identification) with reading from the grand staff. The miniflashes are unique in their expectations of slow/fast reading and playing that prescribes the immediate doubling of the original tempo. Each book is designed to be presented completely at one lesson, then worked on (completely) for several lessons, as needed. Although the number of books is large, each book contains only 8 pages; all 40 books may be completed in approximately 2 years of study.

CLARK, FRANCES, AND LOUISE GOSS. *The Music Tree.* Secaucus, NJ: Summy-Birchard/Warner Bros.

	Time To Begin (1955, 1960, 1973) *Parts A, B, C* (1973). These are revisions of *Write and Play Time* (parts A, B; 1955), *Tune Time* (parts A, B; 1955), *Technic Time* (parts A, B; 1955), and *Look and Listen* (parts A, B, C, D; 1962), with David Kraehenbuehl.
MUSIC MAKER	*Parts A, B* (1986, 1987) Secaucus, NJ: New School for Music Study Press/Warner Bros.
SUPPLEMENTS	Sheet music, solo and ensemble, all levels.

Pitch/Rhythm Reading

PRE-READING	All of *Time to Begin* is a preparation for grand-staff reading. Extensive off-staff reading (on black/white keys); intervallic reading from 2-line through 5-line staves. Use of variable letter clefs evolves to understanding of G, F clefs. 8va from unit 3.
GRAND STAFF	*Part A:* Begins with grand-staff reading. Intervallic reading from landmarks G, F clefs; through fifths only. *Part B:* New landmarks high G, low F (unit 6); intervallic reading through fifths only. *Part C:* sixths, sevenths, octaves.
COUNTING	Unit. From *Part B:* metric. *Music Maker* books: walking, "point and count," "tap and count."
RHYTHMS	*Time to Begin:* Basic note values; time signatures (including 5/4, 6/4). *Part A:* Rests (unit 7). *Part B:* Eighth notes and the dotted quarter. *Part C:* Triplets; compound time. (Sixteenth notes and syncopation in *Keyboard Theory 1,* a text that follows *Part C.*)

Technique

BEGINNING	Whole hand/arm; middle finger.

FIRST LEGATO FINGERINGS	*Time to Begin:* 3-2, 4-3-2. Fingers 1, 5 not used until *Part A,* unit 4.
CROSSINGS	*Part C:* 2/3 over thumb; thumb under. "Technical warm-ups" in each unit (from *Time to Begin,* unit 3). *Parts A, B, C:* Technical warm-ups are at the back of each book.

Theory

SCALE	*Part B:* M/m 5-finger patterns. *Part C:* Major scale (unit 9); (RH) descending.
HARMONIZATION	*Part B:* Accompaniments with fifths. *Part C:* Accompaniments with sixths (V_6, IV_6)
CREATIVE	*Time to Begin:* Original pieces using concepts studied. No writing. *Part B, C:* Accompanying and transposing. *Music Maker A, B:* "Make a Piece" in each unit.

Repertoire

COMPOSERS	Various: George, Goss, Kraehenbuehl, Olson, LaMontaine. None identified with pieces.
FAMILIAR TUNES	*Time to Begin, Part A:* None. *Parts B, C:* A few, often melodies with accompaniment.
ENSEMBLE	*Time to Begin, Parts A, B:* Most pieces have teacher accompaniments. *Part C:* Several teacher accompaniments.

All pieces in *Time to Begin,* many in *Parts A, B, C* have descriptive, metrically suitable words. There is great variety of phrase lengths, range, articulations. Teacher accompaniments are musically interesting and conducive to interpretation of moods, styles, tempi. Without teacher accompaniments, however, student materials remain thin-sounding throughout first three books. The repertoire is admirably sequenced to provide ample reinforcement of all concepts and skills.

Teaching Aids

Teaching the Music Tree, a teacher's manual, offers practical insights into the teaching philosophy of the method and specific teaching strategies for its use. Three-page preface in *Music Maker, Part A,* provides rationale underlying activities in *Music Maker* books.

Features

This course is the classic intervallic method, pioneering an approach to reading that prepares for, rather than begins with, grand-staff reading. The method requires no supplementary materials as it provides (in each book) a variety of activities and supportive repertoire. The organization into units (each of which contains presentation of new concepts, reinforcement material, technical warmups, written and creative/variational activities) clarifies (both for student and teacher) proximate goals and overall pacing. Reinforcement of fundamental rhythmic values is extensive. Eighth notes and dotted rhythms first appear in the third book, *Part B.* The technical approach, while less standard, is integrated into and developed by the repertoire. *Music Maker* books provide supplementary write-and-play activities that can be used with any method.

CLARK, MARY ELIZABETH, AND RUTH PERDEW. *Piano Tomorrow Series.* Boulder, CO: Myklas Music Press.

READING AND REPERTOIRE	*Primer* (1981), *1–3* (1980), *4* (1984)
THEORY NOW	*Primer* (1981), *1–3* (1980), *4* (1985)
RHYTHM NOW	*Primer* (1981), *1–3* (1982), *4* (1983)
SHAPES AND INTERVALS	*Levels 1, 2* (1980)
SHAPES, SCALES AND CHORDS	*Level 3* (1980)
SOLOS NOW	*Primer* (1981)
BASS CLEF BOOK	(1981)

Pitch/Rhythm Reading

PRE-READING	*Reading and Repertoire Primer:* 10 optional black-key rote pieces.
GRAND STAFF	*Reading and Repertoire Primer:* Begins with G-clef G, F-clef F. Develops to include high/low Gs, Fs, and 5Cs as guide notes. Letter names, groupings, intervals shown.
COUNTING	*Rhythm Primer:* Shows all systems. *Theory Primer:* Metric.
RHYTHMS	*Rhythm Primer:* Basic note values, rests, meters. *Rhythm 1:* Eighth notes; 5/4. *Rhythm 2:* Dotted quarter; changing meters; uneven groupings. *Rhythm 3:* Triplets; 6/8; 6/4. *Rhythm 4:* Sixteenths. *Rhythm Now* books, all levels: Separate rhythm

books that contain extensive tapping, singing, and playing and writing activities; games, puzzles, tests.

Technique

BEGINNING *Reading and Repertoire Primer:* 5-finger legato.

FIRST LEGATO FINGERINGS   1-2; 2-1; both hands.

CROSSINGS   *Shapes and Intervals:* 3 over thumb; 1 octave scale. *Shapes, Scales and Chords:* Thumb under/over.

Theory

SCALE   *Theory 2:* Scale pattern; all key signatures. *Reading and Repertoire 2:* Most major, some natural minor scales; some modes. *Theory 3:* All modes.

HARMONIZATION   None.

CREATIVE   None.
Theory Books: Mostly written, some playing activities.

Repertoire

COMPOSERS   Principals: Mary Elizabeth Clark, Anne Shannon Demarest, Ruth Perdew, John Robert Poe. Others: Bartók, Gurlitt, Billie Farrell, Robert Vandall.

FAMILIAR TUNES   Mostly folk materials; included throughout. Some arrangements of classical themes.

ENSEMBLE   Teacher accompaniments. *Reading and Repertoire Primer:* Some rote pieces; occasional others. *Rhythm 1:* Some ensemble rhythm exercises.

Pieces in *Reading and Repertoire* books are grouped around certain notes, or groups of notes. At primer level and level 1 these are the 9 guide notes. At level 2 pitches drilled are those other than guide notes. Primer and level 3 pieces contain more varied textures, styles, sounds than repertoire in other texts or the *Solos Now* primer. Noteworthy is the rhythmic/metric variety (including use of irregular/changing meters) in all materials. Not all pieces in *Bass Clef Book* are for bass clef alone.

Teaching Aids

None.

Features

There is really no core book in this method. The sets of books each attend to separate tasks. Instruction in the reading books does not define rhythmic note values; rhythm books concentrate heavily (especially at early levels) on un-pitched rhythmic reading; technique books are almost entirely exercises. Theory texts, however, do drill concepts and skills from other books. The reading approach calls attention to 9 guide notes: all Gs, Fs, Cs on grand staff plus ledger-line Cs. Each guide note is focused on separately and has its own reinforcing repertoire. The *Rhythm Now* books, because of the use of so much unpitched drill, could be used with any reading approach. The great variety of rhythmic experiences provided by these books could help students stretch rhythmic awareness. The course books at each level correlate, but only in a general sense. Although books at levels 2 and 3 include stress on chords and accompaniment styles, there is no reference to functional harmony or use of it in harmonization or improvisation.

GEORGE, JON, AND MARY GAE GEORGE. *Artistry at the Piano.* Miami: CPP/Belwin.

Introduction to Music/Supplemental Workbook	(1981)
Repertoire Levels 1–4	(1979)
Musicianship Level 1 (1980), *Levels 2–4*	(1981)
Workbook Levels 1–4	(1981)
Ensemble Levels 1–4	(1981)

Suggested order of use at each level: (1) *Workbook*; (2) *Musicianship*; (3) *Repertoire*; (4) *Ensemble.*

Pitch/Rhythm Reading

PRE-READING	*Introduction to Music:* Basics about pitch reading learned before playing. Intervals (from clefless staff) associated with letter names, finger numbers.
GRAND STAFF	*Introduction to Music:* 3C reading moves quickly to 5C reading; four pitches above and below each C; intervallic reading.
COUNTING	Unit. Moves quickly to metric. Continues to combine these. Much attention to stress, non-stress; rhythm linked to language.
RHYTHMS	*Introduction to Music:* Basic note values presented simultaneously. Importance placed on rhythmic figures. Eighth notes, triplets, compound meter also presented simultaneously. (First use of dotted quarter is in compound meter.) Level 1 books:

Dotted quarter, eighth. Level 3 books: Sixteenths.
From level 2: Irregular, changing meters.

Technique

BEGINNING

Introduction to Music: Done away from keyboard.
Exercises for arm, wrist, *flat* fingers. Arch built
gradually. Slurs (fingers 3-2) first practiced away
from keyboard.

FIRST LEGATO
FINGERINGS

3-2, 4-3-2 slurs.

CROSSINGS

Level 2 books: 2 over thumb.
   Levels 1–4: Although there are no separate
technique books, development of technique (by
means of explanation, exercises, repertoire)
pervades this method, often in quite sophisticated
ways.

Theory

SCALE

Musicianship 2 and *Workbook 2:* Tetrachords. Scale
fingering concepts (all keys) explained, charted.

HARMONIZATION

None.

CREATIVE

Introduction to Music: Question/answer.
Musicianship 4: Add inner voice from figured bass.

Repertoire

COMPOSERS

Jon George.

FAMILIAR TUNES

None.

ENSEMBLE

Student-student *Ensemble* book at each level. Much
variation in sound and texture. Requires refinement.
   There is repertoire in all books and a refreshing
mix of short and long pieces from the beginning.
The music, though all by Jon George, reflects
(convincingly) all style periods from early Baroque
through present-day sounds. All pieces in *Repertoire,
Ensemble* books prefaced by sophisticated
descriptions and suggestions. The musical quality is
exceptional.

Teaching Aids

Detailed prefatory remarks in all *Repertoire, Ensemble* books. Tables of contents
in all books organized into "lessons," that show what to coordinate among the

books. Large, loose, check-off charts included with all *Musicianship* books. Flash cards: *Introduction to Music, Musicianship 1.* Cassette recordings (by M. G. George) of all pieces in *Musicianship, Repertoire, Ensemble* books, levels 1–4.

Features

This course is full of surprises: introduction of fundamentals away from the piano; postponement of piece playing until after rhythm, pitch, and technical basics have been covered; a technical beginning with flat fingers, that builds the arch gradually; simultaneous presentation of many rhythmic note values. These and other features necessitate careful study on the part of the teacher intending to use this method. The difficulty of the music develops quickly; level 2 books span late elementary and early intermediate grading. Ear-training activities are sequenced through level 2; rhythmic drills through level 4. The format is often dense. Titles of pieces (mostly abstract, sometimes in other languages) are sophisticated. Instructional commentary seems adult-oriented. The preface recommends the group educational setting.

GLOVER, DAVID CARR. *David Carr Glover Method for Piano.* Miami: CPP/ Belwin.

> *Lessons* (with Jay Stewart): *Pre-reading, Primer, Levels 1, 2* (1988, 1989)
>
> *Performance* (with Jay Stewart): *Primer. Levels 1, 2* (1988, 1989)
>
> *Technic* (with Jay Stewart): *Primer, Levels 1, 2* (1988, 1989)
>
> *Theory* (with Martha Mier and June Montgomery): *Pre-reading, Primer, Levels 1, 2* (1988, 1989)
>
> *Sight Reading and Ear Training* (with E.L. Lancaster and Gayle Kowalchyk): *Primer, Levels 1, 2* (1988, 1989)
> Supplements: Include Christmas, jazz, early American books, others.

Pitch/Rhythm Reading

PRE-READING	*Pre-reading:* Unstaffed notation.
GRAND STAFF	*Primer:* Middle-C approach, C position, G position. Level 1 books: Mostly in 3C range, but all notes on the staff by the end of level 1 books. C, F, and G positions. Level 2 books: Ledger-line reading. C, F, G, D, c, f, g, and d positions.
COUNTING	*Pre-reading:* Unit. *Primer:* Unit or metric.

| RHYTHMS | *Pre-reading:* Quarter, half, and whole notes. *Primer:* Basic note values, rests, meters. Level 1 books: Eighth notes. Level 2 books: Dotted quarter. |

Technique

BEGINNING	*Pre-reading:* 3-2, 4-3-2, 1-2-3. *Primer:* 5-finger legato; from thumbs.
FIRST LEGATO FINGERINGS	*Pre-reading:* 2-3-4; both hands.
CROSSINGS	Level 2 books: With major scale. *Technic* books correlate with *Lessons* books. Mix exercises and short etudes.

Theory

SCALE	Level 1 books: 5-finger patterns (C, F, G). Level 2 books: Tetrachord; regular fingering.
HARMONIZATION	Theory level 1: Limited. Theory level 2: Primary triads; close position.
CREATIVE	None. *Theory* books use writing, playing, listening reinforcement; many games and puzzles. *Sight Reading and Ear Training* books correlate listening and reading with *Lessons* books; stress pattern and interval reading, listening to pitches, rhythms, articulations, dynamics, tempo.

Repertoire

COMPOSERS	Glover and Stewart. Various composers/editors in supplementary music.
FAMILIAR TUNES	Much use of folk, well-known tunes in all books. Simplified arrangements of well-known classics.
ENSEMBLE	Some teacher accompaniments at early levels. Music in the *Pre-reading* and *Primer* books is tuneful, some because it is familiar. Repertoire in the rest of the course is mixed in quality: some pieces are attractive and imaginative; some pieces expand the tonal palette (pentatonic, impressionistic); but many pieces are predictably accompanimental. Repertoire in the supplementary books *Micro-Patterns 1–4* (Glover, Curzon, and Rosco)

introduces current musical and keyboard sounds; "presentation pages" guide both student and teacher in experimenting.

Teaching Aids

Flash cards; assignment book; Music Magic Slate; games; others. All *Theory* books have answers and teacher's listening examples at the end. All *Sight Reading and Ear Training* books include teacher dictation and answer pages that correlate with pages in student books.

Features

This essentially middle-C course incorporates certain multi-key aspects such as the establishment of 5-finger positions in some basic keys, and the presentation and use of functional harmony in repertoire, exercises, and written work. Reference is made throughout the course to intervals (beginning in the *Primer* level books and including limited experience of 6ths, 7ths, and octaves in the *Level 2* books), but the reading approach is not a direct outgrowth of interval awareness. While similar in many respects to Glover's earlier method (*David Carr Glover Piano Library*), this course provides more imaginative and extensive reinforcement in its ancillary volumes, the *Theory* and *Sight Reading and Ear Training* books. The supplementary books written in conjunction with Glover's earlier method are equally useable with this course and allow teachers to coordinate varied materials (sacred, jazz, contemporary, early American, and so on) as they choose.

KISELL, E., V. NATANSON, A. NIKOLAEV, AND N. SRETENSKAYA. *The Russian School of Piano Playing.* Farmingdale, NY: Boosey & Hawkes. Edited by A. Nikolaev. Translated by Nariné Harutyunyan and Martin Hughes.

Book 1: Parts 1, 2	(1978)
Book 2	(1978)
First, Second Repertoire Albums	(1984)

Edited by Nariné Haroutiunian
Book 1: Part 1: First year of study. *Book 1: Part 2:* Second year of study. *Book 2:* Third year of study; works grouped as (1) pieces; (2) sonatinas; (3) studies; (4) duets. This is the piano method officially recommended for use in Children's Music Schools throughout the Soviet Union today.

Pitch/Rhythm Reading

PRE-READING   None. Playing earliest pieces by rote encouraged.

GRAND STAFF   Presented immediately, for student to memorize.

First 28 pages, both hands read from G clef; grand-staff reading follows. No specific reading clues or guides. Pieces are in several keys; many different beginning pitches.

COUNTING	Metric. Uses English and American note names.
RHYTHMS	Rhythmic values first presented in conjunction with words. Time signatures not explained. *Book 1: Part 1:* All note values through sixteenths; all dotted notes; basic meters plus 3/2, 3/8; syncopation. *Book 1: Part 2:* 6/8; 6/4; triplets.

Technique

BEGINNING	Short use of whole hand/arm; middle finger.
FIRST LEGATO FINGERINGS	Middle fingers, varying combinations. Use of thumb, fifth finger somewhat delayed.
CROSSINGS	*Book 1: Part 2:* Thumb under 2. Scale crossings, ad hoc basis.
	Book 1: Parts 1, 2: Occasional short exercises interspersed; *Book 1: Part 2:* A number of studies included among pieces; *Book 2:* Entire third section devoted to studies by usual etude writers.

Theory

SCALE	Concept of scale never presented. *Book 1: Part 1:* Teacher's notes recommend that scale playing begin halfway through first year. Scale fingerings for some M/m scales in appendix.
HARMONIZATION	None.
CREATIVE	None.

Repertoire

COMPOSERS	Wide selection (heavily Russian) throughout entire course. Non-Russian composers are those found in most American intermediate-level books.
FAMILIAR TUNES	*Book 1: Part 1:* Slavic folk music predominates. Arrangements of classical compositions (some even of keyboard works) interspersed in *Book 1: Part 2.*
ENSEMBLE	*Book 1: Parts 1, 2:* Many teacher accompaniments. *Book 2:* Entire last section is duets.
	Earliest pieces are tuneful, frequently with texts.

The pieces in *Book 1: Part 2* and *Book 2* would likely be graded intermediate by American standards. *Book 2* pieces cover a wide chronological range, although none are more contemporary-sounding than Kabalevsky. *Book 2* sonatinas are both classical and mildly contemporary. *Book 2* duets (some composers not identified) are all likely to be unknown to American teachers.

Teaching Aids

Editorial foreward (same in all 3 books) presents the educational logic of the method. Explanatory notes (to the teacher) further define teaching emphases for each year of the course. *Book 1: Part 2* and *Book 2:* Interpretive notes at back of book (or section) give specific teaching advice for each piece.

Features

The method has a no-nonsense approach. Difficulties increase rapidly and there are no illustrations or graphic niceties (pages are often dense-looking). The method relies entirely on the teacher to explain and define concepts and skills. The reading approach falls into no obvious category. Although the preface to the English edition speaks of "the perfectly timed introduction of every aspect of technique," it is difficult to see this happening in fact, since much of the teaching and integrating is not apparent in the books. Reinforcement probably comes more from repetition than from the sequence of materials. The heart of this course is the repertoire.

NOONA, WALTER, AND CAROL NOONA. *Mainstreams Piano Method.* Dayton, OH: Heritage Music Press.

The Pianist 1–4	(1973)
Pencil and Paper 1–4	(1973)
Projects 1–4	(1973)
The Performer 1–4	(1973)
The Contemporary Performer 1	(1976)
The Contemporary Performer 2, 3 (1975), *4*	(1976)
The Jazz Performer 1–4	(1979)
The Duet Performer 1–4	(1977)

Pitch/Rhythm Reading

PRE-READING	None.
GRAND STAFF	*Pianist 1:* Middle-C approach. 3C range. *Pianist 2:* High/low G/F. *Pianist 3:* Ledger lines, entire grand staff.

COUNTING	Metric.
RHYTHMS	*Pianist 1:* Basic note values, rests, meters. *Pianist 2:* Eighth notes. *Pianist 3:* Dotted quarter; triplets; 6/8; syncopation. *Pianist 4:* Sixteenths. Irregular and changing meters, nonmeasured music included in *Contemporary Performer* books.
PENCIL AND PAPER BOOKS	Extensive writing activities.
PROJECTS BOOKS:	Playing and analytical activities.

Technique

BEGINNING	5-finger legato; from thumbs outward.
FIRST LEGATO FINGERINGS	1-2-3; 3-2-1; both hands.
CROSSINGS	*Pianist 3:* Scales; thumbs under/over.

Theory

SCALE	*Pianist, Pencil and Paper, Projects 2:* All major 5-finger patterns (by picture); in groups. *Pianist, Pencil and Paper, Projects 3:* Major scale.
HARMONIZATION	*Projects 2, 3, 4:* "Exploring" sections: Harmonization with Roman numerals, lead-sheet symbols, by ear. Keyboard styles, patterns.
CREATIVE	All *Projects* books: Improvisation, variation, question and answer; styles; group improvisation. All *Pianist* books, and *Performer 2:* Many suggested experiments (change of notes, range, speed; addition of percussion instruments, sounds, effects). All *Projects* books: Completion of short compositions (playing and writing.) *Paper and Pencil* books: Programmed instruction format.

Repertoire

COMPOSERS	*Pianist/Performer 1, 2:* Noona. *Pianist/Performer 3, 4:* Noona; classics (all periods, late elementary and intermediate grading.)
FAMILIAR TUNES	*Pianist, Projects, Performers* books: Considerable use of folk, well-known tunes and hymns.
ENSEMBLE	*Pianist 1:* Some teacher accompaniments. *Duet*

Performer 1—4: Student-student duets, many programmatic; some with texts for primo and secondo.

The tuneful music in the early *Pianist* books is often associated with clever texts. The stylistic variety of repertoire in *Pianist 2, 3* is restricted by its reinforcement of multi-key 5-finger patterns. Music in *Performer* books provides an assortment of keyboard styles and harmonic color. Included classics make clear what editor has added. Repertoire in *Contemporary Performer* books introduces a highly varied spectrum of present-day musical sounds and experiences (unconventional and graphic notation, sound effects inside and outside piano, and so on).

Teaching Aids

None.

Features

The scope of this course is apparent only in the juxtaposition of its multiple sets of books. *Pianist* books are the core texts. *Pencil and Paper, Projects, Performer* books supply complementary stretching materials. The reading approach in the core texts combines middle-C (book 1) with multi-key (books 2, 3) presentation. Directional and pattern reading is encouraged although intervallic awareness is delayed until the presentation of the major scale. The originality of this series lies chiefly in the experience provided in the supplementary books. *Projects* books are divided into 3 sections: exploration, creation, technique. First 2 sections contain abundant material to stimulate ear-training and original music making. Each book includes activities for group improvisation. Some material at level 3, much at level 4, would be considered intermediate by many teachers. Most books contain activities and ideas that would be especially effective in the group setting.

OLSON, LYNN FREEMAN, LOUISE BIANCHI, AND MARVIN BLICKENSTAFF. *Music Pathways.* New York: Carl Fischer.

Piano Discoveries: Books A–D	(1983)
Piano Activities: Books A–D	(1983)
Piano Solos: Books A–D	(1983)

These books are a revision of the elementary books in the original 1974 *Music Pathways* series. Supplementary sheet music: All levels.

Pitch/Rhythm Reading

PRE-READING	*Discoveries A:* Off-staff directional reading leads to partial-staff intervallic reading.
GRAND STAFF	*Discoveries A:* Begins with high and low ledger line intervallic reading. Gradually incorporates middle-C, then treble and bass C guide notes. Intervallic reading.
COUNTING	Syllabic. Later, metric.
RHYTHMS	*Discoveries A:* Basic note values, rests, meters. *Discoveries B:* Eighth notes; dotted quarter. *Discoveries C:* Compound meters; triplets. *Discoveries D:* Sixteenths; syncopation.

Technique

BEGINNING	Whole hand/arm. 5-finger clusters.
FIRST LEGATO FINGERINGS	1-3; 2-4; both hands. Skips before steps.
CROSSINGS	*Discoveries C:* 2 over thumb. *Discoveries D:* Scales; thumb under.

Theory

SCALE	*Discoveries B:* Major 5-finger pattern. *Discoveries C:* Tetrachords; all keys. *Discoveries D:* Regular fingering.
HARMONIZATION	*Discoveries C:* Accompany with fifths, sixths. *Discoveries D:* Accompany with triads.
CREATIVE	Throughout all chapters, all levels: original pieces using concepts studied. *Discoveries B, C:* Additional question and answer, variation activities.

Repertoire

COMPOSERS	Mostly Olson. Terry Winter Owens, Kabalevsky, Salutrinskaya, Gurlitt, Krause, Köhler (with Olson) in *Discoveries D* and *Piano Solos B, C, D.* Sheet music: Olson and others.
FAMILIAR TUNES	Some folk, well-known tunes interspersed throughout *Discoveries A, B.* Most in *Solos A, B, D.*
ENSEMBLE	Teacher accompaniments (simple, but effective) to

many pieces in *Discoveries A,* to most pieces in *Solos A,* and to a few in *Solos B, C, D.*

The partial-staff pieces in *Discoveries A*—with descriptive, rhythmically helpful texts—are melodious and satisfying, most enhanced with teacher accompaniments. The guide-note reading pieces are more built to order. Repertoire in the following books shows variety of length, phrasing, range; noteworthy is the mood and texture change from piece to piece, which nevertheless does not detract from the sequencing necessary to provide adequate reinforcement. *Discoveries C, D,* while attending to the teaching of chords, offer far more varied chord pieces than is usual.

Teaching Aids

A Descriptive Guide to Music Pathways: Provides an overview (by means of brief commentary, reduction of selected student pages) of each aspect of the series—music, reading, rhythm, technique, and musicianship. Last part of book describes the *PATHWAYS* library.

Features

This course is designed to promote the development of informed musicianship at the keyboard. All books are divided into chapters that integrate many types of activities and focus these around key concepts and skills. The approach to grand-staff reading is unique. Intervallic reading techniques are first applied to ledger-line reading above and below staves, then move to include reading of 5 Cs as orientation points. The technical approach is also unique. Whole hand and outer fingers are used before middle fingers. Legato skips precede legato steps. Aspects of multi-key reading are noticeable at levels B through D, yet the repertoire provides far greater variety of textures and styles than is frequently the case in pieces that reinforce the feeling of key.

PACE, ROBERT. *Music for Piano.* Milwaukee: Lee Roberts/Hal Leonard.

Music for Piano: Books 1 (1979), *2* (1980), and *3* (1981)
Finger Builders: Books 1 (1979), *2* (1980) and *3* (1981)
Theory Papers: Books 1 (1979), *2* (1981), and *3* (1982)
Creative Music: Books 1 (1979), *2* (1980), and *3* (1982)
These are revisions of, and additions to, *Music for*

	Piano (Books 1–5; beginning in 1961), *Skills and Drills* (Books 1–5; beginning in 1961), and *Theory Papers* (with Doyle; 1970).
RECITAL SERIES	Original music by a variety of composers (mostly contemporary) to correlate with each level of *Music for Piano.*
RECITAL SERIES DUETS	Original music and arrangements by Pace and others to correlate with each level of *Music for Piano.* Supplements: Christmas music, jazz and others.

Pitch/Rhythm Reading

PRE-READING	A few pages reading from off-staff diagrams stressing finger numbers; 5-finger patterns; multi-key; in all level 1 books.
GRAND STAFF	Level 1 books: Early introduction. Multi-key reading; both hands usually in same 5-finger position.
COUNTING	Nominative. Later, metric.
RHYTHMS	Level 1 books: Basic note values, rests, meters; eighth notes; 6/8; dotted quarter. Level 2: Sixteenths; triplet; irregular meters.

Technique

BEGINNING	5-finger legato; both hands. Equal attention.
FIRST LEGATO FINGERINGS	1-2-3-4-5; 5-4-3-2-1.
CROSSINGS	*Finger Builders 2:* Thumb under (scale).

Theory

SCALE	*Finger Builders 1:* Tetrachords. Level 2: Regular fingering; 1 octave; M/m (all keys). *Music for Piano/ Creative Music 3:* Modes.
HARMONIZATION	Extensive use at all levels including (from level 3) secondary triads and secondary dominants.
CREATIVE	Principally question and answer, variation types. *Creative Music* books present a combination of reading and theory reinforcement and creative work.

Repertoire

| COMPOSERS | Level 1: Pace. From end of level 2: Mix of pieces by |

	Pace with original classics. Various (especially contemporary) composers represented from early levels in *Recital Series,* supplementary music.
FAMILIAR TUNES	Many well-known tunes, especially in early levels.
ENSEMBLE	*Music for Piano:* Some student-student duets. *Recital Series Duets:* Student-student duets by Pace and others. Original music and arrangements.

There is variety in the use of well-known tunes and original music. Although pieces in the core texts are mostly melody-plus-chordal-accompaniment in style, original music (especially in *Recital Series*) is attractive and well-graded. Noteworthy is the early (and continued) use of pentatonic, hexatonic, modal, and 12-tone music.

Teaching Aids

Teacher's Guide: Book 1: This manual presents specific teaching strategies for integrating each page of all four books at Level 1. Reductions of all pages from student's book lie opposite suggested activities. The manual also offers information about the educational aims of the entire course.

Classroom musical background test and student rating form; teacher assignment record; lesson assignment and practice record. Flash cards: Single note; key signatures; triads.

Features

This course is one of the classic multi-key methods. The development of functional skills (harmonization, transposition, improvisation, variation) is built into materials in such a way that the method cannot be used without reference to these skills. The materials are particularly suited for use in group teaching. The language and format of the books seems aimed for the beginner who can read and who is ready for the motor coordination required by early, and extensive, chord playing. It is advisable that an instructor using this method be aware of the teaching processes associated with conceptual learning and the spiral curriculum. The early introduction to contemporary sounds and styles is noteworthy.

PALMER, WILLARD, MORTON MANUS, AND AMANDA VICK LETHCO. *Alfred's Basic Piano Library.* Van Nuys, CA: Alfred Publishing Co.

> *Lesson Books: 1A, 1B, 2*(1981); *3, 4* (1982); *5* (1984); *6* (1986)
>
> *Theory Books: 1A, 1B* (1981); *2, 3, 4* (1982); *5* (1984); *6* (1986)
>
> *Technic Books: 1A, 1B, 2* (1984); *3* (1985); *4* (1986)

Recital Books: 1A,1B (1981); *2, 3, 4* (1982);
5 (1984); *6* (1986)

*Lesson, Theory, Technic, Recital Books: Complete
Level 1* (1983)

Supplements: Christmas books, sheet music, duets,
others.

Software: *Alfred's Basic Computer Theory Program*
(Apple/Commodore).

Pitch/Rhythm Reading

PRE-READING	*Lesson Book 1A:* Off-staff reading (black keys) by finger numbers. Off-staff reading (white keys) by letter names, middle-C orientation.
GRAND STAFF	*Lesson Book 1A:* C position (hands octave apart), G position (hands 2 octaves apart). Reading by intervals. *Book 1B:* Middle-C position (both thumbs on C), new G position (hands 1 octave apart), middle-D position (both thumbs on D).
COUNTING	Both nominative and unit.
RHYTHMS	*Lesson Book 1A:* Basic note values, rests, meters. *Book 1B:* Eighth notes. *Book 2:* Dotted quarter. *Book 3:* (end) 3/8; 6/8. *Book 4:* (end) sixteenths. From *Book 2:* Syncopation (chiefly in pop and blues pieces).

Technique

BEGINNING	Legato on black keys.
FIRST LEGATO FINGERINGS	2-3; 2-3-4; both hands.
CROSSINGS	*Lesson Book 2:* 2 over thumb. *Lesson Book 3:* Thumb under.

Theory

SCALE	*Lesson Book 1B:* Tetrachords. Key signature. *Lesson Book 2:* Descending RH/ascending LH; 1 octave: C, G, D.
HARMONIZATION	*Theory Book 2:* Considerable and varied writing experiences of primary triads.
CREATIVE	None.

Repertoire

COMPOSERS	Palmer. From *Level 4:* Palmer; classics.
FAMILIAR TUNES	Much folk music, many well-known tunes used throughout entire series, all books. Also arrangements of symphonic, chamber, operatic music.
ENSEMBLE	*Lesson Book 1A:* Teacher accompaniments to most pieces, tapering off as student plays more hands-together material.

The technical and musical difficulties of the repertoire are well sequenced and reinforcing. Especially at levels 1A and 1B, texts are rhythmically supportive and instructive. Early music is always tuneful, comfortably arranged, often with catchy sounds and effects. At higher levels the music becomes more predictable (in its phrase shapes, textures, ranges, and so on), especially after introduction of triads.

Teaching Aids

Teacher's Guide to Lesson Book 1A: Provides brief commentary on the method's teaching philosophy; presents specific teaching strategies (indicating goals, key words, emphases, suggestions, student-teacher interactions) for each page of the book. Reductions of all pages from the student's book are placed above teaching suggestions. *Alfred's Basic Flash Cards:* Correlate with levels 1A, 1B.

Features

This course is designed to appeal to the eye as much as to the ear. The graphics are an essential part of the educational plan. Layout, diagrams, and pictures teach as well as amuse. The plan for the teaching of reading combines facets of several approaches: off-staff reading; position (including middle-C) reading; intervallic reading; aspects of multi-key reading. The repertoire places priority on ear-appeal by its heavy reliance on well-known tunes and popular sounds. Materials are sequenced to provide overlapping preparation and reinforcement. *Complete Level 1* books condense the materials and repertoire of the books at levels 1A and 1B for use with students who may be able to move more quickly through the beginning parts of the course. Most books in this series could be used in conjunction with any middle-C method. This is the first course to offer a correlating theory program available on computer software.

CHAPTER 7

The Adult Student

Greater attention then ever before is currently focused on instructional techniques and materials for the person who begins piano study later. Claims are made that within the past few years more adults have begun piano instruction yearly than children. A relatively large number of books have appeared since 1960 whose titles indicate that they are written for the adult beginner. Articles in professional magazines offer advice on what must be borne in mind when teaching the adult beginner.[1] Independent studio teachers are reexamining the merits of offering instruction for the adult beginner, either out of a desire to diversify their teaching schedules or out of necessity. College and university keyboard departments, long accustomed to providing piano classes and/or lessons for music students to whom the piano is a secondary instrument, now are initiating or increasing courses in piano study for the non-music major. The title "adult beginner," however, is elusive. It means different things to different people.

The following widely divergent groups are classified by various teachers as belonging in the category of adult students:

"Slightly older" students—10 or 11 years old and too mature for methods designed for average-age students.

Teenagers—12 years of age and older.

College non-music majors—roughly 18 to 24 years old.

College music majors—roughly 18 to 24 years old.

Adults who play for pleasure—25 years of age and older.

Senior citizens—sometimes considered a special adult category.

Many authors and composers, and certainly all publishers, believe that instruction and repertoire books labeled "for the adult beginner" might be used with equal facility and pleasure by all of the groups listed above. Almost every preface in such publications states that the book can be used with the non-music major, the future elementary school teacher, the music major with a piano secondary, the music education major, the theory keyboard-skills class, or the person who is seeking to play piano recreationally. Further, it is suggested that the book can work well when used in either group or individual settings. Such claims seldom prove to be true in actual practice. Of course publishers cannot afford to offer materials ideally suited to meet the needs of these varied, but small, markets. Therefore, adult-beginner piano books are each slanted with a particular group of students in mind even while professing greater catholicity of intent.

TWO GENERAL CATEGORIES OF ADULT-BEGINNER PIANO BOOKS

All books intended for use with adult students have characteristics that differentiate them from methods designed for children, even though the actual level of the introductory performing and reading difficulties may be similar in both types of instructional material. The adult piano course:

Presents the entire method in very few (sometimes only one) volume(s).

Contains a considerable amount of text that defines, describes, and explains all concepts and most activities.

Includes charts and graphs that often depict an entire body of information, such as the relationship of all note values, key signatures and the entire concept of the circle of fifths, and so on.

Incorporates classics quite early, anticipating that the adult will need to spend less time than the child in preparation for playing such pieces.

Offers few(er) supplementary books.

Moves quickly to the playing of harmony.

Most adult-student books are actually designed for use in either of two teaching situations—the individual lesson or the college class. Ages may vary in either of these situations, but are less likely to vary in the case of the college class. The text that seems intended for use in the individual lesson, then, must appeal to the broadest age differential. It is not simple to design such a text. The teacher searching for the right book for the adult beginner often has a more difficult task than a teacher selecting material for any other student category.

Each group of adult-oriented texts has certain characteristics. Awareness of these may make a search for the right book easier. For reference in this chapter, these two types of texts will be defined as (1) the older-beginner method (for use with varied age levels in an individual lesson format) and (2) the college-adult method (for use in a number of different courses, all of which, however, are taught in a group format).

The older-beginner method:

Is a relatively brief book—perhaps 50 to 100 pages.

Is primarily concerned that the student be able to play pieces, the sooner, the better.

Presents repertoire that consists largely of arrangements of folk, patriotic, religious, and popular melodies.

Seldom contains ensemble music of any kind.

Moves rapidly to presentation of the primary triads played in close position.

Quickly expands reading of harmonic intervals to the octave.

Contains minimal reference to development of technique or the practicing of technical exercises or etudes.

Does not emphasize (if it includes at all) attainment of functional skills such as sight-reading, harmonization, transposition, improvisation.

The college adult method:

Is usually a very substantial book—perhaps 200 to 350 pages.

Is generally cast in a chapter/unit format designed with semester or quarter pacing in mind.

Is primarily concerned that the student be able to integrate playing, reading, harmonic, and improvisatory skills.

Presents repertoire that includes many original teaching pieces along with arrangements of folk, patriotic, religious, and popular melodies; also frequently includes easier original "classics" and pieces using twentieth-century compositional and playing techniques.

Contains a fair amount of ensemble music (often for multiple pianos).

Places some emphasis on development of technique, at times providing colorful teacher accompaniments or background tapes to enhance practice of technical exercises.

Usually provides an abundance of separate rhythmic drills, melodies to sight-read, transpose, accompany, and ideas to guide improvisation and playing by ear.

Those who schedule adults only for individual lessons are not generally inclined to use the college-adult type of method book since it contains too much, or too greatly diversified, material for use in the thirty- to forty-five-minute lesson format. Further, many of the suggested activities (in addition to ensemble playing) work best in a group setting. Those who teach adults in small and large groups in either a studio or college setting are less likely to select an older-beginner type of method book since it does not contain sufficient supplementary material and activities for classes that meet for longer periods or more frequently than once a week. Those who offer group piano instruction to senior citizens often find that although the college-adult-type text includes valuable functional-skill directives and activities, the repertoire is not sufficiently attractive to the older student who wishes chiefly to play well-known tunes for leisure-time enjoyment. Selecting an appropriate method book for the adult beginner may be a matter of some frustration.

THE HISTORY OF THE PIANO TEXT FOR THE ADULT BEGINNER

Piano methods designed for children that began to integrate the teaching of pitch and rhythmic notational reading, as well as the teaching of some functional skills, into the piano curriculum began to appear in the early decades of the twentieth century. (A more detailed account of these methods and their relationship to currently published instructional piano books is in chapter 6.) At nearly the same time, piano courses for the older or adult beginner also began to appear, though not with such frequency or quantity as piano methods for children. Often these adult courses were written by the same authors who had published successful children's methods. The authors of the *Oxford Piano Course* (1928) presented the *The Beginner's Book for Older Pupils* in 1929.[2] The latter books had the same pedagogical philosophy and thoroughness as the former. The book for the older beginner was, in fact, a compilation of materials from the books for children with titles, format, and verbal presentation adjusted to suit the interests and quicker conceptual-learning speed of the older student. Thus the older beginner's course included a multi-key approach to the teaching of reading as well as ample exposure to the learning of practical harmonization and creative keyboard experiences.

The Adult Explorer at the Piano by Ahearn, Blake, and Burrows was published in 1937.[3] All three authors (like the authors of the *Oxford Piano Course*) were leaders in the class-piano movement. This movement, which advocated the establishment of group piano instruction in the public school curriculum, had burgeoned particularly between 1926 and 1930. Such musical instruction was interested in providing a "keyboard experience," not just instruction in the playing of pieces. Consequently great emphasis was placed on functional skills that would enable students to appreciate and understand how music fit into daily life and was an enjoyable means of self-expression beyond, or aside from, performing in recitals. The 1937 book by Ahearn, Blake, and Burrows provided a text imbued with these same concerns but directed specifically to the adult.

> The principles underlying the presentation, and typical examples of the material itself, [had] been tried out in experimental classes with employees of Gimbel

Brothers' and R. H. Macy & Company's department stores in New York City, with adults of varying ages and varying academic background in Columbia University Extension Classes, with young college students in New College of Columbia University, with more mature students in Teachers College, and with many different adult students in private studios.[4]

The book's reading approach centered around an immediate introduction to the five Cs. The pieces and reading examples stressed chordal outlines from the beginning. The reading and use of accompaniment styles including octaves and chordal inversions were introduced early and developed throughout. The pieces were either arrangements of folk tunes or well-known traditional melodies. Verbal explanations were so presented as to make it possible for the book to be somewhat self-explanatory. The teacher was to act as guide, embellishing and complementing what the student was able to learn independently from the text. A later work by Burrows[5] was written with the teenager in mind and completely departed from the C-reading approach, using instead an approach that was built around multi-key reading and transposition from the outset.

Books for the adult beginner offering a format more appealing to the older student but containing the same elements and ideals as contemporaneous children's methods were exemplified by such texts as Wagness's *Adult Piano Course* (1942), Thompson's *The Adult Preparatory Book* (1943), Schaum's *Adult Piano Course* (1946), Aaron's *Adult Piano Course* (1947), Eckstein's *Adult Piano Book* (1953), and Richter's *The Older Student* (1956).[6] All of these books were designed, as were the children's materials by the same authors, for use in the individual lesson. They all contained repertoire consisting of arrangements of folk tunes and traditional melodies, rudimentary harmonic instruction (in some cases merely an introduction to chord playing), very little (if any) technical instruction, and a presentation of reading in relationship to middle C.

After midcentury, however, colleges and universities became increasingly involved in offering group piano instruction to music majors for whom the piano was a secondary instrument. Although group instruction for such students was not altogether new, the emergence in the late 1950s of electronic piano laboratories increased the need for teaching materials appropriate for classroom situations involving simultaneous use of multiple pianos. Methods written with such situations in mind concentrated on presenting the piano as a functional tool on which students could acquire keyboard skills needed in the course of pursuing and practicing a musical profession. Consequently, these method books included an abundance (more or less) of pieces to sight-read and transpose, melodies to accompany, exercises in clef reading, and ensemble music. The repertoire, in addition to initial learning-to-read pieces and arrangements of familiar melodies, was chosen from original easier classics including pieces from the twentieth century.

Utilizing electronic piano laboratories to advantage, colleges and universities also developed more extensive keyboard instruction for the non-music major. Materials to teach these students were (and still are) drawn from numerous sources: adult-beginner books written prior to the 1960s, standard anthologies of easier classics, traditional scale and technical books, duet and other ensemble collections. Gradually, the educational advantage of integrating a certain amount of harmonic knowledge and practice with the development of reading, technical, and interpretive skills led to the desire for books that offered the student a sequentially ordered presentation of materials that coordinated these multiple skills.

In many cases, books designed for use in college-level beginning piano classes attempted (and are attempting) to satisfy the needs of both the music student for whom the piano is secondary and the student who is a non-music major. Achievement standards expected from students in group piano classes vary considerably from school to school. This is not a matter of faculty desire as much as an acknowledgment of the backgrounds and motivations of the students in the classes. Therefore a book that may serve well as a text for non-music-major classes in one university may be equally appropriate for secondary-piano classes in another university. Authors' prefaces have such situations in mind when they state that their books may be used in a variety of teaching situations.

Books to serve the needs of students in these college classes began to appear in the 1960s.[7] Some of these texts provided the first real examples of adult methods that integrated the teaching of functional skills with the teaching of repertoire. Many of these books organized presentation of materials and activities on a theoretical basis: the order of presentation was based on harmonic logic rather than on the practical development of playing and technical ease; functional harmony was introduced early and developed consistently (usually to the point of using secondary triads and sevenths); playing (i.e., harmonizing) from Roman numerals was common; the formation of scales and cadences was presented as harmonic "grammar," but scale and cadence playing was also the basis of the technical regimen; charts, diagrams, and tables figured prominently in the conceptual explanations. Much of the sight-reading and repertoire consisted of "pieces" that were accompanied melodies drawn from familiar (folk, patriotic, religious, march, dance) sources. Easier original classics, sometimes in truncated versions, were introduced somewhat later in the text or offered in supplementary sections or appendixes.

Noticeable in such texts was the departure from the middle-C orientation to pitch reading. Instead, stress was placed on the perception of note groupings, directional reading, intervallic relationships, and early (sometimes immediate) introduction to multi-key reading and playing. Also noticeable was a more extensive orientation to keyboard "geography" and technique. In early pages, students were asked to play only from finger numbers, letter names, or other off-staff directional guides. In some cases, black-key preceded white-key playing. Chords were often introduced via keyboard pictures and remembered and grouped by key-color design before being read from staff notation. Playing by ear was frequently suggested and lists of appropriate tunes were included in most chapters or units. The explanation of rhythmic notational values was usually condensed in "mathematical" tables, with the assumption that because adults could quickly grasp the equivalent relationships between types of notes they could also perform rhythmic groupings readily. Rhythmic reading was aided by the playing of familiar melodies in which the rhythm was less read than remembered. Since many students who used these books were music majors with other musical and performing experience as part of their backgrounds, this presentation of rhythmic reading was rational. Incorrect rhythmic performance was therefore more often a problem of coordination rather than of rhythmic perception.

The true explosion of methods and materials for the older beginner, however, occurred in the 1970s. More than a dozen new methods appeared in addition to updated and revised versions of, or supplementary materials to, methods written earlier. Several of these new methods[8] offered an integrated presentation of materials (like many of the 1960s methods) to teach and reinforce the use of functional skills as well as the playing of repertoire, but did so in formats that might be used as effectively in the individual studio as in the college group-piano class. This meant that the presentation of information (especially harmonic information) was not as condensed as in the college adult methods. Greater emphasis was placed on the playing of pieces than on the development of functional skills per se. The study of keyboard harmony was more a means to reading and playing with understanding than an end in itself. Two of the methods, while presenting some harmonic explanation in the basic text, offered reinforcing and additional theoretical explanations and drills in supplementary theory books. Thus, the adult student (and the teacher of the adult student) could include as much, or as little, of keyboard theory as desired. Graphics and physical layout were designed to make the books seem less dense and serious although the material presented was as thorough, if not as extensive, as that included in other adult texts.

Most of the new 1970s methods and revisions of methods written earlier, however, had several traits in common: greater attention was paid to prereading experiences (aural, technical, and visual); more ensemble pieces were included and many of these were for multiple pianos; rhythmic reinforcement was supported by the inclusion of more rhythm-only drills, many of these geared to developing better coordination in hands-together reading; pop/rock/jazz sounds and forms were added to the harmonic vocabulary and playing repertoire; and there was increasing inclusion of more original keyboard literature both by classic and twentieth-century composers. A few of the 1970s publications offered features unique to that individual text: the inclusion of rote pieces throughout the course of study[9]; a supplementary book of ensemble music for group piano[10]; rhythm background tapes to accompany keyboard drills[11]; a student study guide to be used in conjunction with a television course.[12]

While in many ways similar to the 1960s and 1970s methods, new adult courses appearing even more recently tend to approach the teaching of pitch reading somewhat eclectically (e.g., the promotion of intervallic reading combined with a multi-key presentation; a modified middle-C orientation in the context of some multi-key experiences, and so on). Most of these new methods also offer specific directives for improvisational activities that correlate with the reading, rhythmic, and technical achievements at any given level. The organization of materials into chapters, units, or sections—each of which provides reinforcing exercises and repertoire for concepts and skills new to that chapter, unit, or section—is more convincingly structured than ever before.

THE ADULT AS A STUDENT

It was pointed out earlier that the word "adult" could be used to refer to keyboard students of various ages, interests, and physical and psychological characteristics. The ensuing discussion will therefore refer to two groupings of adults in noting particulars concerning motivation, cognitive skills, physical capabilities, and attitudes. The "young adult" group includes those aged twelve to twenty-four, that is, the junior high school through college (young graduate) student. The "mature adult" category will comprise everyone else, although occasional specifics might apply only to the senior citizen.

The adult category often includes those who are not absolute beginners; that is, those who resume piano study begun in their youth, those who have always remained amateur players, those who have played by ear or for fun and now wish specific guidance or technical direction. Teaching strategies and materials suitable for such students are discussed in chapter 11. This chapter will concern itself only with the adult who is an actual beginner or whose previous keyboard experiences have been so brief or inadequate (or both) that the designation "beginner" remains apt.

Motivation

The young adult may have several reasons for beginning piano study although playing for pleasure is always at the basis of more immediate motivations. The teenager often regards playing the piano as a social asset and may look forward to participating with peers in a group instructional setting or becoming the "life of the party" by being able "to play a few tunes." Desire to study may be stimulated by the wish to perform current favorites, to learn something about reading music and using chords in order to create and/or accompany original songs, to be able to accompany a church choir, or to enjoy a means of self-expression. The college student may share many of the teenager's reasons for choosing to become involved in keyboard instruction, but the immediate motivation is often the practical availability of the keyboard class as a fine-arts requirement, as an "extra," or in the hope of an easy credit. Such students "have always wanted to take piano lessons" but never had the opportunity so close at hand. The young adult seldom pays for such instruction. The teenager is still parentally supported; the college student frequently can take a few extra credits as part of a general fee or package plan or can enroll in a community college for little or no tuition.

The mature adult, on the other hand, often makes a considerably larger investment of time and money to study the piano. Not only is the tuition a personal expenditure, but lesson and practice time fits less neatly into the daily or weekly schedule; it is more than just adding an extra class or another after-school activity. Studying the piano represents a commitment of effort and attention to something quite outside the adult's usual slate of responsibilities. The mature, like the younger, adult also wishes primarily to play for pleasure. Immediate motivation, however, may stem from a number of sources. Quite often playing the piano represents fulfillment of a long-held dream or goal. Today more than ever the mature adult realizes that new adventures may be begun at any time. Occasionally a change of life-style (perhaps the children have left home, a spouse has died, or a move to a new location has taken place) precipitates a fresh examination of personal interests and possibilities. Learning to play the piano may be looked upon as an antidote to loneliness, as a means of increasing self-esteem, as a satisfying hands-on arts experience, as a therapeutic support or outlet, or as an enriching use of leisure time. The mature adult may also be pragmatically motivated. Parents may wish to accompany children who play other instruments or play ensemble music with children who take piano lessons. Preschool or elementary teachers may realize that the ability to play the piano enhances their effectiveness in structuring more direct arts experience into the curriculum. Adults active in civic and religious organizations may wish to learn to accompany singing or dancing groups.

Both the young and the mature adult hope that learning to play the piano will be personally rewarding. Although they also have interest in learning about music, they may have different, perhaps unclear, ideas regarding what "learning about music" means. The teacher therefore is well advised to ascertain each adult's expectations prior to the outset of instruction and to discuss the possibilities and probabilities of meeting these. False promises need not be made, nor is it necessary to accede to each adult's requests. Yet clearing the decks is a good way to begin since adults (unlike most children) come to the lesson with already well-developed likes and dislikes as well as preconceived notions about what learning to play the piano will involve. Neither the adult nor the teacher will be happy if the student is seeking chiefly to play golden oldies and the teacher is urging performance of Bach minuets. Discussing expectations should be bilateral. What the teacher will expect by way of accomplishment (e.g., how many pieces will be learned weekly, that the development of reading and playing will be combined with some attention to technique, that some informal public performance will be expected) should be made clear from the beginning. That way both parties may agree to meet the accepted responsibilities and share in the pleasure of acknowledging the results.

Cognitive Skills: The Adult Learner's Strong Suit

Both the young and the mature adult bring a storehouse of already accumulated information, experiences, and ideas that may be applied to the acquisition of a new skill.[13] Many of these have been learned and expressed by means of verbal communication. The adult has arranged much of this knowledge into categories that have then been evaluated and analyzed. In some areas, the adult may even be an acknowledged specialist, appreciating intricate relationships among myriad details and/or exhibiting consummate proficiency in the performance of specific acts. As the adult functions in most daily situations, (s)he rarely does so as a neophyte. Therefore most adults find the experience of being a "beginner" unsettling rather than exhilarating. They may compensate for this by standing back to observe or discuss the new situation before allowing themselves to act or feel in ways required by the not-yet-understood experience. They frequently analyze and dissect before they *do* or *try.*

Generally speaking, the younger the adult, the greater the willingness to experience something unknown. It is easier to risk at fifteen than at fifty. Generally speaking also, the older the adult, the greater the satisfaction after experiencing the new and finding it good, or even possible. The younger adult, therefore, may respond well when asked to improvise in a group setting, cheerfully willing to discover what works rather than be told what works. Making up one's own mind is still a fairly new experience and it is relished. The mature adult, however, has learned to deal with life on a knowledge-first basis. Trial-and-error learning seems an inefficient use of time and may prove embarassing as well. Nonetheless, the older adult who is encouraged to discover that improvising is possible and, perhaps, quite exciting often has far greater appreciation of the entire experience than the young improviser to whom experimenting seems altogether acceptable. The younger adult is also more willing to learn by rote, assuming that memory will be there when needed. The older adult prefers the security of the printed direction, no matter how difficult to translate, having already learned that memory is not always trustworthy.

In many respects, however, both the young and mature adult possess similar cognitive characteristics. Some of these prove advantageous to learning a new skill; some may be deterrents, if only temporarily.

The keyboard teacher may capitalize in a number of ways on the positive aspects of the adult's cognitive tendencies, and at the same time provide or encourage experiences that will offset those tendencies deterrent to learning or to the establishment of good playing and listening habits.

Teaching Suggestions

Make sure experience precedes definition.

> Rhythmic activities involving the perception of pulse, meter, and rhythm should be provided before pulse, meter, and rhythm are defined and rhythmic notation explained.

> Playing the piano—by rote, by ear, from unstaffed notation, as part of improvisation (any or all of these)—should precede the presentation of single, or grand, staff reading.

Make sure that each lesson or class is as full of musical experience as possible.

> Avoid excessive talking. Try to communicate in solely musical ways, showing and demonstrating rather than explaining and telling.

Adult Cognitive Characteristics

ADVANTAGES	DISADVANTAGES
Fairly long concentration span, especially if activities are interesting and varied.	Often more interested in arriving at a definition than in experiencing and understanding what is defined.
Capable of independent study, can read, and responds readily to verbal communication.	May insist upon labeling each operation and bit of knowledge, trusting neither the senses nor the memory.
Desires to put things in context and arrive at a synthesis.	
Eager to understand relationships; often asks questions that are helpful in satisfying the self as well as indicative to the teacher of areas of confusion or error.	May allow subsidiary interests to deflect attention from the matter at hand.
	Prone to verbalize before acting, explaining and rationalizing in advance what (s)he anticipates is going to happen.
Appreciates accessory information and enjoys the relating of tangential references.	May be resistant to new ideas or less interested in testing unfamiliar sensations and experiences.

Be certain that in each lesson or class the student has had several successful playing experiences, no matter how short or simple these may be.

Choose materials carefully, knowing that the adult is capable of independent study.

Select books that have attractive and adequate, though not overwhelming, explanations, diagrams, glossaries.

Realize the importance of using or suggesting other means of preparing for the lesson or class—give listening assignments, ask the student to tape-record practice sessions, encourage concert attendance, offer sight-reading materials on a lending library basis, and so on.

Communicate sensitively, neither condescendingly nor unilaterally.

Answer questions directly but simply. Do not allow the student to involve you in elaborate discussions of nonpertinent matters.

Ask many questions and listen carefully to the answers. Try to phrase questions that require the statement of an opinion rather than the recitation of a fact or definition.

Motor Skills: Teaching the Adult to Move in New Ways

The adult, unlike the child, has developed and refined a vast repertoire of motor skills, many of which are applicable to playing the piano. The adult is aware of the importance of timing and precision in the use of movements in a way that the child is not. Eye-hand coordination, especially in making smaller movements, has been tested and used in the performance of many activities, such as writing, manipulation of objects, and the formation of expressive gestures. The adult has already mastered many motor skills that involve the relationship of the body to external objects and machines, some of which are large, complicated, or both. The adult also has advantages of size, strength, and height not available to the child.

Yet precisely because the adult has already become accustomed to using the body in certain ways and under certain conditions, (s)he finds it more difficult to change movement patterns and reprogram (if necessary) neural information sent to muscles and limbs. Adult movements—which can be extremely supple and flexible in particular situations—may easily become taut and rigid in other circumstances. Bodily awkwardness or stiffness often reflects psychological tension rather than the actual inability of the adult body to perform specific acts. The adult finds it difficult to be aware of the body's kinesthetic reporting and, moreover, to trust the body to move without a great deal of *inner* instruction and advice.[14]

Sometimes older adults cannot make certain gestures with ease because of arthritis, muscle atrophy, nervous system degeneration, or other physical conditions. Less acute eyesight also affects movement control. The younger adult, on the other hand, is often in prime physical condition, having attained the size and strength associated with physical maturity yet not having lost the muscle resilience and fluidity that is the prerogative of the child. A list of advantages and disadvantages relating to the motor aptitudes of adults must therefore be regarded with considerable latitude.

It is easier for the teacher of the adult to tolerate time and difficulty factors inherent in the learning of new motor skills than it is for the adult to view the same situation with equal forbearance. Telling the adult to be patient is frequently ineffective. The adult needs to achieve success that is self-recognizable in order to move forward with assurance and enthusiasm, if not immediate pleasure. The teacher must provide ample opportunity for the adult to exercise motor skills and, in the process, to begin to establish an accurate and personal feedback system.

Teaching Suggestions

From the beginning, stress posture and attitudes that foster relaxation.

Because the adult is likely to remain highly concentrated during the entire instructional period, bodily tensions and fatigue accrue easily, though not always noticeably. Have the adult occasionally stand, stretch, bend, shake the hands and arms, or otherwise move around to vary the physical sameness of the activities.

Arrange experiences so the adult may observe and feel how his/her body functions naturally: the weight of the hand and arm dropping from the shoulder, the natural curve of the fingers when the hand is at rest, the ten-

Adult Motor Aptitudes

ADVANTAGES	DISADVANTAGES
Fits the piano. The instrument is designed to be played by the adult person. There is no problem in reaching the pedals or keyboard extremities. The adult's height allows maximal peripheral vision.	Frequently tries too hard to achieve immediate perfection, velocity, and power. Unnecessary tensions result.
Possesses the strength and control to produce the greatest variety of tonal resonance and color.	May be unwilling to accept the fact that learning new movements and gestures takes time and repeated trial-and-error practicing. The adult would like understanding of what is to be done to translate immediately into efficient action.
Can physically reach the octave with relative ease. The playing of fuller chords and accompaniment styles may be enjoyed from the beginning of study.	
Can use the relationship between the body and the instrument in order to capitalize on the resources of each.	May be physically tired—or otherwise burdened or distracted—at the lesson or when beginning practice.
Has control over finer movements and tires less easily in manipulating them.	Often unduly self-conscious. Self-criticism frequently impedes progress in learning to attend to what the body reports.
	May reject directive advice, having already attained the ability to make accurate, accomplished movements in other areas.
	Often approaches the learning of an unfamiliar motor skill with preconceived notions of probable personal success or failure.

sion that is required for the fingers to straighten, the relief when that tension is relaxed, and so on.

Work at physical skills (technique) in small doses.

At first the adult, like the child, should be able to direct full attention to making basic gestures. Do not expect the adult to attend to technique, reading, counting all at the same time. Short, memorized technical exercises that do not involve reading and rhythm complexities are best.

Assign specific practice goals. Stress that short, repeated periods of concentration, with full attention to what the body is doing and feeling, are preferable to longer blocks of technical practice. The adult tends to overdo things in this respect.

Plan the lesson or class activities so that the adult may warm up.

The older the adult the more likely it is that (s)he needs to attune to the physical aspects of playing before attending to the learning of new concepts or participating in activities involving reading and rhythmic reinforcement or interpretation.

Warming up need not necessarily mean attending to technique per se. Do not over look the value of having the adult awaken the body by experiencing rhythm while clapping, tapping, swinging, scat singing, or the like. The larger the body motions involved, the better.

Stress awareness of the body, not merely performance of routines.

Encourage the adult to experiment with gestures and fingerings until the body feels good or cooperative. "Play" on the adult's forearms or shoulders so that physical feelings may be communicated directly.

Be alert to whether or not the adult is picking up his/her own bodily feedback. Learn to ask questions that stimulate such attention. Learn also to use language and analogies that recall actual *experiences* rather than depend upon *ideas* about how to do something.

Attitudes: The Adult as a Human Being

Both the young and older adult have *chosen* to learn to play the piano. They have, therefore, definite—and preconceived—ideas about what playing the piano will be like and why *they* are interested in doing so. Each adult expects the experience to be pleasant, but each might define in quite different ways what (s)he hopes will constitute that pleasure. One may be hoping for instant fun and may be satisfied by playing just a few well known melodies. Another has always wanted to know the "secrets" or the basics and feels that (s)he must learn how to read, count, finger, and pedal. Yet another has great curiosity about music in general rather than piano playing in particular and therefore is eager to learn about chording, harmony, and accompanying. None are looking to establish a new career in music, at least not as a pianist, so there is no urgent desire to learn and perfect technique beyond just getting around the keyboard comfortably.

The majority of teachers, however, have been classically trained and find it difficult to envision keyboard instruction that does not include technical development along with learning to perform a solid repertoire. They are accustomed to thinking about the taking of lessons in terms of long-range goals, even though the greatest percentage of their students never really do study for many years. Because they so often deal with the young, they plan in terms of the future, anticipating that hands will grow, concentration will increase, pedaling will become second-nature, reading will become fluent, and musical sophistication will develop accordingly. In agreeing to teach the adult, the instructor must think in terms of more immediate goals since the adult is not likely to take lessons for many years or be willing to work patiently in order to have details fall into place somewhere down the road.

It is important to realize that both the beginning adult student and the teacher have attitudes about playing the piano. (While the child beginner also has some predisposition about what music lessons are going to mean, the child's preconceived notions are apt to be less fixed or less broad in scope than the adult's.) The teacher is likely to be more successful in helping the adult player to achieve results if the adult's attitudes are discerned and acknowledged.[15] This is sometimes a matter of discussion between teacher and student, but may also be a matter of the way the teacher paces the lesson or class activities, chooses materials, designates practice routines, or suggests other actions or arrangements that directly affect what the adult player does and feels while at the keyboard.

Although attitudes vary greatly depending upon age, temperament, culture, accumulated life experience, and many other factors, some predispositions are common to most adults.

The teacher always plays an important role in influencing student attitude(s) and in setting the tone of the lesson or class atmosphere. This is particularly true when the students are children who are more accustomed to responding to suggestion than initiating or controlling actions that involve other people. However, the adult student is generally not so easily led or influenced and brings to the lesson or class a perhaps equally strong predisposition to affect the learning atmosphere.[16] This fact is often forgotten by a teacher who is accustomed to setting the pace. Dealing with the adult student in an adult manner is the teacher's best mode of operation in all circumstances.

Teaching Suggestions

Create an atmosphere of partnership.

> Offer the adult student frequent choices of pieces and activities. This need not mean the omission of anything important. Have ample examples of materials that can serve the same purpose and allow the adult to select those most attractive or meaningful to him/her.

> Allow the adult to be musically responsible as well. Have the adult student occasionally set tempi, suggest fingering, determine dynamics or agogics, conduct an ensemble, or teach a new piece to a fellow student.

Arrange opportunities for feedback.

> Ask questions that call for judgments and opinions. If inappropriate opinions are forthcoming, try them out with the student before suggesting (or insisting) on a different solution.

> Have adult students play for one another, even if they don't study in a group. Allow this playing time to be somewhat social, encouraging discussion and sharing of personal anecdotes related to music making. Participate in this yourself.

Adult Predispositions

ADVANTAGES	DISADVANTAGES
Has made a commitment of time and, usually, money to taking piano lessons. There is great desire to succeed, to get something out of it.	May have unrealistic expectations about the amount of time it takes to achieve technical ease in the performance of motor skills and may become impatient when success is not instant.
Regards whatever (s)he does at the keyboard as a means of personal expression. Opinions, suggestions, and criticisms about the playing, therefore, are taken as reflections on the self. Successful performance is consequently a potent ego boost.	Often inhibited, having already judged the self so often in relationship to the perceived accomplishments, opinions, or attitudes of others.
Capable of setting goals and appreciating the necessity of waiting for delayed rewards. Since cause and effect is better understood, the relationship between practicing and achieving results may be more patiently tolerated.	Fears failure, assuming that what can be done by small children with apparent ease should be done perfectly—and immediately—by the adult. Trial-and-error learning is not acceptable to most adults. The adult who performs incorrectly is quickly frustrated and loses self-confidence.
More adept at expressing opinions, likes and dislikes, and is also more likely to question what is not understood. The teacher is therefore able to read the situation more clearly and to respond accordingly.	Often does not realize how complicated an act playing the piano is. Growing awareness of what it will take to arrive at an acceptable playing standard may result in discouragement.
Often interested in additional background information about whatever is being learned. Thus the lesson may be more enjoyable for the teacher as well as stimulating to the student.	May have forgotten what it means to practice, believing that the application of earnestness or energy will compensate for the discipline of drill.

At all times be encouraging, but honestly so.

Be sure that the material assigned is not too difficult or does not demand concentration beyond the resources of the person to whom the assignment is being made.

Provide many short reinforcing exercises, pieces, or activities so that there may always be several successes in each lesson or class. It is of primary importance that the adult student recognizes this success him/herself and is not wholly reliant upon the teacher for support and/or approval.

Avoid creating an atmosphere in which only perfection is acceptable.

Don't polish every piece. Especially in the beginning, stress different things at different times—sometimes pitch accuracy, sometimes rhythmic or dynamic precision, sometimes tempo, and so on.

Musical activities in which there is no single correct response or solution—for instance, choice of accompaniment style when harmonizing, an original melody improvised over the teacher's (or other student's) ostinato—are valuable in creating a feeling of self-worth as well as serving as an insight into what a student is really able to feel and play.

Probably the single most effective teaching technique in working with adults is to maintain an honest sense of humor. There is nothing as helpful in inducing relaxation, relieving frustration, and fostering realistic self-appraisal than a light word offered at just the right moment. Moreover, humor is contagious and "re-creates" both student and teacher.

METHODS FOR THE ADULT BEGINNER

An arbitrary distinction was made earlier in the chapter between the older-beginner piano method and the college-adult piano method. These categories will be reflected in the reviews that follow. Courses listed as older-beginner piano methods are those in which the organization is based on the playability of pieces and exercises and only secondarily on the development of harmonic knowledge or functional keyboard skills (sometimes presented in ancillary books). College-adult piano methods, on the other hand, integrate skills in reading, playing, harmonizing, and improvising in a single book in which the organization reflects a theoretical - more than a "playing" - plan. The methods selected for review were all created in the 1970s and 1980s, decades that represent an especially fruitful period of adult-piano method development.

Older-Beginner Piano Methods

BASTIEN, JAMES. San Diego: Kjos West.

	The Older Beginner Piano Course, Levels 1, 2 (1977). Each 96 pages.
	Musicianship for the Older Beginner, Levels 1, 2 (1977). Each 48 pages.
SUPPLEMENTS:	*Favorite Melodies The World Over,* Levels 1, 2 (1977); classic themes, religious, and others.
ORGANIZATION	10 units per level. *Piano Course* is in 8-page units; *Musicianship* is in 4-page units. Supplementary

section (6 pieces), in each *Piano Course* book. Reference pages. Dictionary. Manuscript paper.

READING APPROACH
Orientation: Off-staff notation. Grand staff: Two-hand reading in 8 positions: C, G, F; D, A, E; a, d; modified multi-key approach; key signature introduced with G position. Level 2: D-flat, A-flat, E-flat; G-flat, B-flat, B (positions). Level 1 range: All notes on grand staff; ledger lines between. Level 2 range: Ledger lines above and below staff.

SCALES
Level 1: C, G, F (from unit 7); D, A, E (reference page). Level 2: a, d, e (all forms); all major scales (reference page).

CHORDS/ HARMONY
Level 1: From beginning—I IV V_7 (close position). Level 2: Minor, augmented, diminished triads; inversions: C, F, G. Lead-sheet symbols: primary identification throughout.

RHYTHMS
Level 1: Basic, eighth notes, dotted quarter; common meters, 6/8. Level 2: Triplets (unit 4); sixteenths (unit 8); syncopation. *Musicianship:* Some separate rhythmic drills.

TECHNIQUE
Piano Course: Practice directions (for most pieces). *Musicianship:* Short technical exercises coordinated with each unit.

HARMONIZATION
Musicianship: Melody and accompaniment, transposition. Written and played.

IMPROVISATION
Musicianship: Some question/answer (level 1).

REPERTOIRE
Level 1: Arrangements of well-known classical and popular melodies. Level 2: Arrangements of well-known classical and popular melodies; original pieces (Bastien); original classics (Supplementary). No ensemble music.

FEATURES
Piano Course: Adequate core text by itself. *Musicianship:* Provides coordinating theory, technic, sight reading. Practice directions: Pieces (*Piano Course*); technic (*Musicianship*). Multi-key reading (*Piano Course*); stress on intervals (*Musicianship*). Excellent format: larger print size; attractive covers, layout. Presentations thorough, but minimal. Charts (reference pages only). Materials well sequenced, coordinated. Basic reinforcement. Especially suitable for older beginner who wishes to play for pleasure.

CLARK, FRANCES, LOUISE GOSS, AND ROGER GROVE. *Keyboard Musician.* Rev. ed. Secaucus. NJ: Summy-Birchard/Warner Bros. 1980. 208 pages.

ORGANIZATION	22 units, 6–9 pages per unit. Preface to student. Notes to teachers. Glossary.
READING APPROACH	Letter names of keys, basic note values assumed. Intervallic reading: Seconds (unit 1) through octaves (unit 12). Landmarks: F, C, G; low F, high G (unit 10). Range: Ledger lines above and below staff. Sight-reading exercises included in each unit.
SCALES	Major/minor 5-finger patterns (unit 7). Key signature: M (unit 13); m (unit 14); modes (unit 20).
CHORDS/ HARMONY	Major/minor triads (unit 8). I IV V presented as single notes, above/below I; later I, IV, $V_{(7)}$ in close position (inversions); Roman numerals used throughout.
RHYTHMS	Basic; eighth notes (unit 6); dotted quarter (unit 9); sixteenths (unit 18). Meters with eighth as pulse (from unit 16). Separate 2-hand rhythmic drills in each unit.
TECHNIQUE	Short technical exercises included in each unit. Technical exercises played all over keyboard. Finger/ hand independence, slurs, extensions to the octave. Scale fingerings practiced in fragments.
HARMONIZATION	Melody accompaniment with fifths, I, IV, V as single notes; later I, IV, $V_{(7)}$ in close positions (inversions).
IMPROVISATION	Improvising, using concepts studied, included in each unit.
REPERTOIRE	Much single-line texture until unit 7, with frequent teacher accompaniment; thereafter, 2-hand music with intervallic and single-line second parts. Much well written teaching music used throughout; some, but not frequent, use of well-known melodies; single rote piece included in each unit through unit 6; inclusion of short original classics from unit 9; extensive use of classics and twentieth-century originals from unit 14.
FEATURES	Each unit integrates concept presentation, repertoire, rhythm drills, technical exercises, improvising, sight-reading, harmonizing. Especially strong reinforcement of all concepts and skills. Well-sequenced sight-reading exercises in all units. Minimal presentation of harmony (I, IV, V as single notes) until late in the book (unit 17). Musical quality of repertoire is notable, but texture of music remains thin for nearly half the book; bulk of the music is unfamiliar. Later repertoire includes many classics from diverse periods. Everything needed is in one book. Little verbal text; no charts/diagrams. Most

suitable use might be for beginner who is 9–14 years of age.

GLOVER, DAVID CARR. Miami: CPP/Belwin.

Adult Piano Student, Levels 1–3 (1970). Each 96 pages.

Adult Piano Theory, Levels 1–3 (1978). Each 48 pages.

Adult Piano Repertoire, Levels 1–3 (1982). Each 64 pages.

ORGANIZATION | *Piano Student:* No units, chapters. Keyboard charts: scales, chords. *Piano Theory:* Programmed lessons, 1 page each. *Piano Repertoire:* Minimum instruction—some concepts, definitions.

READING APPROACH | Level 1: Modified middle-C presentation; keys of C, F, G (most of book); keys of D, A, B-flat, E-flat (brief, at end); all with key signature. Intervals used, principally in conjunction with technique. Level 2: Intervals in scales. Level 1 range: All notes on grand staff; ledger lines between. Level 2 range: Ledger lines above and below staff.

SCALES | Level 1: C, F, G, D, A, B-flat, E-flat; one octave. Level 2: Minor scales. Level 3: Arpeggios.

CHORDS/ HARMONY | Level 1: From beginning—I IV V₇ (close position). Level 2: Major triads and inversions; M/m cadences (reference). Level 3: Augmented and diminished triads. Lead-sheet symbols plus Roman numerals throughout. Theory books reinforce chord knowledge through written exercises.

RHYTHMS | Level 1: Basic, eighth note, dotted quarter; common meters, 6/8. Level 2: Triplets. Level 3: sixteenth notes, syncopation.

TECHNIQUE | All levels: Technical exercises included throughout to reinforce new concepts, rhythms, keys.

HARMONIZATION | No melodies to harmonize; transposition drills (with chords) in *Piano Student* and *Piano Theory* books.

IMPROVISATION | None.

REPERTOIRE | *Student* levels 1 and 2: Arrangements of well-known melodies; original pieces (Glover); some arrangements of original classics. *Student* level 3: Original classics grouped by periods; original pieces (Glover); short section, practical patriotic music (arranged). *Repertoire* levels 1 and 2: Varied textures; styles. Religious, patriotic, folk, jazz/pop, whole-tone included. Glover is chief composer and arranger. *Repertoire* level 3: Glover originals; original classics; hymn arrangements. No ensemble music in any book.

FEATURES	*Piano Student:* Adequate core text by itself; clear format. *Piano Theory:* Written reinforcement to correlate with *Student* books; not really programmed instruction (no answer card/sheet). *Repertoire:* Could be used to supplement other texts, materials. Directives to teacher included throughout all *Student* books. Little verbal text; charts/diagrams (reference pages only). Combines basic playing/harmonic information, pleasure pieces.

NOONA, WALTER, AND CAROL NOONA. Dayton, OH: Heritage Music Press.

The Adult Pianist, Books 1–3 (1979). Each 49 pages.

The Adult Reader, Books 1–3 (1980). Each 48 pages.

ORGANIZATION	*Pianist* books are in 7- to 10-page units. Reference and dictionary pages. *Reader* books include familiar melodies; Christmas carols; hymns; jazz; classical themes (in book 1); original classics (in books 2 and 3)
READING APPROACH	Book 1: Orientation: Off-staff letters, notes. Guideposts: F, C, G; bass/treble C; bottom/top line F, G. Reference to intervals. C major 5-finger pattern. Book 2: Major 5-finger patterns: C, F, G; D, A, E. D-flat, A-flat, E-flat; G-flat, B-flat, B (reference pages only). Range: Book 1: All notes on grand staff. Book 2: Inner ledger lines. Book 3: Ledger lines above/below staff.
SCALES	Book 2: Tetrachord; regular fingering: C, F, G, D, A, E. Book 3: Minor forms explained. All M/m scales (reference pages).
CHORDS/ HARMONY	Book 1: I V$_7$ (close position) C Major/minor only. Book 2: I IV V$_7$ (close position) C, F, G, D, A, E; major/minor triads I IV V$_7$—all other keys (reference pages only). Book 3: Augmented, diminished triads; major triads plus inversions; sevenths. Lead-sheet symbols: Primary identification. Some Roman numerals.
RHYTHMS	Book 1: Basic, eighth note, dotted quarter; common meters. Book 2: Syncopation; 5/4; 6/4; 6/8. Book 3: Triplets; sixteenth notes. Separate drills (rhythm

	charts) in all book 1 units, some units in books 2 and 3.
TECHNIQUE	Occasional exercises, etudes, references (all *Pianist* books).
HARMONIZATION	Harmonization (project pages) in some book 1 units, most book 2 and 3 units. Book 3, unit 5 stresses lead-line reading/harmonizing.
IMPROVISATION	Frequent suggestion (in all books) to experiment—transpose, change mode, create original accompaniments, études, and so on.
REPERTOIRE	*Pianist* book 1: Arrangements of well-known melodies (most with words); book 2: Arrangements of classical and popular melodies; book 3: Arrangements, lead-sheet tunes, original classics. *Reader:* Arrangements, familiar melodies (many styles) in all books; original classics in books 2 and 3). Original pieces (Noona) throughout all books. No ensemble music.
FEATURES	*Pianist:* Adequate core text by itself, with written, rhythmic, playing drills (project pages); some technique; charts. *Reader:* Supplementary pieces (many styles) to this, or other, texts. Early and continued use of harmonizing and popular piano styles. *Pianist* book 3 includes an introduction to musical styles and periods. Practicing and/or background information included throughout, but not sequenced or printed consistently. Straightforward format; good-size print; pages sometimes crowded. Especially suitable for student who wishes to play in popular styles early, yet includes variety of playing styles, original classics.

PALMER, WILLARD, MORTON MANUS, AND AMANDA VICK LETHCO. *Alfred's Basic Adult Piano Course.* Van Nuys, CA: Alfred Publishing Co.

	Lesson Book, Level 1 (1983). 96 pages.
	Lesson Book, Level 2 (1984). 96 pages.
	Lesson Book, Level 3 (1987). 96 pages.
	Theory Piano Book, Level 1 (1984). 64 pages.
	Theory Piano Book, Level 2 (1985). 64 pages.
SUPPLEMENTS:	Pop, country, Christmas, duets, and others.
ORGANIZATION	*Lesson* books are sectional, though not called units. *Theory* books are correlated (by page) to *Lesson*

	books. *Lesson Book* level 2: Reference section. Certificate of award.
READING APPROACH	Orientation: Single staff; letter names on noteheads. Grand staff: 2-hand reading in 5 positions: C, G, F; a, d. Interval recognition. Playing in keys established before key signature. Key signature introduced at same time as major scale. Level 2 introduces new keys: D, B-flat, E-flat; e.g. Level 1 range: All notes on grand staff; ledger lines between. Level 2 range: Ledger lines above and below staff not presented.
SCALES	Level 1: C, G, F; a, d (relative/harmonic). Level 2: D, B-flat, E-flat; e, g (relative/harmonic); all major/harmonic minor scales (reference section).
CHORDS/ HARMONY	Level 1: From beginning—I V_7 (close position); IV (midway). Level 2: Major triads/V_7 and inversions; sevenths; augmented and diminished triads. Lead-sheet symbols primarily; some Roman numerals.
RHYTHMS	Level 1: Basic, eighth notes, dotted quarter, triplets, syncopation. Level 2: 6/8 (p. 14); sixteenth notes (p. 52). Occasional written/playing drills in *Theory* books.
TECHNIQUE	*Lesson* books: Warm-ups (short exercises) for certain pieces. Occasional practice suggestions in *Lesson* and *Theory* books. Both *Lesson* and *Theory* books give special attention to pedaling.
HARMONIZATION	No melodies to harmonize, although many chord drills: playing (*Lesson* books) and writing and playing (*Theory* books).
IMPROVISATION	None.
REPERTOIRE	Level 1: Arrangements of well-known classical and popular melodies. Level 2: Arrangements of well-known classical and popular melodies; one original classic. Original pieces (Palmer) throughout. No ensemble music.
FEATURES	*Lesson Book:* Adequate core text by itself. *Theory Book:* Provides coordinated (principally written) drills. Excellent format; larger print size; attractive covers, layout. Technical warm-ups are helpfully placed and specific. Materials are well sequenced and reinforced. Harmonic information presented, but harmonization is not a goal. Wide choice of well-known melodies; only one original classic. Especially suitable for older beginner who wishes to play for pleasure.

College-Adult Piano Methods

ALLEN, DORIS R. *Creative Keyboard for Adult Beginners.* Englewood Cliffs, NJ: Prentice-Hall, 1983. 295 pages.

ORGANIZATION	7 units, 26–52 pages each. Pre-reading (3 pages). Glossary. Index.
READING APPROACH	Pre-reading orientation: keyboard, metric basics, posture. Introduces most concepts by rote or improvisation, then defines, presents. Intervallic reading from guidenotes F, C, G (unit 1); treble/bass C (unit 2); high G/C, low F/C (unit 3). Major 5-finger pattern (unit 2); pieces do not use key signature. Major key signatures introduced with scales (unit 4).
SCALES	Major scales played in tetrachords, scale skeletons (unit 4); regular fingering, contrary motion (unit 5). All scales. Minor key signatures, 5-finger patterns presented; not minor scales. All modes, pentatonic, hexatonic scales (unit 6).
CHORDS/ HARMONY	Triads (unit 3); chords as filled-in intervals, Roman numeral identification (unit 4); inversions, seventh chords (unit 5). Unit 7 concentrates on reading lead-sheet notation. Cadence drills (some unusual combinations), from unit 4.
RHYTHMS	Basic (units 1 and 2); eighth notes, dotted quarter (unit 3); triplets (unit 5); 6/8 (unit 6); sixteenth notes, syncopation (unit 7). Rhythm ensemble drill(s), all units.
TECHNIQUE	Specific attention to technical development; warm-up patterns, technic drills in each unit. Practice tips included throughout.
HARMONIZATION	From beginning, accompanying with ostinatos, single lines, chords. Unit 5 devoted to expansion of accompaniment techniques.
IMPROVISATION	Important feature throughout; often precedes conceptual presentation.
REPERTOIRE	Considerable emphasis on folk tunes (international), blues teaching pieces (Allen). Many original classics (wide chronology) almost from beginning. Much ensemble music (multiple pianos), rounds, canons in each unit. Special attention to twentieth-century composers, techniques.
FEATURES	Introduces many concepts and skills by rote or improvisation; then provides presentations,

definitions. Heavy concentration on accompanying, and harmonic and formal knowledge. Introduction to functional harmony is dense; much presented at once. Interesting repertoire/ensemble, especially from twentieth century. Considerable amount of verbal text, use of charts, graphs. Format is inconsistent; some pages clean and open, some crowded. Table of contents not very helpful; topical index more practical. Sequencing, unit groupings seem somewhat arbitrary; not always easy to see logical development of concepts and skills. Especially suitable for multi-culture college classes (many folk songs with foreign texts); many reinforcing ensemble activities.

HEEREMA, ELMER. *Progressive Class Piano.* Rev. ed. Van Nuys, CA: Alfred Publishing Co., 1984. 342 pages.

ORGANIZATION	6 chapters, 36–59 pages each. Supplementary repertoire. Introduction to score reading. Reference pages. Index.
READING APPROACH	Orientation: 15 introductory pages: Intervals, rhythm, major 5-finger pattern, landmarks F, C, G. 2-hand reading in 5-finger positions: C, G, F (chap. 1); D, A, E (chap. 2); A-flat, D-flat, G-flat (chap. 3); E-flat, B-flat, B (chap. 4). Key signature used from beginning. Introduction to score reading.
SCALES	Finger crossings over and under thumb prepare for scale playing, but no scales (as patterns or exercises) presented. Left-hand position (thumb on tonic) allows use of all accidentals in key. Reference: All major, harmonic/melodic minor scales, fingerings.
CHORDS/ HARMONY	Tonic, dominant created by use of fifth, second (chaps. 1–3). Introduction of major and minor triads in chapter 4. Subdominant, chapter 5. Use of figured bass throughout. Cadences/inversions (reference pages)
RHYTHMS	Chapter 1: Basic. Chapter 2: eighth notes, dotted quarter. Chapter 3: Syncopation. Chapter 4: Triplet. Chapter 5: Compound meters. Chapter 6: sixteenth notes. Extensive 2-hand rhythm drills at end of each chapter.
TECHNIQUE	Many short technical exercises at the end of each chapter. Czerny, Hanon, Duvernoy exercises included from chapter 4.

HARMONIZATION	Stressed from outset; important part of each chapter. Harmonizing with intervals develops into use of close position chords.
IMPROVISATION	Stressed from outset; important part of each chapter. Varied and extensive suggestions for improvising in many styles.
REPERTOIRE	Each chapter contains: ample amount of reading pieces following presentational pages; repertoire pieces—longer, offering stylistic variety; 2–4 duets. Much music composed (by Heerema and others) for the book. Well-known and folk tunes used chiefly in melodies to harmonize. Original classics begin to appear in chapter 3, included thereafter. Supplementary repertoire: all original classics.
FEATURES	Each chapter coordinates subject presentation, reading pieces, duets, repertoire, playing by ear, harmonization, improvisation, technique exercises, rhythm drills. Excellent sequencing, reinforcement. Harmonic scope includes only primary major and minor triads, V_7. Major scale not presented, but technique prepares for scale playing. Inclusion of section on score reading makes this book useable in the college music-major (piano secondary) sequence. Much well written teaching material; minimal use of well-known tunes. Excellent format, print size; attractive cover, layout. Repertoire seems especially suitable for younger adult beginners.

HILLEY, MARTHA, AND LYNN FREEMAN OLSON. *Piano for Pleasure.* St. Paul, Minn.: West Publishing Co., 1986. 346 pages.

	Piano for Pleasure, Instructor's manual (1986)
	Cassette to accompany *Piano for Pleasure* (1986)
ORGANIZATION	19 units, 7–27 pages each. Every fourth unit is a shorter "recap" unit. Supplementary repertoire. Index of pieces.
READING APPROACH	Off staff; directional playing from finger numbers, letter names. Partial (2-line) staff; seconds, thirds. Unit 5: All notes, grand staff. Guide notes: F, G; 3 Cs. Unit 9: Ledger lines; stresses A-C-E above/middle/ below staves. Unit 10: sixths, sevenths, octaves as extensions of pentascale.
SCALES	Unit 7: Major pentascale. Unit 10: Major scale as completion of pentascale; use 2 hands to play. Unit

11: Major scale, regular fingering; 2 octaves; hands alone. Unit 13: Major scale, hands together; contrary motion. Unit 15: Relative/harmonic minor; pentascales, with 1-note crossings.

CHORDS/ HARMONY	Playing intervals, from outset. Unit 9: Triads. Unit 11: I IV V triads. Unit 13: Inversions. Lead-sheet and figured bass. Unit 14: All quality triads. V_7. Units 15, 17: Triads in scales.
RHYTHMS	Initial: Tap, tap hold. Basic note values: presented at same time. Unit 6: Dotted quarter. Unit 7/10: Upbeat; syncopation. Unit 14: Sixteenths. Unit 15: Compound meter; triplets. Cassette demonstrates; student practices with cassette background. Extensive 2-hand rhythm drills throughout book.
TECHNIQUE	Built into each unit. 2-hand, even from off-staff notation. Tabletop technique: Finger drills with cassette background; later combined with notated short drills. Prepares hand for scale crossings and inversions before playing such.
HARMONIZATION	Begins in unit 14. Both lead-sheet and figured bass. Most melodies are folk and well-known tunes.
IMPROVISATION	In each unit, from outset. Prepares for, or grows out of, reading, rhythm, technique. Precise, helpful, varied suggestions.
REPERTOIRE	Great variety of styles, textures (even in ensemble music). Does not stress playing of familiar tunes, although these are included. Much original Olson music. Original classics included from unit 7. Extensive ensemble music: some student-teacher; some multiple pianos. Supplementary repertoire to middle-intermediate level.
FEATURES	Each unit coordinates content presentation, reading and rhythm reinforcement, improvisation, technique, theoretical understanding, ear training. Carefully sequenced preparation for reading. Ample reading drills in addition to repertoire pieces. Extensive attention to listening, coordinated to cassette and to student-teacher playbacks (that grow in length, complexity). Written work (and copying) in each unit, from unit 2. Recap units review, solidify contents of preceding 3 units; could be used effectively as tests or material for independent study.

LINDEMAN, CAROLYNN A. *Piano Lab: An Introduction to Class Piano.*
Belmont, CA: Wadsworth Publishing Co., 1983. 293 pages.

ORGANIZATION	12 chapters, 9–17 pages each. Assumes *class* piano course. Introduction to piano (historical development), elements of music. Supplementary: Literature; blues/boogie/ragtime; songs with accompaniments; songs to accompany. Appendixes. Indexes.
READING APPROACH	Orientation: Keyboard landmarks, all Cs, Fs. Off-staff reading from letter names. Group improvisation. Chance music. Chapter 2: Build major 5-finger patterns before on-staff reading. No real reading approach. Read only single-staff melodies. Chapter 3: Grand-staff reading. Many parallel melodies. Read in many positions, keys (accidentals only; no key signature).
SCALES	Chapter 6: Introduces key signature with major scale; all tetrachords. Regular fingering, 2 octaves. All M/m scales (Appendix). Modes; pentatonic, whole-tone, 12-tone concepts/reading.
CHORDS/ HARMONY	Chapter 3: First play chord *roots* from lead-sheet symbols. Chapters 4 and 5: M/m triads. Chapters 6 and 7: I IV V root position. Chapter 8: Inversions (including V_7) presented with figured bass.
RHYTHMS	Chapter 2: Whole, half, quarter, eighth notes. Chapter 4: All dotted notes. Chapter 5: Sixteenth notes. Chapter 7: Syncopation. Chapter 8: Compound meters. Chapter 12: Shifting meters, accents. Separate rhythmic exercises, some chapters; recommends Kodály syllabic counting (Appendix).
TECHNIQUE	Technical exercises in every chapter, all written in CM/m.
HARMONIZATION	From chapter 3 on. Harmonizing with chord roots, triads, close position primary chords. Most harmonizations written out, used for sight-reading. 2 supplements: Songs with accompaniments, melodies to harmonize (lead-sheet symbols given).
IMPROVISATION	Composing project in each chapter.
REPERTOIRE	Folk songs (from many countries), not all well known. Early, and substantial, inclusion of original classics, many out of the ordinary. Some blues/ boogie/ragtime. Many Beatles melodies. Ensemble playing in each chapter, mostly duets or duos.

FEATURES	Each chapter includes concept and skill presentations, composing project, ensemble/ repertoire music, technical exercises, evaluation of skills (playing), evaluation of musical understanding (writing). A great deal of text, many charts and graphs, photographs of historical and modern pianos. Some presentations (e.g., orientation to keyboard and playing) are fresh and attractive; others (e.g., introduction to scales or chord inversions) are dense and highly theoretical. Reading pieces and repertoire are challenging and serious. The format is sometimes crowded, unpredictable, or both. Many suggestions for class activities, interesting tangents. Extensive indexing affords easy location of specific skills and pieces. Clearly a college text, organized for semester or quarter pacing.

LYKE, JAMES, AND DENISE EDWARDS. *Keyboard Fundamentals.* Champaign, IL: Stipes Publishing Co., 1986. 191 pages.

ORGANIZATION	6 chapters, 20–31 pages each. Chapter 7: Patriotic and holiday music. Appendixes. Indexes.
READING APPROACH	Orientation: 2-line staff reading (on black/white keys). Grand-staff landmarks: F, C, G. Attention to intervals. Chapter 2: Major pentachords (C, G, D, A, E), no key signature. Chapter 3: Rest of major pentachords. Reading range extends gradually, without particular focus.
SCALES	Chapter 3: All major scales; tetrachords; with key signature. Chapter 4: Minor pentachords; preparation for thumb crossings. Chapter 5: Major scales; regular fingering; clusters/single-note groups.
CHORDS/ HARMONY	Chapter 3 (late): Major triads. Chapter 5: Primary triads; root position. Chapter 6: V_7. Inversions of primary triads. Use of lead-sheet symbols. Figured bass: primary triads; root position.
RHYTHMS	Chapter 1: Basic. Chapter 2: eighth notes. Chapter 4: dotted quarter; 6/8. Chapter 5: sixteenth notes. Chapter 6: Triplets. Rhythmic reinforcement minimal (except at beginning).
TECHNIQUE	Technical exercises in every chapter. Often go through all keys.
HARMONIZATION	From the outset. At first, single pitches and drones. Chapter 4: Lead-sheet harmonization. Chapters 5 and 6: Primary triads plus V_7.

IMPROVISATION   In each chapter, from outset. Practical, specific suggestions.

REPERTOIRE   Many folk songs. Much ensemble (especially student-teacher duets). Original classics, from Chapter 2. Arrangements and original music by Lyke and Edwards. Solo, ensemble. Contemporary sounds: Mostly pop and blues idioms.

FEATURES   Each chapter includes: concept and skill presentation; reading and rhythmic drills; accompanying (harmonization); technical exercises; suggestions for improvisation; written review. Reading and repertoire suggest a modified multi-key approach. Written reviews at the end of each chapter help pull together main theoretical concepts presented in that chapter. Repertoire presents a pleasing mix of keyboard and musical styles. Most well-known tunes are folk-(rather than pop) oriented. All pop/blues pieces are Lyke/Edwards originals. Much ensemble music is included; many student-teacher duets. Specific and continual attention is given to the development of keyboard technique, mostly through short exercises played in all keys. Format is a no-frills, straightforward presentation, but clearly spaced and printed. Although organized more like a college text, the book could be used in a studio situation.

MACH, ELYSE. *Contemporary Class Piano.* 3d ed. San Diego: Harcourt Brace Jovanovich, 1988. 358 pages.

ORGANIZATION   6 chapters, 24–100 pages each. Appendixes: Score reading; performance terms and symbols; list of compositions. Book index.

READING APPROACH   Small amount of off-staff directional reading from finger numbers. Major 5-finger pattern presented before pitch reading from staff. Grand staff: multi-key approach. Transposition from the outset. Chapter 2: Major/minor 5-finger patterns, all keys. Register guide. Chapter 3: Moves out of 5-finger position. Chapter 4: New notation.

SCALES   Chapter 2: Major/minor pentascale. Chapter 3: Major scales, regular fingering; hands together. Blues scale. Chapter 4: Minor scales, regular fingering; hands together. Modes; chromatic, whole-tone scales.

CHORDS/ HARMONY   Read harmonic and melodic intervals from outset. Chapter 2: Major/minor triads. V_5^6 IV_4^6. Figured bass.

	Chapter 3: Triads on all scale degrees. Triads and inversions. Chapter 5: Letter-name chord symbols.
RHYTHMS	Simple meters; basic, eighth, dotted notes presented at same time. Chapter 2: Compound meters. Chapter 3: Triplets; syncopation. Metric counting from outset. 2-hand rhythmic exercises (without pitch notation) at end of each chapter.
TECHNIQUE	Chapter 1: 5-finger individuation. Chapter 2: Legato and staccato; introduces damper pedal; 2-note slur. Chapter 3: Extensions; major scale; direct and indirect pedaling. Chapter 4: Minor, chromatic scale. Extensive technical exercises at end of each chapter.
HARMONIZATION	Each chapter combines creative experiences with activities involving harmonization. Use of both standard and free accompaniment styles.
IMPROVISATION	In each chapter, from outset. Associated with reading experiences. Incorporation of cluster, aleatoric aspects from outset. Pentatonic, 12-bar-blues, question and answer, bitonal experiences.
REPERTOIRE	Great variety of styles and textures. Familiar tunes: folk, rag, popular, Broadway, TV. Original music by Mach to reinforce skills and concepts. Original classics included from chapter 2. New notation used from the outset. Ensemble music (for 2–4 players) at end of each chapter. Chapter 6: 27 piano classics, from Couperin to Kraehenbuehl.
FEATURES	A multi-key approach to reading, playing, transposing. Register guides (pertinent guide notes placed at the beginning of each piece) to assist pitch placement, reading. Reading, rhythmic, technical exercises at end of each chapter. Extensive and well-planned suggestions for improvisation and creative activities in each chapter. Wide variety of style and texture in repertoire. Notable excursion into different sound systems, including modality, quartal harmony, graphic and spatial notation, aleatoric freedoms. Brief introduction to score reading: open score (3 parts), alto and tenor clefs. Explanations, charts, graphics used effectively.

STECHER, MELVIN, NORMAN HOROWITZ, CLAIRE GORDON, R. FRED KERN, AND E. L. LANCASTER. *Keyboard Strategies: Master Text 1.* Milwaukee: G. Schirmer/Hal Leonard, 1980. 346 pages.

> *Solo Repertoire* Books 1A/B, *Ensemble Repertoire,* Books 1A/B.

Teacher's Guide: The Pedagogy of Keyboard Strategies (1985)

Master Text II (for second-year college music majors) *not* reviewed.

ORGANIZATION	11 chapters, 19–58 pages each. 2 appendixes. Glossary. Index.
READING APPROACH	Orientation: Basic rhythms, drills. Major 5-finger pattern; off-staff notation; directional reading. Improvisation. Extensive preparation. Reference to G, F clefs. Single-line reading. Multi-key approach. Grand staff: A-C-E, G-B-D-F groups, including high and low ledger lines. Complete range, all keys used from beginning.
SCALES	All major/minor; key signatures; extensive work with tetrachords. Chapter 10: Regular fingering, all groups at once, two octaves. Modes; pentatonic, hexatonic scales. Many suggested activities, accompaniments to use with scales.
CHORDS/ HARMONY	Build, play triads before reading; stress key color design. Chapter 3: All triad qualities. Chapter 4: All diatonic triads. Chapter 5: Triads, sevenths and inversions; use of figured bass. Chapter 6: Tonic/ dominant. Chapter 7: Subdominant. Chapter 11: Secondary chords in major. Lead-sheet and Roman numerals used.
RHYTHMS	Basic, eighth notes, dotted quarter from beginning. Chapter 2: 6/8; triplets, sixteenth notes presented together. Rhythms with improvisations.
TECHNIQUE	Chapters 1–3: Combined with rhythm drills. Chapters 4–11: Finger coordination exercises; drills with scale and chord presentations; varied articulations; touches.
HARMONIZATION	From Chapter 2. Section in each chapter, harmonizing from lead-sheet symbols; later also Roman numerals. All melodies from folk or well-known classical literature.
IMPROVISATION	Stressed from outset; important part of each chapter. Extensive suggested activities in each chapter; many accompaniments in varied styles, contemporary sounds; aleatoric techniques.
REPERTOIRE	Each chapter: Reading and sight-reading pieces, canons; solo and ensemble repertoire. All repertoire composed (Stecher, Horowitz, and Gordon) for this

text; original classics are included from Chapter 4.
Ensemble: Duets, duos, multiple pianos.
Supplementary repertoire.

FEATURES

Each chapter coordinates keyboard theory and technique, reading, solo and ensemble repertoire, and creative and improvising activities. Concepts are presented as wholes; details are then defined and reinforced. Many rhythms are presented at once and early on. Extensive verbal text. Use of many charts and diagrams. Sophisticated repertoire. Melodies for harmonization: folk tunes only. Suggestions for improvising are varied, extensive, and attractive. Most suitable use: college or studio group instruction.

PART FOUR

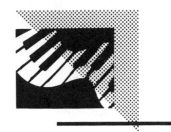

The Intermediate Student

CHAPTER 8

Repertoire and the Intermediate Student

When students arrive at the intermediate level of piano study, they will be ready to explore a higher level of the rich resources of music created for expressive as well as pedagogical reasons. Although much outstanding intermediate-level repertoire is written by educational composers, there are also many accessible works by famous composers who wrote both miniatures and extended compositions.

How far must a student progress before reaching the intermediate level? What is an intermediate student? What is intermediate-level repertoire? This chapter will consider the intermediate level in terms of the music, the student, and the teacher. It will also identify intermediate-level repertoire published in three categories:

1. Method books and coordinated instructional series.
2. Anthologies that feature music of several composers.
3. Collections of music by a single composer.

*M*USIC

When surveying intermediate-level repertoire, it is obvious that different editors grade the same piece in different ways.[1] Since there is little consistency among publications, one can only hope for consistency within given sets of publications. The table offers a frame of reference.

	EARLY INTERMEDIATE	LATE INTERMEDIATE
Bach	Minuets (AMB Notebook)	Two-Part Inventions
Clementi	Sonatina in C Major, Op. 36, No. 1	
Mozart		Sonata in C Major (K.545)
Beethoven	Ecossaise in G Major (WoO 23)	6 Easy Variations (WoO 66)
Schumann	The Happy Farmer, Op. 68, No. 10	Fantasy Dance, Op. 124, No. 5
Kabalevsky	Toccatina, Op. 27, No. 7	Sonatina in C Major, Op. 13

In distinguishing between intermediate and advanced repertoire—or, to borrow the terminology of the French publisher Leduc, between music that is *assez difficile* (rather difficult) and *difficile* (difficult)—it is useful to consider the technical requirements of a composition and to note what makes a piece *difficile*. The following devices are often used effectively in intermediate-level piano music.

Triads in 1 hand, solid and broken, in root position and inversions.

2 independent voices.

Parallel intervals in 1 hand.

Single melody with accompaniment.

Variety of speeds, dynamics, and textures.

Contrasts of touch and dynamics between hands.

Use of the full keyboard.

Expansion and contraction of the hand from a basic 5-finger position.

Ornaments used for expressive purposes—especially mordents, turns, short trills.

These are devices to be avoided at the intermediate level.

4-note chords that spread the hand excessively.

3 or more independent voices.

Rapid changes of intervals in 1 hand.

Complex layers of voices.

Extremes and complex changes of speeds, dynamics, and textures.

Contrasts of touch and dynamics within the same hand.

Awkward leaps at fast speeds, rapid changes of location.

Frequent changes of hand spacing.

Ornaments used to display virtuosity—especially long trills.

There is an abundance of outstanding music by composers who were, and are, fine pianists and astute piano teachers. Much intermediate-level repertoire not only fits the piano, it also fits the pianist. Such music *sounds* pleasing in ways that a listener can perceive and analyze harmonically, melodically, rhythmically, and expressively. Further, it *feels* good in ways that a pianist can appreciate tactilely: such music is comfortable to play. The patterns fit the configuration of the hand (finger length, webbing, thumb and fingers, and so on) and utilize the characteristics of the piano (black and white keys, acoustical traits, registers). Such music prepares students for more advanced repertoire, but it is also music to enjoy now, for its own sake.

Although much intermediate-level music composed prior to the mid twentieth century was intended for children who began piano lessons at about the age of eight, today's intermediate-level student may have started music lessons before entering elementary school (see chapter 5) or may have started or resumed piano lessons as an adult, when time and resources became available (see chapter 7). Thus we find, among intermediate-level students, a tremendous range of goals, interests, physical development, and emotional maturity. This diversity is reflected in the variety of music now available for intermediate-level piano study.

STUDENTS

A well-motivated student may be ready for early intermediate-level repertoire after one or two years of piano study. Such a projection, however, is dependent on a wide variety of factors including age, readiness for study, intelligence, musicality, physical coordination, amount and quality of practice, continuity of study, quality of teaching, emotional maturity, and encouragement from family and friends. The intermediate level itself usually covers three to five years of study and is sometimes subdivided into early, middle, and late intermediate.

Intermediate students who are children have developed many non-musical skills in addition to basic technical skills that enable them to play the piano, decipher notation, and make music. They are experienced in making choices (what to eat, wear, read, or play) They are social creatures who spend much of their time around other people. Peer assessments are important to them. They have become more aware of their changing roles in communities (family, school, nation, world). Both at home and school, they have encountered long- and short-term projects. They have been held responsible for their work and behavior. They have made dramatic growth, both physically and emotionally. They have had exposure to a variety of musical styles, especially as part of their social milieu. They have encountered cultural differences (in real life or via books and television) and may have studied a foreign language. Teachers who work with these students will need to keep such facets of maturation in mind when choosing piano repertoire, planning curricula, and structuring learning activities.

Sometime during the intermediate-level years, students will either decide to continue studying music or they will stop taking lessons. Of those who continue, a few may eventually become professional musicians and teachers of the next generation. They will need both to know how to work independently and to develop a broad understanding of music and its place in society. Those who stop taking piano lessons during their intermediate study likewise are well served by learning how to work independently and how to develop a broad understanding of music and its place in society. Students who only learn how to play pieces often become frustrated when lessons stop. Their technical skills atrophy, and their involvement in music making often fades. On the other hand, students who have learned *how* to learn and how to function as musicians usually continue to be involved in music making and to support the arts in their communities. They perceive music as something that is important to the quality of their lives, not as an expendable frill.

TEACHERS

The teacher's primary role is to facilitate learning. In order to do so, the teacher should know students' learning styles, personalities, strengths, weaknesses, and personal goals. The teacher needs to be familiar with a wide variety of materials and, more important, must know how those materials fit into a learning sequence.

During intermediate-level years of study, it is particularly appropriate to help students develop comfort in using tools that will enhance their ability to function as independent musicians. The tools that will last a lifetime include learning:

To listen to one's own playing.

To strengthen independent skills in reading accurately, maintaining rhythmic stability, and deciphering rhythmic patterns.

To be a functional musician who can improvise, accompany, harmonize songs, and realize chord symbols.

To expand one's expressive range.

How to approach a new piece of music.

How to practice efficiently.

How to use the metronome, tape recorder, sequencer, and computer as tools to enhance musical growth.

About composers, theory, cultural traditions, and historical periods.

What questions to ask and where to get answers.

Sensitivity to the interaction of the body and the instrument.

How to avoid misuse and overuse of the body.

To listen to music, attend concerts, and study recorded performances.

To share music in a variety of situations (e.g., home concerts, informal studio performances, music festivals, recitals, competitions).

To understand the role of the pianist in the creative triangle that links the composer, performer, and listener.

For the teacher selecting repertoire, one frustration is that sometimes intermediate-level students *can* learn to play difficult repertoire. But is that advanced repertoire the most appropriate music in terms of students' readiness and total development technically, musically, socially, and emotionally? Might students become better musicians if foundations were strengthened by working on musically satisfying repertoire that is less difficult?

One approach is to have students work with a variety of materials that reflect several different levels of technical difficulty.

Music for today:	Pieces, just beyond the current level of sight-reading comfort, that will sound good the second or third time a student reads them.
Music for next week:	Pieces that can be polished at home and played, with accuracy and musicality, at the next lesson.
Music for next month:	More difficult material that will be ready to perform after a few weeks of work.
Music for next season:	Long-term projects. Concert and/or contest pieces that need to be lived with and seasoned.

Students need to be challenged. But if they only encounter pieces for next season, then they constantly deal with long-range goals and defer musical gratification. Even more troublesome, they risk being trapped by the mistaken belief that there is an equation between level of difficulty and quality of music.

Ultimately, in order to develop independence, students must become skilled in listening to the sound of their own playing and sensitive to the expressive aspects of music as a language of communication. The process involves helping students learn what it means to be musical beings.

SELECTING MATERIALS FOR TEACHING

The immense variety of piano materials available in this country reflects the tradition of cultural diversity and eclecticism found in the United States. This contrasts sharply with the approach, found in some parts of the world, in which all piano students follow a single, prescribed syllabus throughout their years of piano study. There are advantages and disadvantages to using any set of teaching materials or following any syllabus. Ultimately the teacher must select the approach and the materials to help each student grow musically and develop a secure foundation for future involvement with music.

Before selecting music for intermediate-level students, it is important to make careful assessments of their backgrounds. Where did they begin, what path did they follow, and how far have they traveled? Choice of repertoire should be influenced by the students' technical skills, musical understanding, emotional needs, and physical readiness. It is important to clarify goals (of teachers,' students,' and parents') and to establish realistic timetables for accomplishing these goals. It is valuable to determine supplementary activities and how these will be integrated into the instructional core.

In selecting music, the primary consideration ought to be the quality of the music itself. Does the composer have something to say? Is the music expressive? Is it well-crafted for the piano? The quality of the publication is another factor to consider. Does the work of the editors and publishers reinforce the historical understanding and aesthetic quality of the music? How will various social and psychological aspects of the publication enhance or undermine the student's self-esteem and view of the world? There are also pragmatic considerations including availability and cost of the material.

Method Books

Some teachers choose method books that take students from the beginning through the intermediate level. Occasionally methods are self-contained so that, within the same volume, students deal with several different aspects of study: repertoire, explanations, technical exercises, theoretical information, ensemble pieces, and so on. Other method series present separate books at each level of advancement, coordinating materials that supplement and reinforce the information introduced in the core volume. Some series also supply separate solos that mesh with the levels of the method books.

One advantage in using a method series is that these publications generally offer a complete package of instructional materials that provide a consistent philosophy and continuity of approach. When a teacher's priorities correspond to those of the series, use of a method can be effective. A method can provide a dependable road map, setting out activities step by step, page by page. (This is often helpful to less-experienced teachers.) Although a method may be supplemented, it at least provides a core of material that may serve as a safety net, ensuring against inadvertent omissions of basic information (assuming, of course, that the method itself is thorough and accurate). As students complete each level and begin the next, they may experience a sense of achievement and collegiality with others who have traveled the same path. If, in addition, teachers choose a method from which they themselves studied, they have a teaching model on which to draw in working with their own students. Some series provide teachers' manuals, and many publishers sponsor workshops and clinics to help teachers learn effective ways of presenting what the method contains or advocates. For publishers and music stores, it is easier to develop, advertise, and stock a series than to deal with separate volumes by many different composers.

Extended use of a method series also has disadvantages. Perhaps the worst of all possible reasons for relying on a series is illustrated in the teacher who once exclaimed to the author of a successful method, "Oh, I just love your method. It's laid out so clearly I don't even have to think when I teach!" For some teachers, the very predictability of using a method is a serious shortcoming: it inhibits their creativity and discourages them from individualizing the curriculum to meet the special needs of students. Some teachers prefer not to hear the same pieces played lesson after lesson, year after year. Since intermediate-level books generally contain standard musical literature (perhaps in addition to works by the author), a teacher may have critical disagreements with editorial policies and decisions. Some methods delay introduction of standard repertoire or neglect it altogether, thereby surfeiting students with a diet of banal teaching pieces. Lack of quality music within a series certainly undermines the development of musical sensitivity. Since students progress at different rates and need varied amounts of reinforcement, the same method will not be useful for all of them. Some earlier methods—when viewed from today's perspective—incorporate music, titles, prose, and illustrations that present negative social images and may be considered racist, sexist, and culturally biased.

Reviews of Selected Methods

Most methods listed below were discussed in chapter 6. Since intermediate-level materials build on whatever was presented earlier in a series, readers are encouraged to review the descriptions of these methods.

In general, method books that continue to levels 4, 5, or 6 provide materials technically appropriate at the intermediate level.

BASTIEN, JAMES, AND JANE SMISOR BASTIEN. *Intermediate Piano Course; Levels 1–3.* San Diego: Kjos West, 1982.

	Designed to follow either the *Bastien Piano Library* or the *Bastien Piano Basics.* Each of the 3 levels contains 4 correlated books:
REPERTOIRE	Pieces are grouped by style periods. Standard literature and original works by the Bastiens.

THEORY	Written assignments, music to analyze, material to play.
TECHNIQUE	Studies and etudes, including several by the Bastiens.
MULTI-KEY SOLOS	Recital pieces by Jane Smisor Bastien. Supplementary sheet music and books in many categories: classic themes, folk tunes, hymns, popular, sonatinas, solo collections, Christmas, pop, country, and others. Piano literature volumes are useful anthologies of solo repertoire by European composers.
EXAMPLES OF MUSIC AT EACH LEVEL	1. Bach: Minuet in G Major. Beethoven: Ecossaise in G Major. 2. Schumann: "Merry Farmer." Burgmüller: "Arabesque." 3. Beethoven: "Für Elise." Kabalevsky: Toccatina.
LITERATURE CHOICES	Repertoire books present collections of pieces by standard European composers (Bach to Kabalevsky) and by the Bastiens. Of 32 pieces in book 1, 14 are by the Bastiens. Multi-key solos are impressive recital pieces by Jane Bastien. Technique books include several etudes by the Bastiens.
EDITING	Editors do not distinguish between composers' performance indications and those they have added.

CHRONISTER, RICHARD, AND DAVID KRAEHENBUEHL. Los Angeles: National Keyboard Arts Associates, 1980.

INTERMEDIATE STUDY PROGRAM	Books 41–60 (8 to 12 pages each) cover 2 years of study. Books include no piano literature. Emphasize musicianship, accuracy, facility, continuity, performance, memorization. Books can be purchased singly, in sets of 4 consecutive books, or as a complete volume (including *Teacher Reference Guide*).
INTERMEDIATE PIANO REPERTOIRE	Six volumes (36 pages each) of "authentic music" for piano. Includes 4-hand transcriptions of 2-hand piano music, arrangements of instrumental music, some original solos and duets.
INTERMEDIATE TECHNIC LESSON PLANS	Can be used separately or in conjunction with the *INTERMEDIATE STUDY PROGRAM.* "Technic" is defined as "the way we use our bodies." Specific lesson plans incorporate practice concepts including blocking, skeletal work, fragments, and impulse units. Supplementary music includes sheet-music packets and other collections by Kraehenbuehl

(*Exploring the Blues, Exploring the Masters, Patterns in Blue*).

EXAMPLES OF MUSIC AT EACH LEVEL

1. Tchaikowsky: "The Birch Tree" (theme from Fourth Symphony). 2. Hindemith: "Quickmarch" (*Ludus Tonalis*) (arrangement for 4 hands). 3. Bach: "Bouree" (from Cello Suite). 4. Bartók: "Allegro." 5. Chopin: Waltz in A Minor (arrangement for 4 hands). 6. Bruckner: "Concertpiece." Grieg: "Bell-Ringing."

LITERATURE CHOICES

Music from 5 style periods (Baroque, Classic, Romantic, modern, jazz and rock). Does not include simplified versions of piano music. Offers familiarity with a wide variety of instrumental music by Bach, Telemann, Türk, Haydn, Diabelli, Rossini, Beethoven, Schumann, Grieg, Rebikov, Sibelius, Shostakovich, Kraehenbuehl, and others.

EDITING

Except for recent twentieth-century pieces, most of the repertoire represents arrangements, transcriptions, or excerpts requiring editorial decisions. Scores are clearly presented, in large type, and incorporate musically appropriate suggestions regarding dynamics, articulation, tempo. Includes brief notes regarding composers, influences, and original forms of arranged pieces.

CLARK, FRANCES, AND LOUISE GOSS. *The Frances Clark Library.* Secaucus, NJ: Summy-Birchard/Warner Bros., 1954–1974.

Four sets of books, grouped into 6 levels of difficulty: late elementary (1); early intermediate (2); intermediate (3 and 4); late intermediate (5 and 6). Some of the original volumes, printed separately, are now combined. The letters A and B do not refer to levels of difficulty, but to style and chronology. (A books are earlier compositions; B books are nineteenth- and twentieth-century works).

Supplementary Solos (levels 1–3), first published in 1963, includes pieces by Lynn Freeman Olson, Jon George, David Kraehenbuehl, and others.

Piano Literature 1, 2, 3–4A–4B, 5A–6A, 5B, 6B. *Contemporary Piano Literature* 1, 2, 3–4, 5–6. *Piano Technique* 1, 2, 3, 4, 5, 6. *Keyboard Theory* 1, 2, 3, 4, 5–6.

EXAMPLES OF MUSIC AT VARIOUS LEVELS

PL 2. Bach: AMB minuets. *PL* 3–4A–4B. Clementi: Sonatina, Op. 36, No. 1. Grieg: Waltz. *PL* 5A–6A. Bach: Short Preludes. C.P.E. Bach: "Solfeggietto." *PL*

5B. Schubert: Ecossaise (in A-flat major). MacDowell: "To a Wild Rose." *PL* 6B. Mozart: Variations. Chopin: Preludes in A Major and in C Minor.

LITERATURE
CHOICES

Piano Literature: Includes standard European composers of the seventeenth through nineteenth centuries (Couperin to Grieg). High-quality music, carefully sequenced. *Contemporary Piano Literature:* First published in 1955, this fine collection includes composers who have become classics of the twentieth century (Bartók, Kabalevsky, Finney, Tcherepnin, and others). *Supplementary Solos:* First published in 1963, books at 3 levels include many effective pieces by Olson, Kraehenbuehl, George, and others.

EDITING

With Baroque and early Classic pieces, the editors realize ornaments and provide performance suggestions for articulation and dynamics. Fingering is added selectively. A helpful and responsible teaching edition that retains an appropriate stylistic sense.

KISSELL, E., V. NATANSON, A. NIKOLAEV, AND N. SRETENSKAYA.
The Russian School of Piano Playing Farmingdale, NY: Boosey & Hawkes, 1978.

"Officially recommended for use in Children's Music Schools throughout the Soviet Union today." Although book 2 of this method is described as material for the second year of study, in the United States the repertoire generally would be considered intermediate level. Repertoire, selected from all periods, is considered in 4 categories: pieces (30); sonatinas and variations (6); studies (18); duets (8). Each group is carefully sequenced, by level of difficulty, for gradual development of technical skills. Books also include technical material for daily practice. An anthology that focuses on the music itself.

CATEGORY
EXAMPLES

Schumann: March. Tchaikowsky: "The Sick Doll." Clementi: Sonatina, Op. 36, No. 1.

LITERATURE
CHOICES

In addition to standard European composers, includes pieces by Russian composers who are lesser known in this country. A worthwhile collection.

EDITING

Although not intended as a scholarly edition, pieces are carefully edited with an awareness of stylistic characteristics.

NOONA, WALTER, AND CAROL NOONA. *The Classical Performer; The Classical Pianist; Classical Patterns.* Dayton, OH: Heritage Music Press, 1977.

Three levels (A, B, C) for each book. *Performer:* Repertoire and discovery sheets. *Pianist:* Additional repertoire. *Patterns:* Information about style; worksheets; sets of technical routines.

EXAMPLES OF
MUSIC AT EACH
LEVEL

A. Bach: Minuet. Clementi: Sonatina, Op. 36, No. 1. B. Chopin: Mazurka, Op. 68, No. 3. Heller: "L'Avalanche." C. Bach: Prelude in D Minor. Schumann: "Fantasy Dance."

LITERATURE
CHOICES

Both *The Classical Performer* and *The Classical Pianist* present varying stylistic periods with original pieces by well-known European composers (Byrd to Kabalevsky). "Repertoire and Discovery" sheets direct student's observations of the score and provide information about the music. *The Contemporary Performer,* a collection of pieces by the Noonas, uses varying twentieth-century sounds and techniques.

EDITING

Clear layout focuses on the music itself. Although editorial suggestions are sometimes presented in parentheses, it is not always clear what performance indications have been added, deleted, or changed by the editors. Ornaments are sometimes realized above the score.

NOONA, WALTER, AND CAROL NOONA. *Gifted Pianist: Levels 3 and 4.* Dayton, OH: Heritage Music Press, 1986.

Books present material at a more rapid pace than do Noona's *Mainstreams Piano Method* and *Noona Basic Piano.* Intended to challenge children who "comprise the top 5% to 7% of the intellectual range." Sixteen books, representing 4 levels of achievement.

Gifted Pianist: Conceptual core of the series. *Styles:* Repertoire. *Scriva:* Written skills. *Divertimenti:* Entertaining pieces by the Noonas.

EXAMPLES OF
MUSIC AT EACH
LEVEL

(in *Styles*) 1. Kabalevsky: Melody. 2. Shostakovitch: Waltz. 3. Bach: Minuet (in G Major). Schumann: "Wild Rider." 4. Clementi: Sonatina, Op. 36, No. 1. Burgmüller: "The Chase."

LITERATURE CHOICES	*Styles* presents piano solos, mostly by European composers (Bach to Kabalevsky). Less than 15 percent of these pieces are by the Noonas.
EDITING	Although slurs in Baroque pieces are added sparingly, editors do provide many suggestions regarding dynamics, contrasts, tempo, long crescendos, slurs, articulation, fingering. Large print, clear layout, uncluttered pages, few illustrations.

OLSON, LYNN FREEMAN, LOUISE BIANCHI, AND MARVIN BLICKENSTAFF. *Music Pathways.* New York: Carl Fischer, 1974–1976.

	Levels 3, 4, and 5 constitute the intermediate-level books. Each level is subdivided into 2 levels of achievement (A and B). Coordinates 3 basic volumes (*Repertoire, Technique,* and *Musicianship*) as well as supplementary materials (*Ensemble, Something Light,* and graded sheet-music solos). *Repertoire* books are grouped by stylistic periods. *Technique* books include finger drills, technical exercises, and etudes. *Musicianship* books are organized by modules (e.g., rhythm, melody, harmony, expression).
EXAMPLES OF MUSIC AT EACH LEVEL	3A. Bach: Minuet in G Major. 3B. André: Sonatina. 4A. Beethoven: Ecossaise. 4B. Kabalevsky: "Clowns." 5A. Diabelli: Sonatina. 5B. Schumann: "Fantasy Dance."
LITERATURE CHOICES	Fine balance of original pieces, late Baroque to mid-twentieth century. Mostly standard European composers, but a few representatives of the United States (Cowell, Ganz, Copland, Siegmeister). Effective pieces, appropriately sequenced. Wide range of technical and expressive vocabulary. No pieces by series authors.
EDITING	Does not acknowledge editorial additions (phrasing, dynamics, and so on) for some Baroque and Classical pieces. Realizations given for some ornaments. Selective fingerings that fit the hand and enhance technical freedom. Includes brief historical information regarding composers and periods, and identifies pieces by catalog numbers. Clear layout. A practical edition.

PALMER, WILLARD, MORTON MANUS, AND AMANDA VICK LETHCO.
Alfred's Basic Piano Course. Van Nuys, CA: Alfred Publishing Co., 1981–1989.

Includes multiple books (lesson, recital, theory, technic, and so on at each level, 1A–6). At the intermediate level, supplementing the method books at levels 3–6, are *Masterwork Classics* (anthologies of repertoire from 4 periods) and *Practice and Performance* (accompanying guides for students and teachers), compiled by Jane Magrath.

EXAMPLES OF
MUSIC AT EACH
LEVEL

(*Masterwork Classics*) 3. Bach: Minuets. Schumann: "Wild Rider." 4. Haydn: Scherzo in F Major. Kabalevsky: "Clowns." 5. Beethoven: Sonatina in F Major. Kabalevsky: Etude in A Minor. 6. Clementi: Sonatina in C Major. Prokofiev: "Evening" Op. 65, No. 11.

LITERATURE
CHOICES

(*Masterwork Classics*) Repertoire features standard European composers. These original pieces, technically more demanding than arrangements presented in lesson and recital books at the same levels, use a variety of textures and incorporate contrapuntal interest in both hands.

EDITING

Masterwork Classics has clear pages and large print. The different editors, who are not identified, apply a variety of editorial policies regarding the addition of dynamics, phrasing, articulation, and other performance suggestions. For each composition in *Practice and Performance,* Magrath directs student observations, suggests practice procedures, raises questions for student to answer, summarizes musical and technical goals of each piece, describes the affect or program, and includes a miniature score of the complete piece. Magrath also summarizes characteristics of Baroque, Classic, Romantic, and contemporary periods, provides a glossary, and suggests an appropriate order for presenting the repertoire. The focus is on the music itself; no biographical information is included.

SUZUKI, SHINICHI. *The Suzuki Piano School.* Secaucus, NJ: Summy-Birchard/ Warner Bros., 1972, 1978.

Of the 6 volumes, volumes 2–5 include intermediate level-repertoire. Suzuki's approach to teaching incorporates much more than a systematic presentation of the repertoire. It also involves a set of beliefs and teaching strategies. Students are expected to learn to play the pieces in the first volume by hearing and imitating performances rather than by reading the printed score. Note-reading usually is delayed until students have developed physical comfort in playing the piano and aural sensitivity to the quality of the sounds they produce.

EXAMPLES OF MUSIC AT EACH LEVEL

2: Bach: AMB minuets. 3: Clementi: Sonatina, Op. 36, No. 1. 4: Beethoven: Sonata in G, Op. 49, No. 2. 5: Bach: Two-Part Invention in C Major. 6: Mozart: Sonata in C Major (K. 330).

LITERATURE CHOICES

Volumes 2–6 include pieces by eighteenth- and nineteenth-century European composers. Many pieces by Bach, Mozart, Beethoven, Schumann. Students are expected to learn all the repertoire, generally in the order in which the pieces are printed. Sequence of pieces is not by level of difficulty but by alternation of challenging and easier pieces. Use of pedal is usually delayed until volume 4.

EDITING

No distinction is made between the composer's suggestions and those added by the editors, who are not identified. Editorial additions often contradict those based on historical research of performance practices. Authorized recordings of Suzuki repertoire also constitute editorial guidance regarding articulation, tempo, dynamics.

THOMPSON, JOHN. *Modern Piano Course.* Cincinnati: Willis Music, 1936–1942.

Six basic volumes (preparatory and grades 1–5) and supplementary books. Books 3–5 include intermediate repertoire.

EXAMPLES OF MUSIC AT EACH LEVEL

3: Bach: "Musette." Chopin: Prelude in C Minor. 4: Chopin: Prelude in B Minor. Beethoven: Sonata, Op. 2, No. 1 (first movement). 5: Beethoven: Sonata, Op. 13 (second movement). Debussy: "Reverie."

LITERATURE CHOICES

In addition to original piano pieces (Bach to Debussy), includes familiar songs, arrangements of orchestral works, simplified versions of more difficult piano repertoire. Presents illustrations and popularized biographies. Each piece is selected for a specific pedagogical purpose that is identified, and book 3 includes 24 short "etudes" in all keys. Fifty years ago this was an innovative series that pioneered in helping American piano teachers present a balanced curriculum that enhanced students' appreciation and broader understanding of classical music.

EDITING

Reflects the attitude, commonly held earlier, that editors should "help" students and teachers by sharing their interpretations of the score. Contrasts dramatically with the editorial policies of today's most respected publishers, who uphold the integrity of the composer's score. Additions to Baroque and Classical pieces include long phrase lines, extreme dynamic changes, thick textures resulting from long pedals.

ZEITLIN, POLDI, AND DAVID GOLDBERGER. *The Complete Piano Player Collection.* New York: Wise Publications/Music Sales, 1985.

Four volumes (late elementary to late intermediate). Each volume is an anthology with separate sections: folk songs, solos, etudes, sonatinas, duets. These volumes supplement the 5 volumes of *The Complete Piano Player* (by Kenneth Baker), method books that are "based on today's pop songs and famous light classics." *The Complete Piano Player Theory Book* (1986) presents, in one volume, 3 sets of 15 theory lessons and 15 worksheets. Since correct answers are given in the back of the book, the volume is most useful with students who work well independently.

EXAMPLES OF MUSIC AT EACH LEVEL

2: Clementi: Sonatina, Op. 36, No. 1. 3: Beethoven: Ecossaise in E-Flat Major. 4: Beethoven: "Six Easy Variations on a Swiss Song."

LITERATURE CHOICES

Each volume includes about 50 pieces. Most are by well-known European composers. The etudes include many short pieces featuring a variety of musical challenges. The folk songs in volume 4 include settings by Byrd, Corelli, Villa-Lobos, and others. Familiar music that is not hackneyed.

EDITING

Music is presented without explanations or illustrations. Clear, spacious layout. Selections are well graded within each section. Although not intended as a scholarly edition, these books are edited with appropriate performance suggestions.

Anthologies that Feature Music of Several Composers

When selecting intermediate-level music to supplement or replace a method series, there are many anthologies from which to choose.[2] The word "anthology" is derived from the Greek for "a gathering of flowers." As with a flora bouquet, individual pieces are gathered primarily for the sake of providing immediate enjoyment; they are not intended for strictly pedagogical purposes. Some collections present a large group of pieces unified by a common denominator such as style (Baroque, jazz), place of origin (Latin America, the Soviet Union), era (eighteenth century, 1920s), idiom (one hand, four hands), or level of difficulty (early intermediate). The order of pieces may be organized alphabetically, chronologically, or progressively by level of difficulty. Anthologies often furnish a useful way of introducing students to a wide variety of music by many composers. Some of the pieces may be learned, polished, and performed, but not all of the works need be studied in the same detail or within an immediate time frame, such as the same semester or year.

An anthology may have advantages of economy (many pieces for a relatively low cost), variety (music by many composers), convenience (many pieces from which to choose as needs and interests are discovered), unity (pieces representing a common theme), practicality (repertoire recommended or required for a testing or evaluation program), quality ("real music" as opposed to "teaching pieces" created for specific pedagogical purposes), availability (standard material stocked by music stores), and predictability (consistency of quality for volumes prepared by the same editor and/or publisher).

In contrast with structured method books, anthologies encourage students and teachers to explore music on their own, reading and choosing music at will rather than working through a volume page by page. While this characteristic is advantageous, it may also open the door to problems of sequencing and balance. A teacher opting to use an anthology has the responsibility for planning a well-coordinated curriculum; one that meets the technical, stylistic, and emotional needs of the student. This task is not merely a matter of choosing pieces. Since composers themselves are usually not involved in the preparation of anthologies, the compiler's or editor's role assumes great importance. A teacher should be aware of editorial policies that may ignore or distort the original intentions of the composer.

All **names** are those of the editor(s) and/or compiler(s).

AGAY, DENES. *An Anthology of Piano Music.* 4 Vol. New York: Yorktown Music Press/Music Sales, 1971.
Each volume focuses on a single period (Baroque, Classical, Romantic, twentieth century). Elementary to advanced; mostly intermediate.

―――. *Classics to Moderns.* New York: Yorktown Music Press/Music Sales, 1956. From the series *Music for Millions.* Intermediate-level pieces are also included in *Easy Classics to Moderns, More Easy Classics to Moderns, Classics to Moderns in the Intermediate Grades, Sonatas and Sonatinas, Themes and Variations.*

―――. *The Joy Books.* 33 vol. New York: Yorktown Music Press/Music Sales, 1965–1984.

Each collection covers several grade levels and focuses on a specific period (Baroque, modern), composer (Agay, Bach, Bartók, Beethoven, Chopin, Debussy, Mozart), country (France, Russia), style (ragtime, sonatinas), or idiom (solo, duet, two-piano).

ALLISON, IRL. *Irl Allison Piano Library.* 25 vol. Cincinnati: Willis Music, 1965.
Each volume includes sets of pieces (Classic, Romantic, modern) that are appropriate repertoire for student auditions of the National Guild of Piano Teachers. Complete series includes Elementary (levels A–D), Intermediate (levels A–F, 2 books at each level), and Preparatory (Levels A–D). "Preparatory" designates level immediately prior to the most advanced repertoire, not beginning-level music.

American Composers of Today. Miami: CPP/Belwin, 1965.
Twenty-three piano pieces (1–3 pages) by 23 American composers including Babbitt, Cowell, Gideon, Hovhaness, Sessions, Starer, and others born before 1930.

ANTHONY, GEORGE WALTER. *Composers for the Keyboard,* 4 vols. Bryn Mawr, PA: Theodore Presser, 1967.
All volumes include pieces at early to late intermediate levels. Easy 1: Purcell to Mozart (51 solos); Easy 2: Beethoven to Shostakovitch (53 solos); Intermediate 1: Byrd to Beethoven (27 solos); Intermediate 2: Schubert to Shostakovitch (39 solos).

APPLEBY, DAVID, AND MARTHA APPLEBY. *Bravo Brazil!* 2 vol. San Diego: Kjos West, 1983, 1984.
Twelve short pieces by Brazilian composers (Mahle, Villa-Lobos, Lacerda, Guarnieri and others). Editors include background on composers and compositions as well as practice suggestions. Excellent collection.

BANGS, CHARLES. *The Spectrum Anthology of Short Classics:* Pacific Palisades, CA: Spectrum Music Press, 1985.
Piano Literature for the Intermediate Grades: Baroque to Contemporary. Volume 1, lower and middle intermediate. Volume 2, middle and upper intermediate.

BANOWETZ, JOSEPH. *The Pianist's Book of Classic Treasures.* San Diego: Kjos West, 1981.
Brief background on composers (Haydn to Schubert). Same series includes *The Pianist's Book of Baroque Treasures, Early Romantic Treasures, Late Romantic Treasures, Early Contemporary Treasures.* (Reviewed in *PQ*, no. 125.)

BESSER, KLAUS. *Baroque Masters: Easiest Piano Pieces.* New York: C. F. Peters, 1981.
Works by Froberger, Weckmann, Fischer, Krieger, Pachelbel, Kuhnau, and Böhm. Early to middle intermediate. Series also includes *Classical Masters, Romantic Masters, Twentieth-Century Composers, Sonatina Album.*

BROWN, BILL, AND RICHARD BRADLEY. *Mastering the Classics: An Insight to Learning.* 3 vol. Secaucus, NJ: Bradley Publications/Warner Bros., 1987.

Includes analyses, discussion, and study questions about the music. (Reviewed in *PQ,* no. 138.)

CANIN, MARTIN. *French Piano Music of the Early Twentieth Century.* Milwaukee: Salabert/Hal Leonard, 1976.
A collection of intermediate pieces by Milhaud, Poulenc, Séverac, Koechlin, Schmitt. Good recital repertoire.

CLARK, FRANCES, AND LOUISE GOSS. *Minor Masters: Keyboard Music from the Eighteenth to Nineteenth Centuries.* 3 vol. Secaucus, NJ: New School for Music Press/Warner Bros., 1983.
The volumes are progressive, for second to fourth years of study. Short, well-edited pieces.

————. See also *The Frances Clark Library,* under "Methods," pp. 191, 192.

CLARK, MARY ELIZABETH. *Contempo 1; Contempo 2.* Boulder, CO: Myklas Music Press, 1974.
Technically easy but musically adventurous pieces that incorporate twentieth-century compositional techniques (serial writing, sympathetic vibrations, open form). See also *Contempos in Jade, Contempos in Crimson, Contempos in Sapphire, Contempos in Orchid.*

COULTHARD, JEAN, DAVID DUKE, AND JOAN HANSEN. *Music of Our Time: Parnassus Revisited.* 10' vols. Ontario, Canada: Waterloo Music Co., 1977.
Eight graded student books; teacher's manuals (1–4 and 5–8). A Canadian publication that gently expands the vocabulary of sound and technique. Teacher's manuals provide analyses and technical suggestions. Text in English and French.

EMONTS, FRITZ. *Easy Piano Music of the Romantics; Easy Baroque Piano Music.* Valley Forge, PA: Schott/European-American, 1961.
Romantic: Works by expected composers (e.g., Schubert, Chopin, Grieg) as well as by composers less well known (e.g., Kirchner, Jensen, Haas). A practical and substantial collection. Baroque: Provides a broader picture than most collections of the period. Composers represent French, German, Italian, and English Baroque styles.

FERGUSON, HOWARD. *Style and Interpretation: An Anthology of Sixteenth to Twentieth Century Keyboard Music.* 6 vols. New York: Oxford University Press, 1963–1971.
Volume 1, *Early Keyboard Music* (England and France); volume 2, *Early Keyboard Music* (Germany and Italy) (rev. 1972); volume 3, *Classical Piano Music;* volume 4, *Romantic Piano Music* (rev. 1972); volume 5, *Keyboard Duets* (seventeenth and eighteenth centuries); volume 6, *Keyboard Duets* (nineteenth and twentieth centuries). Each volume includes several pieces of intermediate-level repertoire. Scholarly, sophisticated presentation of performance practices. Extensive introduction and information regarding each piece.

FRASER, SHENA, AND YVONNE ENOCH. *Studio 21: A Selection of Original Piano Music from the Seventeenth to the Twentieth Centuries.* 3 vols. Valley Forge, PA: Universal/European-American, 1986.

All volumes are intermediate but increase in difficulty. (Reviewed in *PQ*, no. 143.)

FREY, MARTIN. *At the Time of Telemann.* New York: C. F. Peters, 1929.
Twenty-eight dance movements by Dieupart, Marchand, Graupner, Grüne-wald, Krebs, Muffat, Stölzel, J. S. Bach, Telemann. See also *Masters of the Baroque* (1937), *Masters of the Rococo,* volumes 1 (n.d.), and 2 (1925).

———. *The New Sonatina Book.* 2 vols. Valley Forge, PA: Schott/European-American, 1936.
Arranged in order of difficulty from early to late intermediate. Each volume includes wide selection of composers and each spans Baroque through early-twentieth-century (Gretchaninoff) music. There is also a sonatina volume at the elementary level.

GEORGII, W. AND HANS MARTIN THEOPOLD. *Easy Piano Music from Two Centuries.* 2 vols. St. Louis: Henle/USA, Inc., 1970.
Volume 1: Earlier composers (e.g., C.P.E Bach, Schubert). Volume 2: Later composers (e.g., Albeniz, Smetana).

———. *Easy Piano Pieces of the Classical and Romantic Eras.* 2 vols. St. Louis: Henle/USA, Inc., 1961.
Although composers included are those most expected, the collection is substantial. Most composers are represented by an assortment of pieces. Volume 2 is more difficult than volume 1.

GOLDSTEIN, FRANCES. *Contemporary Collection for Piano Students.* Secaucus, NJ: Summy-Birchard/Warner Bros., 1963.
Originally published in 2 volumes. Revised edition by Frances Larimer. Compiled for "college-age students with sophisticated taste but limited keyboard facility."

GREEN, et al. *Harris Piano Classics: Levels 1A–7B.* New York: Buffalo, NY: Frederick Harris, 1985.
All level-A books contain Baroque and Classical repertoire; level-B books, Romantic and twentieth-century repertoire. Repertoire in the B books often seems easier than that in the A level. Text in French and English.

HALFORD, MARGERY. *Introduction to Theme and Variations for the Piano.* Van Nuys, CA: Alfred Publishing Co. 1985.
Sixteen sets of variations by European composers (Charpentier to Schumann). Extensive foreword describes types of variants, discusses development of variations. Ornaments realized in gray. Edition based on primary sources. Exemplary publication.

HAROUTIUNIAN, NARINE. *First Repertoire Album. Second Repertoire Album.* Farmingdale, NY: Boosey & Hawkes, 1984.
Supplements the 3 volumes of *The Russian School of Piano Playing.* Fifty-nine pieces, many by Eastern European composers, feature a variety of periods and styles. Careful editing; good fingering choices. Introduction in four languages.

HARRIS, SHIRLEY. *Piano Music for One Hand.* Melbourne, Australia: Allans Music, 1984.

Music by 11 Australian composers. Originally intended for students with physical disabilities, but good music for any student. Excellent etudes in voicing, touch, and independence. Music ranges in difficulty from late elementary to late intermediate. (Reviewed in *PQ*, no. 136.)

HERRMANN, KURT. *Intermediate Piano Book: A Collection of Easy to Moderately Difficult Original Pieces for Connoisseurs and Amateurs.* 4 vols. New York: C. F. Peters, 1980.
Volume 1, *Masters Before J. S. Bach;* volume 2, *The Age of J. S. Bach;* volume 3, *The Classical Period;* volume 4, *The Romantic Period;* volume 5, *Twentieth Century Composers.* Includes many little-known works. (Reviewed in *PQ*, no. 118)

HERTTRICH, ERNST. *Sonatinas for Piano.* 3 vols. St. Louis: Henle/USA. Inc., 1982, 1986, 1989.
Volume 1, Baroque to pre-Classics; volume 2, from Classical; vol. 3, Romantic. Includes many lesser known, but musically valuable, sonatinas. Affords choices other than the usual. Scholarly editing. Introductory remarks and discussion of each work in German, French, English. An excellent teacher resource.

HINSON, MAURICE. *Changing Faces.* Valley Forge, PA: European-American, 1988.
Excellent collection of gratifying pieces by 7 American composers born between 1940 and 1960: Beaser, Paulus, Picker, Rouse, Ince, Schwantner, Singleton. Hinson provides notes about the composers and music, with suggestions regarding practicing. Late intermediate to early advanced.

————. *Masters of the Baroque Period: A Guide to Style and Interpretation.* Van Nuys, CA: Alfred Publishing Co., 1988.
Upper intermediate to early advanced. Foreword includes background regarding style and guidelines to performance (tempo, phrasing, articulation, ornamentation). Series also includes *Masters of the Classical Period, Masters of the Romantic Period, Masters of the Sonatina* (3 volumes), *Masters of the Suite, Masters of the Theme and Variation, Masters of the Character Piece, Masters of the Piano Ballade, Masters of the Piano Fantasy.*

————. *Piano Music in Nineteenth-Century America.* 2 vols. Chapel Hill, NC: Hinshaw, 1975.
Unusual repertoire includes works by Paine, Sherwood, Bethune, Gottschalk, MacDowell, and others. Mid to late intermediate. Preface and biographical information.

————. *Twelve by Eleven.* Chapel Hill, NC: Hinshaw, 1979.
Twelve pieces by eleven twentieth-century American composers (including Crumb, Stevens, Babbitt, Keyes, Finney). Mid intermediate to advancing. A good introduction to a variety of keyboard styles and twentieth-century idioms.

HINSON, MAURICE, AND ANNE MCCLENNY. *Music of the Capital City; Music of the Washingtons.* Miami: CPP/Belwin, 1987, 1988.
Music performed during the early days of the Young Republic. (Reviewed in *PQ*, no. 143.)

HUYBREGTS, PIERRE. *Six Piano Sonatinas by Belgian Composers.* Milwaukee: Associated Music/Hal Leonard, 1981.
A reissue of material published 20 years earlier. Included: Absil, De Bo, G. Lonque, A. Lonque, Peeters, Poot. Composer biographies included. (Reviewed in *PQ,* no. 118.)

JOHNSON, THOMAS A. *The Romantic Pianist.* 4 vols. New York: C. F. Peters, 1985.
Many lesser known compositions. Late intermediate.

LORENZ, G. AND HANS MARTIN THEOPOLD. *Easy Piano Variations from the Baroque and Classical Periods.* St. Louis: Henle/USA, Inc., 1970.
Composers included: Händel, C.P.E., Bach, J. C. Bach, Haydn, Mozart, Beethoven.

MCCLENNY, ANNE, AND MAURICE HINSON. *A Collection of Early American Keyboard Music.* Cincinnati: Willis Music, 1971.
Unusual collection of keyboard music (originally for fortepiano and/or harpsichord) written before 1830 by composers who emigrated to America: Taylor, Moller, Brown, Newman, Hewitt, Reinagle. Editorial indications printed in red; very clean page.

MCGRAW, CAMERON. *Four Centuries of Keyboard Music: A Graded Anthology of Piano Masterpieces from 1600 to the Present.* 4 vols. Boston: Boston Music, 1964.
Volume 1 is early intermediate; volumes 2, 3, 4: mid to late intermediate. Fine variety of repertoire.

MILLER, MARGUERITE. *Mosaics.* Orem, UT: Sonos Music Resources, 1973.
Fine collection of contemporary pieces with background on composers' musical ideas.

OLSON, LYNN FREEMAN. *Applause! Impressive Piano Solos for the Budding Virtuoso.* 2 vols. Van Nuys, CA: Alfred Publishing Co., 1986.
Cassette available from Alfred. Performances by Valery Lloyd-Watts. (Reviewed in *PQ,* no. 138.)

———. *Essential Keyboard Repertoire. One Hundred Early Level Selections in Their Original Form.* Van Nuys, CA: Alfred Publishing Co., 1987.
See also *More Essential Keyboard Repertoire* and *First Steps in Keyboard Literature.*

OLSON, LYNN FREEMAN, AND MARTHA HILLEY. *Essential Keyboard Sonatinas: Sixteen Popular Sonatinas in Their Original Form.* Van Nuys, CA: Alfred Publishing Co., 1988.
From Haydn to Kabalevsky.

ORE, CECILE. *Norwegian Pianorama: Twenty-five Contemporary Piano Pieces.* St. Louis: Norsk Musikforlag/MMB Music, 1981.
Intermediate to advanced. Notes (Norwegian, English, German) regarding composers and music. Recorded by Geir Henning Braaten (NC 4903).

PALMER, WILLARD A. *The Baroque Era: An Introduction to the Keyboard Music.* Van Nuys, CA: Alfred Publishing Co., 1976.
Interesting collection by 18 composers. Includes music from the German,

French, Italian, and English Baroque. Excellent foreword on style, taste, instruments, performance practices. Editorial suggestions in gray. Same series includes *The Classic Era* (with Halford), *The Romantic Era* (with Halford), *Introduction to the Masterworks* (with Lethco).

————. *The First Sonatina Book.* Van Nuys, CA: Alfred Publishing Co., 1971. Composers inluded: Latour, Wanhal, Haslinger, Beethoven, Clementi, Pleyel.

RIEGER, EVA, AND KÄTE WALTER. *Frauen Komponieren.* Valley Forge, PA: Schott/European-American, 1985.
Twenty-two piano pieces by female composers of the eighteenth to twentieth centuries. Collection includes de Laguerre, Szymanowska, Hensel, Schumann, Chaminade, Boulanger, Lutyens, Erding, others. Biographical notes (German and English); pictures of the composers.

SCHWERDTNER, HANS-GEORG. *Sonatinas, Sonatas, Pieces from the Eighteenth through Twentieth Centuries.* Valley Forge: PA: Schott/Universal, 1977.
Works by 25 composers, arranged by periods: Baroque (Scarlatti), pre-Classic (Galuppi, J. C. Bach), Classic (Mozart, Haydn), Romantic (Fibich), contemporary (Honegger, Kadosa). Includes many works not well known in this country. Responsible editing and fingering. Intermediate to late intermediate.

SHEFTEL, PAUL. *Classics, Romantics, Moderns: Eighty Solos for the Intermediate Pianist.* New York: Carl Fischer, 1984.
Twenty composers including Copland, Sessions, Hanson, Cowell. See also *More Classics, Romantics, Moderns; Beginning Piano Solos: One Hundred and Thirty-two Original Masterpieces.*

SOLDAN, KURT. *Bach's Sohne.* New York: Litolff/C. F. Peters, n.d.
"Sons of Bach": A less-usual collection of *style galant* repertoire (late Baroque, early Classics). Rather dense pages.

TEOKE, MARIANNE. *Tarka-Barka. A Microcosmic Collection of New and Extraordinary Pieces for Piano.* Farmingdale, NY: Editio Musica Budapest/Boosey & Hawkes, 1977.
For the adventurous. Most pieces involve new notation. Key to notational signs used given in front of the book. All Hungarian composers.

WEISMAN, WILHELM. *Romantic Masters: Easy to Moderately Difficult Piano Pieces.* New York: C. F. Peters, 1980.
Good assortment, from von Weber to Grieg. Pieces are placed in chronological order, not in order of difficulty.

WILLS, VERA. *The Blue Book.* 2 vols. Milwaukee: G. Schirmer/Hal Leonard, 1984.
From the "Rainbow" series of 25 volumes of piano music. Selected from previous publications of G. Schirmer and Associated Music Publishers. Progressive levels of difficulty: *Blue Book* (2 volumes, early intermediate); *Yellow Book* (3 volumes, mid to late intermediate); *Orange Book* (2 volumes, sonatinas and sonatas); *Purple Book* (2 volumes, late intermediate). Wide variety of repertoire, much of which has been difficult to obtain.

No editor identified. *Celebration Series Piano Repertoire.* Buffalo, NY: Frederick Harris, 1988, 1989.

    Introductory album. Levels 1–10. Introductory album, early intermediate. Levels 9, 10 may be considered beyond intermediate by some. In addition to the repertoire volumes there are *Studies Albums* (Levels 1–10), *Study Guides* (Levels 1–8), and cassettes (performances of all the repertoire in volumes 1–8). This is the official syllabus material for the [Canadian] Royal Conservatory of Music in Toronto. Repertoire books contain an especially broad assortment of twentieth-century composers. (Reviewed in PQ, no. 150.)

Collections of Music by a Single Composer

Single-composer collections may be grouped in various ways.

Unified sets of pieces, compiled by the composer, meant to be performed as a whole [e.g., Pinto, *Scenas Infantis*].

Sets of many pieces, assembled by the composer, that may be performed separately or as an extended group [e.g., Bartók, *Mikrokosmos*].

Groups of pieces, assembled by the composer or by an editor, representing a common idiom [e.g., S. Stravinsky, *Six Easy Sonatinas*].

Collections, usually assembled by an editor, of diverse pieces [e.g., *Dances of Beethoven,* edited by Hinson].

    The piano repertoire is rich, and one can refer readers only to a portion of what is appropriate to the intermediate level. There is a core of well-known European composers whose music is included in many of the anthologies described earlier. During students' intermediate years, it is appropriate for them to become familiar with Baroque pieces by Bach (especially easier dances, short preludes, two-part inventions), classical sonatinas (including those by Clementi, Diabelli, Kuhlau, and Beethoven), romantic character pieces (e.g., by Schumann, Mendelssohn, Grieg), and twentieth-century classics (e.g., pieces by Bartók, Kabalevsky, Prokofiev). However, since collections of pieces by these composers are easily available from several publishers, this section will focus instead on outstanding music that is generally less familiar.

    Works listed below represent music that covers the full range of intermediate-level repertoire, early through late, written for students of all ages, children and adults. The specific use of these works (how and when to incorporate them into the curriculum) is left to the discretion of the teacher. This list gives high priority to the quality of the music and the quality of the editing. It is hoped that this list will encourage teachers to explore composers, works, and publishers new to them. It seems appropriate to stimulate today's students, who live in a global village, to consider the musical contributions of men and women who have written in many styles and who represent many parts of this small planet.

ADLER, SAMUEL (b. 1928). Germany, U.S.A.
The Sense of Touch. Bryn Mawr, PA: Theodore Presser, 1983.
Eight short pieces. Explores twentieth-century techniques. Musically challenging but very pianistic. (Reviewed in *PQ,* no. 125.)

ALBENIZ, ISAAC (1860–1909). Spain
Espana, Op. 165. New York: International, 1950.
Subtitled "Six Album Leaves." Effective, Romantic pieces that re-create Spanish scenes. Late intermediate to early advanced.

ALWYN, WILLIAM (1905–1985). Great Britain
Odd moments; April Morn; Hunter's Moon. London: Associated Board, Royal Schools, 1932.
Three suites, each with 3 or 4 movements, composed in 1920s, 1930s. Expressive and pianistic. From Associated Board's excellent series "Easier Piano Pieces."

AMALDER, JERRY (b. 1939). India
India—Raga for the Piano. Secaucus, NJ: Summy-Birchard/Warner Bros. 1981.
Ten short pieces based on varied melody types *(rāgas)* and rhythms *(tālas).* Sophisticated and musically challenging, but not difficult technically. *Frances Clark Library* supplement.

ARCHER, VIOLET (b. 1913). Canada
Eleven Short Pieces. New York: Peer International, 1964.
Effective pieces presenting varied moods and twentieth-century techniques.

BACH, JOHANN CHRISTIAN (1735–1782). Germany
Klaviersonaten. 2 vols.: Op. 5 and Op. 17. St. Louis: Henle/USA, Inc., 1983.
Six 3-movement sonatas in each volume. Easier than the Mozart sonatas.

———, and FRANCESCO PASQUALE RICCI. (1732–1817). Germany, Italy
Introduction to the Piano: Method or Collection of Elementary Studies for the Forte-Piano or Harpsichord. 4 vol. Edited by Beatrice Erdely. Bryn Mawr, PA: Novello/Theodore Presser, 1987.
Includes scholarly introduction and bibliography. Contains the didactic portion of the method and the music. Outstanding teacher resource. (Reviewed in *PQ,* no. 143.)

BACH, JOHANN SEBASTIAN (1685–1750). Germany
Dances of J. S. Bach: Pieces to Play Before the Two-Part Inventions. Edited by Maurice Hinson. Van Nuys, CA: Alfred Publishing Co., 1986.
Thirty-one dances selected from suites and notebooks. Introduction helpful for teachers and mature students. Editor's suggestions are clearly distinguished. Ornaments are explained in the preface but not realized in the score.

BEETHOVEN, LUDWIG VAN (1770–1827). Germany
Dances of Beethoven: Pieces to Play Before His Sonatas. Edited by Maurice Hinson. Van Nuys, CA: Alfred Publishing Co., 1986.

Nineteen dances. Most published after Beethoven died. Excellent introduction to performance practices of the time.

BENDA, GEORG (1722–1795). Bohemia
Twelve Sonatinas. Edited by Richard Jones. London: Associated Board, Royal Schools, 1987.
One-movement sonatinas, in the tradition of Scarlatti, selected from 6 volumes published in 1780 and 1787. Editor's suggestions are clearly identified as such.

BERNSTEIN, SEYMOUR (b. 1927). U.S.A.
The Earth Music Series. 5 vols. Milwaukee: G. Schirmer/Hal Leonard, 1977–1984.
Book 1, 'Warbles and Flutters—An Introduction to the Trill"; book 2, "Out of the Nest—An Introduction to the Mordent"; book 3, "Early Birds—An Introduction to the Appoggiatura"; book 4, "The Pedals"; book 5, "Dragons." Isolates technical concerns and then incorporates them into imaginative pieces.

BLOCH, ERNEST (1880–1959). Switzerland, U.S.A.
Poems of the Sea. Milwaukee: G. Schirmer/Hal Leonard, 1923.
Three impressionistic pieces. Favorites with high school students.

CARAMIA, TONY (b. 1950). U.S.A.
Fascinatin' Rhythms. San Diego: Kjos West, 1985.
Six idiomatic and attractive pieces in jazz styles. (Reviewed in *PQ,* no. 136.)

CHAMINADE, CECILE (1857–1944). France
Children's Album. 2 vols.: Op. 123 and Op. 126. Paris: Enoch, 1934.
Twelve appealing pieces in each programmatic set. Elementary to intermediate.

CHILCOT, THOMAS (c. 1700–1766). England
Three Keyboard Suites. Edited by Richard Jones. London: Associated Board, Royal Schools, 1987.
Five-movement suites, edited with discretion. Easier than Bach's French Suites.

COLERIDGE-TAYLOR, SAMUEL (1875–1912). Great Britain
Four Negro Melodies Transcribed for Piano. Edited by Maurice Hinson. Chapel Hill, NC: Hinshaw, 1981.
Selected from 3 volumes of 18 melodies originally published in England. Many octaves and full chords; very pianistic. Late intermediate to early advanced.

DELLO JOIO, NORMAN (b. 1913). U.S.A.
Lyric Pieces for the Young. Milwaukee: Marks/Hal Leonard, 1971.
Six well-crafted recital pieces.

DETT, R. NATHANIEL (1882–1943). U.S.A.
The Collected Piano Works. Secaucus, NJ: Summy-Birchard/Warner Bros., 1973.

Not a complete collection, but many of the best-known compositions are included. Music is a reprint of the original plates. Foreword and biography.

DIEMER, EMMA LOU (b. 1927). U.S.A.
Sound Pictures. Farmingdale, NY: Boosey & Hawkes, 1971.
Ten intriguing pieces in which the music reflects the titles ("Clusters and Dots," "Contraction and Expansion," "Angles," "Infinity").

FINNEY, ROSS LEE (b. 1906). U.S.A.
Games. New York: C. F. Peters, 1969.
Thirty-two short pieces that challenge the mind and hands. Some new notation. Beginning to intermediate. (Reviewed in *PQ,* no. 139.)

GADE, NIELS (1817–1890). Denmark
Aquarelles and Other Pieces. Edited by Lionel Salter. London: Associated Board, Royal Schools, 1987.
Fourteen appealing pieces selected from several collections.

GEORGE, JON (1944–1982). U.S.A.
Kaleidoscope. 5 vols. Van Nuys, CA: Alfred Publishing Co., 1973, 1974
Effective pieces reflecting a variety of moods and styles. Progressive volumes. Volumes 3, 4, 5 at the intermediate level.

GILLOCK, WILLIAM (b. 1917). U.S.A.
Lyric Preludes in Romantic Style. Secaucus, NJ: Summy-Birchard/Warner Bros., 1958.
Prepares intermediate students for sound, style, and technique needed in playing romantic literature. (Reviewed in *PQ,* no. 139.)

GLIÈRE, REINHOLD (1875–1956). Russia
Twelve Sketches, Op. 47. Edited by Thomas A. Johnson. London: Associated Board, Royal Schools 1988
Pianistic writing in the grand Russian romantic tradition.

GREENE, ARTHUR (b. 1945). U.S.A.
Seven Wild Mushrooms and a Waltz. New York: Galaxy, 1976.
Intermediate pieces that expand timbral awareness. Score includes clear directions for carefully muting (preparing) a few strings.

GRETCHANINOFF, ALEXANDER (1864–1956). Russia
Glass Beads, Op. 123. Van Nuys, CA: Alfred Publishing Co., 1982.
Unchanged from the original Russian edition. Twelve short imaginative pieces. See also *A Child's Day,* Op. 109.

GRIEG, EDVARD (1843–1907). Norway
Lyric Pieces. 13 vols. New York: C. F. Peters, 1867–1901.
See Maurice Hinson's *Guide to the Pianist's Repertoire* (in appendix 3) for complete listing of titles. Character pieces. Very pianistic. Intermediate to advanced.

HELLER, STEPHEN (1813–1888). Hungary, France
Selected Progressive Etudes for the Piano. Edited by Lynn Freeman Olson.

Van Nuys, CA: Alfred Publishing Co., 1986.
Nineteenth etudes, selected from different collections and grouped by level of difficulty.

HEWITT, JAMES (1770–1827).   England, U.S.A.
The Battle of Trenton: A Favorite Historical Military Sonata Dedicated to General Washington. Edited by Maurice Hinson. Miami: CPP/Belwin, 1989. Programmatic music composed in 1797. Unique recital material.

HOPKINS, ANTONY (b. 1921).   Great Britain
For Talented Beginners. 2 vols. New York: Oxford University Press, 1963. Nineteen short pieces. Musically and pianistically gratifying, especially for adults.

KABALEVSKY, DMITRI (1903–1987).   USSR
Four Rondos, Op. 60. Milwaukee, WI: MCA/Hal Leonard, 1960. Each of these contrasting pieces offers fine music and gratifying technical study.

KAY, ULYSSES (b. 1917).   U.S.A.
Four Inventions. Milwaukee, WI: MCA/Hal Leonard, 1964. Exciting contrapuntal pieces. Late intermediate to early advanced.

KHACHATURIAN, ARAM (1903–1978).   USSR
Album for Young People. Van Nuys, CA: Alfred Publishing Co., 1978. Sometimes called "Children's Pieces." Unchanged from original Russian edition.

KIRCHNER, THEODOR (1823–1903).   Germany
New Scenes of Childhood. Op. 55. Edited by Lionel Salter. London: Associated Board, Royal Schools, 1986. Twenty-five short pieces, originally published in 1881. Polished craftmanship, in the tradition of Schumann.

KUHNAU, JOHANN (1660–1772).   Germany
Biblical Sonata No. 1: The Battle Between David and Goliath. Edited by Margery Halford. Van Nuys, CA: Alfred Publishing Co., 1976. From a set of 6 Biblical Sonatas. Foreword presents helpful background information. Editorial suggestions printed in a gray. Would make unusual recital repertoire.

KURTÁG, GYÖRGY (b. 1926).   Hungary
Játékok. Plays and Games for Piano, 4 vols. Farmingdale, NY: Editio Musica Budapest/Boosey & Hawkes, 1979. Imaginative contemporary pieces that challenge the ear and eye. For the more adventurous. Some regard this as an "updated' *Mikrokosmos."* Recording (by the composer) available from the publisher.

LAST, JOAN (b. 1908).   Great Britain
Down to the Sea. New York: Oxford University Press, 1957.

Effective with adults at early intermediate level. Uses much pedal, wide range.

MACDOWELL, EDWARD (1861–1908). U.S.A.
Eight Sea Pieces, Op. 55. Edited by Lynn Freeman Olson. Van Nuys, CA: Alfred Publishing Co., 1986.
Short, effective, programmatic pieces all of which utilize rich piano sonorities. Mid to late intermediate. See also *Fireside Tales, Woodland Sketches.*

MCCABE, JOHN (b. 1938). Great Britain
Afternoons and Afterwards. Bryn Mawr, PA: Novello/Theodore Presser, 1982.
Seven appealing contemporary pieces. From the series edited by Richard Rodney Bennett. (Reviewed in *PQ,* no. 119.)

MENDELSSOHN, FELIX (1809–1847), and FANNY MENDELSSOHN (1805–1847). Germany
At the Piano with Felix and Fanny Mendelssohn. Edited by Maurice Hinson. Van Nuys, CA: Alfred Publishing Co., 1988.
Twelve character pieces, late intermediate to advanced.

MOMPOU, FEDERICO (1893–1987). Spain
Scenes d'Enfants. Milwaukee: Salabert/Hal Leonard, 1915.
Five short pieces that call for an exploration of color.

MOSZKOWSKI, MORITZ (1854–1925). Poland
Spanish Dances, Op. 12. New York: C. F. Peters, n.d.
Five impressive virtuoso pieces. Many octaves. Late intermediate to advanced.

MOZART, WOLFGANG AMADEUS (1756–1791). Austria
Mozart: An Introduction to His Keyboard Works. Edited by Willard Palmer. Van Nuys, CA: Alfred Publishing Co., 1974.
An edition based on autographs and early sources. Editorial suggestions in light print. A valuable foreword discussing tempo, articulation, ornamentation in Mozart's music. Includes commentary, (by George Lucktenberg), on Mozart's piano.

MUCZYNSKI, ROBERT (b. 1929). U.S.A.
Diversions: Nine Pieces for Students, Op. 23. Milwaukee: G. Schirmer/Hal Leonard, 1970.
Expressive; rhythmically challenging. See also *Six Preludes for Piano* Op. 6; *Fables,* Op. 21. (Reviewed in *PQ,* no. 139.)

NAKADA, YOSHINAO (b. 1923). Japan.
Japanese Festival. Milwaukee: MCA/Hal Leonard, 1956.
Seventeen imaginative character pieces. Late elementary to intermediate. Westernized Japanese music.

PAPORISCZ, YORAM (b. 1944). Israel
Discoveries at the Piano. Vols. 1–3. New York: Broude, 1964.
Challenging and provocative. Many short sketches. Draws on divergent mu-

sical resources (e.g., Ambrosian chant, Hindu *ragas,* organum, music of Central American tribes).

PENTLAND, BARBARA (b. 1912). Canada
Studies in Line. Toronto, Canada: BMI Canada, 1949.
Four contemporary pieces that reflect various linear designs (jagged, circular, and so on).

PERSICHETTI, VINCENT (1915–1987). U.S.A.
Six Sonatinas. 2 vols. Bryn Mawr, PA: Elkan-Vogel/Theodore Presser, 1953, 1957.
Pianistic writing using neoclassical forms. See also *Little Piano Book,* Op. 60 (Elkan-Vogel/Theodore Presser, 1954). (Reviewed in *PQ,* no. 139.)

PERT, MORRIS (b. 1947). U.S.A.
Voyage in Space. Farmingdale, NY: Boosey & Hawkes, 1978.
Twenty adventurous pieces that expand horizons of sight and sound. Effective set to divide among students at various levels (elementary to late intermediate).

SCHUBERT, FRANZ (1797–1828). Austria
Moments Musicaux. Op. 94. Edited by Murray Baylor. Van Nuys, CA: Alfred Publishing Co., 1987.
Based on first complete edition (original manuscript is lost). Editorial suggestions in parentheses. Foreword with pertinent comments for each of the 6 short pieces.

SCHUMANN, ROBERT (1810–1855), and Clara Schumann (1819–1896). Germany
At The Piano with Robert and Clara Schumann. Edited by Maurice Hinson. Van Nuys, CA: Alfred Publishing Co., 1988.
Seventeen character pieces, late intermediate to advanced.

SHOSTAKOVITCH, DMITRI (1906–1975). USSR
Twenty-Four Preludes. Op. 34. Milwaukee: MCA/Hal Leonard, 1932–1933.
Challenging pieces, late intermediate to advanced. Uses same key scheme as Chopin's *Twenty-four Preludes.* Op. 28.

SLONOV, YURI. USSR
Twenty-eight Easy Pieces. Milwaukee: AMP/Hal Leonard, 1974, 1977.
Upper elementary to intermediate. From the series "Teaching Literature of the Soviet Piano School." (Reviewed in *PQ,* no. 105.)

STARER, ROBERT (b. 1924). Austria, U.S.A.
Sketches in Color. 2 vols. Milwaukee: MCA/Hal Leonard, 1964, 1973.
Seven pieces in each volume. Special favorites with many high school students. (Reviewed in *PQ,* no. 139.)

STRAVINSKY, SOULIMA (b. 1910). U.S.A.
Six Easy Sonatinas for Young Pianists. 2 vols. New York: C. F. Peters, 1967.
Twentiety-century sounds in neoclassical forms.

SVOBODA, TOMAS (b. 1940). U.S.A.
Children's Treasure Box. 4 vols. Portland, OR: Thomas Stangland 1977–1979.
Sixty short recital pieces. Beginning to intermediate. Challenging and musically gratifying. (Reviewed in *PQ,* no. 109; see also *PQ,* no. 114.)

TAKACS, JENÖ (b. 1902). Hungary
Sounds and Colors, Op. 95. Nutley. NJ: Doblinger/Foreign Music Distributors, 1977.
Require some degree of experience with aleatoric exploration. Adventurous and imaginative writing. Not especially technically difficult for the midintermediate student. Many pieces also use traditional notation.

TAILLEFERRE, GERMAINE (1892–1983). France
Fleurs de France. Paris: Lemoine, 1962
Eight short character pieces describing various places in France.

TCHAIKOWSKY, PETER ILICH (1840–1893). Russia
Album for the Young, Op. 39. Edited by Ylda Novik. Van Nuys, CA: Alfred Publishing Co., 1976.
Based on original Russian edition. A few additional editorial suggestions in light print. Gratifying miniatures.

TCHEREPNIN, ALEXANDER (1899–1977). Russia, U.S.A.
Ten Bagatelles, Op. 5. Milwaukee: G. Schirmer/Hal Leonard, 1913–1918.
Flamboyant pianism. Upper intermediate to advancing. Also effective as technical studies. (Reviewed in *PQ,* no. 139.)

TURINA, JOAQUIN (1882–1949). Spain
Danses Gitanes, Opp. 55 and 84. Milwaukee: Salabert/Hal Leonard, 1930, 1934.
Ten effective recital pieces. Dramatic range of dynamics (PPP to FFF). Late intermediate.

VILLA-LOBOS, HEITOR (1887–1959). Brazil
Guia Pratico. Eleven separate collections, 1932–35.
For specifics concerning album numbers and publishers, see Maurice Hinson's *Guide to the Pianist's Repertoire* (listed in appendix 3).

WIDNER, ERNST (b. 1927). Switzerland, Brazil
Kosmos Latinoamericano. 2 vol. Milwaukee, WI: Ricordi/Hal Leonard. 1967, 1985.
Ninety-six pieces, elementary to late intermediate, arranged progressively. In the tradition of Bartók's *Mikrokosmos.* Based on Latin American folk music. Challenging, innovative pieces that expand skills and musicianship. Several pieces incorporate improvisation. Spacious layout, very clear notation. An exciting collection.

CHAPTER 9

Technique and the Intermediate Student

Technique interests both students and teachers. Yet students and teachers do not always mean the same thing when they use the word "technique." To the student, technique means something simple and direct. "How do you do that?" "How can I make that sound?" "Show me how to play those chords." Almost always, interest in technique—from the viewpoint of the student—is related to the performance of a particular piece. The student is seeking a short-range plan. The teacher, however, frequently sees technique as a system, as a specific way of doing things, as a necessary discipline—far beyond the needs of any individual piece. So when the student asks for concrete, "right now" directions, the teacher often responds with a more long-range plan, at times involving activities that do not seem at all related to the piece at hand. Both student and teacher are realistic. Few people are eager to acquire skills unless they can see an immediate application of those skills to something they want to do. On the other hand, skill development, especially motor-skill development, often requires attention to physical generalities and consistent, careful practice of particular gestures.

Both short-range and long-range plans are necessary and important. The short-range plan is the motivator. It generates immediate action. The long-range plan is the governor. It regulates, sustains, and appraises action. Neither plan is likely to do the complete job without the other. The student and teacher want the same result: successful performance. The teacher is willing to wait awhile. The student seldom is. They each place value on technique, but have different viewpoints and time tables with regard to achieving it. How a student and teacher manage attendance to both short- and long-range goals will determine whether, and to what extent, the attainment of technical skill is successful.

Technique should always be judged in terms of sound. A good technique is not something that one sees. It is a quality one hears. "In the long run technique, like everything else, is a matter of ear-training."[1] Technique, moreover, is a means to an end, not an end in itself. It is acquired for the purpose of making music. Technique is not just a matter of velocity and power. It calls on the resources of the entire person—the imagination and the inner self, along with the posture and movements of the body.

Technique is not learned from a book. It is learned by listening to sounds made by others and by oneself. Achieving technique may, at times, be aided by looking at gestures and discussing how and why these are made. But "the full acoustic picture of the music must be lodged in the *mind,* before it can be expressed through the *hands.* . . . Playing is simply the manual expression of something [the pianist] knows."[2] Verbalizing about gesture or about particular technical skills, as in this chapter, is many times removed from the actuality of making gestures and acquiring skills.

As much as possible, this discussion of technique will seek to derive information about what specific technical skills need to be developed at the intermediate level from the literature that the intermediate student needs and wants to play. Thus it will focus on the important relationship between the playing of music and the skills necessary to do so beautifully, comfortably, and efficiently.

STANDARD TECHNICAL SKILLS

Syllabi and curricula outlining work at the intermediate level frequently suggest a list of technical skills that are considered pertinent at this stage of the student's development. Similar lists describe elementary-level technical skills. It may be useful to summarize what the majority of these lists contain, although skills itemized in such lists often are not directly related to specific repertoire, or even to particular books of technical studies.

Technical Skills that Prepare the Student for the Intermediate Level

Correct posture of the entire body in relationship to the instrument.

Correct position of the arms, wrists, and fingers (arch).

Legato and staccato playing within 5-finger position, within extension to the sixth, and with alternating hands.

Easy double-note playing (especially seconds, thirds, fifths, sixths).

Some experience of accompaniment styles (e.g., Alberti bass; waltz bass).

Triads and inversions played blocked and broken, in many ranges, both hands.

Release related to the playing of slurs, phrases.

Lateral position shifts; hand crossing.

Experience of basic dynamic range (from *piano* to *forte*).

Experience of crescendo, decresendo, ritardando, a tempo, fermata.

Use of pedal for color and effect.

Limited independence between the hands (dynamics/articulation).

Thumb crossing (thumb under, hand over).

Major scales, regular fingering, 1 or 2 octaves, hands alone (or contrary motion)

Technical Skills that the Student Develops at the Intermediate Level

Legato in extended passage playing.

Experience with finger substitution.

Varied types of staccato playing (wrist, forearm, finger).

Scales, major/minor, regular fingering, up to 4 octaves, hands alone and together.

Trills and ornamentation.

Double-note legato.

Opening of the hand to the octave; some octave playing.

Arpeggio playing, usually hands alone.

Concentrated attention to independence between hands and within the hand.

Voicing (at least of 3-note chords).

4-note chords, blocked and broken, in many ranges, both hands.

Refinement of accompaniment styles.

Rapid changes of register and texture; mobility.

More developed sense of dynamics, color, mood (style).

Syncopated pedaling; rhythmic pedaling; una corda.

Development of velocity, power, endurance, consistency.

A list of skills that need to be worked on during the intermediate years may be of some general assistance when planning a student curriculum. Yet it provides no insight as to how these numerous technical skills relate to one another or in which order they might be taught. Nor does it give any indication of how concentration on each of the skills may be associated with the student's repertoire. It sometimes happens that a teacher using a piano series during the elementary years is able to integrate the teaching of reading, technique, and musicianship with reasonable ease because the method is designed precisely to assist that integration. Textbooks are correlated with supplementary material written in such a way that all books are mutually supportive and reinforcing. As the student progresses into the intermediate years, the teacher may opt not to follow a particular series, or the series itself may not be so hand in glove at higher levels. (That is especially noticeable when looking for the interrelation between the core book of a series, usually the literature book, and that same series' technique book. The content of the technique book often appears only loosely related to that of the repertoire.) Thus the teacher and student who found all aspects of study closely knit during the first few years, and enjoyed that reinforcing mode of instruction, now find the activities of the lesson becoming compartmentalized.

The teacher, with long-range interests based on experience, is not necessarily uncomfortable with this division of labor. The student, with short-range goals related to the playing of pieces, often is. Activities that do not seem to have an immediate connection to music making get less of the student's attention. Practicing scales, exercises, and sometimes even etudes does not always help to smooth away difficulties encountered in the music the student is playing. At this point, to the student, acquiring technique may begin to look as if it is becoming an end in itself.

*R*ELATING *TECHNIQUE AND REPERTOIRE*

Teachers often assign repertoire as if they were using the "four basic food groups" approach. The curriculum must contain something Baroque, Classic, Romantic, and from the twentieth-century. The thinking behind this approach seems rooted in the belief that learning certain keyboard skills is best done in association with, and by means of, playing in particular historic styles.

The hidden agenda for playing Baroque music is to develop independence between two lines (hands), the articulation of short slurs, and the projection of line and color without the use of pedal. Music from the Classic period furnishes multiple opportunities to achieve the niceties of balancing melody and accompaniment (the hallmark of homophonic playing), of exhibiting clean scale and arpeggio passage-work, and of using the pedal as if one "used it not." Romantic (nineteenth-century) keyboard literature is the ideal milieu in which to extend one's hand position, become sensitive to voicing, revel in bravura effects, and rely on the pedal to produce color and resonance. Music of the twentieth-century requires mobility (frequent change of texture and range), an appreciation of freedom (of meter, pitch and rhythm choices, improvisatory moments), the development of new hand shapes (seconds, fourths, sevenths, clusters), and treatment of the keyboard as a percussion instrument. There is some truth in these statements, of course, but they are too often taken as the *whole* truth.

The examination below—of intermediate literature from the standpoint of the technical skills necessary to perform it successfully—may lead, if not to surprises, at least to some less hackneyed observations. Technical training should focus as much on comprehensive areas of development as on separate details. There are three principal areas of technical development: independence, mobility, and tonal control. The skills itemized earlier on the general list will be included in these three broad categories, but should seem less disconnected (either to other specific skills or to the repertoire) once placed in perspective.

(See Appendix 3 for examples relating intermediate literature from all periods and styles to each area of technical development.)

---

*I*NDEPENDENCE

Independence must be achieved in many areas. Because it is manifest in such a variety of contexts, it will be easy for the teacher and student to keep attention focused on the development of independence without frustration or boredom. It is necessary that the listening, as well as the playing, apparatus be trained to distinguish and appreciate independence. If the student cannot *hear* a difference, it is unlikely that his/her efforts to produce a difference will be successful or persevering.

Independence of the Single Hand

An often-overlooked way of making the student aware of what each hand can do is to assign a few pieces written for a single hand. In most cases, pieces of this kind are reserved only for those times when accidents necessitate their use. Every student, at some time, should find out what the single hand is capable of producing. In choosing music for the single hand, the teacher should notice whether the piece is intended for a specific single hand or whether it is written so that either hand may play it. Even when the piece is designated for either hand, the teacher should play through the music to determine if the music really lies well for either hand. At times that is not the case, despite the playing directions. It may be wise to assign pieces for the dominant hand first, so that the student's initial one-hand experience is approached with confidence. The greater necessity, of course, is to challenge the nondominant hand. (For most pianists, that will be the left hand—even with pianists who otherwise are left-handed.) Pieces written for a single hand may help to develop a sense of melody playing, a feel for the difference in weight needed to play in varied registers, an ability to play melody and accompaniment with the same hand, and a keener awareness of pedaling. The student often regards playing with a single hand as a challenge that is both fun and rewarding.

Playing Two Independent Lines

Although many teachers regard the *Anna Magdalena Bach Notebook* as a chief source of music for two-line playing, it is fascinating to note how much music from other style periods also falls into this category. It may help to begin concentration on two-line playing by assigning pieces that have antiphonal, changing-hands effects rather than consistent hands-together playing. Two-part writing that outlines chords may create non-linear-sounding pieces. The need for independence may focus on dynamics, rhythm, articulations, or on all of these combined. It is not necessary to find a book or collection of pieces that fits this category so much as it is important to develop an awareness of how much music is written using only, or nearly only, two-voice texture.

Independence of Dynamics and Articulation

Although most keyboard music requires some attention to the use of different dynamics in each hand, there are certain pieces in which the careful balance of dynamics is the most important aspect. All melody and accompaniment pieces fall into this category. The Classic period is replete with examples of homophonic music in which the hands need to operate on separate dynamic planes. But music from any style period reflects the use of homophony and demands the same balancing skills. Part of the difficulty in learning to handle an accompaniment may be determined by the texture of that part. Playing an Alberti bass requires a different technique than the performance of an extended árpeggio figure. A waltz accompaniment must have a life of its own, not to mention the use of a very discreet pedal. More-dissonant writing in twentieth-century music is not musical when played insensitively. Often this means altering the color of one voice in favor of the other. The pianist who cannot balance dynamic levels is in jeopardy.

In most cases, the projection of melody in relationship to accompaniment is also a matter of maintaining separate articulation. The melodic line depends upon a finger legato or creating the semblance of one (which may be more difficult). Long notes in the melody must keep sounding over changes in the accompaniment and maintain their dynamic connection to the next melody note. At the same time, the accompanying part may be technically fussy in its own right, change textures, require register adjustments, or combine all of these features. "Independence" takes on added meaning. Separate dynamics may be the least of the problem.

Independence Within the Hand: Voicing

Independence within the hand might refer to a number things: observing different note lengths, playing different articulations, using finger substitution, and voicing particular notes or lines. Learning to voice, however, is the technical skill that most often goes unattended until the student is playing advanced music. If that skill is developed gradually the student learns to cope with each type of voicing situation in turn. It may be best to begin with learning to voice the thumb side of the hand since that finger already has a propensity to overproject. Voicing thumb notes is easiest to do when playing broken-chord passages, but it must also be developed in simultaneous chord playing. Another way to approach learning to voice may be to use pieces that allow one finger to sustain a note while the same hand plays softer notes (with other fingers) on different beats. The hand can then develop a feel for more weight on one side of the hand, less on the other. The pianist's ultimate problem, however, is learning to project the weak fingers of both hands since these fingers are responsible for the projection of the bass line (the harmonic foundation for music in most styles) and the upper line (which is frequently the melody and which must also be played on the shortest strings of the piano). Learning to voice is a challenge, but voicing is a technical skill that separates the merely competent from the artistic performer.

Independence of Expression: Freedom to Make Choices

Many keyboard performers are experimenters and improvisers as well as re-creators. In each stylistic era, players have found ways to express themselves directly—through improvising—or to vary what the composer wrote or suggested—through ornamenting, harmonizing, and rearranging. In certain kinds of performance, adding something original to the score was, and still is, expected (e.g., continuo, harpsichord, and jazz playing.) Although twentieth-century composers seem to be those making new demands on the performer, inviting improvisation and decision making in various degrees, composers have always done so. Part of a keyboard player's education ought to include some experience in actively participating in the creative process "alongside" the composer.

In many ways, this kind of ornamenting and improvising is related to technique. The speed, length, and dynamic control of a trill, for example, are directly dependent upon what the fingers can do. Whether a player adds few, some, or many ornaments may also be conditioned by technical agility. A cadenza (originally a matter of improvisation) is exciting because of the technical display. Getting one's fingers ready to be free is another reason for polishing one's technique.

The intermediate student is at just the right place to begin combining freedom of expression and technical dexterity: Baroque literature introduces embellishment shorthand; an early concerto will include a cadenza; nineteenth-century repertoire contains written-in ornamentation; twentieth-century notation is sometimes graphic symbolism of what may be done at liberty. Learning to trill can be exciting as well as necessary. When playing by ear or improvising, a player often uncovers latent technique. Faced with unmeasured music, a young performer may stretch to unsuspected levels of expression. Encouraging some keyboard display may awaken dormant fingers as well as instincts.

MOBILITY

The elementary student has generally spent at least a year playing in specific areas of the keyboard. While these registers may have shifted from piece to piece, the music did not often require many position changes (at least quick ones) within pieces. The intermediate student, however, must learn to make many kinds of rapid moves necessitating adjustments of the entire body as well as of the hands and fingers. The development of finger velocity is sometimes the only aspect of mobility that is given attention at this time. The making of quick chord, register, and texture changes either goes unremarked or is taken for granted.

The intermediate student who is a child is also undergoing particular growth spurts during this period, many of which are themselves unsettling or temporarily uncomfortable. Yet it is precisely this physical growth that enables the young student to begin to fit the instrument in ways that were impossible during the elementary years. The hands grow, the torso and arms lengthen, the use of finer motor skills becomes easier. The technical regimen must take all of these things into consideration.

Velocity

The hands and fingers of the elementary-level pianist have already learned to make certain movements. Much of the time, however, these movements were made with deliberation rather than with rapidity and precision. Part of the excitement of technique-building during the intermediate years is generating speed in the making of these already familiar movements. That, in itself, provides satisfaction. The intermediate student realizes that there is something to build on. Playing "fast" is probably what the student most wants to do.

The first matter of technical concern in the process of developing velocity may be to curb the impulse for speed—or, at least, to regulate it in keeping with what the student is able to do with consistency and control. Scale playing, for example, depends upon the ability to perform five-finger patterns with independence and clarity and to maneuver crossings with efficient and proper gestures. Playing scales before these techniques are well under way often leads to the formation of physical habits that eventually result in tension as well as inaccuracy. Repeatedly both teacher and student must confront the paradox that speed cannot be developed by practicing slowly, and yet practicing slowly (or slowly enough) is one of the safer ways to ensure that listening as well as playing habits remain alert and conscientious.

Scale playing, however, will not provide all the preparatory drill necessary for the development of finger and hand mobility. Attention must also be directed to clarity in arpeggio passages, coordination between alternating hands, speed when playing staccato (as well as legato), and the rapid motions that comprise trills, turns, and other ornaments. Each of these skills must be cultivated in order that the student be able to explore a wide assortment of literature.

Quick Chord Changes

Rapid chord changes (except those involving parallel motion of static hand shapes) demand multiple kinesthetic adjustments. Even the playing of chromatic major triads requires constant refiguration of the hand to fit the varying combinations of white and black keys. Hand shapes involved in moving through chord inversions necessitate adjustments for differing intervallic distances in addition to the white-and-black-key configurations. Practicing chord-change moves does not necessarily require pieces in which the moves themselves must be done at a quick tempo. In the beginning it may be enough that the moves require constant, or near constant, hand-shape alterations. The hand must learn to make efficient moves, adjusting to playing nearer the fallboard or to spending less time moving through the air.

As the hand expands to playing four-note chords, the complexities involving hand-shape adjustments increase. But literature seldom contains consecutive series of four-note chords. More likely the texture of the writing will shift, using chords of varied sizes. Playing chorale-style music presents the most difficult challenge, even though the four-note harmony is divided between the hands. When a student has difficulty with pieces requiring considerable chord changes it is important for the instructor to ascertain the nature of the problem before attempting to determine practice procedures that might solve it. A student may be reading reasonably well but the hands have not achieved a vocabulary of ready chord shapes. It is also possible that the hands can find their way around, but the student's reading habits are undisciplined.

Quick Changes of Register and Texture

Much of the excitement in playing the keyboard derives from having so many pitches at one's disposal and so many registers to explore, each with its own sonority and timbre. Composers often exploit these keyboard assets by writing music that juxtaposes or combines different registers for purposes of drama, color, or humor. The student pianist must become comfortable with using the entire body to make all the registers of the keyboard equally available. This requires attention to the pianist's total posture as well as to the positioning of the feet. The intermediate pianist, especially one who is growing physically, is often eager to test out some of the new possibilities.

Texture often changes when the register shifts. A texture that sounds effective in one area of the keyboard may be blurred or insufficient in another. At the upper end, pitches within thicker chords may be heard distinctly. Pitches within dense chords played at the low end are difficult to distinguish. Single low pitches reverberate easily. Single high pitches may sound harsh or colorless. In all these situations, the pianist's technical approach must be adjusted to what the keyboard is best able to do. Some students have a natural inclination to regard the lower sounds as those requiring force and energy, perhaps because they seem to represent power. Conversely, the same students frequently play too softly at the upper end, not realizing the relationship between higher pitches and shorter strings and the effort it takes to produce a sound at that register. It may take some time before the less-experienced pianist fully understands that to play an even-sounding scale from the bottom to the top of the keyboard, one must feel as if one is making a crescendo.

Students have a natural curiosity to explore the extremities of the instrument. Make sure they have some pieces in which to do so. Provide, as well, literature that demands moves from the keyboard bottom to the top and back. Making these larger movements may free the body to loosen the arms and to approach the keyboard with the weight of the entire upper torso. Guide the student in exploring the manipulations of the hands when they must adjust to playing on top of, over, or under one another.

TONAL CONTROL

The ability to make many different kinds of sound is at the heart of communicative performance. Developing that ability is the reason to strive for technical control. Working at technique should include an exploration of a wide spectrum of sonorities and the means to achieve these. Doing so is perhaps best achieved by stimulating the imaginative and listening capacities of the student rather than by isolating and explaining specific techniques of tonal production. It is important that the intermediate pianist develop a sense of self at the keyboard, since the emergence of self is becoming so much a focus elsewhere in the student's life at this particular time.

The student's imagination is more likely to be aroused if the repertoire expects and allows the student to be dramatic, expressive, and indulge in a bit of fantasy. Learning to play colorfully is not a matter of learning to play loudly or softly, to place accents here or crescendos there, to direct weight from the shoulders or to capitalize on a loose and rotating wrist. Becoming an expressive pianist won't happen until the pianist first desires to *be* expressive. At that point, it may be possible to discuss dynamics, articulations, or physical gestures in light of what motivates the student to make certain sounds or play in certain ways. For the intermediate pianist, the piece itself may be the key stimulus.

Developing a Sense of Drama and Style

What type of piece is likely to excite the student's interest in playing it with a sense of drive, abandon, vigor, or finesse? Most of the time, it will be a piece in which contrast is an obvious feature, in which the opening sounds are arresting, and in which the technical requirements are achievable without undue struggle. Contrast need not be overt. It may exist in the balance between hands as much as in the balance between ranges. The opening sounds are important. (Every successful composer knows this.) The first musical gesture must convey *meaning* and the sense that something is going to happen. If the first measures of any piece are technically accessible to the pianist, it is likely that subsequent measures (despite their difficulties) will be attempted, if not always perfected.

Certain musical gestures are inherently dramatic: a contrary-motion line; the use of keyboard extremities; intense rhythmic propulsion; dissonance; the familiar combined with the unexpected. The intermediate student must hear, as well as see, these musical events. An instructor's performance, or that of a fellow student (in a class or recital appearance), a concert, or a recording is more likely to be compelling motivation than an assignment. An aural art must be communicated through aural, not visual, stimuli.

Balancing Dynamics Throughout the Keyboard Range

A pianistic bugbear is the creation of enough sound on a long, high pitch to carry it through to the next melody note. Learning to listen for, and work with, the piano's natural decay demands attention of the highest order. The intermediate student must discover that playing softly, yet with tonal penetration, requires great concentration and calculation. Having learned how to do this at one instrument only to find that, at another, the weight and balance has to be readjusted may be frustrating as well as challenging. ("It sounded wonderful at home!") Further, the long, high melody note frequently must soar over an involved left-hand accompaniment written in the rich, lower registers. Creating enough depth at one end of the keyboard, but not too much at the other, may make the pianist feel as if (s)he needs to be a divided person. Developing this kind of kinesthetic sensitivity cannot be accomplished if the pianist is not listening or is not aware of whether the balance is successful or not. The ears need as much training as the fingers, arms, and feet.

Exploring Colors with Fingers and Feet

Too often the pianist plays no music that requires softer attacks, the overlapping of textures, or discreet pedaling until the assignment of the first Debussy prelude (probably "La fille aux cheveux de lin"). There is no reason to wait that long to introduce a student to these most natural, and highly effective, uses of the piano's special resources. Even in the elementary years, the student should be encouraged to *stroke* as well as *strike* the keys and to use the pedal as a means of achieving color.

It is valuable for the student to learn what the una corda pedal truly does, to experiment with projecting certain pitches over a wash of others, to enjoy the build-up of different sonorities, to create sounds that ping and ring as well as sing. Stimulating the student's ear and imagination should precede any discussion of the how-to's.

A FINAL COMMENT

The foregoing approach suggests one means by which a technical curriculum may be incorporated within a repertoire plan. Looking at repertoire with a fresh eye may enable the teacher to find ways in which to satisfy the immediate interests of the student (the short-range plan) without sacrificing the planned development of particular, or general, skills (the long-range plan). Working at technique may then become more meaningful to the student and more gratifying to the teacher.

CHAPTER 10

Functional Skills and the Intermediate Student

Most of today's beginning keyboard methods present an assortment of materials that produce a comprehensive musician. In addition to developing repertoire and technical skills, students learn to improvise, harmonize, analyze, and transpose. Acquiring these functional skills helps to produce a musician as well as a pianist. Unfortunately, this aspect of the student's training may end with the completion of the early method and theory books.

Keyboard study at the intermediate level tends to focus on acquisition of a facile technique and development of a wide variety of repertoire from various stylistic periods. It is tempting to devote more and more lesson time to improving technique and polishing pieces. Development of comprehensive musicianship skills may become a low priority. Yet the teacher must be aware of the importance of continued development of functional skills and must see to it that these other avenues of musical growth are not neglected.

When discussing intermediate-level students, the image of a junior high or high school student who has had several years of study usually comes to mind. Indeed this is the age of most intermediate students in the typical independent studio. However, many adults studying piano are also intermediate-level students. This group includes adults who studied piano as children and are returning to keyboard study at a later age for relaxation and enjoyment. They usually perform intermediate-level repertoire and enjoy exploring functional skills as a way of understanding what they are playing. Materials published for this group are readily available, as most adult methods contain diverse and interesting activities to promote musical understanding and develop functional skills.

At the collegiate level, keyboard classes for non-keyboard music majors are geared to cultivating functional skills at the intermediate level. Students whose major instrument is something other than piano have broad music-theory and music-history backgrounds and can progress rapidly. The primary goal of such classes is to give these students skills that will allow them to perform at the piano in practical situations and to use the piano as a teaching or reading tool. It is generally agreed that extended work with sight-reading, improvising, harmonizing, score reading, and accompanying aids greatly in achieving this goal.

HISTORICAL PERSPECTIVE

Keyboard players in the Baroque era were expected to become proficient with a variety of functional skills. We know from treatises of the period that keyboardists were required to realize a score that consisted of a melody line and figured-bass symbols. From this skeleton, an entire composition (often an accompaniment) was created—a practice that began as a means of accompanying singers who sang from part books. Historical accounts of performance practice of the day deal in great detail with melodic embellishment, including the use of ornaments such as the trill, turn, appoggiatura, mordent, slide, and snap as well as with the elaboration of the fermata (a predecessor of the cadenza). The highest improvisatory form was the creation of a complete piece of music. Many Baroque musicians, including Buxtehude, Händel, Sweelinck, Frescobaldi, and J. S. Bach, were renowed for this skill, as were performers in the Classical era. Published accounts of the improvisational skills of Mozart, Clementi, and Beethoven are well documented. Audiences looked forward to attending events in which improvisation (occasionally even in a contestlike atmosphere) was a feature.

The practice of cadenza improvisation grew from a small amount of elaboration (in the Baroque period) to extended display (in the Classical period). Although intended to be a vehicle whereby performers could demonstrate development of thematic motives in an improvisatory situation (particularly when composer and performer were the same person), soloists (especially those other than the composer) began to use the cadenza as a means of personal expression, often to showcase the performer's virtuoso prowess. The idea of composer and performer as two separate people, each with individual specialties, evolved throughout the nineteenth century, even though composers/performers such as Chopin, Liszt, Czerny, Mendelssohn, and Hummel continued to improvise in public.

By the beginning of the twentieth century, the practice of public improvisation had declined significantly and it has remained comparatively dormant throughout most of this century (with some allowance for improvisation by organists as part of the church service and the improvisatory freedoms expected in the performance of certain aleatoric compositions). Jazz is the primary exception to this rule, and the widespread popularity of this idiom attests to the fact that there is renewed interest—on the part of both listener and performer—in the development of improvisational skills.

Today, the traditionally trained pianist usually relies on the printed score for performance information. Any improvisation or demonstration of skills related to embellishment or harmonization must be carefully prepared in advance or is embarked upon with a certain degree of reticence or sense of inferiority. On the other hand, keyboardists in the commercial world, who often read little or no music, rely heavily on "natural" or improvisatory skills to form the substance of public performance. Some of this is facilitated by recent technology. Manipulation of sounds and effects (with MIDI keyboards, synthesizers, sequencers, and the like) facilitates the creation of original musical material, whether in advance or on the spot. The composer and the performer are once again becoming a single person. This may be signaling a transitional era for musicians, one in which the acquisition of certain kinds of functional skills will be paramount.

STANDARD FUNCTIONAL SKILLS

Many keyboard methods and audition syllabi outline specific functional skills appropriate to the development of the elementary pianist. There are fewer such lists at the intermediate level. A brief inventory of functional skills to teach at elementary and intermediate levels may be useful.

Functional Skills for the Elementary Pianist

Sight-read simple repertoire containing concepts studied in the method.

Improvise simple melodies using black keys, 5-finger patterns, or scales as the teacher provides an accompaniment.

Transpose simple melodies and pieces to closely related keys.

Harmonize melodies with primary chords using simple accompaniment styles.

Improvise melodies and simple accompaniments using a question and answer phrase structure.

Play chord progressions that use primary triads in major and minor keys.

Functional Skills for the Intermediate Pianist

Sight-read repertoire and accompaniments beyond the elementary level.

Transpose repertoire and simple accompaniments to closely related keys.

Improvise short examples in the style of composers from various historical periods.

Improvise short examples based on informal idioms (pop, rock, jazz, folk) and twentieth-century idioms.

Improvise melodies from given chord symbols.

Create musical examples that require the use of sequence.

Play chord progressions using secondary chords and secondary dominants in major and minor keys.

Harmonize melodies with secondary chords and secondary dominants using simple accompaniment style.

Create second parts to solo piano repertoire based on analysis of theoretical concepts.

SUCCESS IN TEACHING FUNCTIONAL SKILLS

No matter how or in what lesson format functional skills are studied, they should not be taught in isolation. Relating these skills to theory, technique, and repertoire will ensure that they will not be forgotten. In addition, such knowledge and skill aids in learning, understanding, memorizing, and performing repertoire.

Activities to develop functional skills must be structured to ensure student success. If a proper framework is not provided, the student may lack a sense of direction and feel unsuccessful with activities in which the music is not completely notated. All creative activities should be based on musical concepts that the student has studied or is currently studying. A student can best demonstrate an understanding of a concept by applying it to a new situation.

An understanding of musical concepts, theoretical structures, and musical terms is necessary for successful work in the creative arena. This knowledge should be systematically based upon, and expanded beyond, concepts studied in the elementary years. By the end of the intermediate years, students should have a thorough, practical grasp of the following musical and theoretical concepts:

Major and minor scales.

Major and minor key signatures.

Intervals.

Triads of the key in major and minor.

Chord progressions using primary and secondary triads, secondary dominants in major and minor keys.

5 types of seventh chords.

Modes.

Musical styles (Baroque, Classical, Romantic, contemporary, informal).

The successful teacher will base all functional-skills instruction on these concepts. Ideas for teaching specific functional skills follow.

Teaching Sight-reading

Many beginning methods provide sight-reading material that is correlated at each level. This structured reinforcement of reading skills at the elementary level is often neglected in the intermediate years. Intermediate students will sight-read a new repertoire piece, but rarely are they assigned material specifically for sight-reading.

Sight-reading should be incorporated into the lesson time and assigned for home practice. Examples used should be short. Sight-reading assignments that contain several examples to read each day at home can be part of the regular practice time. Obviously a student can only sight-read an example one time. But continued exposure to the same example helps the student recognize chord progressions, interval shapes, and sequential patterns that aid the reading process.

There are four basic types of sight-reading material. Short examples that reinforce specific theoretical and technical concepts are the first type. Many such examples are provided by today's educational composers and contained in separate sight-reading books or in college class piano texts. A second source of sight-reading material is standard repertoire by composers from various style periods. This repertoire should be easier than the student's current performance repertoire. The reading of such material is also a valuable study of musical style. Hymns and chorales provide a third source of sight-reading exercises. These often prove more difficult than they look. Students may begin by reading single lines before attempting to combine the reading of two or more voices.

Finally, ensemble music is fun to sight-read and can be done at a private lesson with the teacher or at a group lesson with other students. Sight-reading ensemble music forces the student to continue playing when a mistake is made and reinforces the idea of a steady tempo. The intermediate student who accompanies vocalists, instrumentalists, and singing groups is exposed to another valuable type of sight-reading and ensemble experience.

Teaching Harmonization

Harmonizing involves creating an accompaniment for a notated melody or a melody recognized by ear. Prior to harmonizing melodies, students should have played chord progressions involving the chords to be used in the harmonization exercises. At the intermediate level, students should harmonize melodies that have no chord symbols given as well as melodies provided with letter symbols, Roman numerals, or both. When no symbols are given, the choice of chords that a student may use should be limited so that the student may be successful. In either case, the student uses existing knowledge, applying it to performance at the keyboard. By the end of the intermediate years of study, students should have harmonized melodies using primary and secondary triads in major and minor as well as secondary dominants.

Harmonization should also occur in modes other than major and minor.

In modal harmonization, chord symbols should be supplied together with the melody. An excellent assignment for intermediate students is to harmonize a familiar melody with suggested chords in Ionian (major), Dorian, Phrygian, Lydian, Mixolydian, and Aeolian (natural minor) modes. This provides experience with modal patterns, harmonies and chord progressions.

Continued work with harmonization reinforces the study of key signatures, triad structures, and chord progressions. It engages the ear in discriminating between appropriate and inappropriate chords as well as in choosing an accompaniment to fit the style of the piece.

Teaching Transposition

Most pianists who study throughout the intermediate years are asked to serve as vocal or instrumental accompanists. Not only are accompanists required to be proficient at sight-reading, but often they are requested to transpose pieces to other keys. Most methods begin the basics of transposition during the early years. These experiences usually involve transposing single-line melodies within the five-finger pattern, and gradually the range expands to include the entire scale. Transposition of chord structures, with emphasis on the recognition of chord shapes, provides further experience for the understanding of key and modality, which, in turn, aids in transposing quickly and securely.

Practice of transposition should be continued during the intermediate years. It is not always necessary to transpose an entire piece to give the student an experience with the principles of transposition. Short excerpts from vocal or instrumental accompaniments as well as from solo repertoire are appropriate transposition exercises. In studying transposition, students learn to read by interval as well as to analyze harmonically at sight.

Teaching Improvisation

Creative activities and improvisation aid in the development of listening skills and serve to synthesize the students' knowledge of other functional skills. Students who improvise well are able to consolidate concepts that have been learned and demonstrate these at the keyboard. The ear determines successful work in these areas. Most beginning methods tend to neglect the systematic development of the ear that is necessary for developing improvisational skills. Until recent years there have been no published ear-training materials for young students. This is now being addressed in both written formats and with computer programs. The careful listening required to be a successful improviser also sharpens the listening skills used in performance.

Improvisation is a form of spontaneous composition that requires the student to put musical concepts to instant use. Creating a melody from specific patterns or scales while the teacher supplies an accompaniment can be one of the easier types of improvisation. By means of the accompaniment, the teacher sets the tempo, mood, and style. The student begins to improvise only after listening to what has been established. Before the student begins, certain guidelines (e.g., beginning and ending pitches) should be determined. Phrase and rhythmic development is a primary consideration in melodic improvisation, and evaluation of success in these areas is an effective way to judge the activity.

A second type of melodic improvisation involves giving the student a chord progression over which a melody is to be improvised. The student creates a left-hand accompaniment from the progression while improvising a melody in the right. Some students feel more comfortable if specific rhythm patterns are recommended. The teacher may also suggest the use of sequential melodic ideas.

The creation of a theme and variations, by a single student or a group of students, may also synthesize many creative and improvisational techniques. Prior to creating the piece, the student(s) should listen to theme and variation examples from literature, possibly even from varied style periods, to gain insight into what variational devices composers use. The melody chosen for a student theme and variation should be short and harmonically simple, giving the student greater freedom to manipulate the musical materials. Although it is not always necessary to notate the variations, some students may find this procedure helpful.

Creation of a theme and variations may be extended over a study period of several months by having the student prepare one variation every three to four weeks using a different and specific musical variation technique. The list that follows illustrates some typical variation assignments.

Improvise a new melody over the original harmony of the chosen theme.

Change the key, or mode, or both, of the piece. Adapt the accompaniment appropriately.

Change the meter. Adapt the accompaniment to fit the meter.

Harmonize the melody with seventh chords to give a feeling of jazz style.

Accompany the melody with an Alberti bass to give the feeling of Classical style.

Create a ragtime style by using an extended jump bass accompaniment and a syncopated melodic line.

Accompany the melody with a boogie-woogie bass.

Play the melody using octave displacement.

Accompany the melody with quartal harmonies.

Numerous other techniques are possible. These are limited only by the imagination of the student and by his/her understanding of the musical concepts necessary to create musical and formal differences.

RELATING FUNCTIONAL SKILLS TO REPERTOIRE AND TECHNIQUE

All functional skills that relate to the student's performance repertoire will also aid the learning process and ensure more in-depth understanding of that literature. Some direct ways to encourage this correlation include improvisation in the style of a composer and creation of a second piano part for a solo repertoire piece.

Improvising in imitation of a particular composer requires knowledge of the stylistic period in which the composer wrote as well as some awareness of the composer's own music. The student is first given excerpts from works by the composer and asked to complete them in a similar style. The excerpts should be typical of that composer's melodic and harmonic style. Early examples should be no more than four measures long, with the student improvising an additional four measures. Suggested harmonies may be supplied to ensure stylistic appropriateness.

Creating a second part to a piece may serve as a source of student motivation as well as demonstrate the student's understanding of theoretical concepts. In a sense, the student becomes involved in the composition process by first analyzing the harmonies in the original work. The student then creates a two-hand accompaniment based on these harmonies to accompany the performances of the solo by another student or the teacher. The original solo and the created second part may even become an effective recital ensemble.

Teachers should not overlook informal and twentieth-century idioms as stimulating and important sources for the development of functional skills in the intermediate years. Many of these allow the student to stylize the performance according to personal tastes and interests.

CHALLENGES IN TEACHING FUNCTIONAL SKILLS

Teaching functional skills to intermediate pianists has its challenges. A frequently raised issue is the matter of lesson time available for these activities. Time must be set aside consistently to focus on this area. This might be accomplished by extending the lesson time from the traditional half-hour format to forty-five minutes or one hour. Attention to functional skills can also be part of monthly group lessons or musicianship classes. For this second plan to be effective, careful follow-up of concepts covered in these classes must take place at the private lesson. Ideally, experiences with functional skills should constitute an important segment of a separate weekly group lesson.

Keyboard and computer technology may also aid in the development of functional skills. Students may be assigned specific projects to complete on electronic keyboards that have sequencers (e.g., melody, accompaniment, and percussion background can be recorded by the student on separate tracks). This allows sight-reading, ensemble, and improvisation to occur with minimal time taken away from the regular lesson. Since most electronic keyboards can be used with earphones, lesson times may be overlapped to save instructional time and to ensure the inclusion of such activities. Computer instruction may provide reinforcement and drills. Improvised examples may be notated with a computer. Special summer programs can also be designed to explore these and other creative avenues.

Obtaining appropriate materials for teaching functional skills may be another challenge. An abundance of such material exists at the elementary level. At the intermediate level the amount of material is more limited. Teachers are well aware that students who discontinue piano study often do so at the end of the elementary or the beginning of the intermediate years. Consequently publishers regard the production of a great variety of intermediate-level material as a financial risk. Teachers wishing to incorporate the teaching of functional skills at the intermediate level, therefore, may have to create their own materials or gather these from a variety of sources. In addition to the limited number of publications providing functional-skills activities and experiences at the intermediate level, second-year college class piano texts for non-keyboard music majors are an excellent source of this kind of material.

A third challenge is often personal. Teachers sometimes feel that they themselves have not been adequately prepared as "functional" pianists and are hesitant to teach what they cannot do. While no single solution can resolve each teacher's concern, it must be noted that current piano pedagogy classes are addressing this issue in teacher education. Students who graduate from today's piano pedagogy programs usually feel equipped to demonstrate and teach a variety of functional skills, including those specific to intermediate levels of instruction. In-service teachers may avail themselves of opportunities to participate in workshops, seminars, and continuing education programs that offer practical, hands-on experiences in functional skills areas.

CONCLUSIONS

Attention to functional skills at the intermediate level has the potential to save a drop-out, lay the foundation for one of tomorrow's musicians, or sow the seeds for a lifetime of musical enjoyment. It is the teacher's responsibility to ensure that each student is musically literate and able to function at the keyboard. When this happens, both student and teacher find fulfillment and satisfaction.

It is provocative to speculate on just which functional skills the twenty-first-century musician will need. Keyboard and computer technology may alter the focus of musicianship considerably. Will tomorrow's musician need to know how to transpose? (The transposition button on most electronic keyboards easily takes care of that.) Will tomorrow's musician need to be able to notate music? (The computer has the capability of printing out music played into a synthesizer or digital piano through MIDI.) Will tomorrow's musician need to develop accompaniment skills? (The sequencer is able to record and orchestrate accompaniments with sophistication and ease.) Similar questions and others will arise about the interrelationship of performance, functional skills, and electronic technology. It seems certain, however, that musicians will always need to be able to evaluate musical activities, whether these are performed by the individual or with the aid of equipment. That will always be a matter of developing discretion. The "well-tempered" teacher will forever be at the heart of this process.

CHAPTER I I

The Transfer Student

All keyboard teachers accept students who are transferring from another teacher's studio. This change affects both the accepting teacher and the student who is transferring. Even in cases where the new teacher may be using the same teaching materials and strategies as the former teacher, the change is still one of personalities and environment. If the accepting teacher does not use the same or similar materials and strategies, the change is even more pronounced. The accepting teacher, therefore, must first attend to these aspects of change before assuming that instruction may move forward without difficulty or misunderstanding.

Matters affecting change are evident in four processes, each of which is determined by the accepting teacher:

Responding to the request for acceptance into the new studio.

Diagnosing the new student's musical skills and knowledge.

Resolving problems relating to any inadequacies the teacher perceives in the new student.

Integrating instructional activities in a manner that is both effective and encouraging.

RESPONDING TO THE INITIAL REQUEST

When a student who has studied elsewhere requests acceptance into a new studio, it is important for the teacher who has been approached to know why the change is taking place. Many reasons might impel a student to seek a change of instructor.

235

A teacher, sometimes much loved, has moved, ceased teaching, or died.
The search is for someone who in some way resembles the former teacher.

The student has moved.
Many changes affect this student, not only the change of music teacher.

The student and the teacher did not get along.
The search is for a teacher who is different from the former teacher.

The parent is unhappy with the teacher, but the student is not.
Differences between parent and student must be resolved.

The teacher is not teaching something that a student or parent believes should be taught.
The search is for a teacher who fills a particular need.

The teacher has taught the student to the extent of the teacher's own abilities.
The search is for a more professionally competent teacher.

The teacher lacks professional connections or a reputation for teaching winners.
The student and/or parent is (correctly or incorrectly) ambitious.

The teacher feels that the student now "needs someone else."
The student may share this belief or, contrarily, feel pushed.

The list could easily be extended. It should be apparent that, whatever the motivation for seeking a change of teacher, that motivation affects the student's perception of the potential new instructor. If the new instructor is unaware of the issues involved in such a causal relationship, personal (as well as educational) frustrations may arise.

When approached by a new student (or that student's parent), a teacher should make no promises or statements of acceptance until *after* an interview has taken place. A reasonable fee should be charged for such an interview. If the interview is to be thorough, the teacher will need to schedule a decent interval of time, perhaps half an hour or more. A teacher should be compensated for interview and consultation time, as would any other professional. Furthermore, an interview is a two-way communication, one that benefits the student as much as the teacher. It may be that, at the conclusion of the interview, the *student* may decide not to pursue instruction in a particular studio. Decision making, on the part of both teacher and student, should be postponed until after the interview. That fact should be made clear when arranging the interview.

The interview

The interview must include activities that enable the teacher to assess the student's reading and rhythmic ability, general knowledge about music, practice habits, ear, attitudes, learning propensities, and readiness to follow instructions. Too often an interview merely involves listening to the student play self-chosen pieces in a setting that is frequently more social than professional. Some details pertinent to the interview of a transfer student have already been addressed in chapter 2.[1] More specific suggestions follow.

Make clear when arranging for the interview that the student will be expected to play some pieces already learned, demonstrate other technical and musical skills, or both. Ask the student to bring along music that is currently being studied and a repertoire list of books and pieces already completed. Although this list will be no indication of how well pieces have been performed or how securely musical concepts have been learned, such a list does offer an overview of materials to which the student has been exposed.

The interview should begin promptly, at the time arranged. This immediately signifies that the teacher values his/her own time and that of the student. It gives notice that future lessons will also be on time. Do not give the impression that the interview is interrupting one's schedule or is being sandwiched in among other, even professional, activities. If the student arrives late, do not extend the interview beyond the time allotted. If the student's arrival time is unduly late, firmly (but cordially) reschedule the interview. This manner of handling the student's tardiness sets a precedent for acceptable behavior on the part of the student and signifies that studio policy is seriously applied.

Although it is important to be friendly and personal at the outset of the interview, do not spend too much time in conversation. Move as quickly as possible to musical matters. The parent especially may want to offer a history of what has taken place during past musical instruction. This information may be important—particularly in determining the motivation for seeking the change of instructor—but it can be placed in better perspective after the teacher has dealt directly with the student, without having been influenced by parental observation and opinion.

A well-conducted interview need not take a great amount of time if it is planned so that many kinds of activities take place. A successful interview will include various opportunities for observation and assessment. To ensure the inclusion of multiple experiences, it is best to approach the interview with a definite agenda. Even if the plan may not be followed completely, or in the predetermined order, the existence of a plan keeps salient points in the teacher's mind despite the emergence of unexpected, possibly distracting, occurrences while the interview is in progress.

It is best to begin by inviting the student to perform a self-chosen piece. The student will generally play what (s)he really likes or what (s)he feels will impress. That is already indicative of the student's own judgment. Offer a positive (but truthful) comment about the performance. Resist the urge to reteach the piece. Drawing from the music or repertoire list, immediately request performance of a piece that will exhibit the opposite of what the first piece has demonstrated. If such a work is not available, choose another piece, the shorter the better. Do not allow the student to play the same kind of music for an extended length of time even if the performance is interesting, competent, or stunning. Knowledge gained by listening only to a certain style of playing is likely to be one-dimensional.

Move quickly to another type of activity. It may be illuminating to observe what happens when the student's ear, and ability to respond, is challenged. Using another piano, or a different (but not too low) register of the same piano, ask the student to copy back (by playing) short melodic and rhythmic fragments. This may be something the student has never done, and the student's ability to adapt, as well as to respond, may be brought into focus. Begin with dictation that is easy. Success will build confidence. Difficulty should be introduced in small increments and pushed only as far as it can go comfortably. Keyboard-to-keyboard dictation may be based on five-finger positions, scale or triad formations, the pentatonic scale (black keys), or any other keyboard concept to which the student may connect. Remember that it is the *ear* that is being tested. Refrain from expecting the student to define concepts (major and minor, scale and triad, simple and compound meter, and so on) in lieu of, or in addition to, responding by playing.

Ask the student to sight-read. Use short examples appropriate to the level at which the student may be expected to read, based on the level of the student's playing. A fairly wide assortment of materials should be at hand. (This may take the most time and care to plan.) Make sure that these sight-reading examples test the student's ability to read in various ranges, with various clefs, using different textures, and employing different meters and rhythmic patterns. As with the dictation examples, proceed from the manageable to the more challenging. Note the student's preparation before playing, the movement of the eyes, the sense of continuity (not necessarily the correctness of rhythmic figures), the feel for keyboard geography, and the overall response of the student to the unknown. This is frequently the most revealing part of the interview.

Play some improvisatory games. Many students will have had no previous experience with improvisation. Guide the student in the playing of an uncomplicated ostinato figure (use fifths or triads, for instance) While the student plays the ostinato, the teacher should improvise simply, providing a number of feasible melodic and rhythmic models. Reverse the situation. Note the student's ability to adapt to the possibly unfamiliar situation, to maintain the pulse, and to respond to what (s)he plays. Be sensitive to what the student can or cannot do in this impromptu musical situation. The interviewing teacher is seeking information, not specific results.

The teacher's behavior throughout the interview should be governed by the following:

Refrain from making lengthy comments at the conclusion of each activity. Move on to the next experience. Save the assessment until after the student has responded in several musical situations. Instead, make quick notes for use in the final summary.

The teacher's eyes should be on the student, not the music. Step back from the piano, and move around it so that the student's entire posture is observable.

If the student uses music, note eye-hand coordination and whether eye-hand movement is excessive or misplaced.

Throughout the interview read the student's body language. The ease (or lack of it) with which the student holds his/her body while standing, sitting, breathing, or walking is often an important clue to a student's physical coordination and suppleness.

Ask the student pertinent questions. Questions that require explanations or opinions are of more value than questions requiring specific answers. If questions directed to the student are most often answered by the parent, that says much about the parent-student relationship.

Once the student has completed the planned activities, ask a few questions that will offer insight into the student's reason(s) for taking lessons, or for changing instructors, at this particular time. Find out something about the student's practice habits and routine, the type of instrument in the home, the student (or family) interest in attending concerts, recitals, and so on. If a parent has been present, and if the teacher has been communicating directly with the student throughout the interview, take time now to include the parent in the discussion, since the parent has great influence over the home situation and the practice environment.

As the interview draws to a close, offer a brief diagnosis of the student's strengths and weaknesses, how these relate to the aims and expectations of this particular studio, and what the immediate general plan for the student's development would be were lessons to commence in the new studio. If the teacher believes a student would not fit in that particular studio, (s)he should be as honest as possible in explaining why this is so. Be prepared to offer other options. (Recommend another instructor, another type of lesson, a reexamination of goals, a hiatus in instruction, or whatever is appropriate.) Do not feel compelled to accept every student, even for financial reasons. The difficulty and misunderstanding that may ensue in an uncomfortable student-teacher relationship will seldom be worth the extra income.

If it is clear that student and teacher (and parent) are interested in working together, briefly explain the studio and lesson policy. It is especially helpful if the policy is available in printed (or typed) form.[2] Less time need then be taken to spell out details. It is also valuable for the student to have something to take along that will note important points, describe payment plans, and provide other pertinent information. If possible, set the lesson time(s) and indicate what the student is to prepare for, or bring to, the first lesson.

Some teachers recommend offering extra (free) lessons at the outset of instruction that bring the student to the new teacher's studio two or three times a week.[3] During this time the student is requested *not* to practice at home. The extra lessons become intensive practice sessions that allow the new teacher to weed out problems and set the new course of study with greater accuracy. Other teachers offer pre-lesson sessions before a new term begins.[4] Sessions such as these (included in the student's overall tuition) are group experiences during which the teacher works collectively with students having the same difficulties (e.g., rhythm, or practice habits). Students in these groups may be either transfer or continuing students. By providing pre-lesson sessions, the teacher previews what is to come and, at the same time, develops a readiness for, or review of, the skills necessary to begin the new term with interest and confidence.

Conducting such an interview marks the teacher as a professional. The student and parent are likely to regard the opinions and suggestions of the teacher with confidence and interest since the teacher has exhibited care in assessing the student and has been able to indicate an educational and musical philosophy. The teacher has gained important insights into the capabilities and expectations of the new student, saving time and possible false steps in the initial lessons. And, most important, a personal contact has infused what might otherwise have seemed just a business arrangement.

APPROACHES TO SOLVING SOME COMMON PROBLEMS

As lessons with the transfer student begin, certain difficulties frequently require remedial attention. Most of the time, a student needs to do repair work in only some of the following categories. While it is necessary to focus on specific problems until they have been eliminated, other aspects of playing that may not need remedial work should be cultivated concurrently for the sake of interest, balance, and encouragement. Some suggestions for dealing with specific problems follow.

The student has never learned a process for pitch reading although (s)he may be playing relatively difficult (intermediate-level) music.

Teach the principles of intervallic reading (step/skip/repeat as these relate to lines and spaces) together with the names and placement of certain guide notes. Give the student a great deal of music to read that is designed around these guide notes. Make sure that the reading examples are short, varied, rhythmically uncomplicated, and that the difficulty increases very gradually. It is best if the teacher has a supply of music that serves this purpose and the student is assigned a different "library" book every week.[5] The aim is to have the student read the entire book, or a large section of it, during the intervening week. The teacher only spot-checks certain pieces at the next lesson to ensure that development of the reading procedure is taking place. Stress the importance of doing a small amount of new reading every day rather than working intermittently for long periods of time.

Do not expect the student to perfect each piece. A slow, steady, reading pace should be the norm. Do not fuss about articulations or dynamics in these pieces. The aim is to improve the reading process. Let the student concentrate on the single task of reading correct pitches until this can be done with relative ease. Flash cards and reading games are also effective teaching tools. Make an issue of the importance of learning to read pitches, but do not spend the entire lesson time stressing only that.

> **The student has never learned a process for determining or practicing rhythms, meters, and rhythmic patterns. Previous teacher(s) always demonstrated how the rhythm went.**

This problem will take more time to correct than insecure pitch reading, especially if the student is playing music of some difficulty and has come to rely on imitation or guesswork to get the rhythm. Go back to basics if necessary, to ensure that the student grasps the meaning of pulse as related to grouping(s), before insisting that the student be able to translate meters and rhythms into notation, or notated rhythmic symbols into felt rhythmic patterns. Give the student an opportunity to perform many rhythmic examples that do *not* include pitch reading. The student may tap, clap, or drum these or may perform them on the keyboard using any repeated pitches or intervals. Playing rhythms on the keyboard is preferable to tapping or clapping because the longer note values can be heard as sustained sounds.

Do not equate rhythmic understanding with math. Counting is useful only to the extent that the student perceives why it is useful. Most students have some knowledge of metric counting but may not find this helpful in reading rhythmic notation. Introduce a new way to count (such as unit or syllabic counting).[6] This may help the student relate to rhythmic notation in a fresh context. If a student has a chance to work in a group (occasionally or regularly), this will do much to develop and expand the student's rhythmic acumen. Especially in the area of rhythm, take nothing for granted.

> **The student can read and count, but is lacking in basic technique.**

This is a common problem. Most teachers talk about technique; few know how to teach it well. While technical routines and etudes may be suggested in a book, the understanding of technical and kinesthetic gesture is personal. The student's ability to develop an internal cueing and feedback system relating to the establishment of playing technique is a skill that many teachers do not take time, or know how, to encourage.[7] Posture (of the body, torso, arm) may be the best point of referral. Too much, as well as too little, attention may have been directed to the movement and position of the fingers, hand, and arch.

Allow and encourage the student to deal with technical development *apart from reading*. Focus attention on gesture and posture, but also on *sound* as related to gesture and posture. A technical regimen should be prescribed (this need not be forbidding). Make analogies to sports, where warming up is seen as both preparation and safeguard. Musical warm-ups should always be done in a rhythmic context. All gesture is movement. Arhythmic movement is unnatural and therefore harmful. Show the student the importance of coordinating time, gesture, and sound. It may also be profitable to have the student play on the keyboard cover, making all the gestures necessary for the performance of a particular piece (especially if the piece requires moves, crossings, register changes , and the like).[8] Using this technique, a student may be able to concentrate on gesture and mobility without having to be responsible for playing exact pitches.

> **The student has been spoon-fed. Musical self-reliance and personal judgment are undeveloped. The teacher has been the first, final, and only arbiter.**

If the student was unhappy with this arrangement, the situation will be less difficult to change. Many students, however, grow so accustomed to all decision making emanating from the teacher they resist accepting responsibility for choosing and judging on their own. After the performance of each exercise or piece they scan the teacher's face, expecting to read either approval or disapproval. "Students who ... have all errors ... circled (and recircled), and are reminded to follow the printed dynamics and articulations, will not have their imaginations stirred nor their abilities challenged. . . . All students need to ... take an active, not passive, role in their lessons."[9]

Begin by asking simple questions that require judgments. ("Did you really play a crescendo?") If the student shrugs off answering, continue to ask questions, or redirect the situation until the student realizes that a response must be forthcoming. ("Play the passage again. Listen so that you can tell how much of a crescendo you made.") Do not be afraid of silence while the student either thinks or waits for the teacher to supply the answer. Make sure *not* to answer for the student. Learn to remain verbally and facially expressionless until the student has provided an opinion. Then discuss the student's opinion as something deserving consideration.

Provide opportunities for the student to make choices. Ask him/her to:

Determine fingering for a passage, section, or piece.

Select certain pieces among several, or many.

Specify, and notate, original dynamics and articulations in pieces that are not edited.

Play pieces that require the performer to make some decisions (e.g., unmeasured, ad libitum passages, and so on).

Encourage the student to join in making short-term curriculum plans (e.g., for a month, or for a summer break). Suggest that the student occasionally write out a critical self-evaluation, like that on an interview or audition form. Discussing such an evaluation with the student during a lesson might be time well spent.

The student has never learned adequate practice habits.

The best practicing is direct, efficient, and concentrated. At the outset, make sure the student understands that attention and consistency are more important to successful practice than playing for a certain amount of time. Avoid making reference to "practicing for thirty minutes" or "playing this passage ten times." Show the student how to make the practice period goal oriented. ("Warm up on this exercise until you can see that your wrist remains quiet and your thumb is always ready," or "This piece has four parts. We have noticed that parts one and three are the same. Learn each part alone, beginning with the last. Learn it perfectly before going on. By the next lesson be ready to start at any part and play to the end of the part.")

Do not be afraid to spend lesson time making certain that the student goes home with specific goals for each activity or piece. Too often the assignment made is so general ("Make sure that piece is learned by next week") the student only dimly perceives what to do with it during each practice period. Gradually, as the student acquires some knowledge of how and what to practice, less lesson time will be needed to outline practice procedures and routines. Asking the student to keep a practice journal might be motivating.[10] Some students respond well to the idea of creating a practice diary. The teacher may thus gain some insight into how the student uses practice time. A more practical step might be to ask the student to tape-record practice time(s) and bring the tape to the next lesson. If pieces or exercises still contain insecurities or problems, listening to the practice tape may help the teacher uncover what has been going wrong and how to make adjustments or redirect efforts. It may be equally helpful for the student to tape each lesson for use at home to recall sounds, tempos, and specific directions. The taped lesson may also be an aid to the parent in overseeing or encouraging home practice.

The student is playing music that is too difficult.

This may be a diplomatic as well as a musical problem. Music of an accustomed type or difficulty cannot be whisked away and summarily replaced by music that looks and sounds much easier. Even if a student is secretly relieved that less effort and time will be needed to play easier pieces, there is usually some self-devaluation resulting from the awareness that one has not, or cannot, perform something up to standard. Habits have been formed, as much of the ear as of the fingers, and these are not easy to change.

Many times difficult music has been assigned because it seemed important—to the teacher, or student, or both—to perform famous pieces, to enter competitions, to impress parents or friends, or to be at a certain level. It may be helpful to the new teacher to determine what motivation lay behind the choice of overly demanding repertoire. While this information may offer some insight in dealing with the new student's sense of demotion, it does not change the fact that playing easier music is the order of the day.

The teacher with extensive knowledge of repertoire is in a much better position to deal with this situation than the teacher who customarily depends on less varied teaching materials. In selecting easier repertoire, there are obvious pitfalls to avoid. If a student has been working in books that are identified by number or letter, the teacher who assigns a book with a lower number or letter may be inviting resentment. There is so much music from which to choose, however, that finding appropriate unnumbered or unlettered material is not that difficult. One easy solution is to find a book that contains attractive pieces in textures, or styles, or both that may be unfamiliar to the student. Often these may be pieces that sound more modern or popular than what the student has been playing. Go through many pieces quickly, as thoroughly as seems wise. Since the music will be easier for the student to play, concentrate on challenging the student to perform with, for instance, greater color, panache, or velocity. This will make the student feel successful and will also help to build the student's musical and technical security.

If the student has been performing difficult music by well-known composers, choose easier pieces by the same composers, select music by other well-known composers whose pieces are usually shorter and less musically demanding, or interest the student in discovering the music of twentieth-century composers whose pieces require the making of new (to the student) sounds and effects. Once again, make greater performance demands on the student than had been possible for him/her to achieve with music of greater difficulty or complexity. At the same time, work to build technique and increase reading ability. Provide experiences the student may not have had, such as performing ensemble music, improvising, or accompanying.

The student has little or no theoretical background. Such concepts as scale formation, basic harmony, key signature, tempo and agogic terms are either unknown or are only superficially understood.

If there is cause to suspect that a student's theoretical knowledge is sketchy or inadequate, it is best to assume nothing and cover the territory thoroughly from the beginning. There is little worse than working backward, patching in information here and there, only to discover that nothing theoretical was ever very clear to the student in the first place. Since theory is not something the student ever expected to be held responsible for, there is no feeling of inadequacy or frustration if instruction must begin with the basics. On the contrary, the student is often pleased to be learning some of the "mysteries" and equally pleased to discover that doing so is quite easy. This is particularly true if the student is older and can do a certain amount of self-teaching by using books, diagrams, or computer programs.

Many good instructional tools are available to provide explanation and drill; the teacher's time at the lesson should be used in translating theoretical concepts and principles into sound and tactile experience. This is not to relegate the development of general musical knowledge to the fringes of the lesson, but to ensure that theory is related to music making in ways that are vital as well as expressive.

The concept of scale, for example, can be presented in a short amount of time if done in conjunction with a supportive tool (a book or program) that the student uses at home as a text to provide both review and further information. Lesson time can be used to play around the circle of fifths, perhaps in the form of overlapping tetrachords, to link sound and feel with rule and order. The concept and definition of tonic and dominant is straightforward and logical. Drill in building and spelling tonics and dominants can be supplied by a book or program. Appreciating the power and drama of tonic and dominant, however, is likely to occur only at the lesson when examining harmonic function in the musical context of a sonatina, nocturne, or fantasy. Stimulation to do so is provided by the teacher.

*K*EEPING *MANY THINGS GOING AT ONCE*

Solving specific problems, or eliminating certain deficiencies, may not present as much challenge as being able to teach the transfer student at a number of levels simultaneously. The student's reading and rhythmic abilities are adequate, but the technique is lamentable: How does the teacher attend to building the student's technique and yet find pieces that the student is able to play with the technique available? Or the student's fingers are good, the music played is quite difficult, yet the student has no clear idea of how to read or practice: How does the teacher sustain the performance level while equipping the student to learn music quickly and correctly, without overreliance on the teacher's guidance and support? Similar situations could be described by every instructor who has accepted students with a background not totally in accordance with what the accepting teacher might desire.

There is no simple or failproof formula that can be applied to ensure that the necessary juggling will be easy or successful. Yet there are suggestions that may sometimes prove helpful.

Making a correct diagnosis before beginning instruction is key.
Surprises, especially unpleasant ones, prove unsettling.

Take time to interview and assess the student at length. Tell the student what is expected; indicate, at least in general, the manner in which instruction will proceed. Be positive, clear, and firm. If the new teacher is seen to have a long- (as well as a short-) range goal for instruction, the transferring student is likely to have confidence in the new teacher's philosophy. If the student is unhappy with what the new teacher has in mind, it is better for both if this is discovered at the outset.

Do not make promises. ("In two months, you will be reading with ease.") Do not disparage or undermine the student's previous instruction or instructor. This is professionally unwise and also a waste of time. Build and develop rather than criticize and pick apart.

> **Underestimate, rather than overestimate, the student's abilities.**
> **Beware of making assumptions that things have been covered,**
> **concepts grasped.**

Assuming too much is frequently the undoing of many plans. Begin each new presentation with a brief overview of what would have preceded it had the student worked from the beginning in the new teacher's studio. The implementation of this process need not be lengthy or complicated. Begin a demonstration of any technical exercise, for example, with general reminders about the importance of overall posture in relationship to the instrument. Or be sure that the assignment of a new piece includes a discussion of its form together with ways to utilize that knowledge when planning the practice routine.

A well-placed question may be another way in which to uncover what the new student truly knows. ("What is the most important thing to listen for when playing this scale?" "How would you suggest we work out the fingering in this piece?") It may also be informative to ask the new student's opinion about a process or concept. ("Why do you think the editor calls for a crescendo in this particular passage?" "Could you come up with any reason why a dominant is called a dominant?") When the student replies, be sure to listen to the answer. This may sound axiomatic, but it often happens that the teacher is only searching for a *certain* answer, rather than taking into consideration the insight into the student's thinking process that may be gained by noting *whatever* the student says.

> **Involve the student in many different activities early on so that all**
> **facets of the student's abilities or inabilities may surface at the**
> **beginning, even if they cannot all be dealt with at the start.**

It often happens that in working to solve a specific problem (e.g., rhythmic reading and practice), so much time is spent on one type of activity that a student's other talents (e.g., a flair for improvising) may be entirely overlooked. This overconcentration may become discouraging, and it may also keep the teacher from uncovering an ability that could be capitalized on in the overcoming of the original difficulty. Using the ear as an ally in becoming a better reader is a case in point.

Try to involve the student in some group activities. A group session is likely to expose the student to influences that would never occur in an individual lesson. The student gets a chance to react to other students (not just the teacher) and often regards fellow students as more realistic models for what can be accomplished. The social nature of playing, moving, or clapping together is generally more pleasant and supportive than listening only to oneself. A student in a group sometimes becomes quite a different person (musical and otherwise) than the same student in a private lesson.

Learn to determine priorities and implement them reasonably.

Not everything in the student's plan of study is of equal importance. The teacher may decide that, at least for a while, certain activities must be stressed and others can just be carried along. That is a reasonable plan as long as the stressed items do not become the sole focus of concentration. Priorities may also change, depending upon:

the student's progress (reading is improving; attention must shift to the development of velocity and color).

the time of the year (spring is recital and audition time; polishing and developing endurance are necessary).

external activities (the student has begun to accompany the church choir; learning to read choral music and follow a conductor require the acquisition of new skills).

It might be helpful if the instructor regards various activities in an overall plan of study as so many layers, each of which go through certain stages: for example, introduction, drill, development, refinement. While one (or some) skill(s) are being introduced, another is being drilled, yet others are in the process of being developed or refined. Thinking about skill building in this way may allow the teacher to keep a long-range plan in mind while not totally succumbing to the needs of the moment.

At the heart of this concept of curriculum building (and juggling) is the presence of a plan. It is the difference between reacting to what *may* take place at the lesson ("What do you have ready to play today?") and directing what *will* happen even if the student is not prepared ("I have been thinking about this prelude and wondered if we might try the following"). The wise teacher finds ways to communicate the plan to the student. The wisest teacher finds ways to involve the student in making the plan.

Be sure to combine success at one level with challenge at another.

Prioritizing where one directs one's energies has the added advantage of dealing with the realization that not everything reaches the optimum stage at the same time. At some level, the student may be grappling with new skills and uncovering chinks in the armor. It is comforting, as well as truthful, to remind the student (at that precise time) that other goals have been met. ("Look how easily you play this etude now. Do you remember when it was a struggle to get past the middle part?")

No one, it must be admitted, can arrange for another's success. A stimulus (an exercise, a piece, or a question) may be presented, but the student must cooperate, must respond. A student's response is unpredictable. A teacher's value judgment or opinion following upon a response is, furthermore, a subjective evaluation. Nonetheless a student (especially a younger one) generally strives to accomplish the expected and find confirmation of the action or response in the approval of the teacher. "Success" for the younger student is often a feeling derived from having pleased or satisfied someone else. It is therefore important that the teacher seek, as soon as possible, to assist the student in developing a capacity for self-evaluation.

A teacher must also be honest and avoid offering unrealistic praise. "That was a sensational performance" should not stand in as a euphemism for "Well, that was a little closer to an appropriate tempo." Even a young student becomes suspicious of unwarranted superlatives. One way to avoid this pitfall may be to develop a richer vocabulary. For too many teachers there is often little beyond "not right," "pretty good," and "fantastic."

Measure growth and change over longer time periods.

While at times improvement may be dramatic and seem almost instant, development is more often a gradual process. Resist the impulse to evaluate growth weekly, like a dieter who daily checks the scale for evidence of encouraging results. Reward (that is, acknowledge) what may be weekly efforts toward growth, but formulate judgments about a student's progress at the end of more widely spaced intervals. Remember that "diagnostic teaching means considerably more than just an attitude at the first lesson. Diagnosis must be a continuing process of determining what the student has learned, and what steps are to be taken in order to correct anything that will interfere with progress toward the next level of capability."[11]

It might be helpful to set periodic assessment points, at which time the rate and quality of improvement are noted. The end of a semester or term may be a natural juncture at which to do this, but an assessment period might also need to be shorter or longer. A productive way to arrive at an assessment is to somehow include the student when formulating judgments or conclusions. In order to participate in the assessment, the student should be aware, from the beginning, of what goals might be reasonably achievable.

Be as specific as possible when pointing out these aims. "By December, we will check to see if you are a better reader" is a vague statement of direction and motivation. Lay out a realistic sequence of action that will bring results. "From now until December, let's agree that you will spend five minutes each day carefully reading some new music. You will find yourself getting better at this the more you do it. By the time December arrives, you may be surprised to see how much you will have improved."

Making the parent aware of the plan is another positive action. Parents also appreciate knowing what the teacher is projecting, how a goal is to be achieved, and how long reaching the goal may take. Some parents get anxious, curious, or critical as lessons continue, and they become impatient for results. Knowing the expected time frame within which particular skill development is likely to take place may help the parent be realistic about noting and assessing progress.

The teacher must continue to expand his/her acquaintance with an ever-growing body of good literature.

Knowledge of literature and other teaching material should not be limited to what one has always taught, what is recommended by a particular course or syllabus, or what is available at a local music store. The object of seeking out new music is not necessarily so that one may teach the latest. Music new to the teacher may be music that is quite established. Amplifying one's knowledge of Baroque literature, for example, may be a matter of learning to use something in addition to the small dances in the AMB Notebook. An overwhelming amount of easier music is now available in well-edited books and collections; a teacher need not struggle to locate these.

Much may be learned from a course or syllabus prepared by an experienced teacher or a professional organization.[12] However, a teacher should not depend on a single series, method, or list to supply all the literature taught in his/her studio. The good series or syllabus is, rather, a model to be used in building and enriching one's own teaching library. (A syllabus, for example, can offer a way to judge the grading of other pieces or remind one of what musical components constitute a complete course of study).

Keyboard periodicals contain advertisements of current releases and lists of new books and pieces. They generally also include critical appraisals of such.[13] Reviews of new materials often suggest ways in which to use certain pieces and books to best advantage, including references to situations involving transfer students. Some music dealers, publishers, and organizations offer programs for teachers to receive and review new teaching materials.[14] Other music dealers and publishers provide newsletters that keep the teacher apprised of new releases and how these may be effective in meeting special, and occasional, needs.[15] The teacher with knowledge of many pieces, books, methods, and approaches is in a better position to accommodate the transfer student's background and to plan that student's continuing curriculum than the teacher whose knowledge of methods and materials is limited either by choice or experience.

A CONCLUDING THOUGHT

Perhaps the greatest sensitivity to the accomplishments, expectations, and needs of the transfer student is gained by regarding one's own pupils as potential transfer students into the studio of another teacher.[16] How would one's own students be perceived in an interview or audition? What understanding, allowance, or both would one expect a fellow teacher to make on behalf of those students should they ever choose or need to transfer? Would one's own students succeed in reflecting accurately or completely what they had learned? Considerations such as these may enable one to assess the student transferring into one's own studio with professional accuracy and thoroughness, yet with a generosity that bespeaks an awareness of the human situation.

PART FIVE

Professional Preparation

CHAPTER 12

The College Keyboard Major

Whenever a young person decides what major to pursue in college, a commitment is made. That commitment is at least to a strong interest in the discipline and in most cases involves the plan to pursue some professional activity for which that discipline is a preparation. If a major is selected casually, perhaps as a result of mild curiosity, there is strong likelihood that the student will change majors as the rigors of the discipline become apparent. This change may occur several times until a workable match is made. Even if life's demands dictate activities that lead away from the major later on, the period of intense study in the major is a strong influence and is more often than not remembered by the person as a powerful factor in youthful development. How often have we heard someone say, "Oh, I majored in English in college" or "I was a psychology major," providing this information as a key to understanding the viewpoints and opinions of that person.

The choice of music as a major suggests an especially strong commitment, and the choice of musical performance demands intense dedication—perhaps as intense as anything in the entire gamut of human activity. By an assessment of interest and talent, a piano teacher can usually tell if a student is headed toward making this level of commitment. If such appears to be the case, a young person should be counseled to consider carefully both the demands and rewards of this choice, the frustrations and the pleasures. A teacher should try to help the student get some sense of what it means to be a pianist—a musician—in terms of life-style and long-range goals.

The literature is filled with anecdotes that reflect on a life in music, but a few points appear frequently and are basic in considering such a direction:

1. The joy music can bring to one's life is both limitless and of the highest quality. Such a reward combines many levels of human perception, incorpo-

rates varying degrees of intellectual and emotional communication, and acts as a sustaining, positive life force. This joy will be there through triumphs and sorrows, from youth through old age, and even has the potential of acting as a catalyst for spiritual growth and development. Few human endeavors can promise as much in the realm of innermost satisfaction.

2. The demands of music are also limitless, and stringent. These challenges can result in frustration, boredom, anger, and psychological dislocation if they are not handled properly. Such a caveat is inherent in much human striving, but because musical performance is so directly dependent on an intimate, personalized activity, the emotional reaction to disappointment, temporary failure, or not achieving long-range goals can be potent and dangerous. On the other hand, learning to rise above these problems can be an exceptionally positive force for developing strength of personality and spirit.

3. The work involved in arriving at satisfying achievements in musical performance is hard and extraordinarily time consuming, and although levels of achievement can be readily noted, the desire to go on to the next goal is constantly pressing. As a result the amount of time and effort one might possibly invest is endless. Striking a balance between this drive and other aspects of living one's life is oftentimes problematic.

4. In terms of the work involved and the time invested, material rewards for the vast majority of musicians are relatively small, but they need not compare as unfavorably to the rewards of other professions as popular opinion would suggest. This is an important point, which is often viewed from extremes. On the one hand, the student often confuses public attention with monetary reward. Only the few musicians who have large public followings and who offer commercially oriented material make large sums of money. Even the successful, celebrated classical artist earns relatively little when compared with equally successful professionals in other fields. Moreover the plight of the young professional, trying to find a niche, is often both difficult and frightening. On the other hand, a very realistic and persistent approach to the profession by a fully prepared young person will yield an acceptable level of return, one that compares favorably with many other areas of professional endeavor. Musicians can fare as well as other artists and performers, academics, teachers, librarians, and many researchers. In the long run, musicians can probably do as well as many small-business people, personal-service professionals, and white-collar workers. Overall, however, music will not yield the return that might be expected from a career in medicine, law, big business, or high-tech industries. Furthermore, earning an acceptable living will undoubtedly involve some combination of a variety of activities, such as performing, teaching, accompanying, writing, lecturing, composing, arranging, editing, and conducting.

Once these points are understood, it becomes apparent that becoming a music major and subsequently entering the music profession in some capacity very much involves embarking on a life's journey—and the sooner one begins, the better. This preparation will have to become a focal point in the student's life, and the problem of balancing time and effort devoted to music study with other activities will have to be faced immediately.

Where each student will draw the line is an individual matter, but it is obvious that some leisure time and some participation in extracurricular activities will have to be diverted to music study. Balance, however, remains a key concern, because even those students who have an intense desire to practice the piano should weigh carefully the value of interaction with family and friends and should set aside time for living. One cannot escape the demands, emergencies, and even setbacks life will interject at one time or another. Rational thinking, patience, and resilience are qualities that will do more to ensure the maintenance of progress than will attempts to avoid dealing with life as it comes. Learning to stay on an even keel, compromising when necessary, saving as much time for music as possible, saying no to things that can wait but being sensitive to the needs of others and what must be done outside music—skillfully juggling all of these is an important ability to acquire in the early stages of preparation.

Preparing for college entrance examinations is one of the future professional's first big career steps. Most important in preparing any college audition is the preservation of the integrity of the performance. The auditioning student's musical values must be communicated as carefully and effectively as possible, supported by adequate technique, and the whole should represent the student's musical thinking and present level of achievement with a fair degree of accuracy. Trying to impress an audition committee with bombastic playing is doomed to failure, nine times out of ten, because either the committee will be experienced enough to see through such a performance immediately and react unfavorably or the student will be admitted on a performance that belies the actual level of achievement and will be found out later, with attending consequences. Honest representation of a student's best musical capacity is the only approach that will ultimately serve the student's goals.

In the context of honest representation of the student's level and ability, the choice of institution becomes a matter of prime concern. Each school to be considered must be looked at from several vantage points. First, a prospective student should check the quality of the faculty, both in terms of credentials (academic or professional) and reputation. Hearing several student performances, which reflect the faculty's influence, is often a very helpful exercise. A student should check the strength of the theory and history programs at the institution. The college years are the most important years in terms of acquiring supplemental knowledge and skills needed in professional life. In the world of music today, no one depends solely on performance ability to sustain a career. A pianist who neglects developing into as complete a musician as possible is certain to be inadequate to the tasks ahead.

A student should take the time to get a feel for the student life at the institution, especially in terms of levels of peer achievement. At no other time in the development of a young musician will peer awareness be as influential as in the first years of college. Young students at this time move psychologically into an environment where music and musical achievement are a central focus for almost everyone around them. Teachers, most friends, and even many acquaintances seem to equate this achievement with human worth. Thus a student is constantly assessing how he or she measures up and tends to project this assessment into the foreseeable future. Just as Saturday's football heros may or may not be the winners in real life, so the heros of the college recital hall may or may not become professional musicians of significance. Nevertheless their moments of collegiate glory are brilliant enough to eclipse the future temporarily.

How well a student deals with this fitting-in adjustment will depend on how advanced the student is in comparison to peers, on how secure the student is in terms of self-image, and on how mature the student is in being able to view the long haul as opposed to enthusiasms of the moment. Most students, even good ones, go through a period of feeling inadequate in comparison to the achievements of others. The saying "Everyone sounds so great through the practice-room door" is a recognition of this syndrome.

Choosing a school where competition will be vigorous is good for most students. Choosing a school where the level of playing is mostly far below that of the student will likely lead to false security, for vigorous competition will be encountered at one time or another if the student goes on in the profession. On the other hand, choosing a school at which the level of playing is markedly above that of the student very likely will be psychologically damaging, unless the student has an unusually strong sense of self-esteem and is able to see things in proper perspective.

Music students usually form their own community within larger institutional settings, so the pianist will easily be able to identify with a peer group. Members of that group share similar pressures, similar problems, and often similar aspirations. Identifying with these peers can be useful in that the young musician can be stimulated and challenged by the interaction that takes place. On the other hand, achieving a balance between contact with this group of peers and those interested in things other than music is desirable, lest the young musician lose sight of the larger world of diverse interests in which music plays an important but relatively smaller role. Such a balance is easy to effect in the setting of a college or university but less so in the conservatory, where departments or schools centering on nonmusic topics are not close at hand.

Audition requirements differ from school to school. Most schools require a program of between four and seven selections. Usually a Baroque offering is required, often stipulated as a Prelude and Fugue from J. S. Bach's *Well-Tempered Clavier*. A representation from a Classical sonata is often required, this ranging from a minimum of a first movement form from any sonata of Haydn, Mozart, or Beethoven to requiring a complete sonata and excluding some easier works such as Beethoven's Op. 49.

The audition program is generally completed by filling categories. Sometimes an etude or a piece with a technique orientation is required. Often a piece in a Romantic style, sometimes an impressionistic work, and, with increasing frequency, a representative twentieth-century work are asked for. The contemporary category is often one of wide latitude, but usually an audition committee is looking for a stylistic representation rather than a chronological one. It is perfectly possible that a piece written in 1950 would be regarded as less contemporary stylistically than, say, the Op. 11 of Arnold Schoenberg, written approximately forty years earlier. Memorization of the entire program is usually expected, except possibly for the use of a score in an avant-garde twentieth-century work.

Once a young pianist has been admitted as a college music major, growth begins to take place in a number of areas. Pianistic activity is of course intensified: a schedule of three or four hours of practice per day, weekends included, is expected by professors, perhaps even more for bachelor of music piano majors and somewhat less for those in liberal arts or education programs. In addition, accompanying projects are often required, and good readers find themselves besieged with requests from other instrumentalists and singers for services well beyond minimum requirements. Furthermore, courses in music literature, theory, ensemble playing, or conducting may require more time at the piano in preparation of assignments. The practice studio thus becomes the main workplace, and music students even find that much of their everyday socializing is centered in and around the music school.

A program of four to seven pieces is considered about a semester's work in most institutions. The student should have developed reading ability and practice procedure to the level of being able to learn about that much music in a period of four or five months, assuming a practice schedule of three or four hours on most days. Slow learners who have taken many months to prepare their pieces acceptably should beware! Most institutions have incorporated performance as the final examination for each semester's course of study, and inability to prepare and play such a program could result in failure.

The pianistic expectations of professional life will usually come into focus during the first few months of the college pianist's education. Specific technical requirements at the keyboard are often part of the examination procedure. For the first time the young pianist may be confronted with a definitive body of basic technical skills to master. Requirements vary in different schools, but a comprehensive list might well include the following:

Scales

All major and minor, single notes in each hand an octave apart ranging 4 octaves, sixteenth notes at a minimum speed of $\flat$ = MM 120 (all 3 forms of the minor scale: harmonic, melodic, and natural).

Scale groupings in 3s or 6s; the chromatic scale with alternate fingerings.

The same scale routine in thirds, sixths, and tenths.

Scales in contrary motion, 2 octaves out and back.

Arpeggios

Major, minor, diminished seventh, dominant seventh, and often various patterns incorporating other kinds of seventh chords or added notes; all inversions.

Double notes

All scales in double thirds, double sixths and octaves in each hand; the chromatic scale in both major and minor double thirds and double sixths and octaves in each hand.

Other exercise patterns in double fourths, double diminished fifths, and so on, may be incorporated.

Preparation of technical requirements may be left for the most part to the individual student; typically private lesson time will focus primarily upon preparation of literature for performance at final examinations or on recitals. Technical guidance is often offered by professors in the context of the compositions being studied. Remedial advice, too, is frequently given, so the student may well be challenged to alter his/her physical approach to the instrument in order to improve overall technical command. The way the performer sits, shapes the hand, moves the fingers, uses the arms, wrists, or elbows—all may be altered, depending on the degree to which the professor deems change beneficial. In this context, some scales and arpeggios may be studied. Most college-level teachers do not, however, spend a great deal of lesson time teaching or polishing this basic technical vocabulary.

Classes designed to help acquire additional skills in reading, practical keyboard skills, and improvisation are also often required, sometimes as part of a basic pedagogy requirement for all piano majors. The young pianist whose background in these skills is weak may have to spend a considerable amount of additional time trying to improve those abilities to meet minimum requirements.

One thing that may overwhelm the young pianist at first is the vast amount of literature for the keyboard and the realization that the professional pianist is acquainted with a very large segment of that literature. This treasury of masterworks is one of the great blessings pianists enjoy, for it provides more music than any one pianist can learn to play in a lifetime and a vast amount of music to listen to and enjoy. It is during the college years that the young pianist begins to conceptualize the extent of this literature.

The process of becoming acquainted with this body of music is a gradual one, and filling in its details is a lifetime study. Yet graduate comprehensive examinations on the doctoral level assume a good grasp of both the stylistic characteristics of the literature as well as detailed knowledge of a fair number of representative pieces. Achieving a command of this knowledge is helped considerably by having taken courses and seminars at the undergraduate level that focus specifically on keyboard literature and, one hopes, provide a great number and variety of listening experiences.

It is also in the college years that knowledge of musical styles grows and solidifies. Music performance is based in large part on tradition, passing along from generation to generation elusive but easily recognizable characteristics. Although these characteristics are often indicated in musical scores in a general way, the fine points that make a successful performance are often more subtle than the printed page can record.

The studio lesson contributes first and foremost toward the development of these perceptions, for it is here the young pianist will be coached and molded. It is here the young pianist will be brought face to face with a myriad of interpretative demands and problems, such as the use of non-legato, articulation, and ornamentation in Baroque and Classical music; the tempo fluctuations in Romanticism; the development of sonority in the nineteenth and twentieth centuries; and the appropriate balance between restraint and emotionalism in each musical period. The pianist learns that different techniques in handling the instrument are developed to serve varying aesthetic goals.

A college-level teacher expects to be able to communicate the nuances and subtleties of musical thought by means of the music itself and by encouraging the student to observe the details of what is *heard*. This communication and understanding should take place even as the student is beginning to learn how to produce such nuance or subtlety, even before the student can actually mold the music; it is considered by many teachers to be the heart of artistic growth. Early development of keyboard skills that lead to this interaction is among the most important aspects of preparation for college-level study.

Contributing toward understanding are courses in history, performance practices, and in-depth consideration of a specific composer or musical style. At some point the pianist will probably be reading historic documents that describe the performance practices and instrumental techniques of a given era.

The intensity of music study in college often gives rise to a kind of career myopia. Students who are near the end of their college careers, who gain high levels of achievement as musicians, and who are awarded degrees and honors, often wake with a jolt to find that the larger world is relatively indifferent to their hard-won college success. They realize that there is but small demand for their services as solo performers, modest demand for service performance (accompanying, coaching, and so on), and even an extremely competitive marketplace in which to offer their service as teachers.

Faced with these realities, the budding professional often must look further for gainful employment. One of the most neglected and fascinating areas for a student to explore is that of the music industry. Music is a big business, a veritable maze of avenues, all of which present opportunities for the creative mind. Too often, however, students begin trying to understand the complex world of concert management, recording production, music services, film and TV music, publishing, or music merchandising at the eleventh hour, near the end of their college careers. At that time young musicians attempt rapidly to comprehend these industry structures in the context of seeking out a professional niche for their talents. The industry appears hopelessly confusing and too large to be approachable, simply because the graduating student has not carefully established a groundwork of knowledge and experience about it. The earlier a student explores some aspect of the business of music that might be of interest, the more opportunities will appear on the horizon at the critical time; the student will have learned how to scan the horizon and perceive those opportunities.

There is no standard solution to carving a career for a young, gifted musician. A high degree of creative thinking about the marketing of musical skills and knowledge is the young professional's best weapon. Some have done well in organizing community support for music and the arts and have thus established reputations as spokespersons for music (with ensuing patronage for performances and teaching services). Some have established business and corporate connections outside the music profession, offering ideas in creative planning, problem-solving procedures, and related areas (all applications of principles learned from music study), and have achieved tremendous success. Others use their knowledge and taste in developing media programming (radio, TV, film), guiding music publishers, or setting priorities for the recording industry. These alternative career moves are not for everyone, and indeed, each field has its own army of young aspirants that forms competition. On the other hand, as a young musician looks out upon the world in the hope of building a remunerative career, the knack of viewing the marketplace from a broad perspective can lead to the discovery of opportunities that are both useful and personally satisfying.

CHAPTER 13

The Keyboard Pedagogy Major

Certain questions and observations always surface at the outset of any discussion concerning the need for instruction in pedagogy[1]: Doesn't one best learn how to teach by being taught? Isn't taking lessons from an outstanding teacher the most natural way to learn how to teach effectively? Aren't teachers born rather than made? Further questions arise where pedagogy itself is the choice of major. Is the pedagogy major a catchall for the pianist who might not be accepted as a performance major? If the great percentage of keyboard graduates find themselves teaching sooner or later, shouldn't all keyboard majors receive the same training—one that includes pedagogy? Should pedagogy as a major be a choice?

This chapter cannot lay these questions to rest, nor will it even attempt to answer them directly. It will, however, seek to examine matters relating to the preparation of the keyboard teacher in as broad a way as possible yet without wishing to suggest that majoring in piano pedagogy is either a panacea or a necessity.

One way of viewing the practicality of special training in pedagogy is to consider what a keyboard teacher in today's market may be expected to do:

Teach small-group piano classes in independent studio situations.

Teach musicianship classes in independent studio situations.

Teach preschool piano (music) classes in nursery, church-related, or independent studio situations.

Teach popular music classes in a music store or in neighborhood or senior citizen centers.

Teach theory and musicianship classes in community school situations.

Teach group piano classes to music majors at the college level.

Teach group piano classes to non-music majors at the college level.

Teach functional harmony to keyboard and non-keyboard majors at the college level.

Teach (a) course(s) in piano pedagogy at the college level.

Teach small or large group piano classes in a public school program.

While no single keyboard teacher does all these things, many keyboard teachers do (or are able to do) several of them. Most college or university faculty (especially junior-college faculty) are expected to fulfill a combination of such roles. Often, in fact, the person able to function in a number of teaching situations is the person chosen for a position over other candidates who may exhibit greater but more specialized teaching and playing talents. The independent keyboard teacher in whose studio varied types of instruction are offered (small-group and individual lessons, musicianship classes, preschool sessions, ensemble coaching) is also often the teacher whose professional and financial rewards are the greatest. In addition, the independent keyboard teacher may be, for example, a church organist, a choir director, an accompanist, or an electronic or orchestral keyboardist—and each of these positions demands skills related to, but different from, solo piano-playing skills.

A professional keyboard education consisting largely of taking lessons, practicing, and performing provides limited (however musically important) preparation for multiple teaching roles. In order to function in the various instructional roles enumerated above, the teacher must know a great deal of specialized teaching literature, be competent and comfortable in using group teaching skills with assorted age levels, understand the organization of collegiate-level classes involving keyboard instruction and the province of such classes in the music curriculum, and know how to use the keyboard functionally (i.e., to harmonize, sight-read, score read, transpose, and so on). Learning these skills is not the focus of the private lesson. Courses and opportunities connected with a major in pedagogy, however, are structured to help the student attain precisely these as well as other skills.

The most compelling reason to offer courses in pedagogy is to ensure that student teaching takes place—student teaching that is organized, guided, supported, observed, and critiqued. Just as one does not learn how to perform only by talking about performing, watching others perform, reading about performers, and discussing styles of performance, so one does not learn how to teach only by observing others teach, reading about famous teachers, surveying teaching literature, or critiquing the differences among reading approaches. One must be active as a performer in order to understand and perfect performance. One must be active as a teacher in order to understand and perfect teaching. Pedagogy training that does not involve actual teaching on the part of the trainee is neither realistic nor entirely honest.

BASIC CHARACTERISTICS OF THE MAJOR IN PIANO PEDAGOGY

Although specific piano pedagogy curricula may differ depending on the institution and the level of study (undergraduate or graduate), certain components are always important features of the effective pedagogy program:

Performance study and performance experience.

Examination of ideas and theories about learning and teaching.

Observation of teaching.

Study of teaching strategies.

Study of teaching literature.

Student teaching.

Supervision and critique of student teaching.

Experience in both studio and group-teaching situations.

Performance Study and Performance Experience

The most significant factor in the education of the pianist is the development of the pianist as a musician and performer. The heart of that education is usually the individual lesson. Taking piano lessons, however, is only part of the developmental process. The pianist must perform in public, whether studio class, master class, jury, recital, or competition. It is in these situations, playing and listening to others play, that one develops a practical awareness of the art of piano playing, of stylistic performance practice, of the major works in the repertory, and of coping with the excitement and tensions of public performance.

Because playing the piano is such an individual experience, the pianist also needs to make music with others. Ensemble experience may take many forms. It may involve playing chamber music with other instrumentalists, accompanying singers or singing groups, performing in keyboard ensembles, providing (piano reduction) orchestral accompaniments for concerto performances, serving as a continuo player, or playing for dance, exercise, or other movement classes—as well as taking formal instruction in the art of partnering others at the piano. Such experiences develop facets of music making that are not so often the focus of solo keyboard performance.

Examination of Ideas and Theories About Learning and Teaching

An examination of the learning and teaching process is the part of the pedagogy curriculum that may seem most foreign to the piano-teacher-in-training. An introduction to major learning theories is necessary in order to put one's own teaching activities and experiences into some kind of perspective. Study of educational psychology often involves what seems to be heavy research to pianists. Yet knowledge gained in this area appears to be amazingly practical if and when specific learning theories are demonstrated to be the bases of particular studio or class teaching strategies that the student encounters. The import of matters relating to such things as drill, rote teaching, motivation, discovery learning, reinforcement, problem solving, memorization, or sequencing are everyday experiences in a piano teacher's world. The instructor who has gained some insight into the complexities and ramifications of various learning and teaching behaviors is better able to plan, present, and evaluate a lesson or class.

Observation of Teaching

Observation of teaching is usually the first step in involving the pedagogy student in actual teaching. The student observer, however, often needs some guidance in determining what to look at as well as what to look for. The student observer must also be encouraged to record the order in which activities take place and how much time is spent on each. (This is particularly helpful when observing group teaching.) In this way the observer begins to appreciate the use of teaching time and also the importance of sequence and reinforcement. It is wise to have the observer write (that is, verbalize) a general assessment of each teaching situation observed. This provides the impetus for the observer to summarize his/her own reactions to what went on rather than merely to describe which activities took place.

It is important that the pedagogy student sit in on the same class or lesson over an extended period of time. Only after observing the same student(s) week after week will the pedagogy student be able to see the rate of improvement, the need for consistency and reinforcement, the development of skills, and the differences in attitudes and motivational behaviors within the lesson or class under scrutiny. Extended observation also helps ensure that the pedagogy student sees a method (whether this means a specific course of study or an individual teacher's approach) in action. Understanding of "method" thus begins to come into focus.

Study of Teaching Strategies

Observation of a master teacher also allows the less experienced teacher an opportunity to learn how to present material, what language to use, what order to follow, how to incorporate drill, how to organize the lesson or class, how to respond to (or stimulate) questions, how to summarize and make assignments. This how-to aspect of teaching is what will concern the student teacher at the outset of the student-teaching experience. Teaching strategies are means to an end, not the end itself. The beginning teacher, nonetheless, needs to know how to begin, what to say, what is important to teach on a certain page (in a certain piece), how to determine whether the pupil understands (or is doing predict-ably acceptable work), whether to review or drill, when (or whether) to teach by ear or by eye, and a host of similar teaching skills that keep the lesson or class going or determine its effectiveness.

Not all this can be learned by observing a single master teacher. Pedagogy instruction should include discussion and demonstration of different teaching techniques so that the less-experienced teacher learns a variety of ways to act and react at the lesson or in the classroom. Extended observation of a particular class and teacher, together with specific student-teaching assignments, will pro-vide experience with one, or certain, method(s). Some pedagogy teachers feel it is important that the inexperienced teacher begin by learning to teach one method completely and successfully and only after that be exposed to other methods and teaching techniques. Still other pedagogy teachers believe that the student teacher should be made aware of the pluralism of methods and teaching approaches at the outset. Whether one holds to the former or latter view, it remains true that the pedagogy student must ultimately develop an awareness of many methods and teaching styles. The most successful teacher frequently has chosen to incorporate ideas from multiple sources and has learned to select and use compatible teaching materials.

Study of Teaching Literature

In many countries the majority of the nation's piano teachers use the same teach-ing materials. This may be a matter of tradition or custom, or it may be the result of following the syllabus of an organization or institution. In these cases the beginning teacher need not be as concerned with what to teach and in what order to teach it; the concern is with how to teach it. That is certainly not the case in the United States. Piano teaching materials and method books abound. The multiplicity of print materials is not merely a matter of sheer quantity (i.e., many different ways to follow the same general plan or procedure), but a matter of extensive variety in the plans and procedures themselves.

Because the survey of materials must cover so much in so many areas, it should be obvious that an examination of teaching literature cannot be con-tained in a single pedagogy class. Study of teaching literature is most successful if grouped in categories (i.e., materials for beginners, for intermediate students, for college piano classes, and so on) at either the undergraduate or graduate level and done in conjunction with specific observation and teaching experi-ences. Some pedagogy programs, in fact, offer nothing at all in certain areas (e.g., preschool teaching) because they are not adequately equipped to provide observation and teaching experience in these areas.

Student Teaching

Student teaching is the most realistic and valuable component of the piano peda-gogy program. It may begin with tutorial or mini-teaching assignments in the classes or lessons the pedagogy student is currently observing. It may involve short peer-teaching experiences in the pedagogy class itself. It may also incorporate team teaching, either with another pedagogy student (or students) or with the master teacher. In cases where the teaching plan includes offering both group and individual lessons to the same pupils, the master teacher may do the group teaching (with the pedagogy student observing, assisting, or both), and the pedagogy student may teach the individual lesson(s). In most cases, pedagogy students are asked to begin with shorter teaching assignments (whether in group or individual situations) and gradually work up to teaching longer segments, entire classes, and for extended periods of time, such as a week or a month.

Supervision and Critique of Student Teaching

While the pedagogy student's opportunity to teach is itself instructive, greater benefits accrue if the student teaching is guided, supported, and critiqued. Guidance and support may involve assisting the student teacher in setting long-range goals for the semester or term, choosing teaching material, making short-range lesson or class plans, determining teaching strategies to accomplish particular points of emphasis, or preparing pupils for performance. It is especially important that student teaching be observed by the pedagogy teacher (and/or the class or lesson instructor) on a regular basis. Regular observation does not necessarily mean daily or constant observation. But it does suggest that observation be often enough to ensure that the student teacher receives sufficient feedback to assess the teaching experience and to make adaptations or improvements where necessary.

It is both practical and instructive if student teaching is videotaped during at least some of the student-teaching experience. This enables the student teacher to hear exactly what was said, see exactly what took place, and experience exactly the amount of time spent on each activity. Private viewing of the videotape by the student teacher is often revelatory. The pedagogy teacher, in turn, may use the videotape to point out aspects of the teaching either in later private conferences with the student teacher or in conferences and classes involving other pedagogy students.

The after-teaching conference is often when most of the "learning about teaching" takes place. The student teacher begins to realize both the complexities of the teaching and learning process and the necessity of knowing how to use and evaluate specific teaching strategies. Theoretical knowledge of teaching skill is translated into hands-on experience. Suggestions and opinions offered by the pedagogy teacher at such times are particularly meaningful.

Experience in Both Studio and Group Teaching Situations

Whether the pedagogy student goes on to seek an institutional teaching position or to establish an independent studio, it is almost certain that being able to teach in a variety of instructional settings will be an asset and perhaps even a necessity. It seems appropriate, therefore, that a pedagogy program should provide the student with both group and studio observations and teaching experiences.

When interest in group teaching first became widespread in the 1950s and 1960s, some pedagogy programs concentrated on the preparation of group piano teachers—especially those equipped to establish, teach, and supervise college piano classes. Some colleges and universities then inaugurated majors in class, or group, piano. Although there are still some programs that focus more closely (or only) on preparing group teachers, and still some programs that offer mostly (or only) preparation for studio teaching, a greater percentage of pedagogy programs are moving to provide more equitable experiences in studio, large-group, small-group, and small-group and individual piano teaching. Many colleges and universities that formerly offered majors in class piano have not only adapted their programs to include other instructional settings, but have changed the title of the major accordingly.

*T*HE UNDERGRADUATE PIANO PEDAGOGY MAJOR

For some piano students the baccalaureate is the highest degree obtained. If these graduates pursue a musical career, they are likely to establish independent studios. In an extensive investigation prepared by the National Conference on Piano Pedagogy,[2] many undergraduate piano pedagogy curricula were studied and compared with a view to determining the important components of a pedagogy major at this level. In this document illustrative case studies of existing programs are presented, similarities and differences concluded, and recommendations made.

It is noteworthy that the National Association of Schools of Music has since 1985 included in its handbook specific mention of the baccalaureate degree in pedagogy[3] together with a description of its curricular structure. The handbook also enumerates essential competencies, experiences, and opportunities that should be part of or result from this particular program of study.

*T*HE GRADUATE PIANO PEDAGOGY MAJOR

Graduate work constitutes study at both the master's and doctoral levels. These levels are quite different from one another. The master's degree is usually a matter of two years of study. The main purpose of the master's degree is to provide a specialization in the major area. The pursuit of a doctoral degree often involves three or more years of study. The primary focus of doctoral study is to broaden and deepen expertise in advanced scholarship as well as in the major area. It is a time of expansion, intensity, and integration. Programs that offer a major in piano pedagogy at the master's level are relatively numerous. Programs that offer primary specialization in this area at the doctoral level are not.

Pedagogy Study at the Master's Level

The major in piano pedagogy at the master's level is currently in a transitional state.[4] This adjustment process is more acute in some schools than others. Ideas concerning change and development of curricular structure and overall focus of the major are being influenced by the needs and interests of several groups currently looking to specialize in pedagogy at the master's level.

In the first place, the growth and popularity of the baccalaureate major in pedagogy means that more pianists are beginning graduate work with a greater amount of experience and interest in that field than heretofore. At present schools offering a pedagogy major at the master's level do not list a major (or even extensive work) in that same area as a prerequisite for admission. The student who receives a B.M. (major in piano pedagogy), however, is expecting graduate study to expand research and experiences already begun. Such a student is prepared to take on assorted student-teaching responsibilities and to do course work that builds on the orientation already provided by pedagogy instruction at the baccalaureate level.

Second, increased attention to the pedagogical preparation of all undergraduate keyboard performance majors (in the form of mandatory pedagogy coursework, some of it even including student teaching) has stimulated interest in specializing in this area on the part of pianists who, nonetheless, graduate with much less preparation or experience than those who might have majored in pedagogy during the undergraduate years. These students approach graduate study hoping to major in pedagogy for the first time. They do not have many of the observation or teaching experiences of the undergraduate pedagogy major. Graduate study for such students must somehow include these experiences.

Third, a growing number of pianists who have been teaching professionally without benefit of pedagogy training of any kind (having graduated when such was not available), are interested in pursuing graduate work now that majoring in pedagogy is a possibility. They view the master's degree with a major in pedagogy as a viable means of continuing self-development. This group of would-be students has an altogether different background, one that is strong in the area of experience, less complete or current in regard to knowledge of learning theory, use of high-tech equipment, and awareness of group-teaching strategies. They expect graduate pedagogy study to supply what is missing in their teaching backgrounds.

Is is any wonder that programs seeking to attract and meet the needs of such varying constituencies find themselves questioning prerequisites, juggling priorities and course content, weighing and sifting what should be final requirements for graduation? Current programs with a major in piano pedagogy at the master's level may differ widely from one another. Nonetheless some of these programs have begun to move in the same direction regarding course content, teaching experiences, and general focus. The National Conference on Piano Pedagogy study has also examined the pedagogy major at the master's level and presented case studies and recommendations drawn from this examination in a separate handbook.[5] Since the case studies are, once again, those of existing programs, similarities found therein are evidence of the establishment of some common practices and requisites.

Differences among programs are likely to occur in the areas of determining prerequisites or qualifications for admission, means by which shortcomings in courses or experiences may be made up, final requirements for graduation, and the number of semesters or terms that must be spent in residency.

Pedagogy Study at the Doctoral Level

Doctoral programs of study are the most difficult to compare. Schools structure and evaluate graduate work that leads to the Ph.D., the D.M.A., or the D.M. degree in diverse ways. This is true of doctoral study in general, not just of doctoral study in piano pedagogy. It is therefore unwise to comment extensively on the value or focus of specialization in pedagogy at the doctoral level. Although pedagogy programs at this level exist and interest in them continues to grow, these programs are not numerous. Further they are widely divergent in emphasis, entrance and final requirements, and curricula. A particular program of study—its overall scope as well as the focus of specific experiences it provides—usually reflects the expertise and interest of the given program's keyboard and pedagogy faculty.

PEDAGOGY FOR ALL KEYBOARD PERFORMANCE MAJORS

Interest and attention to pedagogy study has not only resulted in the establishment of the pedagogy major, but it is also reflected in the growing number, or greater strength, of pedagogy courses required in curricula for all keyboard performance majors. There are two basic reasons why an institution opts not to offer a major in pedagogy. Since the majority of keyboard performers graduating from professional schools spend some or even most of their time teaching, institutions may feel that it is more realistic to provide all performers with a certain amount of pedagogical training than to establish special programs of benefit to a specific or more limited number of students. A second reason, often unspoken, is that an institution may regard the pedagogy major as a degree only for the less-successful performer. The pedagogy major would then perhaps attract weaker pianists and become a refuge for those not able to meet the performance requirements of the keyboard major.

In schools where the pedagogy-for-everybody philosophy prevails, every pianist is required to study some pedagogy (perhaps even to do student teaching), but every pianist gets less pedagogy than would be the case if pedagogy were a major. Some students may even feel the need for more pedagogy study than is offered. On the other hand, some blue-chip performers who find themselves in pedagogy courses solely because these courses are required discover an interest in, and talent for, teaching that they never knew existed. If left to their own choices, they would not have elected to take these classes. Having taken them, these performers may move to augment their pedagogical knowledge and skills, either on their own or by looking for opportunities to do further directed study in the area of pedagogy.

Attention to the development of pedagogy as a major has given rise to greater discussion of pedagogy in professional forums and publications. Conferences, workshops, and seminars have dealt with such topics as structuring and evaluating student teaching, the history of pedagogy, the development of a pedagogy curriculum, academic job prospects for the currently graduating piano major, and an array of similar subjects. Since the emergence, in 1979, of the National Conference on Piano Pedagogy, keyboard professionals involved with the teaching of pedagogy have a national forum whose function is to disseminate information concerning the training of piano teachers. The existence and activities of this conference have also given piano pedagogy teachers a sense of collective identity and cohesiveness.

Faculty responsible for pedagogy instruction in schools where that subject is not a major have undoubtedly been energized and challenged by such discussion and activity, as have their colleagues who direct programs that offer pedagogy as a major. Without moving either to establish majors or multiply pedagogy courses, these faculty are making the courses already in existence more viable and significant. Training the pianist as a teacher is becoming a matter of general concern among keyboard faculty.

*W*HERE TO MAJOR IN PEDAGOGY

Since not every professional school of music offers a major in piano pedagogy, it is necessary to identify the places where such programs are available and important to learn what each of these programs provide and require. For the benefit of those who have particular interest in this field, the National Conference on Piano Pedagogy has prepared a national directory.[6] The directory lists all schools that offer instruction in piano pedagogy, from those with only one course to those that offer entire degree programs. In addition, under each institutional heading, the directory includes:

names of the applied piano and pedagogy faculty.

titles of required and elective courses in the pedagogy curriculum.

provisions for observation of teaching.

resources and arrangements for student teaching.

provisions for critique of student teaching.

unique features or particular strengths of the pedagogy program.

the name of a person to contact for further information.

In comparing degrees and program offerings in the field of pedagogy, it is important not to give undue attention to the nomenclature of the degree. Titles are numerous and varied: They include majors in performance and pedagogy; piano performance (piano pedagogy emphasis); applied music (piano pedagogy concentration); piano pedagogy. Titles are selected by each institution. There are no standardized labels.

The substance of any program will be revealed in the content of the course offerings, the nature and extent of teaching observation and student teaching, and the final requirements for the completion of the degree. Learning about the pedagogy faculty at a particular school, speaking or meeting with them, visiting the campus, observing pedagogy in action, questioning pedagogy students about the program in which they are enrolled, finding out what graduates of a pedagogy program do as professionals—this is information that will furnish the most telling assessment of a program's direction, effectiveness, and value.

It is equally important that the entire keyboard program of a particular school be considered. Studying pedagogy in a school where performance standards are high, where performance faculty are high-quality teachers and musicians, where music making is of primary importance, where there is opportunity to participate in ensemble performance, and where there are substantive research resources may be a quite different experience than pursuing a pedagogical education apart from these other influences. Piano pedagogy is concerned with the art of playing the piano. It cannot be realistically examined or practiced in a nonperformance context. The piano pedagogy student must hear music, make music, and understand music in order to teach others to do the same.

PART SIX

Competitions

CHAPTER 14

Competitions for the Precollege Student

Piano competitions and festivals for the precollege student have increased markedly within the last few decades. They have become an important means for young musicians to distinguish themselves and gain recognition. The creation of numerous competitions catering to specific musical inclinations and tastes has enlarged the pool of potential participants and contributed to the profusion of competitions. The validity of competitions is corroborated by the prevailing attitude among many students and teachers that participation in competitions is endemic to serious music study.

Precollege competitions often begin locally with sponsorship by state music teachers organizations. Winners from these events proceed to regional and national levels, then to final rounds culminating in public performances featured at annual national conventions. Local arts organizations often hold competitions to select young performers for special youth concerts in their performing arts series. The inclusion of precollege performers draws other young students to these concerts, broadening the traditional base of support for the organization and enhancing future community involvement.

Many colleges and universities welcome the opportunity to host or develop competitions, and they provide faculty members for master classes and adjudications at these events in order to attract prospective students. Numerous other local and national nonprofit organizations have sprung up for the purpose of recognizing excellence in achievement at the same time that they stimulate awareness of the performing arts within the community. Some of these contests are specific to the precollege student; others are subsidiaries to competitions whose major focus is on recognition of the young (usually young adult) artist performer.

COMPETITION AWARDS AND REWARDS: EXPLICIT AND IMPLICIT

Rewards for participation in competitions vary. Most competitions provide some combination of evaluations, cash prizes, certificates, trophies, and performance opportunities. Money, certificates, evaluations, and trophies are tangible evidence of success. Performances may include concerto appearances with local orchestras or recitals in local cultural events. In many cases, these concerto performances represent the first time the precollege student has played with an orchestra, and that opportunity alone provides a new and important learning experience. Occasionally a piano is awarded, and a young musician acquires a valuable practice instrument. Recognition in the form of awards ceremonies and newspaper announcements is public acknowledgement of achievement and counterbalances the many hours of solitary practice that preceded the public performance. These explicit rewards contribute to the less obvious, but powerful, personal reward of enhanced self-esteem accrued through such recognition.

Learning how to cope with playing in unfamiliar surroundings before strangers in a judgmental atmosphere provides practice for dealing with the exigencies and pressures of professional life. The student learns which modes of behavior and which psyching-up procedures work best; how much practice is optimal; how to cultivate a positive attitude in adversity, set priorities, maintain an appropriate perspective, and cope with disappointment. In the rigors of competition, the young pianist reacts and responds to extremes in both advantageous and adversarial circumstances and is forced to confront the ultimate dilemma of deciding the significance of music in his/her life.

TEACHER RESPONSIBILITIES IN RELATION TO COMPETITIONS

Precollege students, with limited musical experience, are more dependent on input from the instructor than are more seasoned performers. This increased dependency implies additional obligations for the teacher. In order to ensure a reasonable chance for productive competition experiences, the teacher must select an appropriate student-competition match. Most competitions feature public performance as part of the festivities. Many times final and semifinal rounds will be played before an audience. Attending the public portion of a contest (prior to entering it some other time in the future) gives both the instructor and student a chance to evaluate expectations in terms of repertoire levels and performance proficiency for individual competitions.

Local competitions, recently inaugurated competitions, or competitions offering small cash prizes may provide the best opportunities for less-experienced performers. The demands of these competitions may be less rigorous than those of more established contests with more sophisticated patronage and lucrative prizes. Also, adjudicators for smaller, newer competitions may be selected from local precollege teachers, who tend to be more familiar with expectations for the younger student than are some college professors or renowned performers chosen to adjudicate more established competitions.

Competitions frequently have several categories to accommodate special interests or age groups (e.g., for the well-motivated student of average ability, for specific composers or style periods, for ensembles, for popular music). Such competitions, with circumscribed repertoire requirements and many limited age groupings, offer another good alternative for the young pianist's initial competitive ventures. Noncompetitive evaluations that customarily offer no prizes or rankings are the least judgmental mode of involvement in auditions. The student receives the benefit of a written critique without the onus of hierarchical placement.

Some students do not flourish in overtly competitive environments. It is therefore imperative that the teacher select carefully not only appropriate competitions for students but, perhaps more important, appropriate students for competitions. Students who work most consistently under pressure may be good candidates. Students who work in spurts run the risk of compulsive last-minute practicing that may precipitate physical injuries. Students who tend to play their best in studio classes, master classes, recitals and other venues may be good candidates. Students who play comfortably only in intimate settings—in lessons, or informally for friends—may not be ready for competitive challenge.

At the precollege level, the parent is often the first to express interest in having the child participate in competitions. Parents, who often have no musical training themselves, monitor progress in terms of their children's peers. If their children's friends are entering competitions, it may seem as if their own children should do likewise. The child may be opposed, reluctant, enthusiastic, or indifferent to the prospect of competing. It is the teacher's responsibility to ascertain whether the student's desire to participate in competition is genuine. Teachers must also be wary of what drives their own desire for students to compete. One must determine whether motivation for competition participation is based primarily on the best interests of the student or on the desire for positive studio publicity. Regardless of the initiator, the student may have a constructive experience if entering the competition is something (s)he wants to do. The ultimate question is: "Who wants to enter this competition, anyway?"

It is incumbent upon the instructor to choose appropriate literature for competitions. The literature must match the stipulations of the competition as well as highlight the special assets of the student. The introspective student whose musicianship is evident in the playing of more reflective music may not fare well in competitions demanding the performance of virtuosic works. Precollege students with an affinity for brilliant concerto literature may not yet have acquired an appreciation of the subtleties of more intimate pieces. The broad

Assets and Liabilities of Competition for the Student

ASSETS	LIABILITIES
Anticipated participation in competitons aids in setting short- and long term goals.	Concentration on acquisition of specific literature may preclude a comprehensive approach to learning the allied, and equally essential, skills of sight-reading, improvisation, and ensemble playing. It may discourage or postpone the exploration of valuable repertoire not suitable for competition performance.
Exclusive attention to polishing details in a circumscribed body of literature enhances discipline and fine-tuning in the final stages of preperformance preparation. Emphasis is on *product*.	Overemphasis on polishing the product may undervalue the *process* of learning and other ancillary benefits, for instance, extrapolation and transference of technical and musical discoveries from current repertoire to a broader choice of prospective repertoire.
Topical competitions featuring the work of a single composer or style period provide comprehensive exposure to that composer or style period and offer the opportunity to learn pieces a student may otherwise not have been motivated to explore.	The narrow focus of specific competitions may inhibit the acquisition of a balanced repertoire.
Performance opportunities in a variety of settings—solo, concerto, ensemble—help promote performance security, poise, flexibility, and self-confidence.	Inappropriately chosen or poorly prepared students may be devastated by public exposure, by the censure of critiques, or embarassed by newly perceived inadequacies.
Playing unfamiliar instruments in different halls with acoustical vicissitudes challenges the student to listen and accommodate to the surroundings with alacrity.	Reacting to unpredictable environment may be beyond the student's capabilities and may lead to further erosion of self-confidence.
Unpredictable interruptions and rapid switch to other repertoire challenges the concentration and security of the most confident performer.	Interruptions and repertoire switching may exacerbate memory problems.
Evaluations and written critiques may supply input to reinforce musical ideas, gauge technical and musical progress, and assess current accomplishment.	Unduly negative comments from judges undermine confidence, resolve, and sense of self-worth. They may also promote a distorted winner-loser paradigm. This predisposition suggests that one is a loser unless awarded first place.

ASSETS	LIABILITIES
Some students may not learn to harness impulsive interpretations until critical judgments about style are manifest in written critiques or low rankings.	Competitions often reward facility and security rather than creativity and spontaneity. This shift to playing it safe can subvert development of personal musical growth and expression.
Competitions provide an opportunity to ascertain one's ranking in relation to peer accomplishment. The student may ask, "Where do I fit in the scheme of things?"	Unrealistic pressures, goals, and expectations may nullify accurate perception of the ranking. To maintain proper perspective, an awareness of the subjectivity and quixotic nature of judging must be preserved.
Competitions provide the chance to reevaluate coordination of one's goals to a standard of excellence and help define the next level of musical aspiration.	The student may come to believe that *only* participation in competitions provides definition of achievement or that standards are determined as a result of external judging.
Competitions offer a foretaste of the demands and pressures of a musician's life and suggest some of the sacrifices and accommodations needed to meet the requisites of the profession.	One cannot do competitions for a lifetime or for a livelihood. Public performance is but one aspect of a pianist's professional existence. Lack of awareness of this balance among performing, teaching, and accompanying may lead to disproportionate training in one aspect of musical activity at the expense of others.
Competitions may provide a sense of camaraderie and opportunity to interact with peers. It is invaluable for young pianists to observe the varied ways in which colleagues handle the demands of practice and pressures of performance.	Personal rivalries and jealousies may arise creating animosity that inhibits personal growth. This is particularly true when the same students are involved in a number of the same competitions.
Competitions increase awareness of, and exposure to, literature. Opportunity to hear a variety of interpretations of the same piece increases perception of musical nuance and aids the student in defining personal choices and aesthetics.	The seeking of a personal voice may cause a student to *use* rather than *serve* the music. The student may distort the intention of the composer or ignore stylistic concerns to highlight technical brilliance or self-expression as a means of self-aggrandizement.
Cash prizes may ease the financial strain on students and families.	Costs involved in participating in competitions (e.g., entry fees, accompanists' fees, travel expenses) may be prohibitive and/or nullify the value of the experience or occasional prize.

Assets and Liabilities of Competition for the Teacher

ASSETS	LIABILITIES
Evaluations reinforce a sense of direction in work with a student and may assist in redefining the student's strengths and weaknesses.	Short-term goals—intense preparation of competition repertoire—may be emphasized at the expense of broader musical skills, leading to vast developmental disparities and the eventual need for remedial work.
Competitions offer opportunities to escape the isolation of the private studio and to associate with other teachers and students.	Rivalries between studios may create nonproductive animosity leading to unethical recruitment practices. The pressure to enter students in competitions and the attention accorded to prizewinners may divert good students away from excellent teachers who are not involved in competition participation.
Exposure to standards of excellence and expectations regarding repertoire levels refine sequencing of literature and attention to detail.	The teacher may be tempted to assign increasingly difficult (and perhaps inappropriate) repertoire to enable students to distinguish themselves. Often the musical demands of pieces are beyond the level appropriate for even the prodigiously talented and musically experienced younger student.
Increased exposure to, and awareness of, a variety of interpretive possibilities enriches the resources of the teacher.	The less-secure teacher may be influenced to have students imitate interpretations or mannerisms of performers who win.
The necessity of creating performance forums for students prior to auditions, and student participation in these events, can lead to studio cohesiveness and the upgrading of the performance skills of the entire class.	Focus on preparation for competition performance may shift perceived emphasis from process to product and lead to a distorted musical value system. Emphasis on contest participation may cause noncompeting students to feel excluded and undervalued.
Competitions provide the opportunity to attract new students and upgrade the the individual studio. Success breeds success. Prizewinning students attract other serious, achievement-oriented students.	The teacher may be tempted to enter the most gifted students in too many, or inappropriate, competitions in order to attract other gifted students. There is also a danger that attracting students in this manner will be perceived as student "stealing."

range of keyboard literature available, and the generous repertoire choices offered in most precollege competitions, usually makes feasible an advantageous match of student abilities and literature.

The teacher must also assist the student in the setting of short- and long-term goals. When competitions require several selections, it is often prudent to limit the number of new pieces assigned and to review previously learned pieces to fulfill requirements. A timetable for learning new notes and memorizing pieces is useful. It is usually wise to begin the longest or most difficult pieces first and add others sequentially throughout the preparation process. Sufficient time must be prescribed for the reviewing and seasoning of all, including older, pieces. The young student usually has fewer old pieces to draw upon, so careful attention to any need for assimilating new concepts as new pieces are added to the repertoire must be considered. A hierarchy of performance tryouts—that is, audio and/or videotaping, studio class, recitals, and mock (simulated or staged) competitions—is useful in monitoring progress toward short- and long-term goals in the acquisition of competition repertoire.

One of the teacher's most important responsibilities is to impart a positive attitude toward the learning process and to provide realistic counsel and support to both students and parents. Encouraging the student to strive for his/her personal best at each incremental stage of preparation deflects attention from product to process and defuses the hazards of a distorted response to the judgmental aspect of the competition.

PARENT RESPONSIBILITIES IN RELATION TO COMPETITIONS

Parents play a significant role in shaping a student's constructive attitude toward competition participation. They must carefully monitor vicissitudes in the student's reactions to the work involved and supply appropriate encouragement and perspective. A competition should be perceived as an opportunity, not an obstacle. Participation in itself implies accomplishment. Competitions are but one of many possibilities for achieving success.

In addition to moral support, parents should provide:

An uninterrupted practice environment on an adequate instrument.

Scores (and duplicates, if necessary) for adjudicators.

Assistance in the timely filing of application forms.

Assistance in the hiring of an experienced accompanist. (Collaboration between the young student and a reliable, accomplished accompanist can vastly increase the student's chance to excel.)

Appropriate concert attire.

Transportation to lessons, rehearsals, and performances.

Housing and supervision when traveling greater distances.

ADJUDICATOR RESPONSIBILITIES

Adjudicators of precollege competitions must bear in mind that what they are hearing probably represents the taste, judgment, and ideas of the teacher as much as those of the student. Judges are therefore confronted with the dilemma of evaluating the proclivities of the teacher as well as the musical potential of the student. At this stage potential is an elusive quality, since perseverance, determination, and discipline are at least as important as talent in the formula for success. Rates of personal and artistic growth, like physical maturation, vary greatly. Judges must weigh concerns about potential in addition to evaluating an actual performance.

Judges are responsible for:

Establishing personal criteria for adjudication (e.g., accuracy, tone production, balance, clarity, poise) and applying these consistently. Interjection of personal taste, fondness for (or dislike of) particular literature, and preconceptions regarding performance should be avoided.

According each contestant the courtesy of a fair hearing and equal time to perform.

Offering a constructive written critique with useful suggestions. Since unrealized potential is difficult to estimate, it is probably best to bestow encouragement and praise as much as possible.

Observing consistency in scoring. Due to the great disparity in physical growth and maturity levels specific to precollege students, one must guard against assigning advantages to a small student or penalizing a larger student of the same age. It is difficult to hold a tiny teen to the same standard as a contemporary who looks like an adult.

Respecting confidentiality. To maintain credibility and integrity in the judging process, deliberations among jurists should not be disclosed.

FINAL CONSIDERATIONS

One argument suggests that the profusion of competitions dilutes the recognition factor: the abundance of winners makes it problematic to identify future stars. At the precollege level, when one is judging potential for development rather than mature artistry, the aim of such competitions should not be to identify stars but to reward achievement and promote talent. The abundance of competitions can be an asset at this level; more competitions provide greater opportunity to encourage large numbers of talented youngsters (many of whom will be avocational musicians and future audiences) to involve themselves in the process of musical discovery and appreciation.

Precollege competitions offer numerous opportunities and rewards to the young pianist who is carefully prepared—musically, physically, and psychologically—to handle competitive challenges. Nevertheless many liabilities implicit in the competitive situation may offset, if not preclude, competition participation. Younger students require special considerations and accommodations. They have more limited experience and are more dependent on guidance and advice. There is often considerable disparity in levels of growth and maturity among younger performers. At best, an isolated performance in competition represents a microcosm of a student's current preparation and potential. Prize-winning in precollege competitions does not ensure success in professional competitions or predict professional viability. Preparing for and entering competitions can be construed as only one expression of a student's seriousness of purpose. The ultimate value of precollege competitions is educational. Competitions can expand exposure to literature, can season performance, and may offer a special kind of self-knowledge.

CHAPTER 15

Competitions at the Collegiate and Young Artist Level

The concept of a competition between performers has a long historical tradition. Whether one recalls the medieval tradition dramatized in Wagner's *Die Meistersinger* or remembers the play-off between Mozart and Clementi staged by the Emperor Joseph, the idea of comparing performances and selecting a winner is a very old one indeed. Yet competitions themselves fall prey to criticism more than most musical activities, criticism not only of the procedures or results of a given play-off, but also of the very philosophy underlying the event. Thus it is pointed out time and again that competitions seduce young musicians into expectations of early glory and thereby dissipate efforts toward long-term, more serious study; that competitions foster attention to gymnastics and a facile brilliance, thereby encouraging neglect of more profound repertoire and musical values; that competitions are notoriously inaccurate in identifying which musicians will succeed as performers over the long haul; and that competitions actually damage the potential growth of young performers by thrusting winners into wide public exposure prematurely.

Nevertheless, major competitions continue to garner the attention of the press and the public. Winners of these events continue to present their achievements in the competition arena as endorsements of excellence, and the concert-going public, including many professional musicians, continues to accept these credentials. Competitions at all levels, from international to local, continue to proliferate.

Since competitive events are interwoven in the fabric of professional life, notwithstanding their shortcomings, perhaps an attempt to reevalute their function is in order. The disadvantages attributed to competitions often have more to do with the *attitudes* surrounding the actual events than with the idea of competitiveness itself. The assumption that competitions are devices for identifying and exploiting star-quality performers is fundamentally destructive. Were professionals to discard this premise, competitions would be relieved of many objectionable qualities.

A competition is, after all, simply an event or a series of events involving evaluations of a group of performers by a judge or group of judges over a given period of time. The event is unique, for those specific groups of performers and judges will probably never be drawn together again, that series of performances can never be repeated exactly, and that segment of time can never be recaptured. Thinking about the event this way can lead to taking a competition pretty much at its face value, encompassing both the good and the bad performances, the acuteness and the dullness of the adjudications, and the appropriateness of the final results.

Just as there are good games and bad games in sports, so there are good competitions and bad competitions. Often extremes are the result of a mixture of human chemistry or of factors over which no one seems to have control. Just as bad weather can take the edge off a football game and influence its outcome, so can the mechanical malfunction of an instrument or a disturbance in an auditorium play a role in a piano competition. Most performers easily recognize the fact that performance seems better sometimes than at other times, for inexplicable reasons. Such variance is also applicable to the concentration of the judges. Moreover the expertise any given judge can bring to the musical values of the literature performed will vary from piece to piece, composer to composer, and period to period, for no person, no matter how conscientious, can bring equal amounts of knowledge and sensitivity to judging all areas of the vast keyboard literature.

Any individual contestant may encounter a host of uncontrollable factors that can influence a performance. Heading this list is dealing with the instrument itself. Large piano competitions may offer each contestant a choice of instrument, from as many as a dozen. Often several makes of instrument are available, and there is usually a brief amount of time allotted to make the choice and get used to the selected piano. Other competitions offer less choice, and sometimes a contestant must simply play whatever is on stage. The fact remains, however, that the degree of comfort a contestant feels with the instrument to be played is a highly individual and influential factor.

Other factors that may influence a contestant are the living arrangements (often provided by the competition administration), the travel schedule to the competition, the order or selection of the repertoire to be heard by the judges, and the order of contestants appearance. There is, for example, a notion that those who play early in a competition are at a disadvantage, particularly the contestant who plays first. The assumption is that the judges are still feeling their way with regard to the level of playing in that particular competition and that even good playing, heard early on, will lose its edge when recalled after other impressive performances.

All of these factors form a psychological profile that can influence the contestant profoundly, regardless of the reality of the circumstances involved. Luck, therefore, seems to become a factor that attends most competitions. With so many variables at work, it becomes apparent that the only rational way in which to regard a competition is to view it in the short range, resisting the temptation to project its results as prophecies for the future. This is not to deny the strengths or weaknesses of performances in any given competition, nor to imply that the decisions of the judges have no significance for the outcome of an event. It is, however, a suggestion that any competition, no matter how highly touted or how exciting, be kept in proper perspective.

Were this premise to become widely accepted, it could open the way for conceiving a host of nontraditional competitions in which less-frequently performed repertoire might be featured, thereby offering arenas for pianists who specialize in early keyboard music, the Viennese classics, or avant-garde repertoire; competitions in which improvised embellishments might be the hallmark of virtuosity, rather than octaves or double thirds; competitions in which enough performance time is invested to be able to judge a contestant's ability to sustain and project one of the great monuments of the literature (the entire *Diabelli Variations* of Beethoven or the entire B-Flat [posthumous] Sonata of Schubert); competitions in which the ability to deal with piano music written since 1950 can be evaluated and which can help establish artistic standards of performance for this music. In short, the professional world could view competitions as serving goals other than that of identifying the next generation of nineteenth-century-oriented virtuosos.

Once this expanded viewpoint gained acceptance, much of the focus of competitions would be on the artistic contributions of the winners rather than the potential commercial value for the threadbare concert circuit. Overexposure in the usual sense would become a moot point. The winner might become an acknowledged master in a given area of specialization but would not be expected to be a rising superstar who played the war-horses more brilliantly than everyone else around.

One of the most powerful arguments for regarding competitions from a short-range viewpoint is the way in which such an approach ultimately reflects on those contestants who do not win on a particular occasion. It is recognized generally that the difference between performances judged for the first prize and second prize can be minuscule. Commonly the first prize is awarded as a result of the way the judges' scores average out, and in a very real sense the winner represents a compromise of differences in artistic opinion among the judges. Those who come in further down the ladder oftentimes exhibit great strength at one point or another in the competition. Sometimes a young musician of markedly individual viewpoint will do less well because of having offended the aesthetic taste of one or two on a panel of judges. Moreover many performers of considerable achievement are overlooked simply because their artistic concepts are not yet entirely solidified. All of these are "losers," in the sense that they did not win the first prize, but too often the hoopla and hype attending the winner produce a negative backlash for these other contestants that is entirely undeserved. A more moderate outlook on the value and implications of winning would lessen the psychological burden others must bear as a result of not having come in first, as well as keep the reality of everyone's achievements in perspective.

Most of the major competitions have requirements that cover a broad spectrum of the repertoire, and long-range preparation should take that into account. Thus serious preparation by any hopeful contestant should address potential problem areas early on. A Baroque requirement, often designated from the works of Johann Sebastian Bach, is almost always present. One or more Classical sonatas may be expected. Virtuoso Romantic works are often designated. In this context there is often an etude requirement designed to display virtuosity. Etude requirements usually draw material from the etudes of Chopin, Liszt, Debussy, Scriabin, or Rachmaninoff. Twentieth-century music is treated quite differently by different competitions. Sometimes there is an impressionist requirement, usually drawn from the music of Debussy or Ravel. Increasingly music of masters of the early part of the twentieth century, such as Prokofiev, Bartók, Stravinsky, or Schoenberg, does not entirely satisfy the expectations for playing contemporary music.

The requirement of a specific competition piece frequently appears in major competitions. The Busoni Competition in Bolzano, Italy, traditionally selects solo music written by the competition's namesake, Ferruccio Busoni. The Van Cliburn Competition in Fort Worth, Texas, has addressed the area of contemporary music by commissioning a required piece from a celebrated composer. The piece is given to all of the contestants at a designated time shortly before the competition, and all are expected to learn it in time to present it at one of the competition rounds. The Queen Elizabeth Competition in Belgium adopts the same procedure using a short piano concerto for its finalists. Obviously the ability to read well, to learn rapidly and securely, and to perform relatively new material under pressure is necessary in these marathonlike situations. Chamber music, too, often forms a portion of the requirement, although here the tendency is to let the contestant select from a short list of standard chamber works using the piano.

Many larger competitions center the final round of the event around performances of piano concerti. Experienced conductors and acceptable orchestras provide the orchestral portions, and the finalists usually underscore their virtuosity by selecting well-known concerti from a list of standards. It is rare that any finalist attempts to beat out competitors with a concerto of Mozart, and the brilliant war-horses of the nineteenth and early twentieth centuries are encountered with great frequency. Often these final events are the best attended and receive the most media coverage. Although they do provide a brilliant finale to a competition that may have lasted days or even weeks, such finales tend to detract attention from superlative performances that may have gone before and only serve to reinforce arguments critical of competition. Nonetheless, any contestant who hopes to play in the finals of a major event such as this must have a couple of showstopper concerti ready to go. A few major competitions do not center their final round on concerto performance, but these tend to be fewer all the time as the popularity of the concerto show rises.

Memorized performance is expected throughout most competitions, except in a few cases involving extremely avant-garde works and sometimes in chamber works. Preparation for a major competition should include not only the ability to memorize securely, but also knowing the music well enough to jump around without getting rattled. Time for each contestant is usually limited in the early rounds of the competition. Judges may wish to hear a wide variety of styles, tempi, and representation from several composers in a time slot of fifteen or twenty minutes. In order to do that, judges may ask the contestant to stop in the middle of a piece, skip to another section, start another movement or another piece. These enforced breaks in concentration can be distracting, but only an inexperienced competitor would ever try to justify being thrown by this procedure. It is to be expected, and preparation must take that into account. The other place where this stop-start facility is useful is in rehearsal for ensemble playing, whether it be chamber music or a concerto. Usually ensemble rehearsal time is minimal, so trouble spots are fixed as soon as they are identified, and the performer is usually expected to be able to continue on from the trouble spot or section rather than dropping back.

Selecting an instrument on which to play in a competition is one of the key factors for success. Every contestant should prepare by seeking out performance situations in which a variety of instruments are encountered. Differences in action, in tonal brilliance, in pedal operation, or in hall acoustics are disturbing to almost all pianists, regardless of their experience. What experience can teach is how to adapt one's aural perception to these differences and how to respond physically with some degree of flexibility. These changes are all fairly automatic if one is following a strong inner aural image, but experience in making them should be sought out before the actual competition. Further, if a performer practices in the same room on the same piano most of the time, an insidious security attended by a feeling of comfort may be built up, only to be rudely shattered when performing conditions change.

If a contestant has the luxury of choosing from among a number of instruments, several factors should be remembered. The instruments are almost always lined up somewhere on the stage, but all of them won't be positioned stage center where the performance will take place. Repositioning the piano will change the performer's acoustical perception. Since what one will hear after the piano has been moved will be a new acoustical mix anyway, it is best to settle on an instrument that seems reasonably comfortable as soon as practical, allowing several minutes to learn the dimensions of that instrument. Last-minute hopping around is usually unproductive. Trying to develop a "new" sound in response to some perceived strength in an instrument is usually dangerous. One will do best under pressure what one has practiced, and the best instrument under the circumstances is the one that responds most beautifully to what one has been preparing to do.

Attentiveness to the acoustical properties of the hall is of utmost importance. If possible, arrange to listen from the front of the house as a few passages are played. One is often surprised to find that the hall is much more alive than perceived onstage. Although the presence of an audience will change acoustical properties yet again, just the sensing of basic resonance in the space of the hall can be very helpful.

Repertoire for any competition should be ready very early (except possibly for the required piece, if it is not made available until a given time). Nothing can substitute for seasoned performance experiences. Even performance under less than ideal circumstances can be helpful in establishing a kind of durability that will act as a bulwark under pressure. Most judges deny that anything as simplistic as wrong notes is the basis for their decisions, but the fact remains that insecure performances, nervous-sounding performances, technically unprepared performances, and memory lapses weigh heavily against any contestant. Judges are interested primarily in the quality of musical projection, it is true, but if that projection is faulty too often, then the ideas simply do not come through. A relentless regime of performance practice helps increase the margin of security. It is a margin that most inexperienced performers do not take seriously enough. To neglect its strength in recital preparation may be sometimes possible, although never wise, but to neglect building it in preparation for a competition—a scene where the entire atmosphere may be charged with nervous excitement—is almost always to assure falling short of one's performance potential.

Athletes train for their competitive events by adopting an all-around lifestyle that contributes to their having the strength and the nerve to meet the challenges they face. Musical performers seldom go so far in terms of their physical preparation, which seems strange when one considers the stamina, the nervous energy, and the high degree of physical and mental coordination demanded by their art. Young pianists often expect the best from themselves under pressure and yet have done relatively little in terms of diet, rest, and exercise to build up any kind of reserve. Performers often strive seriously for mental preparation in other ways, however, and in this context, most experienced young performers tend to keep their own counsel during the days the competition is in progress. This does not by any means imply unfriendliness, but most performers realize that getting caught up in the nervousness generated by other contestants only acts to increase their own sense of insecurity. Many contestants will not allow themselves to listen to other contestants until they themselves have no more playing to do. This is an individual matter, to be sure, but most competitors value solitary practice and contemplation at competition time.

That competitions are going to be part of the musical scene for some time to come is fairly obvious. Their disadvantages can be minimized and their advantages enhanced if clear thinking about their purpose prevails. Competitions will remain, in whatever form, among the most exciting challenges a musician can undertake, and they can provide a panorama of memorable performances and an avenue through which many fine performers may become better known.

PART SEVEN

Historical Overview of Keyboard Pedagogy

CHAPTER 16

Influences on Pedagogy

The history of the pedagogy of playing keyboard instruments has been influenced by several factors:

The aesthetics and function of the keyboard music itself.

The physical characteristics of the instrument(s) for which the music was written.

Research interest of a given period.

The philosophical base of a given period.

Consider the first of these factors. The more utilitarian music is—that is, the more music serves to enhance some other activity—the less likely it is that the music will accrue sophisticated expressive values or complicated technical demands that require explanation, clarification, and direction through pedagogical writings. One has to view this generalization with some degree of caution, because musicians seem to possess an irrepressible creativity that constantly pushes the music into the limelight, notwithstanding the resistance offered by the directors of the activity for which the music was written. The most obvious example of this tug-of-war relationship is the body of music written for religious services. The opinions of church administrators or priests as to what was appropriate music for worship services have been, more often than not, at variance with those of the musicians providing the music itself. As the musicians create music that shows its expressiveness or its virtuosity too powerfully, they are accused of misdirecting the focus of the event. To a lesser extent music written for nobility, for court events, or for entertainment has undergone similar scrutiny. Thus light, cheerful music was often preferred to heavier, serious music as a means to enhance relaxation.

Music kept well contained in a perfunctory role requires but little explanation, and what is required can usually be trusted to the tradition passed from teacher to student in the studio. As music begins to burst forth—either as service music in those situations where composers' creativity prevails or institutional liberalism permits, or in the concert hall, where listening to music is the focal point—musical creation becomes more complex, more expressive, and almost always more virtuosic. In the wake of this rise, after one or two generations, come the pedagogical writings geared to helping the aspiring performer achieve the skills necessary to deal with such music.

This relationship may be seen at work clearly in the nineteenth century, when music was being listened to for its own sake in the setting of the concert hall and when much appreciation centered around the physical skills involved in producing that music. Writings, explanations, exercises, and regimens of various types abound from this period, as a by-product of music written with complex and expressive goals.

Even the pedagogical writings of the twentieth century tend to apply to the nineteenth century. Although methodology may often employ physiological, psychological, and even electronic terms, the audience this methodology addresses still consists by and large of musicians who wish to play nineteenth-century, virtuoso-oriented music. Very few pedagogues have addressed themselves to the past sixty years of serious piano music. The one- to two-generation gap by which pedagogy has followed the demands of musical literature thus seems to be widening, because audiences and even performing musicians have been slow to accept the new definitions of aesthetics evolved by the musical thinking of twentieth-century composers.

The second factor that has influenced pedagogical writings for keyboard instruments is an obvious one: the physical properties of the instrument that was to be played. If indeed Johann Sebastian Bach wrote music for the harpsichord and clavichord, then treatises of the period that explained how to play this music deal with how to make *those* instruments speak in the desired way. Some of what was written may apply to the modern-day piano; some may not. Some instructions may adapt well, other instructions not so well. The piano is yet another instrument with physical specifications that are quite different from either the harpsichord or the clavichord, and it has to be handled differently no matter what music is to be played on it. By the same token early pianos make demands different from later versions of that instrument. Thus every pedagogical treatise must be studied in the context of the instrument for which it was written: the material of that instrument, the construction of that instrument, and the composite sound of that instrument.

If such treatises are truly intended to help us play the *music* of the period, then we may be led to ask some tough questions of ourselves. For example: If weight-technique is indeed a concept espoused by late-nineteenth-century pedagogues and one that is directly applicable to nineteenth-century and twentieth-century pianos, is it then properly used in eighteenth-century music—music written at a time when the piano was made of different materials, constructed differently, and sounded differently? A logical answer is that, since we are playing music of the eighteenth century on a twentieth-century instrument, we can use such a technique if we adapt it in some way to suggest eighteenth-century aesthetics, or sound, or both. Yet not everyone would agree, some suggesting that such adaptation is unnecessary, others arguing that we should in fact seek out eighteenth-century instruments and apply period pedagogy if we intend to deal with music of that period. Even advocates of the middle-of-the-road approach will differ on the degree of adaptation and the way it should be effected.

Projecting the changing physical characteristics of various keyboard instruments against the history of pedagogical writings gives us a whole new set of powerful and influential variables that act and interact upon one another. One can point to obvious relationships: that the pedagogy of the pedal developed only after today's pedal had become a standard part of the instrument, or that the pedagogy dealing with rapid repeated notes came along only after double escapement had been invented and perfected. On the other hand, many relationships are less clear-cut: whether or not the pedagogy of the high finger stroke, espoused right up into the twentieth century, is indeed a tradition carried over from pedagogy of a former time, or whether the pedagogy of the repeated note, developed in the nineteenth century, is applicable to the so-called accelerated action of some modern instruments.

The third factor that has influenced keyboard pedagogy is the research or intellectual focus of the period. That focus influences the format the pedagogy takes and colors its content insofar as what seems important in approaching a complex and multi-faceted subject. The clearest examples of this influence are once again in the nineteenth and twentieth centuries, the periods in which the most voluminous amount of pedagogical material was produced. The overriding research emphasis of both periods has been in various areas of scientific investigation. Thus in the wake of the industrial revolution and the Age of Reason, pedagogues seemed to find it efficacious to speak of "scientific" approaches. Sometimes that science was based on anatomy, sometimes on the mechanics and acoustics of physics, sometimes on psychology, sometimes on neurophysiology. Whatever the underlying field of investigation, the basic assumption, often stated and always implied, is that pedagogical principles derived from these fields of science are totally valid. Thus anatomical study is meant to teach us how to use our playing apparatus in a "natural" way. Mechanics of physics is meant to teach us about the levers and vector motion involved in producing tone at the piano, and how we may approach this action most efficiently. Acoustics is meant to make us aware of the tonal possibilities (and limitations) of the instrument. Psychology is meant to show us something of the cause-and-effect relationship of communicating mood and emotion in music and to reveal how performers may manage their own thinking in attempting to conquer various problems ranging from stage fright to playing fast to memorizing. Neurophysiology explains to us how the brain and central nervous system operate and what may be done to incite desired muscular response in playing the piano.

Each of these areas of research has indeed added to our body of knowledge about how to play the piano, and professional musicians have found help as they have become acquainted with this impressive body of information. Most, however, have been reluctant to attempt to achieve their pianistic goals by total commitment to any one approach. There are probably several reasons for this reluctance. First, musicians will seldom stop making music long enough to isolate and pursue any one approach. Thus they continue to combine the study of any approach with an ongoing learning process that includes much adapted from tradition. Second is that many musicians shy away from subjecting all their thinking about music to scrutiny and analysis. Concepts like "talent," "profound," or "exciting," to name but a few, defy reduction to a nonsubjective base. For most musicians, the essence of music's attraction is precisely what these nondefinable, nonanalytical terms describe. Therefore most musicians prefer merely to flirt with what is termed "scientific investigation" to the extent it can help them over problem areas in their technical approach to the piano, but they hold back in the last analysis as they shape musical concepts. Finally, the various "scientific" approaches themselves were almost all written by nonscientists, mostly by musicians in fact, and are frequently somewhat lacking in both accuracy and completeness.

In pre-industrial Western society, research tended to be mixed with or identical to an underlying prevailing philosophy, the fourth of the influences listed at the beginning of this chapter. Eras whose principle institutions were church and a hierarchy of royalty produced treatises which spoke of Parnassus and Princes of Transylvania. Eras in which time was conceived of in long periods because it took so long to go from place to place, or because a visit meant months, or because there was little with which to fill leisure hours, naturally produced pedagogy processes that demanded enormous amounts of time. These processes were deemed to be efficacious whether or not they were very efficient or effective in achieving desired results. This attitude persisted all the way through the nineteenth century in the guise of Victorian rigor and is often reflected in pedagogy of that time. Charles Hanon probably considered the hour a day he suggests to play his exercises from beginning to end a small price to pay. Perceptions of time as a valuable commodity evolved as a result of industrialization and its emphasis on production within as short an amount of time as possible. This concept has indeed changed our attitude toward learning in all fields. Thus it is almost axiomatic in the twentieth century that being able to learn something *fast* is, in fact, desirable. Pedagogy has, as a result, adopted the premise that it is good to ease the burden of long practice hours as much as possible, and that the more rapidly technical and musical development takes place, the better. Patience is spoken of in terms of reverence but, to be sure, shortcuts are "in." Practice of exercises is often recommended, but in fact such practice is frequently limited by the urgency to learn and play as much concert repertoire as possible. And why not, it is reasoned, if indeed available research suggests—as it does—that much of the benefit of traditional long practice routines is questionable at best and physically damaging at worst. Thus changing philosophical concepts regarding creativity, work, and man's relationship to the world around him have influenced all attitudes toward learning, including those surrounding the learning of how to play musical instruments.

To the four influences just discussed may be added three concepts to which almost all keyboard pedagogical writings subscribe. These concepts tend to be somewhat like the "God, motherhood, and apple pie" syndrome attributed to politicians, in that—once subscribed to—what follows in one treatise may lead in a totally different direction from what follows in the next. Still the frequency with which these ideas appear makes it worthwhile to focus on them.

The first of these is the basic belief in the efficacy of the pedagogy being espoused. Each author sets forth his or her material as law. Indeed belief that results are surefire is good psychological therapy, and conversely, once a rigorous program of achievement has been instituted, especially if a high degree of physical response is a goal, it might be disastrous to question its effectiveness midstream. On the other hand, when one examines a great deal of different pedagogical material and makes comparisons, one is faced very soon with contradictions: some of these approaches may be good, but all of them cannot be. We are thus led to the concepts that what is right for one person may not be right for the next, or what may be helpful at a given stage of development may be rather a waste of time at some other stage. Such variability in human response and reaction is easily observable and accepted in other professional endeavors. What physician can prescribe the same medicine for all patients even when treating the same ailment? Individual reactions differ. So perhaps we must make allowances for such differences in the area of keyboard pedagogy as well, notwithstanding the claims of individual authors.

The second recurring concept is the disclaimer that technical achievement is an end unto itself. This disclaimer is almost always accompanied by a reaffirmation of musical goals. Many authors point to the inseparability of the technical means and the artistic ends. As one examines what follows, however, one is struck by the often sustained focus on mechanics and an inability in the heat of the argument to continue to relate technical goals to the previously acknowledged musical ends. This is true to greater or lesser degrees in various works. Such an observation is not necessarily intended to be an indictment, but rather to point out the difficulty of focusing on detailed analyses or processes for any length of time, especially those centering around physiological response, without losing sight of other goals—notwithstanding intellectual allegiance to ultimate musicality. In this context, *inner* processes (inner hearing, pulsing, and structural concepts) tend to be neglected in pedagogical writings, especially older ones—partly, one is sure, because these processes are so difficult to deal with on the printed page.

Finally, a fair number of treatises acknowledge that the complexity and variability of playing keyboard instruments is so great that getting a grasp of the process, even the core of it, is like dealing with quicksilver. This is not to say that trying isn't worth the time and trouble involved, but rather to point out that everything should be scrutinized to see how much can be helpful in any given case. The late Cecile Genhart, the teacher whose work at the Eastman School of Music produced so many fine pianists, used to put it in a nutshell: "Never believe anything until you hear how it sounds."

CHAPTER 17

From Diruta to C.P.E. Bach

Early pedagogical methods were developed for use with the forerunners of the piano, essentially the harpsichord and the clavichord. The directions given in these early methods are appropriate to playing early music on instruments of the time, and much of what would concern pianists in the nineteenth and twentieth centuries is simply not addressed. The first important treatise was written by Girolamo Diruta (ca. 1554–ca. 1610).[1] *Il Transilvano* was cast in the format of a conversation with an imaginary Prince of Transylvania. It was published in two parts, which appeared in 1593 and 1609.

Diruta distinguishes between organ playing and clavier playing, although much of his advice is applicable to both. He discusses hand position, recommending that the hand be held at the same level as the arm, that the fingers be arched, and that the arm act as a guide for the hand. Slapping the keys is to be avoided, and the hand is to be held loosely and lightly on the keys. In fingering, the middle three fingers are deemed more useful than either the thumb or the little finger, and crossing-over combinations of the second and third fingers or the third and fourth fingers are frequently used. Rules are given for notating melodies, writing counterpoint, improvising, transposing modes, and accompanying a chorale harmonically. Musical examples are drawn from pieces (mostly toccatas) of Diruta, Giovanni Gabrieli, and Merulo.

Almost a century later, in 1716, *L'Art de toucher le clavecin (The Art of Playing the Harpsichord)* by Francois Couperin (1668–1733) was published.[2] The work contains general advice on approaching the instrument, a system of fingering, directions for the execution of ornaments, and eight preludes as illustrative material.

Couperin, like Diruta, suggests that elbows, wrists, and hands should be on one level. Couperin suggests using a small flexible stick to correct one wrist (if it persists in being too high) by placing the stick over the high wrist and passing it under the other wrist. Exercises are recommended for warming up away from the keyboard as well as patterns to play at the instrument. Fingering is discussed in some detail, and fingered examples of Couperin's works are given. Two-finger crossovers are recommended; also the use of the same finger on a given key when the repetition of the key marked the end of one phrase and the beginning of the next. The thumb was used with surprising frequency, and finger substitution on a key to enhance legato is often encountered. Finally, Couperin devotes a large section to the proper execution of embellishments.

Jean Philippe Rameau (1683–1764) published two treatises on technique: *Méthode sur la mecanique des doigts sur le clavessin* (Method for Finger Mechanics at the Harpsichord) in 1724 and a somewhat more general guide entitled *Code de musique pratique* (Practical Music Guide) in 1760.[3] Rameau stresses independent finger action, regularity of action, lifting the fingers as high as possible in early stages of trill practice, freedom, and flexibility.

Friedrich Wilhelm Marpurg (1718–1795) published his two volumes of *Die Kunst das Klavier zu spielen* (The Art of Playing Keyboard Instruments) in 1750 and 1751 and a later work, *Anleitung zum Klavierspielen* (Introduction to Playing Keyboard Instruments) in 1755.[4] These works would probably be regarded as more significant from a historical standpoint were it not for the fact that Carl Philipp Emanuel Bach's volumes on the same subject were published at approximately the same time and essentially eclipsed Marpurg's contributions. A remarkably forward-looking observation that Marpurg makes, however, is that playing correctly requires that the player's nerves be kept entirely passive and the fingers feel perfectly free, as if they had nothing at all to do with the playing.

Johann Nicolaus Forkel's (1749–1818) description of the pedagogy of Johann Sebastian Bach has been questioned, for it represents a second- or third-hand account written fifty years after Bach's death, first appearing in 1802.[5] Yet it is the closest we can seem to come to learning about the teaching of this supremely influential musician.

Forkel's observations are interesting, but his emphasis on legato and tone production suggest that later pedagogical doctrine may be mixed in with earlier practice. Forkel describes a hand position with fingers bent so that each finger can remain at the surface of the key when playing. Fingers should play with equal pressure and draw back toward the palm of the hand. Pressure is to be transferred from finger to finger and is described in a way that suggests complete legato. Tone quality is said to be enhanced by this approach, especially if the fingers glide along the keys with equal pressure. The fingers are to be raised very little from the surface of the keys, and when one finger is in use, the others remain quietly in position.

By far the most influential method book of the late eighteenth and early nineteenth centuries was the *Versuch über die wahre Art das Clavier zu spielen* (*Essay on the True Art of Playing Keyboard Instruments*) by Carl Philipp Emanuel Bach (1714–1788).[6] It was published in two parts, the first appearing in 1753 and the second in 1762. Both parts were republished later in the eighteenth century, and a version considerably edited by Gustav Schilling appeared about

Carl Philipp Emanuel Bach
(1714–1788)

a hundred years later, in 1852. Walter Niemann's abridged edition appeared in 1906, and a complete modern English translation of the work by William J. Mitchell has been available since 1949.

Numerous references to the work by musicians attest to its influence. The most famous of these is Beethoven's instruction to his new student Carl Czerny to bring the *Essay* with him to his first lesson, and Czerny's claim that Beethoven followed the work closely in subsequent lessons. William J. Mitchell estimates that between 1,000 and 1,500 copies of the work were distributed by around 1800, that number being high when compared to other significant publications of the day and also representing widespread use in an age when borrowing and copying books was a common practice.

The *Essay* combines a number of different elements of musical instruction. Part 1 of the work addresses some technical considerations, contains aesthetic advice, and is a source for performance practices of the period, mostly of the *galant* style of C.P.E Bach and his contemporaries, but with some reference to the older, "learned" style of Johann Sebastian. Part 2 is essentially a theory and composition manual, dealing with intervals, thorough bass, accompaniment procedures, and improvisation. In the context of this survey, part 1 of the work is the logical focal point.

The introduction to part 1 contains twenty-five numbered points that range over a variety of topics. C.P.E. Bach is particularly concerned with the ability of the left hand to achieve independence and flexibility. The left hand has the multiple responsibilities of maintaining the pulse, providing the harmonic support, and playing passagework. Recommendations include changing fingers on repeated notes, slow practice, careful attention to fingering, and learning music first without ornaments. (Practicing and adding ornamentation are to come later.)

Basic posture at the keyboard is described as sitting in the middle of the keyboard with the forearms suspended slightly above the keyboard. Fingers should be arched and muscles relaxed. Emphasis is placed on the inclusion of the thumb as a playing unit. Flexibility is recommended for crossing fingers, stretches, and passing of the thumb. Flat extended fingers result in stiffness and awkwardness. Black keys are seldom played with the little fingers and "only out of necessity" by the thumbs.

C.P.E. Bach provides a series of examples that illustrate fingering in scales and similar passages. The musical passages are drawn from the *Probestücke,* a set of pieces written specifically by Bach to provide illustrative material for the *Essay*. Traditional "modern" fingering is put on an equal footing with fingering patterns that cross fingers over each other, mostly in combinations of middle and fourth fingers and index finger and thumb. Scales and examples follow the circle of fifths around from C in both directions (including relative minors in the melodic form). As all twenty-four keys are illustrated and more black keys appear in scale patterns, fingering choices become more limited and traditional "modern" fingering frequently emerges as the only recommended approach.

Examples of double-note patterns provide fingerings that are up to date. In double thirds Bach recommends the 2-1 combination as an extension of a single hand position. He uses 5-2 4-1 sequences in dealing with double fourths and double sixths, and suggests either 1-4 or 1-5 for octaves on black keys. Suggested fingering of basic chords is also presented with traditional fingering. Omitting a finger in scales and similar passages in the sequence of fingering is addressed, as well as sliding from a black key to a white key with the same finger. Repeated notes at a moderate speed may be executed with the same finger, but changing fingers is recommended for rapid repeated notes. All in all C.P.E. Bach's discussion of fingering is forward-looking and useful in that it addresses patterns, combinations of notes, and special problems that occur in much keyboard music of both the nineteenth and twentieth centuries.

The *Essay* is regarded as possibly the most important source for keyboard embellishments for its time. C.P.E. Bach deals essentially with those ornaments that can be notated by a symbol, setting aside cadenzalike embellishments such as those appropriate to a fermata. By 1750 ornamentation was being written out by composers with increasing frequency, a fact of which C.P.E. Bach takes note. He then points out that many passages allow for more than one kind of embellishment and states that prescribing the execution of a given ornament in every context is difficult, if not impossible. Bach suggests developing taste for embellishment by listening constantly to good music, most especially to singers and instrumentalists other than keyboard players. Numerous examples and special cases are cited.

It is literally impossible to condense Bach's discussion of ornamentation, for each point he makes is either basic or applicable to a specific musical context. There is, in short, no substitute for studying this portion of the *Essay* in its entirety. A few of Bach's points, however, may be noted in passing.

Embellishments adjust themselves to the accidentals of the key signature and should be proportioned to the length of the principal note, the tempo, and the expressive mood of the piece. The function of an embellishment is to connect notes. Embellishments written in small notes take their value from the note following the embellishment rather than the preceding one. Embellishments are played with the bass and other parts, a rule, Bach complains, that is often violated.

A discussion of specific types of ornaments is presented by C.P.E. Bach in some detail, covering first general rules of execution and then presenting the ornament in various contexts. He takes up in turn appoggiaturas, trills, turns, mordents, compound appoggiaturas, snaps, and the decoration of fermati.

Appoggiaturas are presented first and are divided into long and short categories. The long appoggiatura should take one-half of the value of the following note in duple time and two-thirds the value of the following note in triple time; but, Bach cautions, there are many exceptions. Short appoggiaturas, appearing most frequently before quick notes, written by two, three, or more tails, are to be played so rapidly that the following note is scarcely robbed of any of its value. Bach recommends that the notation of appoggiaturas actually reflect the value of the note. More than a dozen special cases of the appoggiatura's use are presented.

Basic trills begin on the beat on the note above the principal note. Bach suggests that in practicing trills one should raise the fingers to an equal but not excessive height, begin slowly, and gradually work up speed—but never sacrificing evenness for rapidity. Trills on long notes are generally played with a suffix, played as rapidly as the trill itself. The suffix can be omitted from successive trills, descending successions of notes, particularly if of short duration, and from trills written in conjunction with a triplet figure. Bach then discusses trills that begin from below the main note, which begin with a turn, and a half trill (short trill), offering examples in each case.

Turns are normally played rapidly, beginning on the beat from the note above the principal note. The sign ∞ may be either directly above the note or to its right. This ornament frequently appears in conjunction with the trill or the appoggiatura. It may be used as a substitute for the trill in slow movements, where it can render more expression, and in fast movements, where the turn may be all there is time for. Bach addresses a host of special cases in which the turn is used in conjunction with the trill, the appoggiatura, or the fermata.

The mordent (✱) is executed on the beat; three notes are considered a short mordent and more than three a long mordent. Very short mordents may be executed by striking the two notes simultaneously and releasing the lower one very quickly. The compound appoggiatura and the slide are cases in which the principal note is preceded by two or three auxiliary notes. The compound appoggiatura is most often preceded by a lower and an upper auxiliary, and the slide most often either fills in the interval of a third (two-note auxiliary) or provides the inversion of the turn (three-note auxiliary). The snap is the inversion of the mordent, played quickly on the beat. Bach closes the section on embellishments by providing examples of elaboration on those fermati that appear in slow or moderate movements decorating a melodic voice over another underlying harmonic voice or voices. When a fermata appears over a single voice in a fast movement over rests, however, no decoration should be used.

In the section on performance, Bach tries to place the value of technique in perspective with the values of musical sensibility and emotional expression. He acknowledges the value of highly skilled execution, but he emphatically places such skills properly at the service of musical and expressive values. He once again stresses the importance of listening to a broad spectrum of musical performance, especially artistic singing. He charges that a musician cannot move others without being moved himself, and that a performer's responsibility is to assume the emotion the composer experienced in writing a composition. In addition, a performer should assess his audience and performance conditions in order to strive to satisfy every listener.

In a section on forms of touch Bach explains that detached notes should be held for slightly less than their notated value. Legato notes are to be held for their full value. Portato is described as a legato touch in which each note is slightly accented. Throughout the *Essay,* Bach has championed clear notation and detailed indications of musical intention on the part of the composer. It is in the context of the section on touch that he seems to take a step backward from this crusade, for he allows as a "convenient custom" the marking of only the first few of a succession of detached or legato notes, it being understood that the indicated touch is to continue until another kind of mark is used. The vibrato touch is one in which the key is gently shaken after it has been depressed. It is appropriate to the clavichord, C.P.E. Bach's favorite instrument, in which such a movement causes a change of pressure of the metal tangent resting against the string. A delicate, vibratolike alteration of sound results. This expressive device, known as the *bebung,* is closely associated with C.P.E Bach.

The predominance of non-legato as a basic touch form is exemplified in Bach's instruction that any tones not marked detached, legato, slurred, or with a tenuto over them are to be held for but half of their full value. Even quarter notes and eighth notes in slow movements are to be played in this semidetached way. They should, furthermore, be played with slight accentuation. In general, the short note after a dotted note coincides with the last note of the triplet.

Tempo rubato is explained as the use of more or fewer notes within a time unit than are metrically appropriate. In this departure from metrical division, a subdivision in one hand is usually accompanied by the other's playing in strict time. In these cases the "rubato" hand should give all the notes of the same value exactly equal duration. Only rarely will notes in each hand be played simultaneously.

Dynamics are discussed in terms of indicated levels, such as *forte* or *piano,* but also in the context of the underlying harmonic implications. Thus dissonances are to be played somewhat more loudly than consonances, and melodic tones outside the key are to be slightly emphasized. Repetition of sections and sequences offers the performer opportunities for dynamic contrast.

CHAPTER 18

From Türk to Deppe

It is not surprising that as the piano began to emerge and gain popularity there was an outpouring of didactic material. Method books, finger exercises, directions for fingering scales, arpeggios, thirds, sixths, etudes—all became a regular part of the training world of the pianist. The musical and technical requirements of what was being written for the instrument led to a significant change in aesthetics and the rules that governed good taste.

On the borderline between the old and the new lies the *Klavierschule oder Anweisung zum Klavierspielen* (School of Piano or Instruction in Piano Playing), first published in 1789, by Daniel Gottlob Türk (1756–1813).[1] Türk's suggestions include sitting high enough for the elbows to be above the hands; the middle finger is to be curved, but the thumb is held straight and the little finger straight or curved, depending on its length. Only the fingers should move, the hands and arms remaining quiet. The use of strict legato is praised on the one hand by Türk, and on the other he directs that the finger should quit the key a little before the full value of the note is reached. Türk describes a good tone as full, sensitive, and bright. He also suggests carefully pausing on more important tones for emphasis, a cautious but definite leaning toward the rhythmic flexibility associated with Romanticism. By the same token he looks to the past, devoting a large section of his book to the proper execution of embellishments, much in the style of Carl Philipp Emanuel Bach.

Far more forward-looking was *Introduction to the Art of Playing the Pianoforte,* published in 1803 by Muzio Clementi (1752–1832).[2] Mozart's criticism of Clementi in a letter to his sister dating from 1783 and the fact that Clementi came off second best in the competition between Clementi and Mozart staged in Vienna in 1781 by the Emperor Joseph both suggest that Clementi's style of playing was geared toward a bigger sound and that his technical display, especially of double notes, was considered tasteless. Nonetheless Clementi's influence as a pianist, teacher, and indeed, piano manufacturer, was enormous.

The most remarkable thing about his 1803 publication is its complete alle-

Muzio Clementi (1752–1832)

giance to legato, for he instructs that a key is to be kept down until the next has been struck. Otherwise it contains the usual fingering instructions, directions to keep the hand level with the forearm, to curve the fingers as appropriate, to allow little arm movement, and a number of exercises. Clementi's great work insofar as exercises are concerned was the *Gradus ad Parnassum,* which appeared in parts over a ten-year period starting in 1817. The original work contained not only etudes of mundane patterns, but also compositions of extraordinary originality. Unfortunately the *Gradus ad Parnassum* is known best in a condensation by Carl Tausig, who for the most part cut out the compositions and left only the less-interesting etudes.

One of Clementi's students was Johann Baptist Cramer (1771–1858), whose studies are still prominent in the teaching repertoire because they incorporate a good measure of musical values. Cramer's instruction manual reflects the views of his teacher, albeit Cramer seems to prefer a slightly higher seating position. Finger technique is still set forth as the centerpiece, with as little movement otherwise as possible.

One of the most influential pedagogical writings of the early nineteenth century was the three-volume work published in 1828 by Johann Nepomuk Hummel (1778–1837). Its title is long in itself, forecasting the contents of the work: *A Complete Theoretical and Practical Course of Instructions on the Art of Playing the Piano Forte Commencing with the Simplest Elementary Principles and Including Every Requisite to the Most Finished Style of Performance.*[3] The work contains well over two thousand short exercises and musical examples. In 1861 Theodor Kullak complained in his book about the sameness of Hummel's

Johann Baptist Cramer
(1771–1858)

exercises, suggesting there were too many and that, even so, important technical skills were not touched upon.

Hummel makes several interesting points in his introduction. He suggests keeping one's eyes on the notes rather than the keyboard, not allowing a pupil to play too fast, and training a pupil to mark time with touch (accentuation). Hummel's directions for sitting at the instrument suggest an upright torso with elbows turned toward the body, forearms level with the keyboard, and rounded hands turned slightly outward. He cautions against violent movement of the elbows and against moving any larger playing units except when required by the "quiet" position of the hand. Fingers are to stay rather close to the keys, remain rounded, and strike the keys with equal pressure forward rather than backward.

The many exercises do provide a compendium of fingering patterns, which even today are useful. The last volume of the work deals with interpretation. Hummel argues for beginning all trills on the principal note, one of the earliest written examples of such thinking. He distrusts the damper pedal and would confine its use essentially to slow movements. He also cautions against the use of excessive rubato and embellishment. Finally, Hummel describes the differences between the German and English pianos of his day, attempting to be objective, but favoring the lightness of the German and Viennese keyboard actions.

Hummel's pedagogical contribution has been minimized by writers of the late nineteenth century because it represents a conservative approach to the instrument, one linked with the earlier Viennese style of playing. Mozart was the champion of that style, which placed elegance, lightness, and musical sensi-

Johann Nepomuk Hummel
(1778–1837)

tivity above all other aesthetic values. Mozart's dislike of Clementi's thunderous double notes was genuine, and Beethoven's orchestral use of the instrument had proclaimed a new and different world of aesthetic values. Thus Hummel's work was somewhat old-fashioned by the time it appeared in 1828. On the other hand, there is reason to believe that it represented a way of thinking still very much in vogue at the time and that it continued to influence musicians of the early half of the nineteenth century. Hummel's argument for beginning trills on the main note, for example, proved to be forward-looking rather than old-fashioned. There is, too, evidence that Hummel's influence on the young Chopin was strong, a concept difficult to absorb when we consider the bravura of some of Chopin's music, but one very much to the point when we consider descriptions of Chopin's playing.

Although studies and exercises by Carl Czerny (1791–1857) are well known in the piano studio, the fact that he wrote a four-volume pedagogical work has remained relatively unknown. Yet Czerny's Op. 500 is one of the most important monuments of its time. Published in 1839, it bears a title equal in length to that of Hummel's method: *Complete Theoretical and Practical Piano Forte School, from the First Rudiments of Playing to the Highest and Most Refined State of Cultivation; With the Requisite Numerous Examples, Newly and Expressly Composed for the Occasion.*[4]

Czerny recommends sitting with the upper arm slightly extended, so that the elbows are about four inches nearer the keyboard than the shoulders. The elbows are to be about an inch higher than the upper surface of the keys, and the forearm and hand are to be horizontal. The fingers are to be somewhat

Carl Czerny (1791–1857)

curved, and the hand is to be turned neither inward nor outward. The point of contact with the keys is the fleshy tip of the finger. Finger action is described as a series of finger strokes from fingers held closely above the key, pressing down firmly as the keys are contacted. In addition rapid passages may be played by finger movement like that used in scratching or tearing at something. Although use of the arm is mentioned, Czerny cautions not to move the forearm more than is absolutely necessary for the desired effect.

Volume 2 of Czerny's work is devoted essentially to fingering. Although he still cautions against the use of the thumb and little finger in playing scales on black keys, he does state that the four long fingers of each hand must never be passed over one another, thereby eschewing the older technique. Interestingly, Czerny's recommended chromatic scale fingering, starting on C, is 1-2-1-2 1-2-3 1-2-3-4-1, and he claims the 1-3 1-3 1-2-3-1 pattern is faulty because the second finger doesn't get enough practice and the hand may grow accustomed to a slanting position.

Volume 3 is devoted to musical problems, starting with tempo, expression, reading, and memorizing but ranging as far as transposing, reading various clefs, improvising, and keeping the piano tuned. Czerny includes a historical overview of the styles of playing, starting with Bach, touching upon the Viennese school, on the expressive school represented by Beethoven, and praising the "modern brilliant" school founded by Hummel, Friedrich Kalkbrenner, and Ignaz Moscheles. He further recognizes a "new" school, which combines the best of all approaches and which is represented by the playing of Sigismond Thalberg, Frédéric Chopin, and Franz Liszt. Czerny's fourth volume is devoted mainly to discussion of how to play Beethoven, but it also includes styles of other contemporary musicians.

With the new demands of virtuoso technique in vogue, it was perhaps inevitable that mechanical teaching aids would appear on the scene. Devised to corral wayward fingers and hand positions, these devices were heralded in their day as shortcuts to technical perfection by many professionals. The most widely used was an invention by Johann Bernard Logier (1777–1846). Logier's device, known as the Chiroplast, consisted of two adjustable rails attached to either end of the keyboard and running parallel to it. The hands were wedged between the rails so that perpendicular movement was virtually impossible. In addition, brass plates called "finger guides" supported the fingers and fixed them in place after the thumb and little finger were placed in their slip-through compartments. Thus fingers were kept in position and in close contact with the keys.

Less constrictive was a similar device used by Friedrich Kalkbrenner (1785–1849). Having discovered the efficacy of support by using the armrest of a handy chair (according to Kalkbrenner's own report), he formalized the arrangement by constructing a single support like a rail running parallel to the keyboard upon which the wrists and a portion of the forearms rested. That Kalkbrenner regarded the device as fundamental to his teaching is suggested in the title of his 1830 book: *Méthode pour apprendre le piano a l'aide du guide-mains* (Method for Teaching Piano with the Help of the Hand Guide).[5] The work contains an assortment of five-finger exercises to be used with the hand guide. Then it presents the usual pattern for practicing scales, arpeggios, double notes, and wrist octaves.

Notwithstanding the fact that Chopin left Kalkbrenner after only a few sessions with him, Kalkbrenner's reputation as a teacher was considerable. It is true that his compositions are geared mostly toward a display of virtuoso facility. They do contain, however, musical characteristics that reflect popular expression of the day and that can also be found in Chopin's writing, albeit in much more inspired form. Kalkbrenner's method book even suggests that sensitivity to tone and expression should be placed above bravura.

Fascination with developing the mechanical side of piano playing weighed heavily in the balance of many pedagogical works during the mid nineteenth century. An entire literature developed that emphasized finger action and strength virtually to the exclusion of sensitivity to tone or musical thought. Leading the group was a method published in 1865 by Sigismund Lebert (1822–1884) and Ludwig Stark (1831–1884), founders of the Royal Conservatory at Stuttgart. The method emphasized practicing pieces loudly, without attention to dynamic detail in the early stages, and the authors went on to advocate that fingers be held firmly about an inch over the keys, strike rapidly, strongly, perpendicularly, and quickly return to position. Charles Hanon (1820–1900) offered directions that suggested playing through his entire book of exercises every day, thereby investing in tedium, and he promised that working the fingers vigorously for this hour (or more) would result in evenness and security.

The list of finger-exercise books, scale and arpeggio manuals, and technical regimes appears to be endless and extends right into the twentieth century.

Many of these methods have been used extensively at some point or another. Among them are volumes by Henri Herz (1803–1888), who also invented a finger-support device known as the Dactylion; Louis Plaidy (1810–1874); Josef Pischna (1826–1896); Isidor Philipp (1863–1958); and Ernst von Dohnanyi (1877–1960). In most cases these musicians have been known for more ambitious achievements as performers, teachers, and composers, but the fact remains that their exercise manuals had wide use.

Another long list of prominent musicians could be constructed of those composers who have written studies for the development of technique. These short pieces vary in musical interest, ranging from a dull collection of the most frequently encountered patterns to etudes that are intended for concert performance. These etudes are seldom equal in quality to those of Chopin and Liszt, but clearly they were born of the same impulse, and some of them deserve to be better known than they are. Among this group of composers are Ignaz Moscheles (1794–1870), Henri Bertini (1798–1876), Johann Friederich Franz Burgmüller (1806–1874), Stephen Heller (1813–1888), Adolph von Henselt (1814–1889), and many others.

Fortunately there were teachers and composers in the nineteenth century whose work reflected a more musical, more sensitive approach to the instrument. Although recognizing the importance of developing a virtuoso technique, these musicians seemed to place less emphasis on mechanical exercises, multiple repetition, and building muscular strength. Rather they stressed values such as sensitivity to sound, attention to coordination, and the role of larger playing units. It was out of this thinking that the predominant pedagogical ideas of the early twentieth century were to grow.

Thus in 1837 a method was published by Ignaz Moscheles in collaboration with Francois Joseph Fétis (1784–1871). It was the collection to which Chopin contributed three small etudes, and its approach was based on the idea that technical principles are born of great art and should constantly be altered or updated in response to musical demands.

Adolph Kullak (1823–1862) published three books in the middle of the nineteenth century, the most comprehensive being *Ästhetik des Klavierspiels* (*The Aesthetics of Pianoforte-Playing;* 1860).[6] Unlike his brother Theodor, whose main contribution was a mechanically oriented *Schule des Oktavenspiel* (School of Octave Playing; 1848), Adolf attempted to bring to his writing both historical perspective and musical vision. His approach was undoubtedly influenced by his study with Adolph Marx (1795–1866), a remarkable teacher who also counted Ludwig Deppe among his students. Kullak speaks of cultivating tone production through downward pressure rather than through striking with the fingers. He further states that the weight of the arm aids the pressure and helps with a singing tone. He stresses wrist flexibility and attempts to place his recommendations in the context of earlier methodology. He takes a comprehensive view of technique, stating that one of its most arduous demands is to be able to produce a fine *piano* (soft) sound. A large portion of his writing is devoted to a discussion of aesthetic values, style in playing the literature, accentuation, dynamic control, and tempo control.

William Mason (1829–1908)

A worthy American offshoot of nineteenth-century pedagogical thinking was William Mason (1829–1908). Having received the traditional technical indoctrination in Europe with Alexander Dreyschock (1818–1869), Mason went on to study with Liszt. Mason based his four-volume technical opus on accentuation as it emanated from two-note patterns, an idea he claims to have gotten from Liszt. Indeed Liszt wrote an endorsement for Mason's method that suggests a connection. Mason preserved independent finger action, but he recommended movement close to the keys as the tempo becomes faster. More significantly, he wrote of a "relaxed and limber" condition in which a sensation of freedom is felt, and he discussed the contribution of the biceps and triceps to this state.

Ludwig Deppe (1828–1890) is considered by many the true father of the concept of weight technique. His career was as much oriented toward conducting as piano playing, for he first conducted a choral society that he founded in Hamburg and later secured a post as court conductor in Berlin. His fame as a piano pedagogue was, however, widespread, and several of his students wrote books describing his teaching: notably Amy Fay, in her famous period chronicle *Music-Study in Germany* (1897),[7] and also Elisabeth Caland[8] and C. A. Ehrenfechter,[9] in treatises more directly focused on technique.

Deppe's approach to the keyboard began with an awareness of arm weight. Toward this end, he recommended sitting low enough to bring the forearm to an incline from the elbow to the wrist. In this position, according to Deppe, the fingers are able to produce tone solely by the weight of the hand. The result would be a more "penetrating" tone than that produced by striking the key. Awareness of the role of the shoulder and arm muscles is also stressed, particularly by Elisabeth Caland, who suggests raising the arm high above the head and controlling its descent to keyboard level while concentrating shoulder and back muscles.

The hand position Deppe recommended consisted of a slightly raised wrist, moderately curved fingers, and a slight tilt at the wrist so that knuckles of the fourth and fifth fingers are higher than those of the second and third. In other words, the hand is tilted toward the thumb. Caland cites three dubious advantages to this position: achieving direct muscular connection between the hand and the arm, bringing muscles of the inner forearm into the position most suited for coordination with muscles of the upper arm, and aiding the fingers in attaining complete independence and equality of power.

Caland's exposition of Deppe's principles has in general been regarded as authoritative, although one might question the extent to which she may have interpolated some of her own ideas into her writing. Both Amy Fay and Caland agree, however, on exercises that emphasize conscious control of the fingers, not lifting them excessively, and letting them "fall" onto the keys. In addition, both suggest procedures for passing the thumb that employ lateral flexibility of the wrist rather than snapping the thumb under the palm of the hand.

The term "controlled free-fall" was applied to exercises involving chords. This term suggests taking chords by letting the hand and arm fall from above the surface of the key. These large movements were to be controlled, coordinated, and visually attractive. The wrist was to be elastic and flexible, with enough give to be pliant when the fingers contact the keyboard, but with enough residual set to return to the playing position immediately afterward.

Although there is much that is not completely clear about Deppe's teaching, even if we accept his students' writings at more or less face value, a few things are certain: he was concerned with utilization of the larger playing units, with awareness and control of weight, with flexibility and its effect on endurance, and with sensitive perception of the sounds his students produced. Certainly he was on the forward edge of the wave of weight and relaxation schools, which engulfed pedagogical thinking at the close of the nineteenth century.

CHAPTER 19

Liszt and Leschetizky

Franz Liszt (1811–1886) is remembered for his virtuosity and his ability as a composer. Yet he was a piano teacher for forty years, and his contributions to the field of pedagogy were of enormous importance.

Liszt's first piano lessons were with his father, a land steward of Prince Esterhazy. In 1821 the Liszt family moved to Vienna, and young Liszt began composition and harmony studies with Antonio Salieri and piano with Carl Czerny. His progress must have been notable. After the first twelve lessons, Czerny asked for no payment, saying that "the child's advance amply repaid him for any trouble that he had."[1] This arrangement continued for nearly two years.

In 1823 Liszt was taken to Paris by his father, with the intention that the young musician would further his piano studies at the Paris Conservatory. The conservatory's director, Luigi Cherubini, refused him admittance since the regulations did not permit entry to applicants of foreign birth. Liszt did, however, pursue general musical studies with Fernando Paër and Anton Reicha for a short time. With these lessons his formal training ended in 1824.

Franz Liszt's father continued to supervise his son's development, using Czerny's method as a model: two hours of scales and etudes with the metronome; one hour of sight-reading; the rest composing.

With the death of his father in 1827, the sixteen-year-old Liszt assumed the responsibility of supporting his mother and himself. He began to teach extensively. A detailed account of Liszt's early teaching period comes to light in the diary *Liszt pédagogue* by Madame Auguste Boissier. Madame Boissier, whose daughter Valerie was a private pupil of Liszt's when he was twenty, attended her daughter's lessons and took notes. The record of these lessons was first published in Paris in 1928. In 1930 a German translation, *Liszt als Lehrer,* was published in Leipzig by Liszt's granddaughter, Daniella von Bülow. The English translation, *Liszt as Teacher,* was published in 1973 as part of the volume *The Liszt Studies.*

A description of one of Liszt's lessons with Valerie Boissier provides an example of his teaching during this early period:

Franz Liszt (1811–1886)

In order to make her [Boissier's] hands more flexible and energetic, he had her study first of all certain passages that he considers very important. They consist of octaves repeated rapidly and for a long time on the same key.

With this exercise, he went through all twenty-four keys and the relative keys; he did the same for the arpeggiated octaves. He also wanted to hear chords repeated on the same tones, then octaves both simple and arpeggiated followed by trills with every finger while resting the other fingers on the keys, and, finally, repeated simple notes while again resting all other fingers. He does all this for hours on end, while at the same time reading to avoid boredom. This is the time, as he exercises his fingers, that he meditates over his readings.

He had her play Kalkbrenner's exercise once again, repeating the observation he made the other day, and adding some new remarks. He detests affectation for he wants to hear beautiful sounds; one should give all he can of himself, nothing should be held back; the expression should be free, easy, natural, abandoned, so to speak. When a motif appeared a second time, he made her play faster, but neither too fast nor too excitedly; he did not want a storm, only a soft breeze. Every musical expression was motivated, studied and reflected upon.

Then he played an exercise by Moscheles. "Would you like to try this composition? It's one of my friend's," he said graciously. He played it delightfully, with a certain vagueness, reverie, and offhanded manner, with a touch of inspiration, something soft, tender, unforeseen and artless. The total effect was bewitching. His bass was both sustained, rhythmical and measured like regular waves; not a note, however, was forced or broken off. The upper lines sang out with feeling and candor—for at times it seemed to be dreaming, and then it would enliven itself. One could have believed that thoughts and feelings were passing back and forth that were too fine and exquisite to be expressed other than through music.

Before asking Valerie to start this exercise, he read Hugo's *Ode to Jenny;* through this, he wanted to make her understand the spirit of the composition which he found to have a certain analogy with the poem. He wanted her musical expression to be based solely on deeply felt, true sentiments, and on perfect naturalness. He would frequently have her play certain phrases indifferently, languidly, as if she were weary of feelings: it is very difficult to both speak and be silent at the right moment.[2]

The next glimpses of Liszt the pedagogue come from his fourteen-year period at Weimar, when Liszt concentrated on teaching and guiding the musical careers of talented students. One of his students during the Weimar years was the young American William Mason, who began piano studies with Liszt in 1853. Mason spoke of Liszt's teaching approach in his *Memories of a Musical Life:*

What I heard in regard to Liszt's method of teaching proved to be absolutely correct. He never taught in the ordinary sense of the word. During the entire time that I was with him I did not see him give a regular lesson in the pedagogical sense. He would notify us to come up to the Altenburg. For instance, he would say to me, "Tell the boys to come up tonight at half-past six or seven." We would go there, and he would call on us to play. I remember very well the first time I played to him after I had been accepted as a pupil. I began with the "Ballade" of Chopin in A flat major; then I played a fugue by Handel in E minor.

After I was well started he began to get excited. He made audible suggestions, inciting me to put more enthusiasm into my playing, and occasionally he would push me gently off the chair and sit down at the piano and play a phrase or two himself by way of illustration. He gradually got me worked up to such a pitch of enthusiasm that I put all the grit that was in me into my playing.

I found at this lesson that he was very fond of strong accents in order to mark off periods and phrases, and he talked so much about strong accentuation that one might have supposed that he would abuse it, but he never did. When he wrote to me later about my own piano method, he expressed the strongest approval of the exercises on accentuation.[3]

Liszt's major emphasis on teaching, however, took place from 1869 until the time of his death in 1886. This period is usually referred to as the *vie trifurqueé,* when he divided each year between Budapest, Weimar, and Rome. He was generally in Budapest during the first three months of the year, Weimar in the spring, and Rome and Tivoli from July until November.

In Weimar many pupils came and sought his advice and help. Although Liszt continued giving some private lessons, more of his energies were now devoted to conducting the master classes (Liszt originated the master class). These classes usually met for two hours or more, three or four times a week. Students who attended were required to be there before he arrived, and those who wished to play left their music on a side table. His students were given the freedom both in choice of repertory and in deciding when they were ready to play for the class. Liszt liked to teach Bach and Beethoven—he often taught Beethoven's Sonata in F-Sharp Major, Op. 78, the "Andante Favori," and the Rondo in G Major. He was pleased when his students chose to prepare almost any work of Chopin; he was especially fond of the Preludes. Works by Brahms, Schumann, and the newer French and Russian composers were played in class, along with Liszt's own compositions.

Arthur Friedheim (1859–1932), a Liszt pupil for many years, described these classes:

> Liszt was severely academic at times, and again astonishingly complacent. When he was in a strict mood, he would speak in short, sharp, authoritative sentences of the work under discussion, its relation to other music by the same composer and to the work of his predecessors and contemporaries. He would draw attention to the structure and proportions of the opus and point out its leading moments of eloquence and climax. If a phrase was unsatisfactory in tone or expression, if the attack did not please him, he would have the pupil repeat it three or four times until the desired effect was gained. Those who had the right to desire explicit information and knew how to ask for it, could always have Liszt explain the intricacies and subtleties of pedaling and even get him to suggest useful fingerings. But this he did oftener in his small classes in Rome than before the larger groups in Weimar.[4]

Amy Fay's *Music-Study in Germany* gives another sketch of Liszt as a teacher:

> Never was there such a delightful teacher and he is the first sympathetic one I've had. You feel so free with him, and he develops the very spirit of music in you. He doesn't keep nagging at you all the time, but he leaves you your own conception. Now and then he will make a criticism, or play a passage, and with a few words give you enough to think of all the rest of your life. There is a delicate *point* to everything he says, as subtle as is he himself.[5]

In matters of interpretation Liszt's greatest emphasis was on seeking only natural expression. In accord with this philosophy, he would frequently remark to his pupil Valerie Boissier, "Don't play quite so much."[6] On the other hand, he might say, "Give all that you feel, and do not burden your touch,"[7] or, "Be naive, be simple, do not complicate what you play. Project your tones: do not exaggerate expression but instead be more subtle. Nothing should sound studied."[8]

Students were also advised to cultivate their individuality rather than to imitate. Liszt's goal was to project the music as the composer conceived it. He frequently was to have said, "Never seek success in mere brilliancy of execution, but endeavor to produce the effects which the composer intended."[9]

Another concern of Liszt's was the association between the maturity of the student and the type of music played. For instance at one of the lessons with Valerie Boissier, when she was having some difficulty in the interpretation of a composition, Liszt told her, "When you are so young, you are only able to play with soft feelings, and should play compositions which are suited to these feelings."[10]

As for particulars on phrasing, Liszt called attention to the similarities in matters of speaking and playing, for he believed that the phrasing of themes should always have variety. He insisted, moreover, that the repetition of themes not be phrased in the same manner, and he would make an analogy to clarify his point.[11]

After a score had been analyzed away from the piano, Liszt recommended to his pupils his own step-by-step procedure for becoming acquainted with a new piece. The composition would be played slowly four or five times with careful examination. The first time he wanted the student to become acquainted with the notes. The second time the rhythms would be studied. The third time the nuances would be explored, with all subtle differences indicated and Liszt adding some (since he felt that music was often carelessly marked by composers). The fourth time he wanted the bass part and the upper score studied in order to discover melodies within these parts. The fifth time the tempo should be analyzed. He advocated that it bend according to the expression: accelerate, slow down, follow a natural flow of what each phrase expressed. After a score had been analyzed and scrutinized in depth, the next step was to begin actually practicing it.

In all endeavors he stressed patience. His motto was, "Have patience, place your foot securely on every step in order to reach the heights on a secure footing. Nature works slowly; follow her example."[12]

Liszt's pupils were allowed to use a seat far higher than had generally been used before, so that the forearm sloped down toward the hand. This permitted an increase of force and ease in the execution of arm touches, particularly when there would be a good deal of crossing and interlocking of the hands and when there would be wide skips and thundering fortissimos.

He also emphasized posture, which he said should be upright, with the torso bent only slightly forward: the body was to remain as still as possible. As for the head, it was to be tilted more to the back than towards the front.

With regard to the use of fingers, Liszt emphasized that the fleshy part, or ball, of the fingers strike the keys. He particularly advocated that using the tip of the finger or fingernail be avoided, since the tone produced this way would most likely be rather dry and harsh. Liszt did not lift his fingers as high as other pianists of his time: he believed that in most instances the tones could not be perfectly bound together if the fingers were lifted high. In fingering, Liszt saw no reason why the thumb could not just as well pass *over* the third, fourth, or fifth fingers as under them, or why the thumb could not simply slide from note to note without pulling itself strongly under the hand.

In the execution of octave passages he recommended a whole-arm action with the arm rigid. The joints of the thumb were to be kept as much as possible in a straight line while playing chromatic octaves. In playing rapid ornamental octaves, Liszt produced a special kind of brilliance by holding the fingers almost stiffly, yet allowing them to move with independence; the hand should be thrown onto the keys at the beginning of such passages. In order to emphasize the last note of a broken chord, Liszt had the hand "tear off" the chord.

Liszt classified repeated-note exercises in the tremolo category, since from a technical point of view a repeated-note exercise was one-half of a trill. He set great store by the repeated-note exercise and advised students to practice it for several hours each day if possible. He gave the following instructions for the repeated-note exercise: four fingers should be completely at rest on the keys while one finger played repeated strokes with increasing strength, going from *pianissimo* to *fortissimo;* the finger in use must be self-sufficient, free, and lifted high so that its execution could be strong and full. The fourth and fifth fingers, being the least developed, needed the most practice. He reiterated that the ball of the finger be used in playing rather than its tip, so there could be flexibility and a roundness in the tone.

For octave practice, he prescribed that each octave be repeated while running up a one-octave scale. The entire exercise should be repeated twenty, thirty, or forty times in succession, using a carefully worked out application of crescendo, from *pianissimo* up to the strongest *forte*. All playing of these octaves should be done with a wrist action without arm exertion, using a "dead hand' and tossed fingers.

Octave scales were also to be practiced from one end of the piano to the other, five to eight times through all twenty-four keys, with a good tone quality and crescendo and diminuendo shadings. Octaves were also practiced in arpeggiated and chord patterns.

In addition to the special exercises he gave to particular students, Liszt began in 1868 to set down a series of formal exercises; he completed the twelve volumes of technical studies in 1880. In 1886, after Liszt's death, these exercises were published by Alexander Winterberger through the Schuberth publishing company in Leipzig. Since then several publications of these technical exercises have become available.[13] The distinctive feature of these exercises is the unusual and unique fingerings they outline, fingerings that were intended to lead the advanced student of piano to the epitome of technical proficiency.

The *Technical Studies* and other exercises Liszt devised to ensure the technical proficiency of his students show Liszt as a teacher who easily diagnosed his pupils' weak points and made a concerted effort to overcome them. Many of the characteristics of Liszt's teaching—the insistence on a sound technical equipment, the subordination of technique to musical goals, the emphasis on the achievement of clarity through detailed analysis and systematic practice—have a modern ring, and they are in fact the characteristics of the finest piano teaching today.

An accounting of the most important teachers in the history of piano would certainly include Theodor Leschetizky (1830–1915). Born in Austrian Poland, he studied first with his father and then with Czerny in Vienna. He is said to have begun teaching by the age of fifteen. He was a student of philosophy at Vienna University, but at the age of twenty-two moved to St. Petersburg. There he taught and concertized for sixteen years, joining the faculty of the St. Petersburg Conservatory in 1862. He returned to Vienna in 1878 and remained there for the rest of his active career, which spanned the next forty years. During that time so many of the luminaries of the concert stage were products of his studio that his name became well known in professional circles throughout the world.

Among Leschetizky's famous students were Ignace Paderewski, Ossip Gabrilowitsch, Artur Schnabel, Isabelle Vengerova, Ethel Leginska, Mark Hambourg,

Theodor Leschetizky
(1830–1915)

Fanny Bloomfield-Zeisler, Ignaz Friedman, Edwin Hughes, Arthur Shattuck, Alexander Brailowsky, and Benno Moisewitsch. The list is remarkable not only in that it contains the names of so many successful pianists but also that it encompasses artists of such a wide variety of aesthetic values. Of perhaps less public fame, but equally important, are a group of students closely associated with Leschetizky for other reasons. Of Leschetizky's four wives, three were his students: Annette Essipov, Eugenia Donnemourska, and Marie Gabrielle Rosborska. Still other students wrote about his teaching, providing the chief documentation of what went on in his studio. Ethel Newcomb and Annette Hullah wrote books about their studies with him. Countesse Angèle Potocka wrote an "intimate" biography of Leschetizky. Malwine Bree and Marie Prentner, both studio assistants who prepared students for the master teacher, wrote technical manuals for which Leschetizky penned endorsements. In addition, many performers who had been Leschetizky students spoke of their teacher in public interviews and described some point that was stressed in their lessons.

Leschetizky himself wrote virtually nothing about his teaching. Notwithstanding the various accounts by his students, his pedagogical ideas still defy detailed analysis, for teaching concepts presented through the eyes of others are often colored by the writer, no matter how well intentioned. Moreover, all the evidence points to the fact that Leschetizky had a phenomenal instinct for diagnosis and that his procedure varied considerably from student to student, dependent on what weaknesses he perceived. This conclusion is consistent with the reports of many students who stated that Leschetizky often spoke against the concept of a rigid pedagogical method.

Ethel Newcomb (1875–1959) illustrates this tenet of Leschetizky's thinking in this regard by offering a lengthy direct quotation from him in her book. One might question whether such a quotation was actually taken verbatim by Newcomb or whether she used quotation marks as a stylistic device, having written down what she remembered at a later time. Either way, the drift of what was said is probably accurate and is consistent with other students' observations on the way in which Leschetizky approached each student. Newcomb reports Leschetizky as having said:

> Books could be written about the motions of the wrist, and, although it often required considerable knowledge to cope with an individual hand, in general it was better to let the shape and size of it determine the action of the wrist. Anyway, you can get your softest as well as your strongest tones from the arm with a firm wrist, so in any problem of finger or wrist or arm it is better to reckon with physical characteristics, and be guided by good judgment. I can tell you that I am today a much better teacher than I was ten years ago. One learns from every new pupil, the untalented as well as the talented. Sometimes the pupil who seems stupid in the beginning becomes an interesting student under good training. Often the talented ones find many simple things difficult, so every day I learn something new. Don't have a method; it is far better to leave your mind blank for the pupil to fill in. You will discover more easily, in this way, what he needs. Even in technique it is impossible to have a method, for every hand is different. I have no method and I *will have* no method. Go to concerts and be sharp-witted, and if you are observing you will learn tremendously from the ways that are successful and also from those that are not. Adopt with your pupils the ways that succeed with them, and get away as far as possible from the idea of a method. Write over your music-room door the motto: "NO METHOD!"[14]

Fannie Bloomfield-Zeisler (1863–1927) corroborates this view completely:

> Speaking about teachers reminds me to put forth this caution: Do not pin your faith to a method. There is good and, alas! some bad in most methods. We hear a great deal these days about the Leschetizky method. During the five years I was with Leschetizky, he made it very plain that he had no fixed method in the ordinary sense of the word. Like every good teacher, he studied the individuality of each pupil and taught him according to that individuality. It might almost be said that he had a different method for each pupil, and I have often said that Leschetizky's method is to have no fixed method. Of course, there are certain preparatory exercises which with slight variations he wants all his pupils to go through. But it is not so much the exercises in themselves as the patience and painful persistence in executing them to which they owe their virtue. Of course, Leschetizky has his preference for certain works for their great educational value. He has his convictions as to the true interpretation to be given to the various compositions, but those do not form what may properly be called a method. Personally, I am rather skeptical when anybody announces that he teaches any particular method. Leschetizky, without any particular method, is a great force by virtue of his tremendously interesting personality and his great qualities as an artist. He is himself a never-ending source of inspiration. At eighty he was still a youth, full of vitality and enthusiasm. Some student, diffident but worthy, was always encouraged; another

Fannie Bloomfield-Zeisler
(1863–1927)

was incited by sarcasm; still another was scolded outright. Practical illustration on the piano, showing "how not to do it," telling of pertinent stories to elucidate a point are among the means which he constantly employed to bring out the best that was in his pupils. A good teacher cannot insure success and Leschetizky has naturally had many pupils who will never become great virtuosos. It was never in the pupils and, no matter how great the teacher, he cannot create talent that does not exist. The many books published upon the Leschetizky system by his assistants have merit, but they by no means constitute a Leschetizky system. They simply give some very rational preparatory exercise that the assistants give in preparing pupils for the master. Leschetizky himself laughs when one speaks of his "method" or "system."[15]

Leschetizky begins to come through to us in these quotations as a man of considerable temperament. He was undoubtedly both loved and feared by his students, and he often used his volatile nature as a means to get students to work harder. Mark Hambourg (1879–1960) points to this fact:

Anyone who has faced the fire of Leschetizky has always realized that after this experience one was ready to face almost anything. Nothing could have been more exacting than the demands of Leschetizky. Yet everything he said was tempered with such good common sense, and often with biting wit, that part of the sting was taken away. While with him I always tried to create opportunities to play. Every week I learned a new piece and it seemed as though Leschetizky was equally caustic with each one. . . . During all the time I was with Leschetizky, standing up under a bombardment of criticisms, I knew that he had only my good at heart. When he came to me as I was about to start upon my career as an artist he had a box in his hand. In that box he had deposited every coin I had paid him for my lessons. Not one was missing. He knew that I had a struggle ahead of me to get a start and he offered me back every Heller I had ever given him. Such a man was Leschetizky.[16]

The accounts of Leschetizky's ways in the studio are interesting, but do not give very clear ideas of the substance of his ideas on either technique or interpretation. Of the technical manuals that purport to be derived from Leschetizky's approach, the most famous is by Malwine Bree and paradoxically is entitled, *The Groundwork of the Leschetizky Method.*[17] The book is prefaced with a strong endorsement from Leschetizky, and the forty-seven illustrations of hand positions use Leschetizky's hand as a model. These liaisons raise the reader's expectations that the book offers some substantive insight into the way Leschetizky achieved success as teacher. Unfortunately, such is not the case.

Published first in 1902, Malwine Bree's book seems simplistic at best. The tone of her text is that of a teaching assistant who knows how to state the rules but has little in-depth perception as to why they exist. Such an approach seems particularly anachronistic at the turn of the century, when contemporary literature in the field was attempting to link pedagogy to physiology and psychology. Weight technique is scarely mentioned. Curved fingers are recommended, along with a fairly arched hand position. The thumb is to be snapped under in scale playing. Both prepared touch and unprepared touch are described, but a surprising amount of emphasis is given to an unprepared finger action. Although wrist flexibility is stressed, use of the larger playing units is neglected. The book is filled with finger exercises wherein one is to hold down combinations of notes and exercise a given finger using repeated notes. Scale fingering and double-note fingerings abound. In short, instead of providing insight into Leschetizky's work as a teacher, the book offers nothing more than could be gleaned from any of the many exercise manuals written during the preceding fifty years. This is equally true of the manual by Marie Prentner. Given the fact that Leschetizky achieved so much success in the studio, one assumes that in practice he surely must have gone far beyond the technique described in the manuals he endorsed. Yet relatively few accounts exist that provide further details.

Leschetizky's awareness of tone production is exemplified in a description dating from about 1850 of a Viennese recital by a Bohemian pianist named Julius Schulhoff. Leschetizky described his reaction:

> Under his hands the piano seemed like another instrument. Seated in a corner, my heart overflowed with indescribable emotions as I listened. Not a note escaped me. I began to foresee a new style of playing. That melody standing out in bold relief, that wonderful sonority—all this must be due to a new and entirely different touch. And that cantabile, a legato such as I had not dreamed possible on the piano, a human voice rising above the sustaining harmonies! I could hear the shepherd sing, and see him. Then a strange thing happened, He had finished and has awakened no response. There was no enthusiasm! They were all so accustomed to brilliant technical display that the pure beauty of the interpretation was not

appreciated. . . . Dessauer, coming toward me, a slight sneer of disapproval on his face, asked me what I thought of it. Still very much moved, I answered: "It is the playing of the future. . . ." Schulhoff's playing was a revelation to me. From that day I tried to find that touch. I thought of it constantly, and studied the five fingers diligently to learn the method of production. I practiced incessantly, sometimes even on the table top, striving to attain firm fingertips and a light wrist, which I felt to be the means to my end. I kept that beautiful sound well in my mind, and it made the driest work interesting. I played only exercises, abandoning all kinds of pieces, and when my mother advised me to go back to them, I only answered: "Oh, no! It is not ready—I shall not leave it for three months." In the meantime, Schulhoff had conquered Vienna. Heard in a large hall, his playing produced the proper effect.[18]

These experiments undoubtedly led to an acute sensitivity to sound and to the physical sensations attending the production of sound. Many of Leschetizky's students have commented on the fact that he worked with touch and tone constantly, and the public successes of his students suggest that he developed projection of sound appropriate to the concert hall and concerto playing.

Still, the secret of Leschetizky's magic has remained elusive. As with so much great teaching, his effectiveness was probably inexorably tied with his own personality and how he interacted with students. He was able to make students listen to themselves accurately, to drive them, to change them through his authority, and ultimately to enhance to the fullest every bit of artistic potential each possessed. Such achievements in any age must be recognized as greatness.

CHAPTER 20

Breithaupt and Matthay

By the last decade of the nineteenth century, the new wave of piano pedagogy began to emerge with considerable force. It became obvious to many teachers and writers that dealing with finger independence and strength was not enough. Even the time-honored concept of wrist flexibility did not take into account enough of the overall playing mechanism. It was also apparent that some traditional regimes designed to build technique led to considerable stress.

Furthermore, science had demonstrated that people could save great amounts of time and energy by employing various systematized principles in their endeavors, and many musicians became convinced that understanding and applying scientific principles to piano playing would shorten dramatically the amount of time needed to acquire technical prowess. Exactly which branch of scientific investigation would be most applicable was not entirely clear, and as a result forays were made into the physics of mechanics, anatomy, psychology, and more recently into neurophysiology.

By the same token, dedication to scientific investigation was not so complete that allegiance to traditional concepts was totally abandoned. Thus there are discussions of falling weight that also give attention to tone quality, and there is study of anatomy mixed with concepts of how to induce relaxation into the process of playing. All of this was not as damaging as it might appear, for, scientific precision notwithstanding, loose terminology was often effective in the studio, and the new ideas led to further experimentation that oftentimes helped solve technical problems.

Weight playing, the use of the arm, relaxation, and, for some, rotation were the magic concepts.

The theoretical writings of Rudolf Maria Breithaupt (1873–1945) represent the conceptual epitome of the use of arm weight at the keyboard. Born in Braunschweig, Germany, Breithaupt studied musicology, philosophy, psychology, and law at the universities of Jena, Leipzig, and Berlin. He also studied at the Leipzig Conservatory, making his home finally in Berlin, where he was a teacher at Stern's Conservatory of Music.

Breithaupt did not enjoy an extensive career as a performer, and indeed there seems to be no record of whatever public performances he may have undertaken. Nor did Breithaupt produce performing artists from his studio. He himself claimed that several of the leading pianists of the day, notably Anton Rubenstein and Teresa Carreño, exemplified his principles, but the careers of these pianists were well established by the time Breithaupt began to publish, and there is no record of their having worked with Breithaupt.

Breithaupt's major work, *Die Natürlische Klaviertechnik (The Natural Piano Technique),* was published in three parts: the first part in 1905 in German; the second in 1907 in German, French, and English; and the third, five volumes of exercises, in 1912.[1] That Breithaupt's writings have remained in the classic literature of piano pedagogy and have had considerable influence for more than half a century, particularly in German-speaking conservatories and schools of music, can be attributed primarily to the fact that Breithaupt's writings appeared at the height of the popularity of the concepts of weight technique and relaxation in piano pedagogy and that his writings present these concepts with a tone of authority and revelation.

Breithaupt places concepts of freedom of motion, relaxation, and weight at the foundation of his method. He focuses on arm movements, as well as shoulder and torso flexibility. Once these fundamentals have been instilled, he later incorporates finger action and focuses on the control of smaller muscles. This order was the reverse of prevailing pedagogical doctrine, which began with hand position, finger action, and then moved to wrist and forearm involvement. Indeed, as examination of other pedagogical approaches indicates, much prevailing doctrine never got around to dealing with the role of the upper arm, shoulder, and torso, the very areas Breithaupt considered fundamental.

Breithaupt, like the turn-of-the-century traveling medicine man, promised a cure-all. It is thus no wonder that he found many takers, for a Victorian sense of duty along with the nineteenth-century work ethic had combined to produce a great number of pianists who hoped only for more hours and more energy to invest in traditional regimes. Ambition led to tension, especially in the fingers, hands, wrists, and forearms. Breithaupt offered a method that helped release some of the physical tension and that represented a psychologically "easier" way for pianists to achieve their goals.

As one attempts to discern Breithaupt's principles, directions, exercises, and descriptions, one is very much aware that Briethaupt used language with little precision. Translations tend not to improve much on the original German. Such ambiguity has been the source of a considerable amount of criticism. Analysts who have attempted to pin down *exactly* what Breithaupt meant, by defining carefully each term, have often concluded that many of his statements are confused at best, and wrong—or even anatomically impossible—at worst. Thus, to fathom what Briethaupt was driving at, one must be satisfied with general impressions and be willing to trust one's psychological reaction to his choice of words rather than seek literal definitions. On these terms he does manage to convey his message most of the time. For example, Breithaupt wrote:

The full utilization of the massive weight of the arm (which differs as to quantity and quality with each individual) when combined with elastic muscular tension of the whole physical apparatus set in motion (shoulder, upper and forearm, hand, fingers) constitute the fundamental elements of piano technic.

One may ask what the difference is between "massive weight" and simply weight. Or ask, "What is *quality* of weight?" Are we clear about the meaning of "elastic muscular tension set in motion?" And so one might continue. Such questions quickly expose Breithaupt's lack of precision and could lead to his dismissal. Yet the facts remain that he was enormously influential, that several generations of pianists found at least some value in what he was attempting to convey, and that he reflects a popular turn-of-the-century thinking that has to be reckoned with from a historical standpoint.

If one is simply willing to grasp the whole of what Breithaupt was attempting to say, one can sense his overall point. Studio teachers often use language in the same way in order to get a point across. Unfortunately Breithaupt does not have the advantage of a studio situation: demonstration, reexplanation, and trial and error on the part of the student with corrections by the teacher. As a result, as Breithaupt attempts to get more specific in his instructions, there is more and more room for question, error, or misinterpretation as to exactly what he was communicating.

Given these research problems let us attempt to describe some of his basic concepts and principles.

Breithaupt suggests that the player sit low in the initial stage of training, although he mentions allowances for individual variations in physique. The wrist and the elbow are to be somewhat lower than the level of the keyboard, for Breithaupt believes such a position conducive to suppleness in the joints and relaxation through the passive suspension of arm weight.

Hand position is formed by contracting the extended hand on a flat surface to form an "umbrella." This arch-set functions to carry the weight of the arm. Breithaupt then adds that the hand arch constantly changes as the musical demands change.

Once the hand arch has been formed, Breithaupt directs the player's attention to supporting the weight of the arm by the firmly set fingers. The next step is to support such weight by only the third finger, then the second, fourth, and fifth. Once the sensation of supporting the weight of the arm has been felt by each finger, one "transfers" the weight by shifting the support from finger to finger while the keys remain noiselessly bedded. This is facilitated by permitting the fingers to glide to and fro on the surface of the keys, as well as swinging the arm to and fro.

Now Breithaupt begins to focus on the suspension of weight by lifting the arm from the shoulder. In this context, Breithaupt directs the player to relax the hand and the arch after a note has been sounded, withdrawing the presence of arm weight, and using only enough downward exertion to keep the key from rising. Breithaupt thus sets forth one of the principles that the English pedagogue Tobias Matthay emphasizes as basic, albeit Matthay would not advise playing to the keybeds as does Breithaupt.

Dropping weight into the key must be attended by a sensation of freedom and a flexible wrist. Actions that Breithaupt recommends as basic include the to and fro oscillation of the arm from the shoulder; a recoil action of the forearm as it and the wrist are pushed upward as the key is pressed (this he called "high fall"); the dropping of the wrist and forearm from the key level as the key is pressed ("low fall"); forearm rotation; and a kind of finger action he calls "free oscillation."

As Breithaupt passes from consideration of the larger playing units to the smaller, he once again overlaps Matthay's teaching, particularly in the importance placed on forearm rotation. Such rotation is deemed an essential element in the successful playing of tremolos, trills, all forms of broken chords, thirds, sixths, or octaves, as well as five-finger exercises and scales. Passing of the thumb is effected by rotation in combination with raising the wrist and forearm.

After all the intricacies of shoulder, arm, forearm, wrist, relaxation, and weight balance have been mastered, Breithaupt at this point allows that the fingers may become active to the extent of helping to handle the weight. He suggests what he terms "upward swings" from the knuckle joint, which permit the fingers to rise the maximum of an inch above the surface of the key. This distance will be less above black keys and will be reduced in faster tempos.

Breithaupt cautions continuously against stiff raised fingers. He reminds us that the fingers must become loose the moment the key is sounded. Finally he firmly believes that working extensively with finger action should not be undertaken until the student has completely mastered the use of arm weight in conjunction with supporting, but passive, fingers.

Even a detailed examination of Breithaupt's writing does not yield a clear, noncontradictory picture either of precisely what he meant or how to go about doing each of his exercises correctly. Still his point of departure is definite; the mastery of the larger playing units first, with special attention to the use of arm weight, flexibility (relaxation), and rotation. This procedure tends to lead to a very distinct physical relationship with the instrument, one that may not solve all the complexities of keyboard technique, but one that was very influential in its day and that has colored the thinking and writing of teachers up to the present.

Breithaupt was joined by a host of writers who proclaimed concepts similar to his. In 1905, on the heels of Breithaupt's work, came *Die physiologischen Fehler und Umgestaltung der Klaviertechnik* (The Physiological Misconceptions and Reorganization Transformation of Piano Technique) by Friedrich Adolf Steinhausen, a physician.[2] Steinhausen combined anatomical study with an analysis of the psychological process involved in piano playing. His inquiries were more provocative than his conclusions, however, for he ended up recommending arm movement that relies heavily upon weight and rotation of the forearm. A remarkable analysis appeared as early as the 1890s by a Scotsman, William Townsend. In his *Balance of Arm in Piano Technique* he explored the relative use of the fingers and the larger playing units, attempting to define roles for

Tobias Matthay (1858–1945)

each with considerable success.[3] In 1930, Maria Levinskaya published *The Levin-skaya System of Pianoforte Technique and Tone-Colour Through Mental and Muscular Control.*[4] She attempted to combine the best features of the "old finger methods," as she termed them, and the "modern weight methods," borrowing heavily from Breithaupt for the second category.

Of all the pedagogues who wrote books around the turn of the twentieth century, perhaps Tobias Matthay (1858–1945) is best known to the English-speaking world. Even those who have not studied the history of piano pedagogy in detail know his name and usually associate it with several of the fashionable concepts of his time: relaxation, rotation, and the use of arm weight. In reality, Matthay stands somewhere in the middle ground between tradition and the "new" concepts with which he is associated. He was an original thinker, and he continued to revise his concepts throughout his career. Thus he developed his own special view of relaxation, defined rotation as forearm movement, and viewed the use of arm weight as a mixed blessing. Moreover, Matthay's contributions in areas such as touch, phrasing, the use of rhythm, and pedagogy are significant, though they are often overlooked in reviews of his work.

Matthay's training was begun in London with Edwin Hirst and was continued with Henry Wylde at the London Academy of Music. Matthay was ten years old when he was admitted to the Royal Academy of Music. There he studied piano with William Dorrell and composition, a field equally important to him at the time, with William Sterndale Bennett, Arthur Sullivan, and Ebenezer Prout. Although Matthay continued to compose he turned more and more toward building a reputation as a pianist and piano pedagogue. He had begun to appear regularly on the concert stage in London by about 1884, and by 1888 he began presenting public recitals of his students. During this decade Matthay's writing began to appear in the press, often in reaction to articles about music or piano playing with which he disagreed. His penchant for writing led to the publication of his first major work in 1903, *The Act of Touch.*[5]

Although Matthay, like most of his contemporaries, heralded a "scientific" approach to the complexities of piano playing, he adopted a style of writing that seems far from precise. His sentences are long, involved, and interlaced with descriptive words and phrases that are not clearly defined. The format of his presentation is filled with a confusing concentration of rules, summaries, maxims, parenthetical thoughts, and footnotes. Furthermore Matthay continued throughout his career to refine his ideas and to rewrite his concepts. Shifts of emphasis occur in his writings as a result of his having believed that he was misunderstood on some point or another, and throughout his life he relished engaging in controversies in the press.

Thus Matthay's writings are neither easy to read nor to encompass. Yet one senses clearly Matthay's concern for detail, his intense desire to be of help, and his patience in explaining time and time again, often in different words, the principles in which he believed. As Matthay's influence grew, he became the object of criticism and interpretation. Ambrose Coviello wrote a small volume entitled *What Matthay Meant,*[6] and one finds references to Matthay's teaching in many of the pedagogical works of the first half of the twentieth century. Furthermore, a great number of Matthay's students had become prominent teachers by the 1930s and 1940s, and their devotion to their mentor's ideas has built a Matthay tradition in many private studios.

The impressive success Matthay had as a teacher is undoubtedly due to the fact that he built a rapport with each individual student that provided answers to musical, technical, and psychological problems. Like many other great teachers, he claimed to have no method, meaning undoubtedly that he gave neither the same regimen nor the same advice to all of his students. Matthay furthermore stressed musical concepts in addition to technical ones. Once again like many great teachers, he became known for a technical approach, and with a passing nod the other concepts were but mentioned.

Matthay sought first of all to develop sensitivity to sound and to touch at the instrument. He regarded the piano key and its mechanism as a complex set of levers. He sought a "controlled" key descent, which he defined as one of constant acceleration to the point where the hammer is disengaged from the key mechanism in its movement toward the string. That point can be felt as slight extra resistance when one presses the key down slowly. Matthay labeled it the "key spot." Matthay stressed sensitivity to this way of handling key depression as opposed to what he conceived as "slapping" or "hitting" the keys. He furthermore disdained "key bedding," or continuing to exert downward force on the key bed after the tone had sounded. Matthay recommended playing to the "key spot" rather than the "key bed."

Matthay remained convinced to the end of his life that the pianist has control of tone quality at a given dynamic level. Like most professional pianists of his day, he balked in the face of contemporary experiments such as those of Otto Ortmann, Sir James Jeans, and William Braid White, which offered evidence to the contrary. Thus he taught that a "singing" (beautiful) tone could be achieved by a key descent that increases speed gradually and that a "brilliant" (less beautiful) tone was the result of more rapid acceleration. In the latter case the string is "hit" by the hammer, but, Matthay cautions, even here the *key* should not be hit.

Other concepts of tone production that Matthay taught were less controversial. He pointed out that as the speed of the key descent increases, the volume of tone increases. He recommended "aiming" the key to the beginning of the produced sound, for by the time the sound is perceived by the player, the hammer has fallen back, away from the string, and it is then too late to "influence" the sound, except with regard to its length.

Matthay distinguished between the effort necessary to produce sound and the effort necessary to hold the key down in order to prolong the sound, the latter being considerably less. He urged students to perfect a technique of "weighing" the keys, thus sensitizing touch to the key resistance. From this concept, he focused on key "rebound" to effect staccato and on "sliding down" to obtain extremely soft tones.

The closest Matthay ever came to the weight-transfer concept of Breithaupt was in describing "tenuto-resting transferred." Matthay conceives transferring the weight of the hand alone from key to key. He directs the player to stop using the effort needed for holding the key down by one finger at the very moment the weight passes on to the next. Matthay's hypothetical directions here reflect the discomfort with which he approached the concept of weight transfer. Late in his career, he was sharply critical of Breithaupt and the weight-transfer concept.

Matthay described three types of movements involved in piano playing. Calling them "species" in his earlier books, he categorized them as finger movement, hand movement, and arm movement. He pointed out that finger movement alone was most appropriate to rapid passagework and that arm movement was appropriate for producing full sound. Between these two extremes are various combinations of finger and hand movements with the arm being self-supported. Matthay emphasized the interaction between these combinations in his later writings.

Matthay's concepts were so varied that it is somewhat difficult to focus generally on what distinguishes his approach from that of other pedagogues. A very good case can be made, however, for the fact that the concept most nearly unique to Matthay's teaching is that of "rotation." The term was precisely defined by Matthay and refers to forearm rotation only.

Matthay believed that forearm rotation could be either visible or invisible. The former is obvious. The latter he conceived as extremely small movements and/or release of muscular tension. Rotation was conceived as being in the direction of the finger to be used with a small preparatory movement away from that finger. Thus if one moved from the third finger to the fourth, the preparatory movement would be toward the thumb side of the hand and the activating movement toward the little finger side of the hand. These invisible impulses were thought to take place even in rapid passagework. Matthay viewed rotation as such an important element in basic technical training that it appears early in all of his teaching materials for beginners. He believed it to be the correct way to achieve basic finger independence.

Matthay discussed the use of the fingers, but two observations point to the fact that he did not give development of traditional finger technique extremely high priority. First, discussions of finger action come surprisingly late in Matthay's ordering of subjects. Second, finger action is discussed only in terms of flat-finger as opposed to bent-finger position, leading respectively to a "pulling" action and a "thrusting" action. Although recognizing both as useful, Matthay strongly preferred the former; that is, the flat finger and the pulling action.

It should be noted that "flat" meant only flat enough to permit use of the finger pad just opposite the fingernail. Thus visually the finger might not appear flat at all. By the same token "bent" meant bending the finger at the midjoint and nail joint sufficiently to ensure that the point of key contact was at the very tip of the finger, which would probably involve the cutting edge of the nail.

Although Matthay's technical concepts have fallen to criticism, his pedagogical and musical ideas are more universally held in esteem. They are set forth for the most part in his book *Musical Interpretation*.[7] Matthay speaks of the imagination and judgment that must be used for every note. He believed that dynamic levels are, in general, too *forte*. He recommended matching the dynamic level of a tone to the end of the preceding tone (that is, the level of decaying sound) in order to achieve smoothness. He focused on differentiation of levels between notes of an octave or a chord, as well as between accompanying material and more important material.

Matthay's view of rubato was reasonably conservative in that he believed that flexibility of beat must not change the time span of the overall phrase. He also gave considerable attention to a concept he called "progression." The term described for him the conceptual flow of music at all unit levels: short groups of notes to the next beat, weak beats to strong beats, groups of notes into phrases, phrases toward cadences or other structural points, and structural units toward climactic points, or a conceptual whole, or both.

Matthay's views of pedaling are interesting but not unusual. At times he seems to use the terms "half-damping" and "half-pedaling" interchangeably, although he recognizes the difference between pressing the right pedal only a portion of the way down as one technique and as another technique the releasing of the pedal from its bottom-most position and repedaling very rapidly so that some sound is carried over.

Matthay's influence has been greatly enhanced not only by his written works, but also by his successful work with students. He was particularly helpful to pianists who were suffering from tension problems; his innate kindness and astute perception cast him in the role of guiding mentor. Moreover, Matthay was genuinely dedicated to serious and refined aesthetic goals. Thus students found relief from tension, ways to improve technique, musical growth, and high ideals.

By the same token, Matthay's fame has resulted in both misunderstanding and criticism. As a result of Matthay's emphasis on relaxation and rotation he is often perceived as an advocate of weight technique. In fact, he attempted to take a middle-of-the-road position with regard to both the use of arm weight and muscular relaxation. His theories about those subjects, as well as those on rotation, the heart of his technical approach, have been open to dispute by later investigators. To be sure, Matthay often falls short of completely clear explanations of the movements he discusses, partly because of the language he employs and partly because of what Matthay himself characterizes as the "merging" of movements one into another along with an "invisible" component.

In retrospect, however, Matthay's contribution is enormous. He stands as one of the most effective teachers of his time, and his writings continue to open up many avenues of thinking for those who explore his work. His legacy also includes a large number of students who base the content of their teaching on his ideas.

CHAPTER 21

Ortmann and Schultz

Notwithstanding the impact of the new thinking about technique in the early twentieth century, it would be a mistake to believe that older traditions were completely swept away. Quite the contrary, there were many studios in which finger training dominated, and there were many teachers who distrusted the efficacy of the new cure-all concepts. The tradition of finger training was particularly strong in France. Isidor Philipp, Alfred Cortot, and Marguerite Long all wrote piano methods or exercise books that are based on training the fingers to be strong, independent, and supple. Certainly the use of the larger playing mechanisms are mentioned, but the basic orientation of such work is more toward the use of the fingers than of those larger units.

Still others took issue directly with the theories of the weight school. Thomas Fielden published his book *The Science of Pianoforte Technique* in 1927.[1] In it he criticized both Breithaupt and Matthay for not understanding physiology; he reinstated the role of the fingers, but then tied the entire process to the concept of timing the entry of arm weight. Thus after opposing the arm-weight school's loss of finger movement, he seemed to join forces with that very school. Later James Ching, primarily opposing Matthay's views, wrote a 1934 book entitled *Piano Technique: Foundation Principles.*[2] Ching advocated the use of continuous hand and arm pressure instead of weight and recognized that tension should be present in the playing process under certain conditions.

Possibly the most controversial research in piano technique was that of Otto Rudolf Ortmann (1899–1979). Born in Baltimore, he studied at both the Peabody Conservatory of Music and the Johns Hopkins University. He continued to build his career as a piano teacher in Baltimore, being appointed to the faculty of Peabody in 1913 and serving as its director from 1928 to 1935. In 1925 his first book, *The Physical Basis of Piano Touch and Tone,* was published.[3] In it he questioned the validity of tone quality at the piano, and he set the stage for his major work by revealing his dedication to the scientific process as an approach to examining the pianist's problems. *The Physiological Mechanics of Pi-*

ano Technique appeared in 1929 and over the next few decades became a celebrated, hotly debated classic.[4]

Ortmann's writing appeared at a time when prevailing doctrine centered around concepts of tone color, weight, relaxation, and rotation at the keyboard. Matthay was still teaching, and there were many active professionals who had been students of Matthay, Breithaupt, Leschetizky, or others who had stressed such doctrine. Ortmann's first book set forth experimental evidence that suggested the only factors operating in the production of a given tone at the piano are intensity and duration. Thus he joined the ranks of those who were calling into question a long-cherished tradition of tone production at the piano, a tradition that was attended by a colorful vocabulary used to elicit "different" tone qualities: "crisp," "bell-like," "singing," "penetrating," and so on. The annoyance inspired by Ortmann's first book turned to anger with the publication of *The Physiological Mechanics of Piano Technique,* for readers already conditioned to dislike the results of Ortmann's scientific approach were confronted with research that not only "attacked" the tone-production tradition, but purported to deal with the entire question of piano technique.

It is probably safe to conclude that piano teachers disliked the methodology of Ortmann's research more than its results. Indeed there are probably a fair number of professionals who became vehemently opposed to *The Physiological Mechanics of Piano Technique* after having merely thumbed through it. Even a larger number may have recognized the book's possible contributions but admitted to being intimidated by the thought of wading through it.

At the root of this recalcitrance is the belief that there exist hidden dangers in undertaking this study, and that there is a safer, more direct way to achieve technical and musical goals. Many piano teachers fear that detailed examination of the playing process from a physiological viewpoint will lead to the proverbial centipede's confusion in not knowing which leg to move next after having thought about it. Moreover, in view of the fact that the ultimate goal of piano playing is the creation of an artistic whole, professionals suspect that such intense focusing on the physiological means tends to warp the mental process to a degree that will damage the clarity and intensity of musical concepts. Finally, one can point to a well-established tradition of coaching performance dependent upon physical response and to those successful practitioners who swear to the superiority of psychological suggestions over physiological directions.

Ortmann was aware of these attitudes and addresses them. In his preface he argues that clear understanding of the physics attending tone production at the piano and the physiological process used in playing the piano is the only logical basis from which to arrive at psychological suggestions. He returns to this line of thinking in the closing section of the book, where he points out that the next step of investigation should be how the physiological facts lead to psychological images and effects. Although Ortmann was barely thirty years old when he projected this continuing research, he never published any other results, if indeed he ever undertook further investigation, even though his career as a piano teacher in Baltimore continued for several decades after his early written works were published.

Ortmann's first exposition in the *Physiological Mechanics of Piano Technique* deals with the physics of mechanics. He then moves to physiology, explaining skeletal and muscular location and function of the torso, arms, hands, and fingers. He touches upon matters of concern for the pianist such as fatigue, rigidity, and relaxation. As he draws conclusions he points to commonly held misconceptions regarding physiological properties, errors that he believes have led to incorrect and sometimes damaging piano teaching.

As Ortmann discusses the neural and circulatory systems, he concludes that repetition in piano practice is a necessary part of the learning process, for it transfers the neural impulses of a movement from the higher brain centers to the lower spinal-reflex centers. He furthermore points to the desirability of coordination of the entire neural system with corresponding response in movement in the torso as well as the arm, hand, and fingers. Efficiency in muscular response is partly dependent on good circulation, and Ortmann suggests that in some cases technical difficulties may be traced to circulatory problems.

Ortmann points to the fact that curvilinear movement is less restricting than angular movement, and he suggests that it should be favored at the keyboard as much as time allows. In musical passages that call for repetition, Ortmann notes and endorses a pianist's tendency to shift the positions of playing units in order to relieve tension. He furthermore points to the efficacy of slow practice, especially in the early stages of learning, as a means of reducing fatigue.

Ortmann examines the relationships between action and reaction at the keyboard and concludes that fixation is a necessary part of piano playing. It is here that he begins to offend the proponents of prevailing early twentieth-century doctrine. Ortmann continues to point out that passivity leads to little, if any, learned muscular coordination, that coordinated movement must consist of a balance between muscular contraction and relaxation, and that excessive attention to relaxation is just as inefficient as too much tension. Coordinated movement, furthermore, is highly fluid and the balance between tension and relaxation constantly changes with each change in speed, range of movement, and force delivered to the keyboard.

Having redefined the role of relaxation, Ortmann treads further on sacred ground by discussing the "relaxed arm" and its companion "arm weight" at the keyboard as variants in distribution of weight, pointing out that fixation and muscular tension must be ever-present. He describes in accurate detail the muscular effort needed to "drop" the arm onto the keyboard or to move the arm laterally along the keyboard. Similarly the weight-transfer touch that formed the basis of Breithaupt's teaching is presented as not only involving muscular contraction but as being seriously compromised by any attempt to produce articulation, intensity of sound, or speed. The implication is clearly that in virtually all musical contexts weight transfer is simply not the basis of effective piano playing.

After using mechanical apparatus that simulates the playing mechanism or which is affixed to a human subject, Ortmann reports his study of the motions used in various types of frequently encountered technical demands. He describes the muscles and joints involved in each motion, taking into account speed and intensity and the changes that occur as these factors are increased. In this manner he observes motions pertaining to arm legato, tremolo, staccato, finger stroke, scales, and arpeggios.

Much of what Ortmann concludes from these experiments comes as no great surprise. His results reinforce the impression that his research was controversial sixty years ago because his methodology seemed foreign to traditional investigation and because of his insistence on accounting for muscular tension and fixation in joints at a time when focus was directed toward relaxation and freedom of movement. Ortmann's observations with regard to tension and fixation were by and large correct, but his contemporaries simply did not wish to think about those aspects of physiology. By the same token, Ortmann is not willing to report his findings without throwing a few stones. Frequently he criticizes prevailing teaching techniques and suggests that they are ineffective at best and harmful at worst.

It follows, then, that Ortmann concludes in his section on arm legato that it is not "arm weight," the popular term, that is transferred from key to key in legato playing, but rather a force resulting from muscular contraction. Similarly, the rotation used in tremolo playing results from muscular contraction rather than a shifting of weight. Furthermore, if a shift in position is involved in tremolo movement, as would take place in a broken-octave passage that moves up or down a scale, finger action is combined with the forearm rotation. Ortmann describes both finger tremolo and whole-arm tremolo, two types of tremolo often ignored. He points to the problematic aspects of the first and the usefulness of the latter.

In discussing staccato touches, Ortmann reasons that the crucial test of any motion is its effectiveness in changing from the downward direction needed to produce the tone to the upward direction needed to release the key. In all staccato touches, whether they be hand, arm, or finger, the shoulder muscles are active in suspending arm weight. Vibrato touch, a very rapid succession of staccato movements, is analyzed and found to be possible only with virtually uniform muscular contraction.

Ortmann confirms the traditional notion that finger independence is one of the fundamental skills to be acquired in learning the piano. He points to the fact that the flexor and extensor muscles of each hand have four tendons, one for each finger, and the capacity to coordinate disintegrated action varies widely among individuals and is often regarded as a measure of talent in learning piano technique.

Actions of the fingers are analyzed by Ortmann by examining what he calls "flat finger-stroke" and "curved finger-stroke." The former is an action in which the knuckle joint acts as a fulcrum, and movement at the midjoint and nail joint is minimal. Ortmann's analysis suggests that this type of finger action is capable of considerable speed, but with a loss of force due to the mechanical disadvantage with which it contacts the key. Using high finger strokes with this position, however, is an effective method to exercise the hand muscles. Furthermore, since this position tends to place the finger cushion rather than the finger tip in contact with the key, surface noise is kept at a minimum. Thus this approach is especially effective in producing "singing" tones. Its chief disadvantage is the lack of a forceful (efficient) angle between the finger and the key. If one makes up for this deficiency of sound by raising the fingers higher, one may gain in tonal intensity, but then one loses speed.

The curved finger stroke is defined by Ortmann as a position in which the finger is curved in its three joints enough so that the nail joint is held vertically. The fingertip thus comes into contact with the key through a straight, approximately vertical line. Ortmann suggests that this is the "typical curved finger touch of modern pedagogy," a generalization that is probably questionable. Although the curved finger stroke results in greater surface noise, since the fingertip rather than the pad is the point of contact, this disadvantage is offset by the fact that a greater quantity of tone can be produced from initiating the action at the key surface, thereby reducing percussion impact. The advantageous angle of contact results, in fact, in a considerable quantity of tone, the chief advantage of the curved finger stroke.

Ortmann addresses the classic problem of the "breaking" (bending in) of the nail joints by confirming that it produces an undesirable hiatus in the transmission of muscular force to the piano key, thereby diminishing tonal control. Since this condition is an indication of lack of muscular activation of the flexors rather than actual weakness, he recommends working on the problem using the flat finger position. In this position the student can train the flexors to contract at the instant of contact with the key, thereby providing the resistance to ensure a firm finger. Often a student is advised to correct the problem by playing on the fingertips. Although this appears to be a solution, what actually happens is that the bone of the fingertip is forced end to end against the bone of the second phalanx, resulting in little if any contraction of the muscles. Thus the fingertip is braced rather than muscularly active.

Ortmann mounts experiments that illustrate several other physiological relationships, thereby "proving" the efficacy of pedagogical practices that by now had been well adopted into the mainstream of piano teaching. Thus he suggests that the use of excessively high finger action is inefficient, that the use of what he terms an "elliptical stroke" (the snapping back of the fingertip in order to produce the tone) is useless for strength but can be useful for repeated notes in conjunction with changing fingers on the same key, that a very high wrist makes a high finger stroke more difficult, that a high finger stroke is a deterrent to speed, and that an arched hand position provides the most efficient base from which to operate the fingers.

Part of Ortmann's work focused upon detailed analysis of movement used in playing various kinds of frequently encountered musical passages: scales, arpeggios, sequential patterns, and so on. With the aid of a light attached to the middle finger, Ortmann studied photographs that showed the track this light traveled while playing these passages. Variables such as speed and intensity were introduced to examine the ways in which they altered these patterns.

This phase of Ortmann's work would be enhanced had it been practical to include sound recordings correlated with these visual, graphlike displays. For the most part, however, Ortmann's conclusions in these experiments simply reinforce observations he had made in other contexts: that a constant balance between the use of the larger and smaller units (arm weight and fingers, for example) must exist with frequent shifts of emphasis depending on the pattern to be performed, that technically proficient players produce movement that appears to be "smooth" and "coordinated," that for every change in speed or intensity there is a corresponding alteration of coordination, and so on.

Ortmann makes the point that the general principles he has attempted to establish must be considered in the light of individual physiological differences, and indeed, it is those differences that often concern the teacher of piano. Those physiological differences in players are great. Ortmann noted arm-weight differences of between six and fourteen pounds in his own adult students, for example. He goes on to examine a number of factors that influence muscular coordination in piano playing: differences in weight, size, and length of the torso, arm, hand, and finger; in musculature framework and nervous system; in circulation and metabolism. He concludes that *all* pedagogical principles are subject to alteration when viewed in the light of the individual pianist's physiological characteristics.

Ortmann was acutely aware that his attempts to analyze the physiological characteristics of piano playing quickly led to thresholds of vast areas of further research, many of them involving psychological perception of signals and many of them intimidating in their complexity. As his work began to touch upon stylistic differences that occur in different performers' playing of selected passages from the standard repertoire, he decided further investigation was appropriate. He shows that the physiological response from different pianists varies as each plays the same passage, and indeed that repetition of the same passage by the same pianist varies somewhat. These conclusions are not surprising to the experienced pianist or teacher.

Had Ortmann chosen to pursue his work further, he certainly would have had to include sound recordings as a part of the experimental package. Projecting physiological differences against a background of stylistic values or investigating how certain sounds become psychological symbols that translate into emotional meaning becomes pointless without evidence of how the performance under examination actually sounds. The matter is complicated even more by the fact that such evidence, once presented, would probably not be universally regarded as having been based on the ideal performance, for consensus as to the perfect goal toward which to strive would be difficult if not impossible to attain. Once individual taste was introduced investigation would become limitless, for any conclusions one would draw would necessarily be confined to a given interpretation and the validity of such conclusions linked to the desirability of emulating a particular performance.

In retrospect Ortmann's work was a heroic effort to bring rationality and an attitude of impartial investigation to piano pedagogy at a time when prevailing doctrine was steeped in subjective imagery of a pseudo-physiological nature. He went a long way toward checking the momentum of methodology based on "relaxation," "arm weight," and their synonyms. He was heralded by some as a savior, by others as a fanatic. In perspective we can recognize his work as important, far less radical than originally perceived, influential, and far from complete, something Ortmann himself recognized. The segment of investigation he did complete, however, stands as an intelligent body of work that goes a considerable distance in helping us understand how we play the instrument.

Yet another important American pedagogical writer was Arnold Schultz (1903–1972). Schultz was born in Winona, Minnesota, received his early training locally, and went to Carleton College. His career was centered around private teaching in Chicago. As he encountered technical problems in his own playing he sought out teachers who were exponents of the prevailing doctrine; that is, of the methods of Breithaupt and Matthay. The instruction he received did little to solve his problems, he felt, and it was not until he discovered Ortmann's work that he began to formulate his own principles. In 1936, a few years after the appearance of Ortmann's work, Schultz's principal work was published. *The Riddle of the Pianist's Finger*[5] sets forth an approach similar to Ortmann's in that an examination of the physical process of piano playing is undertaken from a physiological point of view. Schultz includes in the book essays that evaluate the work of Leschetizky, Matthay, Breithaupt, and Ortmann, the first three pedagogues being targets of sharp criticism and Ortmann being lauded except for disagreement in a few minor details.

After an examination of the physiological properties of the playing mechanism, Schultz sets up seven categories that represent his analysis of basic movement at the keyboard. He regards the playing mechanism as a series of levers each acting against a base of the next: fingers against hand, hand against forearm, forearm against upper arm, full arm against the torso or the entire body. Schultz reasoned that force could be applied to the base by muscular contraction and that the base was formed by the application of either weight, pressure, or muscular fixation. If the base remained stable and unmoving when acted upon, Schultz used the term "contra," which had three types: contra weight (muscular contraction against an unmoving base of weight), contra pressure (muscular contraction against an unmoving base of pressure), and contra fixation (muscular contraction against an unmoving base of fixation). If the base moved when being acted upon, Schultz used the term "trans," giving rise to three more categories: trans weight (muscular contraction against a moving base of weight), trans pressure (muscular contraction against a moving base of pressure), and trans fixation (muscular contraction against a moving base of fixation). To these six categories Schultz added a seventh: movement caused by weight alone.

This rather complicated set of relationships was evaluated against three criteria: affinity with true legato (which Schultz insists is what is commonly perceived as tone "quality"), refined control of tonal intensity (which is linked to "expressive" playing), and ability to sustain velocity. He finds that the two forms involving fixation are the most efficacious, and for most playing contra fixation is best. Here is how he reasons.

The use of weight alone, defined as movements caused *only* by the pull of gravity, is possible at the keyboard only when the full arm is utilized, a touch form ruled out because it is cumbersome and because no individual finger action is possible. In contra-weight movements, the muscular action of the fingers or the hand are balanced against the weight of the large base and need constant adjustment. Thus, although careful legato is quite possible, velocity and rapid changes in intensity are impaired. Contra-weight movements are, incidentally, the ones suggested by Breithaupt in "weight transfer." Permitting the base to move upward in reaction to the use of the hand or fingers (trans-weight movement) does little to correct the problems in the areas of intensity control and velocity and adds an additional tendency to forego legato.

Schultz dismisses pressure movements without much ado, stating simply that the only difference between weight and pressure movements is that the downward force is supplied by muscular contraction rather than by the force of gravity pulling on the arm. Thus contra-pressure and trans-pressure movements exhibit the same undesirable faults cited for contra- and trans-weight movements.

As Schultz begins to develop the advantages of contra-fixation movement, he explores each possible type: using the finger as a playing unit against a fixated hand, using the hand against a fixated arm, and using the arm against the torso. Contra-fixation finger movement can provide refined control of legato touch, of intensity, and of velocity. It falls somewhat short when high levels of intensity are desired. Contra-fixation hand movement is good for intensity and velocity control, but it too has a limited range of tonal intensity. Contra-fixation arm movements are at least equal to weight or pressure movements in control of velocity and intensity.

At this point Schultz admits trans-fixation movement to the desirable category; for when both velocity and high intensity are required, trans-fixation can provide a short-term solution, especially when used in rapid alternation with contra-fixation. Such a rapid muscular vibrato is afforded by the strength of the fixation as antagonistic muscles pull against each other. Schultz also recommends trans-fixation for staccato playing. He cautions, however, that trans-fixation movement is to be used sparingly, and although the best of the trans-movement forms, it, like all trans movements, has velocity but impaired control of tonal intensity and legato.

The area of investigation in which Schultz is perhaps most noted has to do with the use of the fingers. He first examines the muscles of the hand, which he divides into three categories: the long flexors, consisting of those muscles that originate in the underside of the forearm and lead to the second and third phalanxes; the small muscles, consisting of the lumbricales and the interossei (the former originating in the palmar base of the hand and leading to the first set of phalanxes and the latter existing in both palmar and dorsal sets); and the extensor (originating in the dorsal side of the forearm and leading to the nail phalanx).

Schultz finds that there are seven possible combinations of these muscle sets. He examines each of these for degree and control of intensity, velocity, legato, and effect on hand movement. As he does so he rules out as impractical three coordinations; those which use the flexor alone, those which use the extensor alone, and a "bent finger" approach in which the extensor operates alone in conjunction with the use of the small muscles. As Schultz discards this last coordination, he theorizes that it is recommended unwittingly by many teachers and theorists when they train their students to approach hand position from a starting point in which the hand is curled up.

The four finger coordinations that Schultz deems practical are the use of small muscles alone, the use of small muscles plus long flexors, small muscles moving a finger fixed by the long flexor and extensor, and a finger fixed by the flexor and extensor but moved by an excessive contraction of the long flexor. By pointing to the possibility of using the small muscles alone, Schultz presented a theory heretofore unexplored by pedagogical theorists, one that Schultz evaluates as being capable of high degrees of velocity and of tonal control of all types, which interferes minimally with hand movements but lacks high degrees of intensity. The addition of the use of the long flexors to the small muscles results in slightly diminished velocity and tonal control; it interferes more with hand movements but adds the capability of more intensity. Thus using the long flexors and the small muscles is frequently a useful compromise. The third and fourth categories, in which the finger is fixed by the flexor and extensor muscles, show marked reduction of velocity and tone control, relatively great interference with hand movements, and accordingly are not recommended by Schultz.

Discrimination between the various combinations of muscular coordination is often difficult, because the outward appearance of the playing units offers but little indication of what is taking place muscularly. In order to isolate the sensations of using the small finger muscles, Schultz offers a number of exercises. The one most basic to the use of the small muscles is one wherein the hand is resting on the thigh, and the fingers, extended in a flat position, are pressed forward so that the midjoint and nail joint are "broken." Schultz suggests that as this finger action becomes habitual, the resulting feeling will be one of freedom on the dorsal side of the hand, pliability and sensitivity in the fingers, lightness of the wrist, and a remarkable sensation of separation between the hand and the arm. Schultz also describes less comforting sensations of fatigue and sharp pain at the base of the palm as the small muscles are trained to do the work of key depression.

Schultz explored a variety of other topics in his writing, taking points of view that were similar to those presented by Ortmann. Thus Schultz negated the widespread belief that tone color or quality could vary. He believed the perception of differences in tone quality to be, in fact, perception of differences in legato. In his study of rotation, he concluded that its proper use should be confined to tremolo figuration. He advocated a moderately flat finger for legato playing and spread chords. He pointed to the greater efficiency of a more bent finger for intensity and velocity.

Schultz's critical essays may have rendered a hostile audience for research, because he was not only critical of the principles of weight-touch, relaxation, and rotation, but also of their most revered representatives, Breithaupt and Matthay. In addition, Schultz targets Leschetizky as represented by Malwine Bree's *The Groundwork of the Leschetizky Method.* This attack was set forth at a time when a great number of students of these men were professionally active, and Matthay was still teaching. It is no wonder that many ignored Schultz's work and others regarded it as unnecessarily quarrelsome. Schultz himself mellowed in his attitude toward the targets of his youthful attacks; in an extended essay that formed the introduction to the 1962 edition of Ortmann's *The Physiological Mechanics of Piano Technique,* Schultz suggested that many of the mistakes he identified in the work of these pedagogues were prompted by their sensitivity to problems of nervous coordination, problems which these men attempted to solve in mechanical or muscular terms.

Like Ortmann, Schultz never attempted to document any of his theory with recorded examples of music. Rather Schultz set up standards of efficiency by which to judge various muscular combinations. Schultz supplied no hard data with regard to those standards. Thus readers were assumed to be willing to try the recommended exercises in order to gain greater control of tone, velocity, or legato. Presumably prompt results were to prove the case. Since Schultz addressed an audience that by and large found his clinical approach and critical attitude odious, many dismissed his work without testing it, claiming that it led to "unmusical" results. Unfortunately, too, unlike other theorists such as Matthay or Abby Whiteside, Schultz seems not to have produced a group of prominent student followers who wished to champion the theories of their teacher. Thus the ranks of pianists and teachers who are even knowledgeable about the details of this body of research remain small, and the number who incorporate its use consciously into teaching and playing even smaller.

CHAPTER 22

Other Twentieth-Century Pedagogy

Later twentieth-century books on piano playing have represented a mixture of historical theory, newly explored psychological and physiological concepts, and personalized thought on the subject. Many are distillations of ideas collected after years of studio teaching and, in some cases, have been influential in the formation of public performers whose careers have been noteworthy. A few pedagogical works are more the product of abstract theory and lack the in-depth experience of having worked with many students.

In the 1930s two short books were published by Karl Leimer (1858–1944), whose most famous student was the German pianist Walter Gieseking (1895–1956). Consolidated and republished in 1972 as *Piano Technique,* the method borrows heavily from traditional weight technique and emphasizes the guiding factors of careful listening and intense concentration.[1] Unusual in Leimer's approach is the degree of detailed analysis he applies to the score as one first encounters it. Such detailed study leads to clear musical imagery, rapid memorization, and, according to Leimer, total security. Study away from the instrument can become almost as effective as practice at the keyboard.

Another modified approach that grew out of the weight-technique school is that of Abby Whiteside (1881–1956). She was trained in the United States, except for a period of study in Germany in 1908 with Rudolf Ganz. Her career was centered around private studio teaching, first in Portland, Oregon, and then, from 1922 until her death, in New York City. In 1929 her first book, *The Pianist's Mechanism,* was published. Her most influential book, *Indispensables of Piano Playing* was completed in 1948 and published in 1955.[2] A third book, *Mastering the Chopin Etudes and Other Essays,* was published after her death in 1969, having been prepared from manuscripts by Joseph Prostakoff and Sophia Rosoff, two of Whiteside's students.[3]

344

(left to right) *Karl Leimer* (1858–1944) *and Walter Gieseking* (1895–1956)

The widespread influence of Abby Whiteside's ideas can be attributed not only to their originality and strength, but also to the fact that Whiteside's approach flies in the face of tradition, thereby creating controversy. Pianists who know Whiteside's writing are apt to remember first of all the ideas Whiteside disdains, for she does not believe in stressing fingering, developing hand position, slow practice, counting, or the use of time-honored technical materials such as the works of Hanon or Czerny, to mention but a few. She agrees with the research that questions "tone quality" at the piano, and she questions the teaching of "touch." She even calls for careful reconsideration of concepts such as rotation, relaxation, and weight technique.

What Whiteside offers is an approach that attempts to integrate the entire playing organism into movement driven by inner aural images and basic rhythmic impulse. Such movement is closely connected with upper-arm and torso guidance. Balance and follow through are also important. Whiteside points to the performances of superb athletes as examples of total coordination. She also admires those jazz pianists who tend not to worry about mechanical details such as fingering, but whose performance is generated by intense inner hearing and strong rhythmic drive.

Whiteside's concept of rhythm is undoubtedly at the heart of all her ideas. This she defines as an undulating action that impels the music forward and that is intertwined with musical concepts. Thus this concept is not synonymous with either note values or meter. She considers the physical response of large playing units (torso, whole arms, buttocks) necessary for capturing this rhythmic flow. She believes that total involvement in this rhythmic momentum results in emotional response, control of dynamics and touch, and proper balance between large and small playing units.

Learning a rhythm so that one becomes physically involved with it depends on identifying pivotal points that Whiteside calls "rim tones," responding to these points by "rocking," and, as the details of the rhythmic pattern are filled in, never allowing these points to become secondary. Harmonic outlining in conjunction with these points becomes part of the process, so that a sketch of the music consisting of important chords that outline the progression becomes an overall driving force. As music is approached in this way, the forward motion of the rhythm tends to activate the entire playing mechanism from the large levers downward, starting with the upper arm and its fulcrum, the torso.

Whiteside approaches more detailed analysis of technique by first focusing on ways in which to involve the larger playing units. She suggests contraction and relaxation of the muscles around the ischial bones in the area of the pelvis as a means of setting up torso response to rhythm and meter, to dynamics, and to the molding of phrases. The active upper arm, or "top arm" as Whiteside calls it, is identified as the unit that provides continuity for musical thought, gauges distance and power, enables more important and less important tones to fall into place, and acts as a fulcrum for fast articulation of the forearm. Whiteside emphasizes that upper-arm involvement and control is at the heart of coordinated piano playing, and she provides detailed analysis of ways in which such orientation may be achieved.

Whiteside points to the coordination between the forearm and the wrist, in what she calls "alternating action," as the answer to problems of speed and brilliance. She describes both active wrist motion and passive "loose wrist" as the muscles in the forearm and upper arm take over, and she provides analysis of this complex relationship in the context of musical examples. As Whiteside approaches the problems usually associated with finger coordination, she continues to regard solutions to these problems as by-products of the playing techniques of the larger units. In her discussion of the problem of passing the thumb under the hand in scale passagework, Whiteside believes that most of the responsibility can be taken by the larger units with but slight adjustments of the smaller ones.

Imagery of sound and guidance by the larger playing units are the recommended bases for memorizing and pedaling, according to Whiteside. She also tends to eschew the use of the damper pedal, to the point of declaring that the better the playing, the less the damper pedal is used.

In applying her ideas to various types of specialized problems, Whiteside reiterates again and again torso and upper-arm guidance, sharp aural imagery, and never allowing the movements involved to deteriorate into "reaching" for the keys or a series of separate actions by small playing units. She continues to emphasize attention to the spatial parameters: the complete width of the keyboard, in and out distances, and vertical distances. She emphasizes that the ability to repeat patterns through use of the larger playing units, along with inner rhythmic drive, lies at the heart of efficiency. It is in this context that Whiteside addresses problems associated with trills, octaves, double notes, arpeggios, and scales.

Whiteside's approach to piano playing might be accused of over emphasizing larger physical and mental concepts at the expense of mastery of detailed coordination. On the other hand, she elucidates with great conviction processes that are central to successful handling of the instrument and that are often neglected in teaching firmly rooted in historical tradition. Regarded in proper perspective, Whiteside's views can be enormously helpful.

Following the theoretical lines of Ortmann and Schultz, but far more accessible for the reader, is a small handbook titled *The Pianist's Problems,* by William S. Newman (b. 1912).[4] Published in 1956 and reedited in 1974, the book is a simple, direct exposition of the issues of piano playing set forth in uncomplicated, clear style. Newman organizes his discussion around five topics: musicianship, technique, practice, performance, and methodology.

In the section on musicianship Newman points to the importance of developing the skills of playing by ear and sight-reading, offering several suggestions to assist those who find these activities difficult. In addition he urges pianists to expand their activities to include ensemble playing and to take time to study appropriate research in such matters as style and choice of editions.

Newman's approach to technique starts with a consideration of the lever mechanisms inherent to human physiology. He thus sets the stage in much the same way Ortmann and Schultz did, albeit with characteristic directness and simplicity. Newman bases his recommendations for finger action primarily on Schultz's theories, and the use of such concepts as relaxation, weight technique, and rotation are carefully limited to specific demands of the music.

Newman questions the extensive use of exercises and traditional technique-oriented material such as that propounded by Hanon or Czerny and offers in its place carefully thought out exercises that focus on coordinative skills and acute observations of the playing process. In this context he explains how fingering evolves for scales in single and double notes, arpeggios, and chords. He recommends developing exercises out of difficult passages as they are encountered in musical works.

A meticulous discussion of practice procedure emphasizes first the importance of practicing in ways that will foster the student's ability to become independent of the teacher's corrections. Newman suggests that accurate learning of the notes and rhythm of a piece, along with good fingering, should be perceived as the student's responsibility. Newman emphasizes heavily the skill of learning to place rhythmic patterns in the context of metric pulse. He recommends both the use of the metronome and the development of the ability to count aloud while playing.

Like Ortmann and Schultz, Newman points out that the piano is incapable of qualitative change in tone, so that an individual pianist's alleged "tone quality" is nonexistent, popular perception to the contrary notwithstanding. Newman suggests that five factors contribute to the illusion of "good" or "bad" tone quality: relative intensity of each tone compared to other simultaneous or succeeding tones; degree of legato; use of the pedals; the performer's projection of phrasing, rhythmic grouping, or harmonic inflection; and the presence or absence of noise made by the impact of the fingers on the key surface, the keys on the key bed, or the foot on the pedal. In this context he describes a controlled key descent as one that employs only one lever at a time, avoiding any "give" at other lever hinges, and one that initiates the key descent from the key surface rather than from above it.

Pedaling is an art that is developed by assigning primary responsibility to the ear. Use of the pedal will change with each instrument, each hall, and each composer's style. These factors combined with the change in the instrument over the past two centuries make pedal markings in editions, particularly older ones, fairly unreliable. Developing a fine pedal technique is thus not so much a matter of following printed directions or even of learning muscular response as it is a matter of attentiveness of the ear, combined with an active imagination in the area of "color" effects.

Newman offers practice suggestions that include advice about developing an ability to recognize possible mistakes *before* they occur, organizing practice time around problem areas in order to conserve time, and continuing to utilize slow practice even after a piece is learned well enough to play it moderately fast. Newman discusses various types of memorizing—by ear, by feel, by analysis, by visualization—and reiterates the fact that all of these combine to produce a secure memorized performance. He urges the inclusion of memorizing as a regular part of the practice routine, not as an after effort once a piece is near completion.

Newman devotes attention to a careful analysis of various factors that contribute to the completion of learning a composition and its successful performance. He elaborates on the learning process by outlining nine steps in learning a new piece, taking the pianist through the process of choosing the piece; analyzing and fingering it; learning it physically (including memorizing it); and finally bringing it up to tempo rhythmically, polishing it, and establishing overall interpretative values. He deals in detail with the application of these principles to short pieces of Bach, Mozart, and Chopin. Finally, Newman provides a short but useful bibliography of books that will enrich the pianist's knowledge.

Possibly one of the most abstract studies of piano technique ever published was the 1953 *New Pathways to Piano Technique,* written by Luigi Bonpensiere with an introduction by the celebrated novelist Aldous Huxley.[5] Taking the position that motor responses occur as a result of completely clear images and perceptions of spatial relationships, Bonpensiere approached note patterns by studying selected symbols that triggered mental images and released physical responses. He theorized that conditioned reflexes would inhibit the physical response and impair its accuracy, but once that conditioning was set aside the hand and fingers would obey as unerringly as they do in so many daily tasks of a less complex nature.

After elaborately setting up this theory of "ideo-kinetics," Bonpensiere examines special keyboard problems in detail and suggests experimental exercises for the execution of skips, some traditional note patterns, chords, and octaves. He eschews the idea of planned fingering in favor of spontaneous response, and he offers exercises to be practiced with the eyes closed. Although Bonpensiere's approach ignores much that is rudimentary in piano study, his study can be beneficial in dealing with mental imagery for complex passages, skips, and a host of sophisticated problems. His work, although far from providing complete answers, is highly provocative.

Heinrich Neuhaus (1884–1964) enjoyed a reputation as a pianist and teacher in his native Russia, for he trained several Russian pianists who enjoyed international reputations on the concert stage, notably Radu Lupu, Emil Gilels, and Sviatoslav Richter. Neuhaus's own family was musical. His father, Gustave, had studied with Ferdinand Hiller, who in turn had been a pupil of Beethoven, and his mother, Olga Blumenfeld, was the sister of Felix Blumenfeld, who trained Vladimir Horowitz. The chief influences on Heinrich Neuhaus's development were Felix Blumenfeld and Leopold Godowsky, with whom Newhaus studied in Germany just before World War I. Neuhaus's early playing career was centered in Germany and Russia, but a neurological disorder of his hand put an end to his performing. He spent most of his career teaching at the Moscow Conservatory.

Neuhaus's one pedagogical work, *The Art of Piano Playing,* is essentially a collection of ideas gleaned from years of work in the studio.[6] The volume does not offer a methodology that can be strongly associated with either Neuhaus or a "Russian" approach to the keyboard, notwithstanding the number of famous students he produced. His approach is both personal and eclectic; he borrows heavily from the piano-culture tradition, interlacing his prose with stories of master pianists and experiences with his students. Although many of Neuhaus's ideas are helpful, they are nevertheless loosely organized and oftentimes presented with less than complete clarity of detail. One senses, however, that Neuhaus himself was a superlative musician and a highly effective pedagogue.

Neuhaus begins his volume with a discussion of the importance of clear musical conception as the key to all piano playing. He returns to this theme again and again, placing it as the driving force behind all technical development. In this context he stresses inner aural perception, working with the score away from the instrument, and reflection on the emotional content of the music as well as the intellectual content.

Next Neuhaus turns to considerations of rhythm and tone. His approach to the former is strongly influenced by eurhythmics, and he emphasizes the value of learning to conduct the scores one intends to play. He addresses common problems such as dotted rhythms, polyrhythms, and tempo control. In his discussion of tone, Neuhaus links the perception of quality to dynamic control, type of attack, perception of the continuity of the piano's tone, and levels of projection.

It is in the context of tone that Neuhaus introduces his "scientific" variables: f (force), m (mass), v (velocity), and h (height). Although Neuhaus refers to these variables at several points in his book, he never attempts to define them clearly from a physiological standpoint. Generally speaking, f is linked with pressure, m with the mass of the playing unit, v the speed of the motion used to depress the key, and *h* the height from which the playing unit activates the key. Neuhaus claims to have used these concepts frequently in the studio, but in the context of the written word they offer only a few clues to his physiological approach. Furthermore, his apologies for lapsing into "physics" suggests that he was not entirely comfortable with his attempts to analyze his teaching in these terms.

Neuhaus recommends studying all possible movements of the playing mechanisms and even provides a few general exercises to induce flexibility. His approach includes beginning with a "natural" hand position shaped around a whole-tone scale built between the notes E and B-sharp. He suggests slow, heavy practice to induce security and fingers strong enough to support a weight-technique initiated from use of the arms, shoulders, and torso. At one point he even describes the ability to do (what seem to be) push-ups on the fingers as evidence of desirable strength for pianists. He compares the arm from shoulder to fingertip as a flexible hanging bridge, the fingers supporting the structure firmly on the keyboard. "Flexibility" and "relaxation" are emphasized in the context of various kinds of motions. Neuhaus goes on to analyze eight elements of technique: playing simple notes, playing two- to five-note patterns, scales, arpeggios, double notes, chords, skips, and playing polyphonic textures. Octaves are to be played with a dome-shaped hand maintaining the wrist lower than the palm, even for small hands.

Neuhaus was obviously a man who lived for his work. His book is filled with observations, anecdotes, suggestions, and commentary regarding student-teacher relationships, conservatory life, and public performance. He writes of a second book in his preface, but he apparently was not able to undertake the work before his death in 1964.

József Gát was born in Hungary in 1913, studied with Bartók and Kodály at the Franz Liszt Academy in Budapest, concertized in Europe, and taught at the High School of Music in Budapest. His pedagogical ideas are summarized in a single major work, *The Technique of Piano Playing,* first published in 1958.[7] The book contains more than three hundred photographs and film strips of famous pianists' keyboard postures and hand positions. In addition there are more than two hundred musical examples and figure sketches.

Gát begins by addressing the controversy regarding change of tone quality at the piano and, after some detailed examination of the piano's action and the physical properties of tones, he concludes that very little, if any, qualitative change can take place in a given single tone. The subjective perception of quality change he attributes to dynamic control, agogics, and the "mixture" of these elements as they occur in more complex patterns involving both the successive and simultaneous sounding of many tones.

The basis of Gát's physical approach to the piano is what he calls the "swing stroke." Three factors are involved: a firm base established by a good posture and a firm bench; an elastic support established by a series of elastic joints in the body; and a swinging unit starting from one of the joints. If the swinging unit is such that the finger stays in contact with the surface of the key, the swing stroke is called "direct" by Gát. If the finger is not on the surface of the key as the stroke movement begins, the stroke is "indirect." If the stroke is supplemented with the aid of the arm or the body, it results in what Gát calls "weight-effect." As the tempo of the music increases, so does the importance of weight-effect in helping to mold dynamic contours.

The weight-effect is constantly changing as dynamic nuances and tempi change. Adjustments in weight-effect are made constantly between larger and smaller playing units. These "synthesizing" adjustments, according to Gát, are small, virtually unnoticeable, and made mostly through movements controlled by the upper arm. Equally important are another set of "adapting" movements, those that adjust the swinging unit to different key positions and help the fingers achieve an advantageous position for striking the keys, controlling surface-noise effects in the process. Gát provides specific musical examples to which these various movements might apply and illustrates the movements by means of about ninety photographs from a film strip of Sviatoslav Richter playing a Schubert passage.

Gát discusses sitting position at the keyboard, recommending a position in which forearm and upper arm are free and the body can move forward and backward easily. In such a position adjustments of the torso can bring the elbow somewhat higher than the keyboard, with the upper arms stretching forward (for octave and chord playing), or can bring the elbow and forearm somewhat lower than the keyboard (for velocity and dynamic control in finger passages). The sitting height depends upon the length of the upper arm; the distance back from the keyboard depends upon the length of the forearm. These lengths vary with each individual, and appearances often lead to deceiving conclusions in cases where using a high bench or a low bench is only compensating for the arm proportions of the individual. Photographs and excerpts from film strips of more than a dozen performers illustrate Gát's discussion.

The effect of legato at the piano is enhanced by a pauseless succession of tones, by the elimination of noises, the adaptation of dynamic levels of successive tones with careful attention to tone decay, the appropriate choice of a general dynamic level, and the careful shaping of melodic contours. By contrast, staccato playing should contain pause between tones, is enhanced by noise effects, needs to commence vigorously, should be at a fairly high dynamic level in rapid tempi, and is somewhat more independent of melodic contours. Legato playing in slow tempi can be effected by swing strokes involving the upper arm but is most easily effected at all tempi by the fingers. Staccato is most easily played by upper arm or forearm swing strokes. Fingers are not suitable for staccato playing, although, in light passages they may be used to supplement swing strokes of the forearm.

After Gát establishes his physiological approach to the piano, he embarks on a discussion of the relationships of the body's inner response to the music and the instrument. He points to the importance of establishing musical meaning, emotional responses, and strong inner aural perception. The body will reflect emotional content in its posture and movement, and it will seek to carry out musical ideas by the most appropriate physical responses. Breathing, the direction of the eyes, adapting to variances in space and acoustics are all tied to the strength of the musical perception. Gát insists that the pianist's focus should not be on the keys, but rather should be on the strings, the source of the sound, and that "key playing" leads one into a morass of complex problems that interferes with music making. By concentrating on the strings, one comes closer to the source of musical concepts.

In a section on practicing Gát warns against excessive repetition, saying it dilutes the intensity of the emotional response to the music. Thus each repetition must be carefully prepared and should be accompanied by a clear musical concept and its attending movement. Slow practice is valuable to perfect the automatization of movement, to improve control so that velocity may be achieved, and to facilitate memorization. However, slow practice distorts other factors, usually limiting coloring and dynamics as well as thinking in longer musical contours. It must be used, therefore, with intelligence and reduced to the smallest possible extent. Synthesizing movements are apt to be neglected in slow practicing but actually should be attended to carefully since they represent the strongest link with the musical concept. By the same token, slow practice encourages the exaggeration of adapting movements, leading to a completely different set of movements from those needed in playing at tempo. This duality can interfere seriously with the facility of proper adaptation. Gát's cautions toward slow practice are equally applicable to practicing in varying rhythms.

A "fixed" arched hand position is recommended for octave and chord playing. Octave playing is primarily a function of the upper arm and forearm, according to Gát, with the wrist playing a supplemental role, being flexible or unmoving depending on the dynamic demands and the length of the musical passage. Similarly a firm hand, shaped to a chord position, is required for tremolo playing. The axis of rotation for tremolos should be the elbow, with either an unmoving upper arm or a passive shaking of the upper arm, the latter to be used for passages requiring higher dynamic levels. Skips, too, Gát considers a subdivision of octave and chord playing, for effective execution of skips depends on firmness of the fingers and a shaped hand.

Gát presents sections that analyze the special problems encountered in playing double notes, trills, repeated notes, and selected passages from standard literature, concentrating heavily on difficulties found in Chopin and Liszt. He presents this material as an extension of the techniques set forth in his previous discussions, adding observations on fingering, the value of etudes, and types of trills. He repeatedly returns to his concern for keeping musical values uppermost as goals and suggests constant renewal of the musical goals as one analyzes technical components.

Gát believes strongly in the efficacy of calisthenics, general exercises to be performed away from the instrument on a regular basis. He provides a section that is, in fact, a small exercise manual, setting forth gymnastics for the shoulders, arms, wrists, hands, and fingers. This approach is reflected also in Gát's suggestions for beginners, which involve numerous activities away from the instrument both for conditioning the playing apparatus and perception of musical values. This advice is combined with surprisingly traditional techniques for counting (one-and, two-and), cautions against burdening the student with too much technically oriented material, and recommendations for improvisation, listening, and development of musical perception.

The Art of Piano Playing by George Kochevitsky was published in 1967 and opens with a foreword by Sumner Goldenthal, M.D., in which the tone is set for a book about piano playing that focuses on the role of the central nervous system.[8] Goldenthal states that although there is not yet complete agreement among neurophysiologists as to the workings of the central nervous system, there are relatively firm conclusions on many aspects of voluntary motor activity that can be applied to musical performance. The theoretical basis of Kochevitsky's approach is thus clearly laid down.

From this point of departure Kochevitsky briefly summarizes the history of keyboard technique, beginning with the change from the harpsichord to the piano—with continuing emphasis on finger activity and strength—through the use of weight and relaxation techniques and the physiomechanical approaches of the early twentieth century. In a separate discussion Kochevitsky traces the history of the gradual, and oftentimes sporadic, emergence of the concept of the role of the mind in directing muscular response.

In embarking on his own approach, Kochevitsky likens the cerebral cortex to an extremely complex switchboard. The reaction to stimulus is an electrochemical process in which nerve fibers conduct impulses to the central nervous system from which, in turn, orders for motor activity are transmitted along nerve fibers to peripheral organs. Thus even the simplest acts are the result of an extremely complex interplay in the central nervous system. Stimulation can be tactile in nature, but also visual and auditory, including impulses from the semicircular canals of the middle ear. The system can become efficient enough to allow the mind to devote its full attention to something that has seemingly little relation to the muscular activity being performed. In most acts we are not conscious of how this system functions so much as we are conscious of the purpose or goal of our action.

In a complex activity such as piano playing, the interference of levels of the conscious mind is very often necessary to set up the process. During this process new connections must be established between the higher and lower areas of the system, and at first the resulting muscular response may be slow, awkward, and attended by concomitant movements as well as muscle tension. Gradually the cortex "learns" the new connections, and the resulting response becomes more rapid, flexible, and automatized, eliminating unwanted responses and refining those that serve the purpose of the guiding impulses.

As we perform movements directed by signals from the nervous system, a relay of the sensations of these movements is sent back to the cerebral cortex. These "proprioceptive" sensations, as they are called, are extremely important for logging in the appropriateness of the action and its sensation. In order to train the skills involved in piano playing it is important that the proprioceptive sensations are as clear and distinct as possible. At this stage of setting up the response system, several devices serve to reinforce the proprioceptive sensations: slow, deliberate, and somewhat exaggerated movement as well as tactile sensations, such as pressure. Several time-honored practice devices thus find new validity, not for physiological or muscular strength, but rather, to reinforce proprioceptive sensations.

Kochevitsky continues with an explanation of the balance that must be maintained between excitation, the process wherein stimuli result in a series of impulses, and inhibition, the process by which responses are regulated, timed properly, and focused. Excitation is established more quickly and tends to be less stable than inhibition. This fact results in the tendency to play too fast, to short-circuit the ends of trills or runs, or other symptoms of a "nervous" or uncontrolled performance. The antidotes Kochevitsky recommends are practice patterns in which one stops before strong beats and also patterns that work backward from strong beats in convenient, short metrical groups. These methods strengthen the inhibition, thus preventing the premature anticipation of strong beats or the beginning of a new series of signals.

When one is establishing new motor acts, the nervous process tends to involve not only those muscles necessary to perform the act but also various other regions, resulting in unnecessary movements and needless contractions. The natural tendency to "irradiation," as it is termed, ultimately becomes weaker until the action is concentrated on only those units needed to perform the motion, resulting in smoothness and economy of motion. Balances often have to be maintained, such as that constant variable between the use of fingers and the use of the upper arm.

Kochevitsky repeatedly emphasizes the importance of inner aural activity. The sound must be the activator of the impulse, which anticipates the muscular movement, which in turn produces the sound. If a visual stimulus is present (notes on a page), it must *not* be the stimulus that leads directly to muscular action, but rather the stimulus that leads to inner sound, which, in turn, starts the process. After the tone has sounded, it is then appropriate to use the aural perception as an evaluation device, comparing the actual sound with the inner aural image. Corrections can then follow. The process when described appears to be more cumbersome than it actually is. It flows continuously when correctly activated.

Velocity in piano playing depends on training the weaker, inhibitory process more than the excitatory one. Slow practice, gradually increasing speed, frequent dropping back to a slower tempo, clearly defined muscular movements, and deep legato practice are all valuable techniques in developing fast playing. Dividing a passage into metrical groups and practicing stopping on strong beats are also recommended techniques.

As Kochevitsky addresses various aspects of the pianist's technique, he moves away from the underlying theory of his approach and focuses more directly on practical suggestions for solving specific problems. He emphasizes the necessity of flexibility in dogma, of tailoring the pedagogical method to the individual student. He points out that theory of movement is a necessary base for understanding, but that in actual practice the complexity of movement is such that much must be gleaned from live demonstration (rather than written description) and, of course, from strong auditory perception. Awareness of the physical sensations of the playing apparatus, although often elusive, must also be developed. Ultimately technique must be molded by artistic goals.

The tonal control often described as "qualitative" and often associated with an individual's playing is dependent primarily on mental conception. Kochevitsky asserts that the playing apparatus will ultimately obey the strength and sharpness of inner tonal concepts. He acknowledges that use of the term "quality" is meaningless in describing a single tone, but suggests that a complex of many tones leads to the impression of quality.

"Relaxation" and "weight playing" are concepts that Kochevitsky describes as reactions to the principles of the old finger school, but he considers them dangerous terms. He points to the fact that there is constant muscular contraction and relaxation in playing and that the use of the larger playing units must be coordinated with finger movement and strength. Finger strength must be combined with a flexible wrist to effect adjustments to a variety of keyboard positions, and Kochevitsky offers solutions to a number of specific problems drawn from the literature that involve wrist adjustment, position flexibility, and skips.

Finally, Kochevitsky offers suggestions in conceptualizing various kinds of passages. Accentuation is suggested for passagework involving figurations similar to scales. Examples of facilitation by regrouping notes are applied to several types of passage: fragments of notes that move in one direction; repetition of similar movements; notes that can be played in one hand position; constructions in which the last note of a group comes on an accent. Careful analysis of the music, regulating practice tempi so that every element is under control, and practicing in sections short enough to ensure complete concentration are further recommendations. Kochevitsky makes the final point that careful analysis, constant control, and diligent preparation are the best defense against stage fright.

On Piano Playing, by Gyorgy Sandor (b. 1912), was published in 1981, but the book is strongly influenced by early-twentieth-century weight doctrine.[9] Beginning with the premise that a few basic motions are fundamental to coordinated movement at the keyboard and that these are, in turn, linked to musical results, Sandor addresses technical matters by an analysis of "free-fall," a use of the entire arm, hand, and fingers from above the keys. This he views as growing out of the weight-technique concepts of Breithaupt. Flexibility and elasticity of the hand and wrist are stressed, and individual finger strokes are to be made with an adjustment of the wrist, forearm, and upper arm. The wrist is to be lowered for thumb movement, and traditional passing of the thumb under the hand is eschewed in favor of a wrist flexibility that aids the thumb in initiating a new hand position.

Notwithstanding these adjustments of the larger playing units, Sandor cautions that the fingers must uphold their share of the work with independent movement. He also stresses this balance throughout a discussion of forearm rotation. Octave technique is described in terms of a staccato action involving the entire arm in addition to the wrist and hand. Sandor offers a series of extended examples from the literature in which he indicates by the use of added symbols the detailed application of the basic motions he has described. He also offers suggestions on the use of the pedals, tone production, memorization, practicing, articulation, and phrasing.

The parade of books on piano playing provides a never-ending panorama. Any attempt to survey this great expanse of writing must necessarily end in a degree of frustration, for no overview can touch upon every volume of value or mention every worthwhile idea. The preceding accounts have attempted to trace the general line of historical thought about piano pedagogy, including summaries of a few of the more celebrated writings along the way and also some examples of eclectic contemporary thought. The omissions are great, however, for the field is both vast and diverse. It will continue to be so as long as piano playing and teaching form an important part of our culture.

PART EIGHT

Contemporary Thoughts

CHAPTER 23

Great Pianists of Today: Thoughts and Viewpoints

In this chapter, twenty-five internationally acclaimed pianists discuss their lives as concert artists, their ideas about piano playing, and their thoughts on teaching, and speak about their art and careers. Because these artists have devoted their lives to music making of the highest order and because their names and performances are renowned throughout the contemporary music world, their words deserve attention.

Over the period 1977–1988, special interviews with these pianists were conducted that culminated in the two volumes of *Great Pianists Speak for Themselves*.[1] What follows are excerpts drawn from the interviews, selected and grouped according to topics pertinent to the content of this book. The thoughts and viewpoints of these artists, presented in their own words, should be of interest to pianists, teachers, students, and aspiring young artists alike.

ON LEARNING MUSIC

You have to start with an absolute faithfulness or loyalty to what the composer wanted by studying the early editions, the manuscripts and the facsimiles. . . . This fidelity and loyalty to what the composer wanted is only a basis on which the artist builds his own vision, his own idea of the work. But the vision must not jeopardize his respect for the text, or what he might know about the intentions of the composer. Some pianists "use" the original music and change it into a form of self-expression only. This is wrong. Others seem to be so awed by the composer that they do the opposite—they play nothing *but* notes. This is wrong, too. A good artist goes into a flight of imagination on his own, but he never destroys the integrity of the work as the composer saw it.

Claudio Arrau

I try to look at each piece as naïvely as possible. I do not try to analyze it first. I think that analysis, becoming aware of the processes in the composition, should be the result of such acquaintance, not the input. So I become more and more aware of the pieces the longer I play them, and yet I try to maintain the naïvete. . . .

What it all comes down to is that I learned that the music dictates the terms. It tells you what to do with fingering, pedaling, and hand movements. That's why I do not believe in the intentional slowing up of the tempo in practice or in warm-up. If I slow down the musical process, the fingering may be wrong; the movements may be inadequate. On the other hand, to try to discover fingering by playing in slow motion a piece which goes rapidly is basically wrong.

Alfred Brendel

I study the music carefully first to form an idea of what it is all about. Then I seek passages or sections which offer the most difficulty, especially in regard to fingering. For me, the fingering is very important. I may decide on using a certain finger to produce a particular tone, but if it doesn't work, then I have to change the fingering accordingly. That's why I don't advocate practicing away from the piano as some pianists do.

Alicia de Larrocha

I do advise practicing in a slower tempo. I think it's a good idea because, in the first place, you can overcome some bad habits which can creep into your playing. Secondly, when playing slowly, you can concentrate more on the function of the fingers and on the quality of tone than you do at a faster pace.

Rudolf Firkusny

I like to practice *pianissimo*. This forces more concentration, and you pay more attention to what you are doing, I think, because you have to listen more carefully. Consequently, I keep everything *pianissimo*. In fact, the first study of Chopin I learned only by *pianissimo*. When you are playing a lot of the same notes, the *pianissimo* is helpful because the sameness of the tone comes through.

Youri Egorov

I think it's better in working progressively, thinking first about certain elements like rhythm or harmonic structures. Take one linear aspect at a time, and then add to it. Then take a second linear aspect alone. Now put the first and second linear aspects together. Then move to a third aspect of the music; now put the third with the first; then put it together with the second. If you build in this manner, the music becomes a more clear progression, and there is more continuity, coherence, to the piece.

Leon Fleisher

Claudio Arrau

ON TECHNIQUE

What helps is to dissect a really difficult passage—one that has a lot of notes—away from the keyboard. Don't dissect it by playing it again and again or by

Alfred Brendel

playing it slower. Get away from the piano, and if you know what the notes are, don't even look at the score. Envision the notes as you would envision a dancer taking steps. Find out *how* you're playing—what note it is—what you always miss or which note it is that doesn't always speak or that speaks too much. Then find a motion to correct it. For instance, know that you must give a little extra to the right side of the hand with the fourth finger when you get to that place, or whatever.

André Watts

If I have real problems, I work with a passage in all sorts of rhythmic patterns. Some people say that such a system doesn't work, but I have found that it works

Rudolf Firkusny
(photograph:
Sue A. Warek)

for me. So with that particular passage, the very basic way of practicing with the rhythm would be to start with the triplet—to stop on the first note and play the second two notes at regular speed, then stop on the second note and play the first and third at regular speed, then stop on the third, and so on. . . . If both hands are to play the same notes rapidly an octave apart, put them two octaves apart and practice them like that. Or practice them cross-handed, so that the left hand plays the notes that the right hand plays and the right hand plays the notes that the left hand is supposed to play. Or change the key. If you can play a difficult passage in any key, you're pretty secure in the original one!

Stephen Hough

If I were to advise *young* pianists, I'd tell them to work on technical exercises. Through the years, I think that technical exercises are very important, not only scales and arpeggios but also certain parts of the most difficult, the most demanding piano works like Chopin etudes, Liszt etudes, and so on. Difficult sections from, let's say, the Chopin etude for the thirds, the G-sharp Minor, the most difficult parts of certain Liszt etudes, as well as finger exercises written by

Leon Fleisher
(photograph: Paul
J. Hoeffler)

Dohnanyi and the famous ones—Czerny, Clementi. I would say they are very, very important in the early years of learning the piano.

Zoltán Kocsis

The actual stance or position of the hands and fingers has much to do with the final effect of the performance. The Russian school, in imitation of Rubinstein, uses a higher bridge and a flatter finger than we do. The only variance is the Leschetizky school, which uses a very curved finger. As for me, I have no preference. When I play, I use anything that works. Half the time I'm not even aware of what I do. However, I believe very much in the correct use of strong weight in playing. I don't mean that one should attack the keyboard, but use strong weight which gives a much richer and less percussive sound than merely hitting the keys.

John Browning

André Watts

I don't know about others, but I do know that *I* have never solved a major mechanical or interpretive problem at the keyboard. I have always solved it in my mind. . . . I've even experimented, mentally, mind you, with playing some notes with the left hand that are written for the right—things like that. But never at the keyboard.

Jorge Bolet

There is that technique, the ability to play scales rapidly up and down the keyboard, which is necessary, but which becomes very boring after two or three minutes of listening. That instrument is capable of sounds which are loud and soft; but in between there are many, many degrees of sounds which may be played. To be able to produce many varieties of sound—now that is what I call technique, and that is what I try to do. I don't adhere to any methods because I simply don't believe in them. I think each pianist must ultimately carve his own way, technically and stylistically.

Vladimir Horowitz

Zoltán Kocsis

Each finger must be capable of every type of touch while every other finger is doing another type of touch simultaneously. The dynamics must be such that a different quantity of tone can be produced at different levels of playing so that the texture and quality of tone, although different for each finger, can be interrelated and can blend in the different motifs that are going on simultaneously. The finger's touch, tonal quantity and quality must relate as the lines move horizontally and contrapuntally to each other as, for example, in a four-voiced fugue. They must relate harmonically as they move in a harmonic progression from one section to another. Even within short phrases they must relate contrapuntally and harmonically so that, although each phrase, long or short, is an entity in itself, the differences in touch create a complete unified structure. This is a microscopic view of my technical style for a Bach performance on the piano.

Rosalyn Tureck

John Browning conducting master classes at Northwestern University
(photograph: Rich Sato, Northeastern Illinois University Photo Department)

ON MEMORIZATION

I memorize in three ways: I have a visual memory, I have a harmonic memory, and I have a digital memory—that is, I know what chords are involved and I know the fingering. I've worked so hard that I know just where the notes are.

Janina Fialkowska

When it comes to memorizing, I do 95 to 98 percent of it away from the piano. I look at the score, study it, go through it in my mind, and piece it all together.

Bolet

Sometimes I have to play a piece very slowly to solidify the memorization of the part. Slowness also helps to check note accuracy and phrasing, because

Jorge Bolet
(photograph:
Francesco
Scavullo)

when you play in slow motion—just as in viewing a movie run slowly—you see every detail and, at the same time, reinforce the memory. . . . The memorization of the rhythmical accents in every phrase is a very important memory aid, but not quite as reliable as the memorization of the phrases, cadences, and form. I don't believe much in vision memory. It seems unsure and leaves me feeling rather insecure. Also I don't practice above the keys, omitting the aural aspect, that is. I may do this on occasion when I'm afraid I'll disturb someone, but it seems too unnatural.

de Larrocha

I try to let the composition run through my mind whether I'm on a plane, a train, or just relaxing. I don't necessarily have to look at a score because I don't have to see every note. I try to understand structural relationships and move through the piece slowly, especially if it's a difficult one. Then, at the piano, I just play it.

Vladimir Ashkenazy

On a larger scale, I break down the form of the piece into its larger structural sections. In the smallest possible sense, I memorize intervallic relationships and harmonic blocks that are common throughout the entire movement of the complete piece. If, for instance, the piece is based on the interval of the sixth, then

Rosalyn Tureck as conductor and performer

that interval will permeate the entire movement and form harmonic units. And whenever it crops up, it not only contributes to an understanding of the piece, but offers a way to memorize it. Thus, I memorize harmonic structures which are related to intervallic structure so that when I come to fixed points of harmony, I am not memorizing senseless details, but rather blocks of harmonic sound along with all the secondary units surrounding that vital point. So even if I lose some details in that first couple of days of work, my mind remains fixed on those big blocks and I have a picture not only of the harmony, but the hand relative to these main blocks.

There is, however, a kind of "learning" that takes place before the breaking down is undertaken. I play through a complete work a few times, even badly if it's a difficult piece, to give me an idea of the overall shape of it. Then if it's a technically problematic piece, I'll single out the places that are the most awkward technically and I'll work on these as intensely as possible so that they become as easy as any other part of the piece. Consequently, they become second nature to me as I look at the overall structure of the piece. I'll make a daily exercise of a given passage if it's really a stickler.

Possible memory failure is certainly an unpleasant thought and I'm sure there's no one who would say that he or she had always played spotless performances and had never forgotten anything. . . . But if the artist is as perfectly prepared as possible with a complete understanding of the harmony and rela-

Janina Fialkowska
(photograph:
Christian Steiner)

tionship of parts, and if the artist is rested and reasonably relaxed, and then still forgets something, then he's human, thank goodness!

Misha Dichter

Students often think there is some secret formula that the masters use to learn a work. If there is, I never found it. I simply play a piece over and over until I know it by heart.

Browning

ON NERVOUSNESS AND PRECONCERT TENSION

Before a concert, as long as the general atmosphere is good, I'm not really nervous. But if there's a problem with the instrument, yes, then I'm nervous. Remember, you're changing the piano every time you give a concert, and you must get accustomed to that particular piano. There's also the fatigue factor. If you perform every evening, the weariness soon catches up with you. But after every concert, one should relax.

Cécile Ousset

*Vladimir
Ashkenazy*

Working hard at practice is also the best defense I know against preconcert nervousness which can never be entirely eliminated but can be psychologically prepared for by convincing oneself that one has done all the homework necessary for a solid performance and everything will work out all right.

Ashkenazy

I have always been nervous before concerts, and I continue to this day to be so. I've never found a cure for it. But I find that by being reflective and meditative about it all, I can do it.

Emil Gilels

I have to admit that sometimes before a concert I get nervous. I try to avoid the jitters by preparing myself psychologically for the event. I begin my preparation about a week before the concert. I imagine myself already on the stage actually playing the concert. So then I go upstairs to my Steinway and, sure enough, the nerves begin the tingle, because I pretend that I'm on my way up to the stage and to the piano at which I'll sit and play the music. I also concentrate, as I would on the night of the concert, on the music itself and review one more time just how I will perform it. So the last week before the concert is consumed by my playing the intended compositions over and over again, all the while imagining that the audience is right there listening to me. Some nervousness is still there, but I can cope with it because I have more control over myself. The thing with nervousness is that when it occurs, the mind begins to speed up, and that leads to many mistakes.

Egorov

I might be geared to play well when suddenly the piano sounds as if I'm striking the keys too hard and then I begin to play badly. It is the most miserable feeling I know, and the only way out of it is to become completely involved in the music. The music will carry me through. However, I can never predict what will happen during a performance. If I try to talk myself into being more calm, I start getting nervous. And if I begin with a case of nerves and just go out and play, I enjoy the concert and it seems to come off well.

de Larrocha

Every performer is nervous before a concert, and one way to occupy your mind is to think of failure. If you fail, you think, it's bad for your career and the future of your concerts. So you can be very strained and feel almost hostile toward the people out there because some of them might be waiting for you to mess up.

On the other hand, you can take the attitude I prefer, which is to prepare the program, go on stage, and proffer your music to the audience. I try to avoid expecting too much from the public and just play in the most open way I can. But a concert always is an incredible exposition of one's daring and insides. If you're not willing to do that, or if you feel uncomfortable about it, then there's a limit to what you can offer the people. . . . A performer has to learn to live with cases of nerves. It may be the program, the hall, the conductor, or anything else. But the artist must work it out for himself.

Watts

I guess you could call it taking more of a positive mental attitude than sheer courage, bravado, or competitiveness. Even when I'm walking onstage to play, I try to think courageous thoughts. I think only of smiling at the audience. What kind of feeling is it? I call it defensive optimism. I'm generally quite happy by the time the concert arrives. It's the two hours before that that I've been unhappy. I don't become ill or anything like that, but I get this feeling that I'd like to go away, to hibernate, to go to the movies, to sleep. It's the escape thing that gets to me. Yet when I become jittery, I become almost too relaxed; I grow sort of "soft." That's when, right before I go onstage, I go and get a cup of coffee. People tell me they could never do that because they'd be too jittery. Sometimes I'm asked whether or not I could eat just before I went onstage, and my standard reply is, "I can eat anytime."

Garrick Ohlsson

. . . I also have some thoughts to share about concert performances, particularly what goes through my mind before I walk onstage. Imagine, I am so excited that I have the feeling of being so faint, so helpless, as if the very candle of my life is going to snuff out. I feel as if I couldn't lift an arm, move a finger, and as

Garrick Ohlsson
(photograph:
Martin
Reichenthal)

if I'd never seen a piano. It is as if I'm lost and don't know what to do. But when I walk out and see the friendly grin of those eighty-eight keys reassuring me, inviting me, I love them, and then everything falls into place.

I never eat anything before a performance because I believe that every fiber of your body has to serve the performance and you cannot burden your stomach by making your digestive juices work. If you do, you function too much in the stomach and not enough in the spirit and the brain.

Lili Kraus

There seem to be artists who subscribe to the biorhythm theory. I don't. There are other artists who rely on their astrologer's predictions so intensely that they make all their important concert dates coincide with the astrologer's prophecy of success. It makes no sense to me and, even if it did, I wouldn't want to know what might happen to me tomorrow.... I have no pet superstitions or good luck charms that will put the gods to my service. I prefer to be well prepared. My routine is simple. After I rehearse, I usually take a short nap. A half-hour or so before the concert, I warm up to activate my hands. I wouldn't like to go onstage without having played a little. This system has worked rather well for me.

Brendel

*Paul Badura-
Skoda*

ON CONTEMPORARY MUSIC

I'm interested in contemporary music. I believe our age . . . is very creative in
music, but not every piece of created music is good, as was also the case in the
time of Mozart. Out of ten thousand works which were created, only a very few
survived. . . . So, too, today there is an enormous output of music. And if only 1
percent survives, it's very much. American composers are very productive, but
some aren't so well known. One who, perhaps, is little appreciated by the vast
majority but is one of the best is Roger Sessions. Or Ned Rorem. Of course,
everyone knows Copland just as everyone knows Barber and Griffes. . . . The
second and third piano sonatas of Sessions are gigantic works, extremely difficult to perform. Everyone knows Barber's Piano Sonata. Copland wrote many,
many good works. And don't forget Ives, whom I still consider contemporary
because he died not so long ago. . . . Another particular favorite of mine is the
Swiss composer, Frank Martin.

Paul Badura-Skoda

For a modern composer, I like Steve Reich with Philip Glass a little behind him.
Reich has more grit in his compositions. . . . I'm also very busy now with Boulez,

especially his Second Sonata. A lot of work! Then I'm doing some Russian avant-garde music. I'll be doing some Babadganian (he's an Armenian) and some Gubaidulina. Very interesting music.

Egorov

In 1970 we established the New Music Studio in Budapest, a group of young composers and performing artists. This was the group that performed in Budapest, for the first time, Cage's "Water Music," "Water Walk," "Music Walk," "Winter Music," "Music for Amplified Toy Pianos," and many others. We've also done other American composers such as Philip Glass, Morton Feldman, and Christian Wolff. Among the Europeans, although we do them all, we go mostly with Boulez and Stockhausen, and sometimes Penderecki and Lutoslawski.

Kocsis

One of the reasons I enjoy working with modern composers is that I can get to know one of them and ask him what he meant by this marking or indication, or what do you mean here or there, or what do you really want done in this place. And you don't know how stimulating it is to work with music of living composers and being around them to find out how *they* think the music should be and how they listen to music, which I've found out is very different from the way the pianist thinks of music. . . .

If new music is a little bit too strenuous for a classical audience, the 2 percent, remember it took them a long time to get to Beethoven, too. Yet they should hear new things occasionally. However, I'm not a believer in giving concerts consisting of all-new music. And when I see them being offered, I become quite irritated and I run from them, because I find them exhausting. I'm as lazy as the next guy. New music should be integrated with the old, because I believe in the universality of music and its impulses, thought processes, and feelings. For me, to work on Bartók is not radically different from working on Beethoven.

Ohlsson

In my musical tastes, I am a progressive person. I don't like reactionary music, music which sounds as if I had already heard it before. Schoenberg, Berg, and Webern were great composers. I admire some of Bartók's music, too, though I am not so fond of his latest works. I prefer what he wrote up until the time he left Hungary. I think his First Piano Concerto is superior to the other two. . . . But this is the new music of our grandfathers!

Brendel

My tastes in contemporary music . . . are really very limited. . . . The integration between line and harmonic balance is very apparent in the best of Schoenberg's works. In fact, one could say that the pursuit of that kind of integration is one of Schoenberg's trademarks, and I'm not just speaking of the twelve-tone works. But as far as what attracts me is concerned, I guess I'd have to say that I'm attracted to different aspects of his art at different periods of his life. . . . I should add, by the way, that I don't think any of his best works are for the piano, includ-

Glenn Gould (photograph: Don Hunstein)

ing the Concerto, and that's probably because Schoenberg tended to use the piano as a quick and dirty medium for trying out new techniques. But I do think that the Piano Suite, Op. 25 is a marvelous piece, all the same.

Glenn Gould

In every period of history, there is a so-called avant-garde group of composers. For example, look at Scriabin and Prokofiev. At one time they were thought to be contemporary avant-garde composers. And now they are considered classical. Even Bartók is now considered a classicist. For me, Stockhausen and Penderecki are the most interesting names in contemporary music, but time alone will tell whether it will live on.

Gilels

ON COMPETITIONS

In my time, there was nothing like that at all. Each artist had to fight his way, step by step, to make a career. Now the youngster can gain a foothold, *if* they have promising talent. And the competition toughens them. After all, the pianists who go through the competitions are excellent players, and they have to pit their own talent against that of their peers.

Kraus

The leading competitions are still a starting point for a career in concert piano playing. . . . And, in this respect, I particularly like two competitions. One of them is Santander, in Spain (Paloma O'Shea competition). The main prize in this one consists of getting a guaranteed number of performances—about twenty, I believe. The same is true of my other preference, the Busoni, in Italy. Before that competition is over, the directors have already lined up some twenty cities of concert organizations not only for first prize, but even at times for second prize, too.

Badura-Skoda

I don't really hate competitions, at least not as much as some of my colleagues do, but I certainly would not have entered one on my own. . . . It's just that I do not find them a pleasant activity. Yet I know that competitions, or at least a certain number of them, are necessary to help artists get playing engagements. At least in competitions a group of musicians, not agents or recording companies, are making the decisions, and that is certainly an advantage of the system.

Murray Perahia

I've been in many competitions. . . . especially the first Van Cliburn in 1962. I took third place in that one. After I had won, I went to New York to line up a manager. But all responses were negative, absolutely negative. "You are a woman," I was told, "and you are very young." I soon learned that at that time young pianists received no consideration at all, especially not younger women pianists.

. . . It seems that even today, a career is possible before age twenty or even after age forty or forty-five. But in between is a kind of never-never land in which it's really difficult to get established. I don't know why that is, but it is. Of course, all artists must struggle for recognition, and in the case of women, managers do not trust them between the ages of twenty and forty, because those

Murray Perahia

are the childbearing years. Managers don't want artists who will stop for a number of months and try to start up again. . . .

I don't think, either, that were I to win a competition today, my career would take a different direction. There simply are too many competitions. To win a big one, like the Tchaikowsky Competition or the Chopin Competition, that would be something else. It's ironic that there are more competitions but fewer opportunities.

Ousset

It used to be that there was a small handful of important international competitions. They were very relevant, very consequential, then. It meant something to win one of these competitions, especially in terms of management. If you won an international competition in the 30s or 40s, you'd find management and managers at your every door. Then in the 60s came more and more competitions, and managers figured out some excuse to avoid all of these young players. At one time, the young would-be artist heard, "Go win an international competition and we'll take you on." But now every other street corner has its own competitions with the result that management is becoming ever more cavalier.

Fleisher

It has nothing to do with the music or the artist. It's like an Olympic which is artificial and mechanical. It's just work to make the competition, but then what? If the pianists are any good, they don't need a competition. Besides, if they do win, they merely receive a prize and a series of concerts which sometimes turns the pianists into mere machines. That isn't music, nor is it art.

de Larrocha

Too much commercialism has crept into the picture to allow the young artist sufficient time to develop. Music has become too big a business. Now young people win a prize and are expected immediately to live up to expectations. They are supposed to be ready-made great artists, which obviously they cannot be. They need time to mature. Instead, they are pushed into a tour of fifty or sixty concerts with only one or two programs, which is as unhealthy a situation as you could find. I suppose that, with the number of young gifted people available, it is quite difficult to make a career without winning a competition. But there ought to be another way, too.

Arrau

Another element that is capable of hurting the artist is the competitions. From a managerial standpoint, it helps to capitalize, to have a winner, and then launch a career. But from the musical point of view, I don't like them because they select not by excellence, but by elimination. There was a big competition at the end of the nineteenth century, I believe it was the Anton Rubinstein Competition in Moscow. Busoni played and took third prize. First prize was won by Mr. Heinz. Do you know who Busoni is? Do you know who Heinz is?

Horowitz

On Teachers and Teaching

A strong teacher needs a strong pupil as a strong mother or father needs a strong child. Frequently, people with talent study too long and too late in life anyway. I stopped my studies with Horowitz when I was twenty. Actually, it was he who influenced my decision. "You'll go out and make mistakes," he said, "but that's okay. They'll be your mistakes. Let them be yours. Say something with your music—it doesn't matter what, but say something that's *you*."

Byron Janis

You ask how [Martin] Krause taught me. Well, to begin with, he showed me the many ways Liszt used to play trills. He stressed the fact that trills had meaning;

they were not merely adorned to a work but had expressive purpose. The trills had to be played at different speeds to fit the mood of the work being performed. Some were fast, some were slow, some were loud, and some very soft. The technique was determined by the character of the piece. And, in playing scales, arpeggios, and general passage work, Krause advised that the arms should be like snakes so that together with loose wrists there would be no interruption of the flow of movement anywhere. The whole picture was one of fluidity and effortless playing, whether you were rendering a great chord or the smallest package of notes. It is the way Liszt himself is supposed to have played.

Arrau

This is one of the qualities I admired in Edward Steuermann's teaching—he made his students learn passages at a fast tempo, but he subdivided the passages into smaller bits. He'd tell the student to go up to a certain place and play in a specific manner. Next he asked the student to play the second bit and connect it with the first, but not in slow motion. This went on until the student had finished the passage. This system may also be beneficial for memorizing the whole work.

Brendel

You'll find that the musical doctrine of Schnabel was a similar line as that of Fischer, but I would say more on the intellectual side, whereas Fischer had a great confidence in the artist's intuition. That became a powerful message with Fischer. "Trust your intuition. Have your dreams, have your visions. And be not overly concerned with your career."

Badura-Skoda

What I remember most about [Marcel] Ciampi was that he was tremendously sensitive to playing onstage. And as a consequence, when he taught you fingering, or style, or technique generally, he taught them in the light of how the music would sound to an audience. Another memorable trait was Ciampi's talent for driving his students to the limit of their ability, their potential. I remember a radio broadcast I did when I was eleven. I was to play Liszt's "Mazeppa," and since I'd never done anything even remotely similar to it, I knew I was tempting fate to work it out on a broadcast. Even two days before the broadcast, some sections were giving me trouble. But all at once everything jelled. Ciampi was very pleased, because now he saw that I had reached a crossroad in my progress.

Ousset

My teacher, David Saperton, always used to say that you should just take your normal position at the keyboard, drop your hands to your lap, relax, and then bring them up and put them on the keyboard. "That," he said, "is your normal position." And I believe the body should be kept relatively still, too. The more you move around, the more you're asking for trouble.

Bolet

Cécile Ousset

When you start playing music, you begin with simplicity—how to produce the notes themselves. Then you gain a sense of expression, of wanting to articulate the emotions behind the music. And then with certain pieces like those of late Beethoven or Schubert or certain Mozart pieces, you have to go beyond human expressivity into an almost spiritual realm of purity, or of ecstasy, I suppose. At that time, I simply thought, "This is such a beautiful melody." And I proceeded to play it like a Chopin nocturne. [Gordon] Green taught me that day a truly meaningful lesson which was potent to a youngster, and which has stayed with me until now.

Hough

Fleisher felt that your approach to your instrument in the morning, or at any other time for that matter, set certain patterns that would carry over into every practice session. His idea is to start the session by playing some music—read through something gently, slowly, until you're warmed up. After you've warmed up, then you can do some exercises if that is what is in your regimen. That's the time to work on your trills or octaves or whatever.

Watts

Stephen Hough

When I reached age five, my parents once again took me to Jacob Tcatch who, as it turned out, was one of the greatest influences on my career because of the firm foundation he gave me. . . . I was given many scales and forms of scales as well as all the various studies which I practiced devotedly. And this is where my foundation for technique was developed.

Gilels

One of my former teachers told me something that I will never forget, that a pianist is much better off developing all of his life, not merely sticking to the repertoire and playing for fifty years or so. That is one way in which one may experience an evolution. After all, the music you know today may be reviewed from quite another aspect in twenty years. Then he added another point. It is very hygienic for the pianist who wants to progress continually to always have the pieces of the virtuosic and the polyphonic in his repertoire. These two directions should always be represented, because the one helps to keep the hands in order, the other helps to keep the brains in order. The thought process must continue all the time.

Ivo Pogorelich

Ivo Pogorelich

To work with Arrau is to work with a real master, to feel the pressure of his consciousness upon you. I suppose of all the teachers I've had, I would say he could hear more than anybody else. I'm not just talking about notes. I'm talking about nuance and intentions and implications and musical understanding. And having had so much experience, he was also in some ways the most practical of my teachers, even though he is hardly a mechanistic person. He could actually tell you, "That's a beautiful fingering, but it is risky for this reason." . . . And it's also because he never illustrates, so you can slavishly imitate him. He always wants you to find answers yourself. . . . He wants *you* to connect with *yourself,* and that's very demanding. A lesson with him usually lasted about an hour and a half, which was a very exhausting period for both of us. He is very philosophical but also very practical, because he believes very much as I do in the unity of mind and body in terms of your technique, your whole mode of expression. He wasn't divided. He's a very unified person. He doesn't say, "This is technique, *and* this is musical expression, *and* this is philosophy." It all weaves into a big tapestry, which I believe in entirely. Music, like all art, has to be one. There are no unconnected parts.

Ohlsson

I would say that the single most important notion I learned from [Arthur] Rubinstein was the idea of projection. Being onstage and playing beautifully what you think is beautiful does not mean that the person in the back of the hall hears the same thing. And he made me aware of the audience at all times, aware, that is, of what *they* are hearing, not what *I* am hearing. He made me aware that to play too quietly on stage—this is a very simple and elementary example—forces people in the back of the hall to strain to hear you. And that's a no-no because audiences don't like to strain just to hear the notes. Consequently, you somehow have to play much more loudly on the stage yet give the impression both to the people in the last row and to those nearest you that you're playing a delicate *pianissimo*. Now, that's difficult to learn, and you learn it by playing a great deal and by experimenting. Rubinstein didn't show me how to do it. He merely made me aware of the problem, and the necessity of having a beautiful singing tone to help overcome it. Color and imagination were extremely important to him, I guess, because he himself had such great imagination with music.

. . . One of the most important ideas I learned from him is a sense of pulse in a piece, not metronomic rhythm, but a feeling for the rhythm all the way through. For example, in a polonaise, the first beat comprises a dotted-eighth, and then a sixteenth, and so on. However, to give it the tremendous polonaise feeling, you hold that long note a smidgen longer, and it sounds perfectly in rhythm. It isn't really, but it gives the measure so much more of a rhythmic quality. No one could play a polonaise like Rubinstein. He never counted one, two, three. Again it was a matter of the feeling he wanted to give the audience.

Fialkowska

Schnabel was incredible. He taught in a very special way. He rarely heard a piece two weeks in a row, because at each lesson he told the student everything he knew about the piece. You see, what it comes down to essentially is, "Do you teach the student, or do you teach the music?" When I teach, I generally do both. One must be aware of the particular problems of each student in achieving the musical goal. It becomes a combination of teaching the music *and* teaching the student. However, when one played for Schnabel, it was a different experience altogether. I like to cite the example of the first time I played Beethoven's Opus 81a, the "Les Adieux." We stayed on the opening Adagio for three-and-a-half hours. That's only three lines of music. And he didn't repeat himself! . . . My head and emotions were so filled with all of this that I felt transported out of myself. It was what I would imagine it to be if one were on some kind of chemical substance—a high, a transformation. It was truly incredible. Great artists achieve through concentration, discipline, and inspiration what many of the younger generation of today seek to achieve through chemicals. Through some natural transformation, they actually arrive at other states of awareness.

. . . I think, in a sense, that teaching is one step beyond performing. Teaching entails more responsibility. There's a greater obligation in teaching than in being a very great and successful performer today, because if you are a performer and if you have something to say (teach) that is meaningful, you will have the success. But if you're a performer, and if you can play your instrument, whatever it be, marvelously, and have nothing or very little to say, I don't think you'll remain a success very long. That's something that is a one-to-one relationship between performer and public. It simply sifts itself out. However, if you're a teacher, and you pass on nonsense, then I think you commit a grave sin. Yes, in that sense [being] a teacher is far more serious and responsible because it's something that is passed on to the next generation, which will itself pass it on, and so forth.

Fleisher

CHAPTER 24

Keyboard Teaching and New Technology

In the past several decades, electronic technology has made new tools available to the keyboard teacher. The traditional piano, now called an "acoustic" piano in some circles, has changed little. Computers and electronic musical instruments, on the other hand, have changed considerably, becoming smaller, more portable, more versatile, and less expensive. Electronic instruments, widely used in commercial music as well as serious composition, are assuming new roles in music education. Children are growing up with computers at home and at school, using them to learn programming and a variety of other subjects, including music. This chapter will briefly survey the technological tools that may be used in teaching piano and will examine the challenges, opportunities, and consequences of this developing technology.

ELECTRONIC INSTRUMENTS AND OTHER TOOLS

The earliest *electronic pianos,* many of which are still in use, produced sound by striking metal bars with hammers, much as piano hammers strike strings. This quiet sound was then electronically amplified and reproduced through built-in speakers and headphones. More recent electronic pianos synthesize sounds electronically or use sampled sounds. (Samples are digital electronic recordings of the sounds of an acoustic piano, combined and tuned for each desired pitch.) Instead of using hammers, modern electronic pianos measure the velocity of the key descent, adding weighted keys to make the touch more realistic.

386

Electronic pianos are used frequently in teaching laboratories, where instructors and students can hear one another and communicate through the teacher's console. Consoles generally allow for flexible groupings of students and have connections for microphones, tape recorders and metronomes. Many teachers use consoles regularly, others only infrequently. But most music schools and colleges—and some independent studios—consider such equipment indispensable.

Although the design of modern electronic keyboards has changed greatly, the most significant element in this development is not the creation of better "imitation pianos," but the creation of musical instruments with new capabilities. The best known of these new instruments is the *synthesizer.* Synthesizers create sounds electronically, either by combining simple waves or by altering, filtering, and processing more complex waves. The tone or timbre can then be further altered by *modulators, signal processors,* and *envelope generators,* which add distortion, delay, and variations in attack and dynamic shape.[1]

Unlike pianos, synthesizers can generate any frequency. They can "bend" pitches within a given range. They can create sounds that sustain like a flute, crescendo like a gong, or decay like a piano. They can simulate other instruments and can create sounds that no other instrument can make. The individual timbres of a synthesizer are called its voices, and the number of preset voices in a synthesizer can range from a few dozen to hundreds. Many synthesizers are further programmable by the user, making the number and variety of voices unlimited.

Modern synthesizers generally are equipped with keyboards. But the development of *MIDI* (Musical Instrument Digital Interface) allowed electronic instruments of all kinds to be connected to and controlled by one another. MIDI is a language of musical events rather than a representation of actual sounds. MIDI conveys digital information about the details of a performance: the exact time that a note is played, the key velocity, when the note is released, whether it has "pitch bend," and the channel that will send it to the desired synthesizer voice. This digital data, transmitted and processed electronically, tells the synthesizer when, how long, how loud, and at what pitch it should make a given sound.[2] By allowing synthesizers to be combined with other instruments, MIDI makes them more capable, more flexible, and easier to use.

For piano teachers, synthesizers can be a source of interesting and useful sounds; for instance, of simulated harpsichord, clavichord, or organ sounds that can be used in playing Baroque keyboard works. Piano music can be judiciously transcribed for the synthesizer, particularly pieces with textures reminiscent of other instrumental idioms. Synthesizer sounds may also stimulate student composition. They enable students to hear compositions with a variety of instrumental timbres, not just with traditional keyboard sounds. In improvisation, they provide opportunities for students to discover the idiomatic characteristics of various voices. Synthesizers are more useful in these creative, less structured, or composition-oriented activities than they are in aiding the technical mastery of particular pieces or skills.[3]

Synthesizers are especially effective when used in conjunction with a *sequencer.* Not a musical instrument as such, a sequencer stores and plays back

MIDI information through another instrument, such as a synthesizer or electronic piano. A sequencer is roughly analogous to a tape recorder, but with several important differences. Since it records data instead of sound, a sequencer allows independent editing of pitches, rhythms, dynamics, tempi, and timbres. A student can play back a performance at a slower or faster tempo without changing the pitch. When slowed down, passages that are uneven or poorly coordinated are even more evidently flawed than when heard at tempo. Passages performed slowly can also be played back faster, giving an idea of the eventual sound and tempo of a work. Used this way, sequencers can help develop listening ability and a higher standard of accuracy, and can help make the conceptual leap from slow practice as drudgery to slow practice as a window onto the details of a performance.

Most sequencers also have a feature called timing correction. When individual-note attacks occur slightly before or after the beat of the built-in metronome, the sequencer can correct them to the nearest beat with mathematical precision. If an attack is far enough off to be closer to another beat, it will be "corrected" to the wrong beat. While this may seem useful in reinforcing rhythmic precision, artists do not play with computer-like rhythmic accuracy. Effective, rhythmical playing comes from skillful timing of attacks and use of agogics. Rhythmic energy and flexibility (appropriate or not) are lost to timing correction. The flatness of this mechanical rhythm is often disturbing to classical and jazz musicians alike.

These applications of rhythm correction and variable-speed playback are largely remedial, not creative. The real potential of sequencers ranges from the merely convenient to the potentially enlightening. Sequencers can record accompaniments to improvisation activities, freeing the teacher to give full attention to students instead of playing at the same time. Accompaniments or ensemble parts can be made available for practice in a lab or (if the student has the proper equipment) at home. A student can also create and record his/her own backgrounds for improvisation or single-handedly record and assemble all the parts of an ensemble. The speed adjustment can help adapt each of these activities to the needs and abilities of the individual student.

It is often useful to "think orchestrally" at the piano. Yet without exposure to orchestras, students may find this concept abstract at best. Orchestrating a piece of piano music with sequencer and synthesizer can stimulate awareness of voicing and color. The process of identifying characteristic parts of a texture and choosing appropriate sounds for those parts can help students to understand structure and contrast. Hearing the parts together will help them to learn to differentiate color and dynamic levels.[4]

Other technological tools are of use to piano teachers, many of which use a MIDI format. With a *music notation program* for a personal computer, one can write music at a MIDI keyboard or at a typewriter and it will be printed in musical notation. These programs are often found in combination with sequencing programs. Notation programs vary widely in ease of use. Programs used to transcribe music played directly from a MIDI keyboard also vary in the accuracy of what they write. For teachers who compile theory notebooks, write textbooks, or compose music, such programs can help edit, print, and even publish these materials.

Samplers are a technological extension of *Musique Concrete,*[5] using sounds from natural or preexisting sound sources to create new sounds too complex or unique to be synthesized. Samplers digitally record the sounds of voices, tin cans, or any other object, and then mix, transpose, and reshape these sounds to different pitches and sonorities. Samplers generally have keyboards that are used in transposing and playing back sampled sounds.

Drum machines are devices that reproduce sampled or synthesized percussion sounds. They are played through special pads or buttons or through any MIDI keyboard. Drum machines usually also have some features of sequencers, and are capable of playing back rhythm patterns recorded by the user or programmed on a disk.

While electronic pianos, synthesizers, and sequencers remain the principal technological teaching tools, the most popular instruments in young people's hands today are *portable electronic keyboards*. Portable keyboards are small synthesizers with short keyboards and several dozen voices, usually featuring percussion sounds, preset rhythm patterns, automatic accompaniment patterns, and automatic chords. They usually do not have touch-sensitive keys, but some keyboards have MIDI, built-in sequencers, samplers, and a surprising number of features for the price. These "folk instruments of our time"[6] now outsell acoustic pianos more than twenty-five to one.[7]

Serious musicians often dismiss portable keyboards for their undistinguished sound and mechanical "auto-play" features, but these instruments can be useful. Preprogrammed rhythms can be used as metronomes, but metronomes with more appeal to youngsters. Students can transcribe or reprogram the preset rhythm and chord patterns, developing important ear-training and rhythmic-cognitive skills by doing so. Built-in sequencers can be used to record ensemble parts and accompaniments. The limited sounds of portable keyboards are usually superior to the sounds of most computers, making MIDI-equipped keyboards useful with many educational computer programs. The flexibility, convenience, and low cost of portable keyboards have made them central tools in many school music programs.

Getting Started

Outfitting a teaching studio with a reasonable quality electronic keyboard, synthesizer, and sequencer will require an investment of several thousand dollars. Better-quality portable keyboards are available for well under $500. Bear in mind that electronic instruments are usually heavily discounted, and discounts of 20 percent to 40 percent are not unusual. Shop around and bargain.

Keyboard

A touch-sensitive electronic piano will probably be the largest single investment of a MIDI-equipped studio. Quality of touch varies considerably between the products of different companies, so try several instruments carefully, choosing one that feels, responds, and sounds best. Within wide price ranges, the "actions" of most manufacturers' electronic pianos are often identical. Thus it is not necessary to buy the top-of-the-line electronic piano to get a good sound or touch. Differences in price within a product line are affected by the size of amplifier and speakers, the finish of the cabinet, and the number of "features," such as voices and automatic rhythms. If the electronic piano will be used with a synthesizer and a sequencer and will be connected to a stereo system in the studio, the corresponding features of the electronic piano need not be elaborate. If the synthesizer will be connected to the speakers of the electronic piano, the keyboard must have line-in connections. The line-out connections allow the keyboard to be heard through an external amplifier and speakers.

A more specialized instrument is the *keyboard controller*. A controller usually has weighted keys and excellent touch response, but makes no actual sounds itself. Instead it is designed to be a full-featured tool for controlling other MIDI instruments such as synthesizers. Intended for the serious MIDI user, a controller usually has more professional MIDI features than an electronic piano. But without speakers or sounds of its own, it cannot be used independently as a free-standing instrument.

Synthesizer

The best way to choose a synthesizer is to go to music stores and try out as many as possible. Listen to every voice, preferably with the same amplifier and speakers. Consider:

Are the sounds interesting, appealing, and useful?

Do voices that carry instrument names sound realistic?

Is the synthesizer easy to understand and use?

Are the manuals and guides clear and comprehensible?

Can the synthesizer be programmed with other voices? Does this require a computer, special equipment or programs?

Some synthesizers are available as modules. This means that they have no attached keyboard and are designed to be played through another MIDI keyboard. In the continuing trend toward miniaturization, synthesizers are even appearing as computer cards, included or installed in personal computers. In evaluating options, consider convenience (portability, adaptability, compactness, and availability of expansion slots in your computer) and price. If the electronics are the same, the sound will be the same too, whether the unit is in your computer or in a box of its own.

Sequencer

Sequencers are available either as stand-alone units or as programs for a personal computer. "Dedicated" sequencers (the device is dedicated to a single purpose, sequencing) offer ample sequencing capability and tend to be relatively simple to operate. Most machines will lose what has been recorded when they are turned off, so they should have some way of storing information. Look for sequencers that use standard computer-type memory media: either $3\frac{1}{2}''$ or $5\frac{1}{4}''$ disks, both of which are inexpensive and widely available. Tape storage is clumsy and slow, and odd-sized memory disks are expensive and limited in availability.

Sequencing programs for personal computers generally offer more features and flexibility. If portability is not needed in a sequencer, this option may be the better investment. The computer screen enables you to use features such as graphics, charts, or even musical notation. Sequencing and notation programs are available for most popular computers. Rather than buying several different programs, choose one full-featured program and use it until you have exhausted its capabilities. To use a sequencing program, a MIDI interface is needed to connect the computer to the instruments. The interface is included on some computers, some sequencing packages, or in internally mounted synthesizers.

Electronic devices of all kinds—and musical instruments especially—tend to become quickly outmoded or obsolete. When shopping for equipment one must learn to distinguish important and useful new sounds and features from interesting but transient ones. The basic concepts of playing, sequencing, and synthesizing may remain the same, but new products, features, and sounds are created almost daily. Programmable or expandable synthesizers can help keep up with new sounds, if that is important to you. Separate components make it easier to upgrade the individual parts of a setup. "MIDI workstations"—keyboards, sequencers, and synthesizers combined into single units—can be more convenient and portable than separate pieces, but can also be less flexible when it is time to replace or add equipment later. In all cases, keep a clear idea of the planned educational applications. Student and teacher skills developed on this equipment will be transferable to newer technology when it is created.

COMPUTER-ASSISTED INSTRUCTION

The use of computers in teaching is called "computer-assisted instruction," (CAI). CAI programs generally consist of drills or games designed to teach or practice specific ideas or skills. Most CAI programs in music are for learning basics of pitch and notation, theory, or ear-training. Some are sold as sequential sets; other programs appear singly, presenting or reinforcing a certain skill at one or more levels. Some programs are accompanied by written texts or workbooks or are designed to accompany current piano-teaching methods.

Technically and educationally well-designed programs can be of great value as an adjunct to group or private instruction. A computer program can be an inexhaustible source of drills and questions to test and expand the student's knowledge. Graphics can enhance the presentation of musical concepts with moving notes or shapes. Musical work in a non-keyboard environment can add variety to the student's studies. Game-like elements, including records of high "scores," can make repetitive drills more enjoyable. Positive comments reward work done well. And the "toy element"—the novelty of making a fancy machine do fancy things—can pique the interest of many students.

The nonhuman, mechanical interaction of computer with user can also be used to good purpose. Computers can time a student's response to a question or can wait indefinitely for a student to consider a difficult answer. A computer can repeat a question as many times as needed and can create unlimited new questions by means of random processes. Computers are scrupulously honest and never equivocal about errors. A computer response to a student answer carries no overtones of approval, disapproval, or embarrassment.

There are also drawbacks to computer-assisted instruction. The drill format may be disguised as a game but the disguise may wear thin. Drills generated by random processes are often musically uninteresting. Positive comments from a computer ("great job!") become trite and reinforce expectations of instant gratification. While capable of creating endless drills, computers can only display explanations that have been written into the program. The inherent emphasis on "right" answers does not stimulate creative thinking or the discovery of artistic limits.

The instructor should choose, supervise, and follow up on computer-assisted instruction, just as with other materials. Terminology and methods should be compatible with the instructor's. The skills covered should be appropriate to the student's level and should be reapplied by the instructor in actual musical contexts. Records of successful or unsuccessful completion of work should be kept. In choosing programs, consider both content and presentation.

Content

Is the content well ordered and thoroughly explained?

Are exercises and activities of real benefit?

Are terms and concepts clear and consistent with the level of the material?

Do questions challenge the student to think without being confusing or ambiguous?

Are incorrect answers explained or corrected?

Is the student's active participation an integral part of the program?

Presentation and User Interface

Is the program user-friendly or does it require the student to memorize arcane commands?

How do the program and the computer sound?

Are choices presented to the student clear and logical?

Are there entertaining features such as graphics and animation?

Are there annoying or confusing features that reduce the convenience or enjoyment of the program?

Does the program respond too slowly or too quickly to student answers?

Does the program keep track of the student's work?

Does the program allow the teacher or student to select the level of difficulty? Can it automatically adjust to how well the student is doing?

It is possible for someone with limited computer experience to write his or her own instructional materials as well as to use commercially available programs. Simplified languages enable instructors to write their own lessons for classes or individual students.[8] *Hypermedia,* programs that combine text and graphics in a kind of electronic card-filing system, allow teachers to compose programs where the student moves from one "card" to another (on the computer screen), exploring a subject in a number of different ways. And, for futurists on a big budget, *videodisc* technology offers much promise, combining the best features of instructional videotape with the flexibility of computers.

Getting Started

In making intelligent, effective decisions about using computers, the first question is whether to use computers at all. Many students find CAI programs and sequencing applications very appealing and enjoyable. Computers can also be great time-saving devices for writing, billing, record keeping, and business and household management. But equipment and programs require a certain investment of time and money. The following questions should be helpful both for private instructors planning personal studios and for college teachers submitting proposals to administration:

Do you see a specific need for computer-assisted instruction or feel that it could be helpful?

Are you personally interested in computers and CAI?

Do you feel that computers would interest and motivate your students? Might they distract or intimidate some?

Will you find computers helpful for other uses as well?

Are there specific programs you want your students to use?

Do sequencing and synthesizing also interest you?

Will the investment pay off economically, either by attracting additional students, generating lab fees, or saving time?

Do you have available space for students to use computers before or after lessons or at other "lab" times?

Before purchasing a computer, study the available software first. Buy the hardware (computers and equipment) to fit the software (programs). Be specific about what you want the software to do. Do you want an integrated music theory or music basics package? If so, do the order and timing of ideas in the program coincide or clash with your current methods? Do you instead want individual skills drills that can be assigned for each area or level? What skills should be included, and how? Read about the programs and ask people you know and respect for information. Try out the programs to be sure they meet your needs. *Write down* each of your requirements and preliminary evaluations so you do not lose track of your goals.[9]

In selecting programs, carefully note the complete equipment requirements of each one you examine. Each program requires a certain amount of memory (RAM), the amount of information a computer can work with at one time. Some may require a color monitor, others black and white. Some may require a joystick or mouse (devices for moving the cursor around the screen). Some require special interfaces (such as MIDI), synthesizer cards, or other devices. Figure all of these equipment requirements into the estimates of your final cost. When in doubt, refer to the checklists and advice in TESS (see "Further Resources," below).

Another important consideration is how the programs *sound* on the computers for which they are written. The intonation and tonal capabilities of computers vary widely, and they usually are not very good.[10] Programs that use MIDI instruments generally improve the sound and flexibility of the setup.

After choosing the software, you will know exactly which computer and peripheral equipment you will need. Well-meaning friends may tell you that *their* brand of computer is easier to operate, or more capable, or better in some way, than what you have chosen. Bear in mind that most people tend to prefer what they know and have used. By choosing your music software first, you will have satisfied your specific needs.

Frequently manufacturers, music stores, colleges, and individuals offer workshops in electronic music. These workshops can help you learn about new products and applications, and better understand the possibilities of computer applications. They can also put you in contact with others who are learning and exploring in this area, giving you an opportunity to share notes and information. Such workshops can be the best place to get hands-on experience with programs and equipment without having to buy them first.

CONCLUSION

This chapter has surveyed just a few applications of technological tools in piano teaching. The most promising uses have less to do with the mechanics of playing and more to do with exploring, composing, and unlocking the structure of music. These applications may be seen as a natural extension of changes in pedagogy in this century. Greater emphasis is currently placed on the development of musical understanding and general musicianship and less on the mere acquisition of technique. But if a teacher does not address conceptual and compositional aspects of music in his or her teaching already, that teacher will be no more likely to do so with synthesizers and sequencers.

Computer tutorials and electronic instruments should solve a clear problem and meet a clear need or they will be little more than an expensive distraction. Electronic pianos, synthesizers, computers, music printers, sequencers, and other devices can provide powerful tools for learning, analyzing, composing and arranging. Some teachers will welcome these tools but others will fear that they may ultimately distract students from an intimate mastery of the piano and its literature. In evaluating the promise of electronic technology, we should carefully evaluate our work as musicians and teachers—

In continuing a tradition of artistic and humanistic values.

In stimulating students to understand and compose music on their own.

In encouraging students to explore new paths of musical expression.

In helping students to gain poise and self-knowledge through discipline and concentration.

In developing artistry and all that is associated with this term.

In establishing goals for students, and in helping them to realize goals they have set for themselves.

In sharing what we ourselves find enriching in music.

The success or failure of teaching with technology will be highly dependent upon the attitudes and skills of both instructor and student. Computers and synthesizers will inspire some and disquiet others. Used as ersatz flash cards, tape recorders, and toys, electronic equipment will be an unnecessary distraction. These tools will not make ineffective teaching effective or an unsuccessful teacher successful. But used to enhance the creative aspects of a program of instruction, electronic technology can be a powerful and valuable resource for those who choose to explore and evaluate its possibilities.

*F*URTHER RESOURCES

For further reading about electronic instruments, educational computing, and their use in teaching music, the following list should provide a good starting point.

Books

ANDERTON, CRAIG. *MIDI for Musicians.* New York: Amsco Publications, 1986.
    This book is an excellent discussion of MIDI for serious users.

CARDEN, JOY. *A Piano Teacher's Guide to Electronic Keyboards.* Milwaukee: Hal Leonard, 1988.
This is an introduction to keyboard and synthesizer uses in the piano studio, with specific suggestions for lesson activities.

The Educational Software Selector (TESS) is published by the Educational Products Information Exchange (EPIE).
TESS lists all kinds of educational software, and contains references to software reviews, addresses of suppliers, hardware requirements, and invaluable advice on selecting software. There are helpful forms and checklists at the end of the volume for use in software selection. Address: EPIE Institute, P.O. Box 839, Water Mill, NY 11976.

HOFSTETTER, FRED T. *Computer Literacy for Musicians.* Englewood Cliffs, NJ: Prentice-Hall, 1987.
Written by an educator who is an acknowledged expert in both computers and music, this is an excellent beginning guide to understanding computers and music programs.

PAPERT, SEYMOUR. *Mindstorms.* New York: Basic Books, 1980.
Papert's ideas are seminal for anyone interested in using computers in creative environments. His ideas, while centering on the teaching of mathematics, have strongly affected all computer applications in education today.

Organizations

The *Association for Technology in Music Instruction* (ATMI) is a special-interest group within the Association for the Development of Computer-Based Instructional Systems (ADCIS).
ATMI publishes a directory of courseware for music, listing hardware and software requirements. ADCIS has a university-level emphasis; ATMI addresses music educators at all levels. ADCIS also publishes the *Journal of Computer-Based Instruction.* Addresses: ADCIS, 409 Miller Hall, Western Washington University, Bellingham, WA 98225; ATMI, Dr. Charles G. Boody, President, Evaluation Center, Hopkins Public Schools, 1001 Highway 7, Hopkins, MN 55343.

The *Music Educators National Conference* (MENC) has offered numerous presentations on technology at its conventions. In addition, the *Music Educator's Journal* features frequent articles on technology as well as a regular review called "Floppy Discography." The address for subscriptions is 1902 Association Drive, Reston, VA 22091.

The *Music Teachers National Association* (MTNA) has begun to examine the area of music technology enthusiastically. The 1988, 1989, and 1990 national conventions featured symposia on CAI in music and published a thick booklet with practical information on CAI, advice for CAI implementation, and reviews of programs. Address: MTNA, Suite 1432, 617 Vine Street, Cincinnati, OH 45202-2434.

Periodicals

Clavier features an occasional column titled "On Line," with information about equipment and resources and reviews of instructional and other music programs. *Clavier,* 200 Northfield Road, Northfield, IL 60093.

The *Computer Music Journal* is a highly technical periodical, providing information about composers and activities on the intellectual and artistic forefront of music technology. There is no pedagogical emphasis. Address: *Computer Music Journal,* M.I.T. Press, 28 Carleton Street, Cambridge, MA 02142.

The Electronic Music Educator began in September 1988 as an occasional supplement to *The Instrumentalist* and *Clavier.*

Electronic Musician and *Keyboard* are two important magazines in which the latest instruments, programs, and gadgets are discussed, evaluated, and advertised. Discussions can range from the basic to the highly technical. Subscription addresses: *Electronic Musician,* P.O. Box 3747, Escondido, CA 92025-3747; *Keyboard,* 20085 Stevens Creek, Cupertino, CA 95014.

The Music and Computer Educator began publication in January 1990. It is designed specifically as a resource for keyboard and other music teachers who use electronic technology in their teaching.

Other periodicals devoted to general uses of computers in education include *Technical Horizons in Education, Classroom Computer Learning, Journal of Computing in Education, The Computing Teacher,* and *Educational Technology.*

APPENDIXES

APPENDIX I

Selected Articles About the Business of Teaching

FEES

From **Clavier**

October 1980. "The Private Studio: Fees and Studio Policies," by Martha Lewis.

November 1981. "Why Not Raise Your Rates?" by Dean Elder.

July–August 1983. "Give Yourself a Raise," by Jean Oelrich.

July–August, 1984 "You Deserve a Break—With Pay!" by Barbara Hacha.

December 1986. "Dollars and Sense," by Katherine K. Beard.

December 1989. "Piano Teaching: Hobby or Profession?" by Katherine K. Beard.

From **American Music Teacher**

January 1989. "The Billing Contest: Mixing Fun with Finances," by Michael Freeman.

June–July 1989. "Late-Payment Fees and Payment Plans," by Michael P. Marsh.

August–September 1989. "Tuition Fees," by Michael P. Marsh.

TAXES AND FINANCE

From American Music Teacher

January 1981. "Should You Have an IRA?" by Richard Norton.

November–December 1982. "Tax Advantages for the Private Music Teacher," by Donald L. Mellott, C.P.A.

January 1988. "Individual Retirement Accounts," by Michael P. Marsh.

February–March 1988. "Simplified Employee Pensions," by Michael P. Marsh.

April–May 1988. "Cash Flow Management," by Michael P. Marsh.

June–July 1988. "Risk Management," by Michael P. Marsh.

September–October 1988. "Investment Planning, Part 1," by Michael P. Marsh.

November–December 1988. "Investment Planning, Part 2," by Michael P. Marsh.

January 1989. "Advice for Planning the Coming Fiscal Year," by Michael P. Marsh.

February–March 1989. "Business Cents," by Michael P. Marsh.

April–May 1989. "The Family Business," by Michael P. Marsh.

From Clavier

January 1981. "The Private Studio: Record Keeping," by Martha R. Lewis.

February 1981. "Preparing Your Income Tax, Part 1," by Martha R. Lewis.

March 1981. "Preparing Your Income Tax, Part 2," by Martha R. Lewis.

February 1982. "Keeping Tax Records," by Donna Bashaw.

July–August 1982. "Start Planning for Retirement Today," by Donna Bashaw.

October 1982. "Business Advice for Private Teachers," by Ron Sepic.

November 1982. "Teaching Music for Profit," by Elzey Roberts.

March 1983. "Tax Reforms Aren't Tough," by Barbara Kreader.

May–June 1986. "Living in a Material World," by Eileen Duggan and Rhonda Barfield.

September 1986. "Making Ends Meet—and More," by Elaine Guregian and Barbara Kreader.

From Keyboard

April 1987. "Taxes: Musicians and the New Law," by Jim Aiken.

September 1987. "Home Studios and Income Tax: A Guide Through the Labyrinth," by Steve B. Harlan.

February 1988. "A Musician's Guide to the New Tax Law: Pay It Again, Sam," by Steve B. Harlan.

STUDIO POLICIES, PROFESSIONALISM, AND MARKETING

From American Music Teacher

February–March 1982. "Studio Policy," by Sara Marantz.

June–July 1982. "The Professional Piano Teacher," by Anne Simpson.

January 1986, February–March 1986. "Independent Music Teachers Forum," by Carol Winborne.

February–March 1986. "Professional Responsibility and the Independent Piano Teacher," by Robin Rausch Sheets.

November–December 1986. "Marketing Strategies for the Music Teacher," by Mary F. Mobley and Thomas D. Tolleson.

January 1988. "Taking Control of the Telephone Inquiry," by Mary Ann Walker.

February–March 1988. "Brochure Basics," by Frances Scott.

April–May 1988. "Teaching Leave: Create Your Own," by Alison Barr.

September–October 1988. "Moving Your Studio: A Calendar for Success," by Deborah Fishbein.

November–December 1988. "Studio Recitals as Promotional Vehicles. Music Classes for the General Public," by Elizabeth Manduca.

January 1989. "Toward Independent Teaching," by Alison Barr.

February–March 1989. "What to Do When the Teacher Is Sick: Handling Illness in the Studio," by Constance W. Murray.

April–May 1989. "The Piano Popularization Program: You're Part of the Network," by Don Dillon.

April–May 1989. "Your Next Professional Meeting: How Will You Get There?" by Shirley Raut.

June–July 1989. "Beating Burnout," by Rebecca Johnson.

June–July 1989. "When Students Relocate: Paving the Way for Parents and Pupils," by Patricia Florig.

August–September 1989. "Sales Techniques for the Independent Music Teacher," by Susan Capestro.

October–November 1989. "Building Effective Student—Teacher Relationships in the Private Music Studio," by Kenneth Bruscia.

February–March 1990. "Teachers and Parents as Partners: The Key to a Successful Parent—Teacher Relationship," by Kikuyo M. Power.

February–March 1990. "Support Personnel in the Private Studio," by Jean Fox.

From Clavier

September 1980. "The Private Studio: Advertising and Promotion," by Martha R. Lewis.

November 1980. "The Private Studio: Details of Studio Management," by Martha R. Lewis.

October 1981. "The Business of Teaching: Making the Most of Your Teaching Day," by Patricia Taylor Lee.

September 1982. "Studio Operation on a Large Scale," by Kristi Thielen.

October 1982. "Business Advice for Private Teachers," by Ron Sepic.

March 1984. "Be Professional!" Part 1," by Martha R. Lewis.

April 1984. "Be Professional!" Part 2," by Martha R. Lewis.

May–June 1984. "Relocating Your Studio," by Ronald Stinson Moir.

April 1985. "Semi-Private Lessons," by Judith Lessin.

January 1986. "The Quality Music Teacher," by Lynn Freeman Olson.

April 1986. "Closing the Credibility Gap," by Dee Ann Brown.

September 1986. "Ten Steps to Professional Well-Being," by Alison S. Barr.

April 1988. "From Private to Group Lessons," by Claudia J. McCain.

November 1988. "How We Had the Law Amended," by Jerome Stassen and Betty Kowalsky Stasson.

February 1989. "Promoting Your Studio," by Steven H. Roberson.

October 1989. "Running a Business," by Joanne Marie Barnaba.

January 1990. "Tips for the Traveling Teacher," by Martha Baker.

February 1990. "Preparing Teachers for the Twenty-First Century," by E. L. Lancaster.

From Proceedings of the National Conference on Piano Pedagogy

October 1982. "How Can We Better Prepare Future Piano Teachers to Work in the Real World of Music Business?" report of the Committee on Music Business Practices, Bill B. Ramal, Chair.

October 1982. "Music Teachers' Associations: A Valuable Means of In–Service Training for the Independent Piano Teacher," by Carol Winborne.

October 1984. "An Application of the Managerial Grid to Piano Pedagogy," by Steven H. Roberson.

October 1984. "A New Career from Two Points of View: How to Make a Living after Graduating with a Degree in Piano Performance," by Karen Simsonsin and "Was It Guilt or Altruism?" by Fran Schuler–Ellis.

October 1986. "Finishing Our Professional Wall," by Harriet F. Green.

October 1986. "Crippling Contradictions in the Piano Teaching Profession," by Marsha Wolfersberger.

From Keyboard

January 1985. "The Business of Teaching Piano," by Paul Rinzler.

From Keyboard Arts

Autumn 1984. "Dear Parents," by Richard Chronister.

---

*E*QUIPMENT

From American Music Teacher

February–March 1984. "Computers for Piano Teachers," by Hanley Jackson.

June–July 1985. "Music Computer-Assisted Instruction," by Dinah Embry.

June–July 1988. "Computer Applications in Music," by Randall Faber.

November–December 1988. "A Traditionalist's Guide to Electronic Keyboards," by Larry Harms and Samuel Holland.

January 1989. "Word Processing and Piano Lessons," by Guy Wuellner.

February–March 1989. "The MTNA Symposium on Computer–Assisted Music Instruction," by Christine Hermanson.

December–January 1989. "Buyer's Guide to Electronic Keyboards," by Frederick Bianchi.

From Clavier

December 1984. "Synthesizers: A Primer for Teachers," by Sam Holland.

September 1985. "Does Your Studio Need a Computer?" by Jim Kunitz.

April 1986. "Why Not a Harpsichord for Your Second Studio Instrument?" by Lee Jordan-Anders.

April 1986. "What Are We Going to Do About Those Synthesizers?" by Donn Laurence Mills.

September 1986. "Help! I've Been Amped," by Virginia F. Campbell.

October 1987. "An Armchair Shopper's Guide to Synthesizers," by James Warrick.

January 1987. "New Tools, Traditional Goals," by Nancy Cree.

February 1988. "A Look at the Latest in Electronic Keyboards," by Larry Kettlekamp and Donn Laurence Mills.

April 1988. "Moving in a Small Studio," by Marta E. Perez-Stable.

November 1988. "The Portable Keyboard: Pandora's Box or Teacher's Best Friend," by Betsy Allums Widhalm.

July–August 1989. "Summer Synthesizer Projects," by Sandra Bowen.

From Keyboard

December 1985. "The Piano: Can It Survive in the Electronic Age?" by Bob Doerschuk.

June 1986. "Setting Up a Home Studio," by Ted Greenwald.

June 1987. "Sequencer Basics: A Guide for the Mystified," by Jim Aiken.

June 1988. "Plug In Here: The ABC's of Techno–Music Literacy," by Jim Aiken.

June 1988. "Teaching and Learning Music," by Kyle Kevorkian.

August 1988. "In Praise of the Piano," by Bob Doerschuk.

August 1988. "Piano Builders Sound Off," by Bob Doerschuk.

June 1989. "Roland HP-5000S & MT-100," by Mark Vail with "A Pianist's Perspective," by Robert L. Doerschuk.

From The Piano Quarterly

Summer 1989. "MIDI Equipment for the Classical Pianist," by George F. Litterst.

Fall 1989. "Tackling Technology: Sequencing and the Classical Pianist," by George F. Litterst.

From Myklas Times

January–February 1987. "Easing the Independent Studio into the Twenty–First Century" by Gayle Kowalchyk.

ALTERNATIVE AND/OR SUPPLEMENTARY CAREERS

From Clavier

May–June 1985. "David Arden: Pianist in a Ballet Tapestry," by Carol Montparker.

December 1985. "The Piano: Springboard to Alternative Careers," by Carol Montparker.

February 1986. "Circuit Rider Teacher," by Susan Henry.

February 1987. "Career Choices," by Julie Jaffee Nagel.

March 1987. "On Stage," by Julie Jaffee Nagel.

March 1988. "Paid to Play: The Ballet Accompanist," by Mary Koepke.

November 1989. "Careers in the Music Industry," by Alfred Reed.

February 1990. "Team Up with an Organ Teacher," by Marie A. Asner.

From American Music Teacher

February–March 1990. "The Best Seat in the House," by Marsha M. Evans.

From (Contemporary) Keyboard

February 1980. "Dance Class Piano," by Dennis R. Passmore.

December 1980. "Where the Jobs Are, Part 5—Piano Tuning," by John Svec, as told to Bob Doerschuk.

January 1981. "Where the Jobs Are, Part 6—Touring Staff Organist," by Tim Harris, as told to Bob Doerschuk.

February 1981. "Where the Jobs Are, Part 7—Music Stores," by Bob Doerschuk.

July 1981. "Where the Jobs Are, Part 11—Rehearsal Pianist," by Bill Grossman, as told to Bob Doerschuk.

October 1981. "Where the Jobs Are, Part 13—Electronics Technician," by Marvin Jones, as told to Dominic Milano.

February 1987. "Rebecca La Brecque Teams Piano and Synth In Recital," by Bob Doerschuk.

From Keyboard Arts

Winter 1988. "Bloom Where You're Planted," by Thomas McBeth.

Resources: Intermediate

Literature

ALBERGO, CATHY, AND REID ALEXANDER. *Intermediate Repertoire: A Guide for Teaching.* 2d ed., rev. Champaign, IL: C & R Music Resources, 1988.

The American Music Scholarship Association. Offers *Piano Guides,* with suggestions of materials for each level. Available on request. AMSA, 1826 Carew Tower, Cincinnati, OH 45202.

American Music Teacher. Journal of the Music Teachers National Association. Suite 1432, 617 Vine Street, Cincinnati, OH 45202-2434.

The Associated Board of the Royal Schools of Music. Publishes books of examination pieces (grades 1–8), books of other examination requirements (e.g., *Scales & Broken Chords, Aural Tests, Questions and Exercises on Theory of Music),*and other piano collections. 14 Bedford Square, London WC1B 3JG. Available from Theodore Presser, Presser Place, Bryn Mawr, PA 19010.

The Australian Music Examinations Board. Publishes *Manual of Syllabuses* dealing with the teaching of music (all instruments, voice, speech, and drama), an Australia-wide system of graded examinations (preliminary, grades 1–8). Warren Thomson, AMEB Chairman, N.S.W. State Conservatorium of Music, Macquarie Street, Sydney, N.S.W. 2000.

BURGE, LOIS SVARD. "Contemporary Piano Repertoire: A Guide for Teachers," in *Keyboard* (August 1981), pp. 44–46.

CANADAY, ALICE. *Contemporary Music and the Pianist.* Van Nuys: Alfred Publishing Co., 1974.

Clavier. 200 Northfield Road, Northfield, IL 60093.

Educo Records. Box 3006, Ventura, CA 93006.

FRISKIN, JAMES, AND IRWIN FREUNDLICH. *Music for the Piano: A Handbook of Concert and Teaching Material From 1580 to 1952.* Reprint. New York: Dover Publications, 1973.

FUSZEK, RITA M. *Piano Music in Collections: An Index.* Detroit: Information Coordinators, 1982.

GRIESINGER, FREDERICK, AND TINKA KNOPF. *A Graded List of Suggested Repertoire for Preparatory Piano Levels.* Baltimore: Peabody Institute, 1973.

HINSON, MAURICE. *Guide to the Pianist's Repertoire.* Bloomington, IN: Indiana University Press, 2d ed., rev. 1987. *Guide to the Pianist's Repertoire: Supplement,* 1979.

————. *Music for More Than One Piano: An Annotated Guide.* Bloomington, IN: Indiana University Press, 1983.

————. *Music for Piano and Orchestra.* Bloomington, IN: Indiana University Press, 1981.

————. *The Piano in Chamber Ensemble: An Annotated Guide.* Bloomington, IN: Indiana University Press, 1978.

————. "Editions of Keyboard Music." In *How to Teach Piano Successfully,* by James Bastien. 3d ed., rev. San Diego: Kjos West, 1988. Pp. 287–298.

KEMMERLING, SARAH ELLEN MOORE. *Selected Piano Compositions Written Since 1960 for the Intermediate Piano Student.* DMA diss., University of Texas, Austin, 1980. UM 80201385.

KERN, ALICE M., AND HELEN M. TITUS. *The Teacher's Guidebook to Piano Literature.* Ann Arbor, MI: Edwards Brothers, 1954.

Keyboard Arts Magazine. Published by National Keyboard Arts Associates, Box 24 C 54, Los Angeles, CA 90024.

LINCOLN, CLARICE YOUNG, AND DAVID C. KORTKAMP. *Certificate of Merit Syllabus and Guide for Piano Teachers: The Music Teachers Association of California.* Available from MTAC, 414 Mason Street, Suite 605, San Francisco, CA 94102. First published in 1953. Various revisions through 1988.

MAGRATH, JANE. "Avant-Garde Teaching Materials for Piano." *The Piano Quarterly,* no. 123 (Fall 1983): 46–51.

MAXWELL, CAROLYN, ed. *Haydn Solo Piano Literature* (1983). Available from Maxwell Music Evaluation, 1245 Kalmia, Boulder, CO 80302. 1983. Other volumes, with William De Van, include *Schumann Solo Piano Literature* (1984), *Scarlatti Solo Piano Literature* (1985), and *Schubert Solo Piano Literature* (1986).

————. *Maxwell Music Evaluation Notebook* and *Maxwell Music Evaluation File.* 1245 Kalmia, Boulder, CO 80302.

MORHANGE-MOTCHANE, MARTHE. *Thematic Guide to Piano Literature.* New York: G. Schirmer. Vol. 1, *Easy Pieces of J. S. Bach and Handel; Sonatinas and Sonatas of Haydn,* 1982. Vol. 2, *Mozart and Beethoven,* 1982. Vol. 3, *Chopin and Mendelssohn,* Vol. 4, *Schubert and Schumann.*

Music Minus One. 423 West Fifty-fifth Street, New York, NY 10019.

National Federation of Music Clubs. 310 South Michigan Ave., Room 1936, Chicago, IL 60604. Graded lists, prepared for NFMC Festivals. Encourages performance of works by American composers.

National Guild of Piano Teachers. Box 1807, Austin, TX 78767. The *Irl Allison Piano Library* (see p. 199) includes twenty-five graded volumes grouped as sets of repertoire for Guild Auditions.

National Piano Foundation. *New Music Review Library.* 4020 McEwen, Suite 105, Dallas, TX 75244–5019.

The Piano Quarterly. Box 815, Wilmington, VT 05363.

PIERCE, RALPH, AND RITA FUSZEK. *The P-F Guide,* 1982. Distributed by Ralph Pierce Music, 616 North Azusa Avenue, West Covina, CA 91791.

REIF, JEAN FRANCIS. *A Compendium of Piano Concertos,* 1981. Distributed by Von Franc Enterprises, P.O. Box 25896, Richmond, VA 23206–5896.

Royal Conservatory of Music Piano Publications. Frederick Harris Music, 340 Nagel Drive, Buffalo, NY 14225–4731.

Schmitt Music Centers. 88 South Tenth Street, Minneapolis, MN 55403.

THOMPSON, ELLEN. *Teaching and Understanding Contemporary Piano Music.* San Diego: Kjos West, 1976.

UNGER, JOYCE. *Galaxy of Composers: Biographical Sketches of Modern Composers of Piano Educational Materials,* 1988. 430 East Vine Street, Mulvane, KS 67110.

ZAIMONT, JUDITH LANG. "Twentieth-Century Music for the Developing Pianist: A Graded Annotated List." In *Teaching Piano,* by Denes Agay. New York: Yorktown Music Press/Music Sales, 1981. Pp. 389–436.

Examples Relating Intermediate Literature to Areas of Technical Development

In the outline that follows, each area of technical development in keyboard learning is examined in conjunction with intermediate literature from various periods and styles. Although certain repertoire is used as an example, this is not meant to imply that the selected pieces are intrinsically better than others in achieving the stated goals. Any teacher may plan a similar curriculum with materials (s)he knows, values, or has on hand.

INDEPENDENCE

Independence of the Single Hand

"Susan Bray's Album," MIRIAM HYDE. *Piano Music for One Hand.* Melbourne: Allans Music.

Late elementary or early intermediate. Ten pieces for left hand that explore antiphonal effects, changing dynamics, articulations, ranges. Requires little or no pedal.

Entire volume, LYNN FREEMAN OLSON. *SINGLE-HANDED.* New York: Carl Fischer. Early intermediate. "Serenade" offers opportunity to balance dynamics and make quick register shifts. Pedal must be used. "Londonderry Air" requires much dynamic adjustment, more subtle pedaling, some double-note playing.

"Scherzino," "Contemplation," "Discussion," ERIC GROSS. *Piano Music for One Hand.* Melbourne: Allans Music.
Middle, late intermediate. These pieces would make a good set (fast/slow/ fast). They require some sophistication, rapid adjustments, and within-the-hand independence. Pedaling is not marked. Not much is necessary except in "Contemplation."

Playing Two Independent Lines

Pieces suggested avoid quoting from the most obvious sources—that is, music from the Baroque period in general, music by J. S. Bach in particular—since most teachers would automatically choose such literature to develop this type of technical independence.

"Escerzio," JON GEORGE. *Artistry at the Piano: Repertoire, Book 4.* Miami: CPP/ Belwin.
Early intermediate. Left/right hands answer each other. Written in the style of Scarlatti. Affords a clear picture of binary form.

"Walking on Sand," ANDRZEJ DUTKIEWICZ. *Seascapes.* San Diego: Kjos West.
Intermediate. Opportunity to project dotted eighth and sixteenth against steady eighth notes in compound meter. Colorful harmonic shifts. Requires careful reading of accidentals. Some use of hemiola.

"Interlude," WILLIAM GILLOCK. *Lyric Preludes.* Secaucus, NJ: Summy-Birchard/ Warner Bros.
Intermediate. A short, moody sketch calling for projection of independent phrases. Uses middle register of piano effectively. Requires sensitive pedaling, some rubato.

Entire volume, JEAN BERGER. *Seven Inventions.* Delaware Water Gap, PA: Shawnee.
Middle intermediate. Each invention has similarities to those of Bach: imitation, hands-together episodes, reading of accidentals, and a "hard part." Some differences: less usual and changing meters, unexpected harmonic shifts.

"Blues," ERICH KATZ. *Piano for the Developing Musician 2.* St. Paul, Minn: West.
Middle intermediate. A blues canon. Requires careful fingering, some finger substitution, and a sense of style. For the student who can't stand Bach.

Independence of Dynamics and Articulation

The following suggestions call attention to homophonic pieces in which the accompaniment is a little less usual.

"Spanish Donkey Driver," JENÖ TAKÁCS. *Studio 21: Book 1.* Valley Forge, PA: Universal/European-American.

Early intermediate. Left hand "guitar" is technically simple, but effective. Pedal markings are unusual (noncontinuing lines). Interest lies in uneven phrase lengths and major/minor mixtures. A clear-cut case of right/left hand polarity.

"From Afar: A Little Serenade," DONALD WAXMAN. *New Recital Pageants: Book 2.* New York: Galaxy.

Intermediate. An opportunity for the student to learn to play a quietly repeating left hand. Includes the use of some less usual sonorities. The right hand roams freely, often over the left hand, thus creating different balance and legato problems.

"A Song for Duke," TONY CARAMIA. *Fascinatin' Rhythms.* San Diego: Kjos West.

Intermediate. A suave stride bass supports a bluesy melody. Especially effective in teaching balance because returning sections change their overall dynamics. This is a melody/accompaniment piece for someone who may not wish to play Mozart or Chopin.

"Folk Song Op. 12, No. 5," EDVARD GRIEG. *Master Series for the Young.* Milwaukee: G. Schirmer/Hal Leonard.

Middle intermediate. Grieg's *Lyric Pieces* are not used as much as they might be to ease the student into exploring complexities of projecting nineteenth-century keyboard writing. Melody line requires rhythmic care, some ornamentation. Left hand accompaniment (basically a waltz) changes texture constantly. Cadential measures require subtle voicing.

"Unfinished Phrase," TOMAS SVOBODA. *Children's Treasure Box: Book 3.* Portland, OR: Stangland.

Middle to late intermediate. A very sophisticated piece for a collection titled as it is. Each hand demands the ultimate in legato versus staccato. The legato hand maintains 2-voice writing in which inner balance is a factor and finger substitution a necessity. In the middle of this short piece, the hands switch parts. Beautiful, but not easy.

Independence Within the Hand: Voicing

"Soaring," WILLIAM GILLOCK. *Lyric Preludes.* Secaucus, NJ: Summy-Birchard/Warner Bros.

Intermediate. Right-hand thumb projects a melodic line as it plays arpeggiated chords through middle and upper registers. Left hand and pedaling are uncomplicated.

"Homage to Schumann," DONALD WAXMAN. *New Recital Pageants: Book 4.* New York: Galaxy.

Intermediate. Single fingers sustain notes while other fingers (often the thumbs) play on off beats. Chance to develop a feel for weight on the hands' weaker sides. Schumann himself calls for similar techniques in *Album for the Young*.

"Etude in D Minor," STEPHEN HELLER. *Selected Progressive Etudes*. Van Nuys CA: Alfred Publishing Co.
Middle intermediate. Melody on weak side of right hand must project over repeated chords (divided between both hands). Often the top pitch has the opportunity to begin the phrase alone. The music of Heller, while somewhat harmonically predictable, affords the student a variety of pieces in which to explore sonorities and techniques.

"Lonely Wanderer," EDVARD GRIEG. *Edvard Grieg: An Introduction*. Van Nuys, CA: Alfred Publishing Co.
Middle intermediate. Thumbs in both hands sustain notes while other fingers, in both hands, project the melodic line in octaves, tenths. Cadential measures require adroit fingering and pedaling.

"Sarabande," from Sonata in A Minor, J. S. BACH. *Dances of J. S. Bach*. Van Nuys, CA: Alfred Publishing Co.
Late intermediate. This demands great sophistication in voicing separate lines, sustaining and voicing suspensions (inner lines), and considerable finger substitution to avoid overuse of the pedal.

Independence of Expression: Freedom to Make Choices

"Arietta," VINCENT PERSICHETTI. *Little Piano Book*. Bryn Mawr, PA: Elkan/Theodore Presser.
Early intermediate. The right hand is invited to be a "singer" in this short, unmeasured piece. Repetition allows the making of further dynamic or rhythmic changes. Left hand plays quiet, descending thirds. May be pedaled freely.

"Mountains," ROSS LEE FINNEY. *Thirty-two Piano Games*. New York: C. F. Peters.
Intermediate. New notation, but easy to read because the "picture" is clear. Technical skill of player will determine how long to trill, how far crescendo or decrescendo may be stretched. Encourages imagination, experimentation. Create a piece like it!

"Menuet en Rondeau," JEAN-PHILIPPE RAMEAU. *The Baroque Era*. Van Nuys: Alfred Publishing Co.
Intermediate. Learning to play *notes inégales* will make the study and performance of this piece attractive as well as informative. It will also teach the ear to distinguish between even and uneven eighth notes. The student will enjoy "swinging" Rameau.

"Aria," BERNARDO PASQUINI. *The Baroque Era*. Van Nuys, CA: Alfred Publishing Co.
Intermediate. A quite easy piece to which optional passing and changing

notes may be added on the repetitions. This excellent edition offers models, suggestions, and historical background for many such experiences.

Entire Volume, PAUL COOPER. *Cycles*. St. Louis: Chester/MMB Music.
Late intermediate. Contains 11 short sections, some of which invite freedom, some of which do not. Freedoms include: rhythm, improvising with given pitches, clusters. At times performer plays inside the piano or uses the palms. Player must be tall enough to damp strings with one hand, play with the other. Requires use of middle pedal. For the more experienced.

Mobility

Velocity

"Innocence," JOHANN FRIEDRICH BURGMÜLLER. *Beginning Piano Solos*. New York: Carl Fischer.
Early intermediate. Short finger patterns interspersed with phrases involving an octave scale afford variety with relaxation between efforts. Since most right-hand passages are descending, fingers move more readily.

"Etude in A Minor Op. 45, No. 2," STEPHEN HELLER. *Selected Progressive Etudes*. Van Nuys, CA: Alfred Publishing Co.
Intermediate. This perennial favorite ("The Avalanche") requires the rapid linkage of 3-note patterns, alternating hands, ascending and descending. The opening patterns are short, each moving to its "landing" note. Octave reach is necessary for chords.

"Sonata K. 431," DOMENICO SCARLATTI. *Scarlatti: Introduction to His Keyboard Works*. Van Nuys, CA: Alfred Publishing Co.
Intermediate. This short G-major sonata demands right-hand agility in playing broken chords. The 3 2-octave arpeggio passages descend and thus are not very difficult. An easy left-hand part includes some octaves.

"Droplets," PAUL SHEFTEL. *Preludes, Interludes, and a Postlude*. Van Nuys, CA: Alfred Publishing Co.
Intermediate. Left hand (black keys), right hand (white keys) must alternate rapidly and softly to create the "style." While left-hand patterns remain constant, right-hand patterns shift, requiring quick adjustments. Gentle off-beat accents provide occasional sparkle. Easy to memorize.

"Chatter," ROSS LEE FINNEY. *Twenty-four Piano Inventions*. New York: C. F. Peters.
Intermediate. Staccato 3-note figures shift from hand to hand, join, separate, and interact. Two long legato passages (one each for right and left hands) interrupt with a sinuous, highly chromatic gesture. A calm ending.

"Bagatelle Op. 5, No. 10," ALEXANDER TCHEREPNIN. *Bagatelles*. Van Nuys, CA: Alfred Publishing Co.

Late intermediate. Short bursts of chromatic ascending passages, sequential turn-around patterns, and 2 long descending scales keep the right hand alert and busy. Tense staccato chords provide contrast. Quick moves, octave reach also necessary. This must be played like a breathless romp!

Quick Chord Changes

"Prologue," VINCENT PERSICHETTI. *Little Piano Book.* Bryn Mawr, PA: Elkan/Theodore Presser.
Early intermediate. Mostly major triads, but different ones in each hand. Change in texture to 4-note chords, two notes in each hand. Brash, contrasted with gentler, sounds. A very short piece.

"The Sun Wakes the Sea," ANDRZEJ DUTKIEWICZ. *Seascapes.* San Diego: Kjos West.
Intermediate. Broken chords move quickly through keys, shapes, inversions. Right- and left-hand figuration overlaps. Hands take turns leading. Requires alert moves and a sense of color.

"Patriotic Song," EDVARD GRIEG. *Master Series for the Young.* Milwaukee: G. Schirmer/Hal Leonard.
Middle intermediate. Teachers often assign this well-known piece without realizing how difficult the chordal passages are for many students. Textures change almost constantly. Since there may be some struggle with these changes, the piece is often performed too slowly.

"Winter Morning Op. 39, No. 2," PETER ILICH TCHAIKOWSKY. *Master Series for the Young.* Milwaukee: G. Schirmer/Hal Leonard.
Late intermediate. Difficult chord changes, which, at the same time, shift registers in each measure. Only 2 notes in each hand, but reading and playing the varied sevenths demands agility. Further, each seventh and its resolution must be finger-phrased.

"Etude in D Minor Op. 45, No. 15," STEPHEN HELLER. *Selected Progressive Etudes.* Van Nuys, CA: Alfred Publishing Co.
Late intermediate. Chord shapes range from 3 to 5 notes in each hand. Student must be able to reach octaves easily. Constant register changes, from very low to high. Big sonority required. This is the "poor man's Rachmaninoff."

Quick Changes of Register and Texture

"Seashore," ROSS LEE FINNEY. *Thirty-two Piano Games.* New York: C. F. Peters.
Intermediate. Uses some 5-finger clusters as well as the highest and lowest pitches on the keyboard. Helps to establish how much (or little) energy and weight it takes to play at top and bottom. Use a rote-note approach and more pedal than the composer suggests.

"Above, Below, and Between," ROBERT STARER. *American Composers of Today.* Milwaukee: Hal Leonard.
Middle intermediate. The hands do just what the title suggests. Moves and dynamic adjustments must be lightning-quick to create an effective performance.

"No. 22," THEODOR KIRCHNER. *New Scenes of Childhood.*Bryn Mawr, PA: Associated Board, Royal Schools/Theodore Presser.
Middle intermediate. Texture and register change nearly every half bar in this wispy scherzo. In 32 measures there is uncommon variety of spacing, articulation, and sonority—and also one delightful surprise. Kirchner's music is in the same category as that of Heller—many keyboard experiences within short pieces.

"No. 5," ROBERT MUCZYNSKI. *Diversions,* Op. 23. Milwaukee: G. Schirmer/Hal Leonard.
Middle intermediate. A syncopated rollick contrasting registers, marcato and legato, and dynamic extremes. Must be played with great freedom and imagination.

---

*T*ONAL *CONTROL*

Developing a Sense of Drama and Style

"Maestoso," J. C. BACH/FRANCESCO P. RICCI. *Fourteen Pieces.* Chapel Hill, NC: Hinshaw.
Intermediate. The contrary-motion motive suggests drama at the outset. In a contrasting middle section, broken chords over a pedal point build to a climax, then recede. Repetitions make this piece easy to learn.

"Night Journey," WILLIAM GILLOCK. *Lyric Preludes.* Secaucus, NJ: Summy-Birchard/Warner Bros.
Middle intermediate. A taut broken-octave motive punctuated by sharp chords explores many registers. Key of B-flat minor creates its own color. Dramatic possibilities within this short prelude.

"Gargoyles," JON GEORGE. *Patterns for Piano.* Van Nuys, CA: Alfred Publishing Co.
Middle intermediate. Excitement provided by irregular rhythmic groupings (3 + 3 + 2). Single lines in each hand mirror one another, making this piece technically easy. Rhythmic motive interrupted by hand-crossing thirds. Creates a big impression without being difficult. Short enough so that drive can be sustained.

"No. 6," ROBERT MUCZYNSKI. *Diversions,* Op. 23. Milwaukee: G. Schirmer/Hal Leonard.
Middle intermediate. Sixteen measures of quiet intensity. Phrases unfold

seamlessly at low and high registers. Demands sensitivity to dissonance and thoughtful pedaling.

"Kum-Bah-Yah," arranged by Jack Butler. *Piano for the Developing Musician 2.* St. Paul, Minn: West.
Late intermediate. Richly colorful harmony makes the pianist "sound good." Repetitions of the last phrase bind this arrangement together. Writing centered in middle and lower registers. A piece that the student will play for friends.

Balancing Dynamics Throughout the Keyboard Range

"Serenade," William Gillock. *Lyric Preludes.* Secaucus, NJ: Summy-Birchard/ Warner Bros.
Intermediate. Opportunity to develop the long singing note in both high and middle registers. Three dynamic levels must be maintained: one for the upper line, one for the bass notes, and the third for the supportive chords.

"Cantabile in B-Flat Major (posthumous), Frédéric Chopin. *Chopin: Introduction to His Piano Works.* Van Nuys, CA: Alfred Publishing Co.
Middle intermediate. Melodic line incorporates ornamentation. It is necessary to create 3 dynamic levels. Left-hand chords shift constantly and occasionally require special voicing.

"Gymnopedie," Erik Satie. *Introduction to the Masterworks.* Van Nuys, CA: Alfred Publishing Co.
Late intermediate. The left hand has an opportunity to set its 2 dynamic levels in the introduction. (Play the chords with the left hand from the start.) In this piece, registers for the "3 levels" never change. Cool sophistication, rather than great drama, required.

Exploring Colors with Fingers and Feet

"In the Forest," Vladimir Rebikov. *Miscellaneous Short Pieces.* Bryn Mawr, PA: Associated Board, Royal Schools/Presser.
Intermediate. In this bitonal piece, the right hand must dominate, but softly, as it searches for the way out of the forest. Although unmeasured, this piece easily groups itself by the right-hand phrases and direction of the lines. Pedal freely, but often.

"Mist," Tomas Svoboda. *Children's Treasure Box: Book 3.* Portland, OR: Stangland.
Middle intermediate. Both hands must float and allow the moving notes in the broken chords to project here and there. Accidentals must be read with care. Music is measured, but rhythm plays little part in shaping this piece. Color is all. Follow the composer's pedaling suggestions.

"Moonlight Mood," WILLIAM GILLOCK. *Lyric Preludes.* Secaucus, NJ: Summy-Birchard/Warner Bros.

Middle intermediate. The reference to "Clair de lune" is unmistakable, yet provocative. Watch out for accidentals and clef changes. The sweeping scales (B major, whole-tone) are easy to play and make effective tonal gestures. The composer has provided careful pedaling.

"Fortune Telling," DARIUS MILHAUD. *The Household Muse.* Bryn Mawr, PA: Elkan/Theodore Presser.

Late intermediate. Student may enjoy discovering that the second half of this piece is a retrograde of the first. Cluster playing accompanies mysterious "other" sounds. Opening and closing musical gestures are dramatic. Use of the pedal requires experimentation; none is suggested.

"Nuages Gris," FRANZ LISZT. *Liszt: The Final Years.* Milwaukee: G. Schirmer/Hal Leonard.

Late intermediate. Not everything in this collection is suitable at the intermediate level, but many students might be able to play several pieces. Requires a comfortable octave reach. A most unusual cadence! Pedal a little more freely than indicated.

Materials Useful in Teaching the Transfer Student

Books Useful for Teaching and Reviewing Pitch Reading

BURKES, JOYCE M. AND THERESE DALEY. *The Music Machine: Primer, Grades 1, 2.* Boston: Boston Music.
  The format of these small books allows for "mix and match" measures. The split page accommodates many graded choices. Fun, and practical.

CLARK, FRANCES AND LOUISE GOSS. *Music Maker: Books 1, 2.* Secaucus, NJ: Summy-Birchard/Warner Bros.
  Helps to develop feel for keyboard geography, as well as pitch and rhythm reading. Part playing book, part workbook.

CLARK, FRANCES AND LOUISE GOSS. *Readers: A, B, C, D.* Secaucus, NJ: Summy-Birchard/Warner Bros.
  Short (never more than 8 measures) examples built around landmarks. Explanatory headings direct student's attention to reading and rhythmic elements on each page.

CLARK, MARY ELIZABETH AND RUTH PERDEW. *Reading and Repertoire: Primer, Levels 1–4. Bass Clef Book.* Boulder, CO: Myklas Music Press.
  Pieces are organized around 9 assorted guide notes. *Bass Clef Book* stresses bass-clef reading, but music is written using both clefs.

KAPLAN, BURTON. *A Basic Skills Pitch Sight-Reader.* New York: Perception Development Techniques.
This is a self-paced skill builder for players of all instruments. A unique approach to increasing coordination of mind and body. May be easier to use with older students.

OLSON, LYNN FREEMAN. *Right From the Start: A Rapid Piano Reader.* New York: Carl Fischer.
Short pieces, some requiring the student to write in his/her own fingering. Quick-read book to make sure that nothing basic has been skipped.

PEARCE, ELVINA TRUMAN. *Intervaludes.* Secaucus, NJ: Bradley/Warner Bros.
Good-sounding short pieces that develop feel for intervals. Covers grand-staff reading.

SHEFTEL, PAUL. *Easy as A, B, C.* Chapel Hill, NC: Hinshaw.
Pieces built on certain pitch names, with that pitch occurring in several octaves. Good for extending range to grand-staff reading. Fun.

WILLS, VERA. *Fat Cat.* Chapel Hill, NC: Hinshaw.
Develops extension of reading range and reading of patterns. Each piece includes preparation for reading and observations that point out differences, ask questions.

Books Useful for Teaching and Reviewing Rhythmic Reading

CAMP, MAX. W. AND LYNN FREEMAN OLSON. *Guidelines for Developing Piano Performance: Books 1, 2.* Chapel Hill, NC: Hinshaw.
Early and late elementary pieces. Step-by-step practice procedures for developing inner grasp of pulse and rhythmic groupings. Rhythm and pitch combined.

CLARK, MARY ELIZABETH. *Rhythm from Myklas: Books 1–4.* Boulder, CO: Myklas Music Press.
Pieces with rhythm accompaniment. Pieces notated; rhythm accompaniments unpitched.

CLARK, MARY ELIZABETH AND RUTH PERDEW. *Rhythm Now: Primer, Books 1–4.* Boulder, CO: Myklas Music Press.
Mostly non-pitch reading. Contains hands-together reading with different rhythms for each hand. Mostly playing; some games and writing. Fun done in a group, with rhythm instruments. Advances to less usual rhythms and meters.

CRESTON, PAUL. *Rhythmicon: Volumes 1–4.* Miami: Franco Columbo/CPP/Belwin.
A dictionary of rhythms. Contains explanations, practice drills, and short pieces. By book 4, pieces are difficult and use unusual meters. Mostly pitched rhythm reading.

KAPLAN, BURTON. *The Rhythm Sight-Reader: Books 1, 2*. New York: Perception Development Techniques.
Begins with basics and provides many unpitched rhythm exercises (some to study, some to sight-read, some to perform in ensemble). Book 2 introduces 2-line reading. May be used by all instrumentalists.

STARER, ROBERT. *Basic Rhythmic Training*. Milwaukee: Hal Leonard.
Systematized instruction in rhythm reading from basic pulse to 16th-note groupings. All rhythms shown in relationship to basic pulses. *Rhythmic Training* is the follow-up to *Basic Rhythmic Training*. Unpitched rhythm reading.

Books that Invite Choices and Freedoms

COOPER, PAUL. *Cycles*. St. Louis: Chester/MMB Music.
A few pieces in this cycle of eleven require using inside-the-piano effects; many invite rhythmic freedoms; all expect the performer to participate in the creative act. Student must be tall enough to depress keys, at the same time reaching inside to play on the strings.

FINNEY, ROSS LEE. *32 Piano Games*. New York: C. F. Peters.
Many of these pieces incorporate new notation, allowing for improvisatory extension relating to pitches, dynamics, and length. Good models for stimulating creativity as well.

GLOVER, DAVID CARR, B. J. ROSCO, AND CLARA CURZON. *Micro-Patterns: Levels 1–4*. Miami: CPP/Belwin.
Introduces 20th-century musical and keyboard sounds. Designed for young students. Teachers may appreciate the elements aimed at engaging the student's imagination.

MILLER, MARGUERITE, ed. *Mosaics*. Orem, UT: Sonos.
Explores many 20th-century compositional and playing techniques. Intended to stimulate experimentation and original composition. Includes a cross-referenced subject index.

NOONA, WALTER AND CAROL NOONA. *Projects: Books 1–4*. Dayton, OH: Heritage Music Press.
These books offer a mixture of activities, exploratory and technical. "Exploring" and "creating" sections range from musical storytelling to using standard variation techniques.

SHEFTEL, PAUL. *Sight-Reading Folk Songs from Around the World, Levels 2, 3*. Van Nuys, CA: Alfred Publishing Co.
Suggestions to vary the folk songs are quite specific, yet may unlock variation techniques for the more reticent. Emphasis is on fun as much as experimentation.

TAKÁCS, JENÖ. *Sounds and Colours,*Op. 95. Nutley, NJ: Doblinger/Foreign Music Distributors.

Some pieces are played on the standard keyboard, others use inside-the-piano effects. They require willingness to examine and project new textures, "sounds," and "colours."

The following lists are short since they are meant to serve primarily as models of what type of material may be effective as substitutes for other, or more difficult, literature.

Unlettered or Unnumbered Early Books

GEORGE, JON. *A Day in the Forest.* Secaucus, NJ: Summy-Birchard/Warner Bros.

GEORGE, JON. *A Day in the Jungle.* Secaucus, NJ: Summy-Birchard/Warner Bros.

OLSON, LYNN FREEMAN. *Menagerie.* New York: Oxford University Press.

PEARCE, ELVINA. *4 O'clock Tunes.* Secaucus, NJ: New School for Music Press/Warner Bros.

PEARCE, ELVINA. *Solo Flight.* Secaucus, NJ: New School for Music Press/Warner Bros.

Numbered Books, but Usable Since They Do Not Look Like "Methods"

CARAMIA, TONY. *Sounds of Jazz: Books 1, 2.* Secaucus, NJ: New School for Music Press/Warner Bros.

CLARK, FRANCES AND LOUISE GOSS, eds. *Supplementary Solos: Levels 1–4.* Secaucus, NJ: Summy-Birchard/Warner Bros.

FRASER, SHENA AND YVONNE ENOCH. *Studio 21: Volumes 1–3.* Valley Forge, PA: Universal/European-American.

WAXMAN, DONALD. *New Recital Pageants: Books 1–4.* New York: Galaxy.

Unlettered or Unnumbered Intermediate Books Offering Experience in Playing in "Styles"

COLLEY, BETTY. *Styles for Piano.* San Diego: Kjos West.

GILLOCK WILLIAM. *Lyric Preludes in Romantic Style.* Secaucus, NJ: Summy-Birchard/Warner Bros.

GROVE, ROGER. *Jazz About.* San Diego: Kjos West.

OLSON, LYNN FREEMAN. *Four Sonatinas in Varying Styles.* Van Nuys, CA: Alfred Publishing Co.

ROCHEROLLE, EUGÉNIE. *Montage*. San Diego: Kjos West.

SHEFTEL, PAUL. *Interludes*. New York: Carl Fischer.

Easier Pieces by "Standard" Composers

BACH, J. C. AND FRANCESCO RICCI. *Introduction to the Piano: Volumes 1–4*. Edited by Beatrice Erdely. Bryn Mawr, PA: Novello/Theodore Presser.

HELLER, STEPHEN. *Selected Progressive Etudes*. Edited by Lynn Freeman Olson. Van Nuys, CA: Alfred Publishing Co.

HALFORD, MARGERY, ed. *Edvard Grieg: An Introduction to His Works*. Van Nuys, CA: Alfred Publishing Co.

HINSON, MAURICE, ed. *Dances of J. S. Bach*. Van Nuys, CA: Alfred Publishing Co.

HUGHES, EDWIN, ed. *Peter Tchaikowsky (Master Series for the Young)*. Milwaukee: G. Schirmer/Hal Leonard.

KIRCHNER, THEODOR. *New Scenes of Childhood,* Edited by Lionel Salter. Bryn Mawr, PA: Associated Board, Royal Schools/Theodore Presser.

PALMER, WILLARD, ed. *Frédéric Chopin: Introduction to His Works*. Van Nuys, CA: Alfred Publishing Co.

Music by 20th-Century Composers

CARAMIA, TONY. *Fascinatin' Rhythms*. San Diego: Kjos West.

DUTKIEWICZ, ANDRZEJ. *Seascapes*. San Diego: Kjos West.

GEORGE, JON. *Patterns for Piano*. Van Nuys, CA: Alfred Publishing Co.

MUCZYNSKI, ROBERT. *Fables,* Op. 21. Milwaukee: G. Schirmer/Hal Leonard.

PERSICHETTI, VINCENT. *Little Piano Book*. Bryn Mawr, PA: Theodore Presser.

STRAVINSKY, SOULIMA. *15 Character Pieces for Piano*. New York: C. F. Peters.

NOTES

Chapter 1. Career Possibilities

1. The periodical *Keyboard* (formerly *Contemporary Keyboard*) is a graphic example of this reality. The periodical contains articles and advertisements that bridge and include the worlds of pop, commercial, and serious keyboard music and musicians.
2. Donn Laurence Mills, "What Are We Going to Do About Those Synthesizers?" *Clavier* 25 (April 1986): 38.
3. Bradford Gowen, "Playing, Teaching, Surviving, Dreaming," *The Piano Quarterly* 133 (Spring 1986): 40, 42.
4. For more information about piano-teacher training, see chap. 13.
5. Patricia Taylor Lee, *A Business Manual for the Independent Music Teacher,* rev. ed. (Dallas: The National Piano Foundation and the National Association of Music Merchants, 1984). pp. 21–31.
6. Gowen, "Playing, Teaching, Surviving, Dreaming," p. 40.
7. Connie Arrau, "Where are the Jobs? A Look at a Changing Marketplace," *Clavier* 24 (October 1985): 52.

Chapter 2. Functioning as a Professional

1. Patricia Taylor Lee, *A Business Manual for the Independent Music Teacher,* rev. ed. (Dallas: The National Piano Foundation and the National Association of Music Merchants, 1984). p. 9.
2. Sue Moser, "Latchkey Kids," *Clavier* 25 (March 1986): 15–16.
3. Ronald Stinson Moir, "Relocating Your Studio," *Clavier* 23 (May–June 1984): 50.
4. Lee, *A Business Manual,* p. 31
5. Ibid.; Beth Gigante, *A Business Guide for the Music Teacher* (San Diego: Kjos West, 1987); Linda Clary and Larry Harms, *Business Manual for Independent Studio Teachers* (Loveland, OH: Baldwin Piano and Organ Company, 1987). The following are available from the Music Teachers National Association, Suite 1432, 617 Vine Street, Cincinnati, OH: *The MTNA Book of Policies, Letters and Forms; A Publicity Handbook for Music Teachers; A Brief Tax Guide for the Independent Music Teacher; Review of Public School Credit and Released Time.*
6. Martha R. Lewis, "Be Professional! Part 2," *Clavier* 23 (April 1984): 46.
7. Susan Henry, "Circuit Rider Teacher," *Clavier* 25 (February 1986): 24–25.

Chapter 3. A Survey of Learning Theories

1. Gilbert Highet, *The Art of Teaching* (New York: Vintage, 1950), p. 5.

2. John Dewey, *Experience and Education* (New York: Macmillan, 1938), p. 1.

3. Robert F. Biehler, *Psychology Applied to Teaching*, 2d ed. (Boston: Houghton Mifflin, 1974), p. 268.

4. Morris L. Bigge, *Learning Theories for Teachers*, 4th ed. (New York: Harper & Row, 1982), pp. 55–56.

5. Biehler, *Psychology Applied to Teaching*, 2d ed., p. 207.

6. Robert M. Gagné, *The Conditions of Learning*, 3d ed. (New York: Holt, Rinehart and Winston, 1977), p. 15.

7. Interview with Elizabeth Hall, "Will Success Spoil B. F. Skinner?" *Psychology Today* 6 (November 1972): 65. Hall quotes then Vice President's Agnew's description of Skinner as "advocating radical surgery on the national psyche," and states that others regard Skinner's theories as a "blueprint to hell."

8. Gagné, *The Conditions of Learning*, pp. 74–75.

9. Ibid., p. 12.

10. Arthur W. Combs and Donald Syngg, *Individual Behavior*, rev. ed. (New York: Harper & Row 1959), p. 11.

11. Jerome S. Bruner, *The Process of Education* (New York: Vintage, 1960), p. 17.

12. Ibid., p. 17.

13. Biehler, *Psychology Applied to Teaching*, 2d ed., p. 266

14. Bruner, *The Process of Education*, p. 9.

15. Jerome S. Bruner, *Toward a Theory of Instruction* (Cambridge, MA: Harvard University Press, Belknap Press, 1966); *The Relevance of Education* (New York: Norton, 1971); *On Knowing: Essays for the Left Hand*, expanded ed. (Cambridge, MA: Harvard University Press, Belknap Press, 1979).

16. Biehler, *Psychology Applied to Teaching*, 2d ed., p. 126.

17. Robert F. Biehler, with Jack Snowman, *Psychology Applied to Teaching*, 5th ed. (Boston: Houghton Mifflin, 1986), pp. 85–90.

18. Arnold M. Cooper, Allen Frances, and Michael Sacks, "Chapter 1, The Psychoanalytic Model," Section 1, "The Personality Disorders and Neuroses," in *Psychiatry*, Vol. 1, rev. ed., edited by Robert Michaels, et al. (Philadelphia: J. B. Lippincott, 1989), p. 9.

19. Ibid., p. 1.

20. The opinions in this paragraph are the result of conversations with Sherwyn Woods, M.D.

21. Judd Marmor, M.D., "Psychoanalytic Therapy and Theories of Learning," in Judd Marmor, M.D., and Sherwyn Woods, M.D., eds., *The Interface Between the Psychodynamic and Behavioral Therapies* (New York and London: Plenum Press, 1980), pp. 36–37.

22. John Holt, *How Children Fail* (New York: Pitman, 1964); Neil Postman and Charles Weingartner, *Teaching As a Subversive Activity* (New York: Delta, 1969); and Charles E. Silberman, *Crisis in the Classroom* (New York: Random House, 1970).

23. Biehler, *Psychology Applied to Teaching*, 2d ed., p. 73.

24. Abraham H. Maslow, *Toward a Psychology of Being*, 2d ed. (Princeton, NJ: Van Nostrand, 1968), p. 55.

25. Biehler, *Psychology Applied to Teaching,* 2d ed., p. 676.

26. Carl Rogers, *Freedom to Learn for the 80s* (Columbus, OH: Charles E. Merrill, 1983), p. 20.

27. Biehler and Snowman, *Psychology Applied to Teaching,* 5th ed., p. 420.

28. This observation was the result of conversations with Dr. Richard Clark, University of Southern California School of Education.

29. Gagné, *The Conditions of Learning,* p. 16.

Chapter 4. The Keyboard Teacher and the Process of Teaching

1. The examination will be somewhat loosely based on Gagné's conditions of learning. See Robert M. Gagné, *The Conditions of Learning,* 3d ed. (New York: Holt, Rinehart and Winston, 1977). See especially chapter 2, "What Is Learned—Varieties."

2. Gagné, *The Conditions of Learning,* p. 219.

3. Ibid., p. 219.

4. Annie (Mrs. John Spencer) Curwen, *The Teacher's Guide to Mrs. Curwen's Pianoforte Method.* 16th ed. (London: J. Curwen & Sons, 1913), p. 5.

5. Some isolated examples of older books move in that general direction, though none does so in language that would call to mind words like "internal cueing and feedback." See Tobias Matthay, *The Act of Touch in All Its Diversity* (London: Bosworth & Co., 1903), also Matthay's *The Visible and Invisible in Pianoforte Technique.* (London: Oxford University Press, 1932); Annie (Mrs. John Spencer) Curwen, *Psychology Applied to Music Teaching* (London: J. Curwen & Sons, 1886).

6. See W. Timothy Gallwey, *The Inner Game of Tennis* (New York: Bantam paperback, 1974); W. Timothy Gallwey and Barry Green, *The Inner Game of Music* (Garden City, NY: Doubleday, 1986); Eloise Ristad, *A Soprano on Her Head* (Moab, UT: Real People Press, 1982); Seymour Bernstein, *With Your Own Two Hands* (New York: Schirmer, 1981).

7. Curwen, *The Teacher's Guide to Mrs. Curwen's Pianoforte Method,* p. 6.

8. Gagné, *The Conditions of Learning,* p. 124.

9. Ibid., pp. 200, 201.

10. Grosvenor Cooper and Leonard B. Meyer, *The Rhythmic Structure of Music* (Chicago: University of Chicago Press, 1960).

11. Gagné, *The Conditions of Learning,* pp. 155, 156.

12. Ibid., p. 172.

13. Ibid., p. 44.

14. As quoted in Benjamin S. Bloom, ed. *Developing Talent in Young People* (New York: Ballantine, 1985), p. 31.

15. David P. Ausubel, *Educational Psychology: A Cognitive View* (New York: Holt, Rinehart and Winston, 1968), pp. 365, 366.

16. Robert F. Biehler and Jack Snowman, *Psychology Applied to Teaching,* 5th ed. (Boston: Houghton Mifflin, 1986), p. 531.

17. Gagné, *The Conditions of Learning,* p. 245.

18. Hrair M. Babikian, M.D., "The Psychoanalytic Treatment of the Performing Artist: Su-

perego Aspects," *Journal of the American Academy of Psychoanalysis* 13, 1 (1985):148.

19. Bloom, *Developing Talent,* p. 61.

20. Abraham H. Maslow, *The Farther Reaches of Human Nature* (New York: Penguin, 1976), pp. 184–185.

21. Edward L. Walker, "Response," in the documentary report of the Ann Arbor Symposium, *National Symposium on the Applications of Psychology to the Teaching and Learning of Music* (Reston, VA: Music Educators National Conference, 1981), p. 129.

Chapter 5. The Preschool Student

1. The Better Baby Program is associated with the Institute for the Achievement of Human Potential (Philadelphia), directed by child development specialist Glenn Doman. The institute is also a proponent of the Suzuki method of talent education. See Glenn Doman, *How to Teach Your Baby to Read* (New York: Random House, 1964).

2. Ezra Bowen, "Trying to Jump-Start Toddlers," *Time* 127 (April 7, 1986):66.

3. Émile Jaques-Dalcroze, *Rhythm, Music and Education,* translated by Harold F. Rubinstein (London: The English Dalcroze Society, 1967), p. viii.

4. James A. Keene, *A History of Music Education in the United States* (Hanover, NH, and London: University Press of New England, 1982), pp. 333–334.

5. Robert M. Abramson, "Dalcroze-Based Improvisation," *Music Educator's Journal* 66 (January 1980):62.

6. Ibid., p. 63.

7. Keene, *A History of Music Education,* p. 335.

8. Margaret C. Brown and Betty K. Sommer, *Movement Education: Its Evolution and a Modern Approach* (Reading, MA: Addison-Wesley, 1969), p. 39.

9. Ruth Zinar, "Highlights of Thought in the History of Music Education. Part 11: Carl Orff," *The American Music Teacher* 33 (April–May 1984):20.

10. Keene, *A History of Music Education,* p. 344.

11. Ibid., p. 345.

12. Zinar, "Carl Orff," p. 19.

13. Lois Choksy, *The Kodály Method* (Englewood Cliffs, NJ: Prentice-Hall, 1974), p. 8.

14. Ibid., p. 9. These early collections were by Gyorgy Kerényi and Benjamin Rajeczky: *Enekes ABC* (1938), and *Eneklo Iskola* (A singing school; 1940).

15. Ibid., pp. 9–10.

16. This system of hand signals did not originate with Kodály. Most references acknowledge the English nineteenth-century musician and pedagogue John Curwen as the source. While Curwen did, in fact, inaugurate the hand signals (probably sometime around 1870), he was but the adaptor and developer of a *sol-fa* system of notation devised earlier by Sarah Glover. Kodály, in turn, accommodated the teaching strategies of Glover and Curwen as part of his own system of teaching vocal sight-reading. See Peggy D. Bennett, "Sarah Glover: A Forgotten Pioneer in Music Education," *The International Journal of Music Education* 4 (November 1984):27–35.

17. Ruth Zinar, "Highlights of Thought in the History of Music Education. Part 10: Zoltán Kodály as Music Educator and Patriot," *The American Music Teacher* 33 (April–May 1984):18.

18. Barbara Maris, "The Suzuki Method . . . and Piano School," *The Piano Quarterly,* no. 127 (Fall 1984):34.

19. Ibid., p. 39.

20. Ernest Van de Velde, *Méthode Rose* (Tours, France: Éditions Van de Velde, n.d. [Maris suggests after 1924]). Available in the United States through Ability Development, Box 887, Athens, OH 45701.

21. Lorraine Landefeld and Martha Stacy, "Response," *The Piano Quarterly,* no. 127 (Fall 1984):48.

22. Ibid., p. 49.

23. Maris, "The Suzuki Method," p. 36.

24. E. L. Lancaster, "The Yamaha Music Education System," *The Piano Quarterly,* no. 128 (Winter 1984–85):19–20.

25. Genichi Kawakami, *Children Are the Best Teachers* (Tokyo: Yamaha Music Foundation, 1981), p. 91.

26. Betty J. Looney, "Response," *The Piano Quarterly,* no. 128 (Winter 1984–85):32.

27. Lancaster, "The Yamaha Music Education System," p. 22.

28. Looney, "Response," p. 32.

29. Lancaster, "The Yamaha Music Education System," pp. 21–22.

30. Ibid., p. 19.

31. Barbara J. Alvarez, "An Historical Perspective of Early Childhood Music Education and Research in the United States," *The International Journal of Music Education* 5 (May 1985):9.

32. Louise Robyn, *Teaching Musical Notation with Picture Symbols* (Chicago: Robyn Teaching Service, 1932).

33. Louise Robyn, *Keyboard Town* (Bryn Mawr, PA: Ditson/Theodore Presser, 1934).

34. Ibid., p. iv.

35. Ada Richter, *Kindergarten Class Book* (New York: Witmark/Warner, 1937).

36. May B. Kelly Kirby and John Kirby, *Kindergarten Piano Method* (Oakville, Ontario: Frederick Harris, 1939).

37. Montessori was active in the early decades of the twentieth century. She taught disadvantaged children and developed a teaching method that would now be described as using discovery techniques.

38. Described later in this chapter. See "Some Preschool Piano Methods."

39. Ibid.

40. Landefeld and Stacy, "Response," p. 48.

Chapter 6. The Average-Age Student

1. W. S. B. Mathews, *Standard Graded Course of Studies* (Bryn Mawr, PA: Theodore Presser, 1892–1894).

2. John Williams, *Very First Piano Book* (Boston: Boston Music Co., 1925).

3. Dorothy Gaynor Blake, *Melody Book* (Cincinnati: Willis Music Co., 1916).

4. Angela Diller and Elizabeth Quaile, *First Solo Book* (Milwaukee: G. Schirmer/Hal Leonard, 1918).

5. Louise Robyn, *Teaching Musical Notation with Picture Symbols* (Chicago: Robyn Teaching Service, 1932); and *Keyboard Town* (Bryn Mawr, PA: Ditson/Theodore Presser, 1934).

6. Ernest Schelling, Gail Martin Haake, Charles J. Haake, and Osbourne McConathy, *Oxford Piano Course* (New York: Oxford University Press, 1928).

7. Raymond Burrows and Ella Mason Ahearn, *The Young Explorer at the Piano* (Cincinnati: Willis Music Co., 1941).

8. John Thompson, *Teaching Little Fingers to Play* (Cincinnati: Willis Music Co., 1936). Also John Thompson, *Modern Graded Piano Course* (Cincinnati: Willis Music Co., 1936–1942).

9. Frances Clark, *Time to Begin* and *Write and Play Time* (Secaucus, NJ: Summy-Birchard/Warner Bros., 1955).

10. In one method, however, use is made of a counting system that chants the name of each note (quar-ter, half-note, two-eighths) as well as the use of metric counting. Bernard Wagness, *Piano Course:* Book 1 (Bryn Mawr, PA: Ditson/Theodore Presser, 1938).

11. For further information about Dalcroze and eurhythmics see chapter 5, pp. 76–77.

12. Schelling, et al., *Oxford Piano Course; Teacher's First Manual* (New York: Oxford University Press, 1929).

13. Robyn, in fact, stated pointedly that "during the early period, children should not be taught to count time-values." *Keyboard Town,* p. ii.

14. Marienne Uszler, "The American Beginning Piano Method: A Pause and a Look Back," *The Piano Quarterly,* no. 126 (Summer 1984): 26.

15. For further information about reinforcement in the conceptual learning cycle see chapter 4, p. 60.

16. Abby Whiteside, *Indispensables of Piano Playing,* 2d ed. (New York: Coleman-Ross, 1961); Grosvenor W. Cooper and Leonard B. Meyer, *The Rhythmic Structure of Music* (Chicago: University of Chicago Press, 1960); Marilyn Pflederer Zimmerman, "Percept and Concept: Implications of Piaget," *The Music Educators Journal* 56 (February 1970); Max W. Camp, *Developing Piano Performance* (Chapel Hill, NC: Hinshaw Music, 1981).

17. Mathews, *Standard Graded Course:* Grade 1, pp. 2–3.

18. William Mason, *Touch and Technic* (Bryn Mawr, PA: Theodore Presser, 1890–1892).

19. John Williams, *First Year at the Piano* (Bryn Mawr, PA: Theodore Presser, 1924; rev. ed. 1942), pp. 3–5.

20. Dorothy Gaynor Blake, *Keyboard Secrets* (Cincinnati: Willis Music Co., 1927); *First Steps in the Use of the Pedal* (Cincinnati: Willis Music Co., 1925).

21. Louise Robyn, *Technic Tales:* Books 1 and 2 (Bryn Mawr, PA: Ditson/Theodore Presser, 1927, 1930).

22. Schelling, et al., *Teacher's First Manual,* pp. 55–56.

23. Ibid., pp. 59–60.

24. John Thompson, *Keyboard Attacks* (Cincinnati: Willis Music Co., 1936); *First Grade Etudes* (Cincinnati: Willis Music Co., 1939).

25. John Schaum, *Hanon-Schaum* (Miami: CPP/Belwin, 1946); *Technic Tricks* (Miami: CPP/Belwin, 1950).

26. David Hirschberg, *Technic is Fun* (New York: Musichord, 1941 ff).

27. June Weybright, *Technic for Pianists* (Miami: CPP/Belwin, 1947).

28. Edna Mae Burnam, *A Dozen a Day* (Cincinnati: Willis Music Co., 1950 ff).

29. Guy Maier and Herbert Bradshaw, *Thinking Fingers* (Miami: CPP/Belwin, 1954).

30. Thaddeus P. Giddings and Wilma A. Gilman, *Public School Class Method for the Piano* (Boston: Oliver Ditson, 1919); Helen Curtis, *Piano Class Course* (Kansas City, MO: publisher unknown, n.d.); Helen Curtis, *Fundamental Piano Series* (Chicago: Roosa, 1926).

31. Schelling, et al., *Oxford Piano Course.* Each line of printed music is a phrase even to the extent of having incomplete measures at the end of one line and the beginning of the next. See pp. 11, 16, 18, 23.

32. Burrows and Ahearn, *The Young Explorer at the Piano;* also, *Young America at the Piano* (Cincinnati: Willis Music Co., 1945, 1946, 1948).

33. John Thompson, *Modern Graded Piano Course,* see note 8 above.

34. Leila Fletcher, *Theory Papers,* books 1–3 (Boston: Boston Music Co., 1943, 1946, 1947).

35. John Schaum, *Theory Lessons,* books 1–3 (Miami: CPP/Belwin, 1946); *Harmony Lessons,* books 1, 2 (Miami: CPP/Belwin, 1949).

36. John Thompson, *Note Speller* (Cincinnati: Willis Music Co., 1946); *Scale Speller* (Cincinnati: Willis Music Co., 1947).

37. Marvin Kahn, *Theory Papers,* books 1–3 (Miami: CPP/Belwin, 1955, 1958); *Note-Speller and Ear-Training Book* (Miami: CPP/Belwin, 1959).

38. Frances Clark, *Time to Begin, Write and Play, Tune Time, Technic Time* (Secaucus, NJ: Summy-Birchard/Warner Bros., 1955); Robert Pace, *Music for Piano* (6 books: 1961, 1962, 1969), *Skills and Drills* (4 books: 1961, 1962), *Recital Series* (sheet music, various dates) (Milwaukee: Lee Roberts/Hal Leonard); James Bastien and Jane Smisor Bastien, *Pre-reading Experiences* (1963), *Reading Books* (3 books: 1963, 1964), *Writing* (3 books: 1963, 1964), *Magic Finger Technic* (3 books: 1966). San Diego: Kjos West.

39. Bert Konowitz, *Jazz for Piano,* (Milwaukee: Lee Roberts/Hal Leonard, 1962); David Kraehenbuehl, *Jazz and Blues* (Secaucus, NJ: Summy-Birchard/Warner Bros., 1963); David Carr Glover, *Jazz (Etc) on 88* (Miami: CPP/Belwin, 1975).

40. *The Piano Quarterly,* 142 (Summer 1988): See "Reviews of Educational Jazz Keyboard Materials," 11–14.

41. To cite one instance: A method that uses the middle-C approach to the teaching of reading is unlikely to include reading on two, three, or four lines prior to the introduction of grand-staff reading.

42. Each method, for example, expects the student to perform five-finger legato. Whether this playing technique is presented at the outset of study, or results from a gradual expansion of two- or three-finger legato, is information that can be identified by a glance at the summary of any individual method reviewed.

Chapter 7. The Adult Student

1. Andrew M. Brown, "Teaching Piano to Adults," *Clavier* 28 (May–June 1989): 24–25. Brenda Dillon, "The Adult Music Student: Bridging the Gap Between Wishing and Doing," *American Music Teacher* 39 (October–November 1989): 22–23; 55. Teresa

D. Marciano, "A Sociologist's Exploration," *American Music Teacher* 39 (June–July 1990): 24–27. Marienne Uszler, "Andragogy?" *American Music Teacher* 39 (June–July 1990): 12–15. Three videotapes, "The Adult Piano Student and You," "Teaching Adult Piano Students," "Make It Come True," are available from the National Piano Foundation, 4020 McEwen, Suite 105, Dallas, TX.

2. Ernest Schelling, Charles Haake, Gail Martin Haake, and Osbourne McConathy, *The Beginner's Book for Older Pupils,* (London & New York: Oxford University Press, 1929).

3. Ella Mason Ahearn, Dorothy Gaynor Blake, and Raymond Burrows, *The Adult Explorer at the Piano* (Cincinnati: Willis Music Co., 1937).

4. Ibid., p. iii.

5. Raymond Burrows, *Piano Series for the Older Beginner* (Cincinnati: Willis Music Co., 1950).

6. Bernard Wagness, *Adult Piano Course* (Chicago: Rubank, 1942); John Thompson, *The Adult Preparatory Book* (Cincinnati: Willis Music Co., 1943); John Schaum, *Adult Piano Course* (Miami: CPP/Belwin, 1946); Michael Aaron, *Adult Piano Course* (Miami: CPP/Belwin, 1947); Maxwell Eckstein, *Adult Piano Book* (New York: Carl Fischer, 1953); Ada Richter, *The Older Student* (Secaucus, NJ: Witmark/Warner Bros., 1956).

7. Russell N. Squire and Virginia Mountney, *Class Piano for the Adult Beginner* (Englewood Cliffs, NJ: Prentice-Hall, 1964); Robert Pace, *Music for Piano for the Older Beginner* (Milwaukee: Lee Roberts/Hal Leonard, 1967); James Lyke, Ron Elliston, Elisabeth Hartline, *Keyboard Musicianship: Group Piano for Adults* (Champaign, IL: Stipes, 1969); Alex Zimmerman, Russell Hayton, and Dorothy Priesing, *Basic Piano* (Dubuque, IA: William C. Brown, 1969).

8. David Carr Glover, *Adult Piano Student* (Miami: CPP/Belwin, 1970); Frances Clark, Louise Goss, and Roger Grove, *Keyboard Musician* (Secaucus, NJ: Summy-Birchard/Warner Bros., 1976); James Bastien and Jane Smisor Bastien, *The Older Beginner Piano Course* (San Diego: Kjos West, 1977).

9. Clark, et al., *Keyboard Musician.*

10. James Lyke, *Ensemble Music for Group Piano* (Champaign, IL: Stipes, 1971).

11. James Lyke, Ron Elliston, Tony Caramia, *First-Year Piano Patterns (With Rhythm Background)* (Champaign, IL: Stipes, 1974).

12. Allen Giles, *Beginning Piano - Adult Approach* (Bryn Mawr, PA: Theodore Presser, 1978); *Telecourse Student Study Guide,* (Bryn Mawr, PA: Theodore Presser, 1979).

13. Malcolm Knowles, *The Adult Learner: A Neglected Species,* 3d ed. (Houston: Gulf Publishing Co., 1984), pp. 57–59.

14. W. Timothy Gallwey, *The Inner Game of Tennis* (New York: Bantam Books, 1979), p. 13.

15. Raymond J. Wlodkowski, *Enhancing Adult Motivation to Learn* (San Francisco: Jossey-Bass Publishers, 1988), pp. 22–28.

16. K. Patricia Cross, *Adults As Learners* (San Francisco: Jossey-Bass Publishers, 1981), pp. 120–122.

Chapter 8. Repertoire and the Intermediate Student

1. Muzio Clementi's Sonatina in C Major Op. 36, No. 1 appears in the following volumes: James Bastien, *Sonatina Favorites* (book 1); A. Nikolaev, et al., *The Russian School of*

Piano Playing (book 2); John Thompson, *Modern Piano Course* (book 3); *Suzuki Piano School* (book 3); Frances Clark, *Piano Literature* (book 3); Denes Agay, *Learning to Play Piano* (book 4); Michael Aaron, *Piano Course* (book 4); Walter and Carol Noona, *Gifted Pianist* (book 4); Walter and Carol Noona, *Classical Performer* (level A).

2. Several resources furnish information and lists. Check appendix 2, "Resources: Intermediate Literature." Note especially Albergo and Alexander, *Intermediate Repertoire: A Guide for Teaching,* 2d ed., rev. (Champaign, IL: C & R Music Resources, 1988); Fuszek, *Piano Music in Collections: An Index* (Detroit: Information Coordinators, 1982); Hinson, *Guide to the Pianist's Repertoire,* 2d ed., rev. (Bloomington, IN: Indiana University Press, 1987), "Anthologies and Collections," pp. 367–398.

Chapter 9. Technique and the Intermediate Student

1. Annie Curwen, *The Teacher's Guide to Mrs. Curwen's Pianoforte Method* (London: J. Curwen & Sons, 1886), p. 5.

2. Josef Hofmann, "What Is the Purpose of Music Study?" *The Etude* (November 1944):617.

Chapter 11. The Transfer Student

1. See chap. 2, pp. 20–21.

2. Ibid., pp. 18–19.

3. Marion Brown Stone, "Transfer Students' Troubles, Part 1," *Clavier* 22 (September 1983):39.

4. Frances Clark, "Questions and Answers," *Clavier* 24 (October 1985):56.

5. Another recommended practice is to have the parent prepare a list of music already available in the home, some of which may also be used as sight-reading material. See Stone, "Transfer Students' Troubles," p. 39.

6. See chap. 6, p. 11.

7. See chap. 4, pp. 53–55. Note the commentary regarding phases of learning, especially that of the reinforcement phase.

8. Frances Clark, "Questions and Answers," *Clavier* 23 (May–June, 1984):52.

9. Ruth S. Edwards, "The Independently Prepared Piano," *The American Music Teacher* 35 (January 1986):43.

10. Carolyn Britton, "The Practice Journal," *Clavier* 23 (September 1984): 28–29. Burton Kaplan, *The Musician's Practice Log,* New York (P.O. Box 1068, Cathedral Station, NY 10025): Perception Development Techniques, 1985.

11. Sandra Bostrom, "Diagnostic Teaching," *The American Music Teacher* 34 (June–July 1985):23.

12. Examples that include both syllabi and print materials: Associated Board of the Royal Schools of Music (London), available from Theodore Presser, Presser Place, Bryn Mawr, PA 19010; Royal Conservatory of Music (Toronto), available from Frederick Harris Music, 340 Nagel Drive, Buffalo, NY 14225-4731; *Irl Allison Piano Library,* appropriate for the national auditions of the National Guild of Piano Teachers, available from Willis Music, 7380 Industrial Road, Florence, KY 41042. Examples of syllabi only: National Federation of Music Clubs, 310 South Michigan Avenue, Chicago, IL

60604; American Music Scholarship Association *Piano Syllabus,* 1826 Carew Tower, Cincinnati, OH 45202; Australian Music Education Board, available from Warren Thomson (Chair, AMEB Board) New South Wales Conservatorium of Music, Macquarie Street, Sydney, N. S. W. 2000.

13. Maxwell Music Evaluation File, Update Notebook, Composer Collection, 1245 Kalmia, Boulder, CO 80302. While not a periodical, the Maxwell Music Evaluation materials offer extensive information about piano-teaching literature, including grading, teaching suggestions, best uses, number of pages and pieces, recital pleasers, cross-referencing, and so on.

14. Publishers offering review packets: Piano Review Service, Hinshaw Music, Inc., P.O. Box 470, Chapel Hill, NC 27514; Piano Teachers Association, Willis Music, 7380 Industrial Road, Florence, KY 41042; Piano Preview Plan, Hal Leonard Publishing Corp., 8112 West Bluemound Road, P.O. Box 13819, Milwaukee, WI 53213. A dealer that offers review packets: Texas Music Supply, Box 620, Pittsburg, TX 75686. An organization offering a review library: National Piano Foundation, 4020 McEwen, Suite 105, Dallas, TX 75244-5019. All of the above charge some fees and have different privileges.

15. Publishers' newsletters: *Noteworthy,* Kjos West, 4382 Jutland Drive, San Diego, CA 92117; *Keynotes,* CPP/Belwin, 15800 NW 48th Ave., Miami, FL 33014; *Update,* Hinshaw Music, Inc., P.O. Box 470, Chapel Hill, NC, 27514; *Myklas Times,* Myklas Music Press, P.O. Box 929, Boulder, CO 80306. Dealer newsletter: Ralph Pierce Music, Division of Morton Burt Music Center, 616 North Azusa Avenue, West Covina, CA 91791.

16. Richard Chronister, "Getting Every Student Ready to Transfer," *Keyboard Arts Magazine* (Winter 1987):10–11.

Chapter 13. The Keyboard Pedagogy Major

1. Pedagogy is defined in *Webster's New World Dictionary,* 2d ed. (Cleveland: William Collins, 1979), p. 1046, as "the art or science of teaching, especially instruction in teaching methods." The etymology of the word more aptly underscores its true meaning. *Paidagogos* derives from two components: *pais* (child) and *agein* (to lead).

2. Marienne Uszler and Frances Larimer, *The Piano Pedagogy Major in the College Curriculum: A Handbook of Information and Guidelines.* Part 1, *The Undergraduate Piano Pedagogy Major* (Princeton, NJ: The National Conference on Piano Pedagogy, 1984). Available from The National Conference on Piano Pedagogy, 51 White Pine Lane, Princeton, NJ 08540.

3. *Handbook* (Reston, VA: National Association of Schools of Music, 1985).

4. Uszler and Larimer, *The Piano Pedagogy Major.* Part 2, *The Graduate Piano Pedagogy Major* (1986), p. 26.

5. Uszler and Larimer, *The Piano Pedagogy Major.* Part 2, *The Graduate Piano Pedagogy Major,* pp. 7–25.

6. Available from The National Conference on Piano Pedagogy, 51 White Pine Lane, Princeton, NJ 08540. This directory began in the 1988 conference proceedings. It will be updated bienially in subsequent conference proceedings.

Chapter 17. From Diruta to C.P.E. Bach

1. Girolamo Diruta, *Il Transilvano,* translated and edited by Murray C. Bradshaw and Edward J. Soehnlen. (Ottawa, Canada: Institute of Medieval Music, 1984).

2. Francois Couperin, *L'Art de toucher le clavecin,* edited and translated by Margery Halford (Van Nuys, CA: Alfred Publishing Co., 1974).

3. Jean Philippe Rameau, *Code de musique pratique, ou méthodes pour apprendre la musique* (Paris: De l'Imprimerie Royale, 1760); *Méthode sur la mécanique des doigts sur le clavessin* (Paris, 1724).

4. Friedrich Wilhelm Marpurg, *Anleitung zum Klavierspielen der schöneren Ausübung der heutigen Zeit gemäss entworfen* (Berlin: Haude und Spener, 1755); *Die Kunst das Klavier zu spielen* (Berlin: Haude und Spener, 1751).

5. Forkel comments on Bach's teaching in *The Bach Reader,* edited by Hans T. David and Arthur Mendel (New York: W.W. Norton, 1945).

6. Carl Philipp Emanuel Bach, *Essay on the True Art of Playing Keyboard Instruments,* translated and edited by William J. Mitchell (New York: W.W. Norton, 1949).

Chapter 18. From Türk to Deppe

1. Daniel Gottlob Türk, *Klavierschule oder anweisung zum Klavierspielen fur Lehrer und Lernende, mit kritischen anmerkungen,* facsimile edition (Kassel: Barenreiter, 1962).

2. Muzio Clementi, *Introduction to the Art of Playing the Pianoforte* (New York: Da Capo Press, 1973).

3. Johann Nepomuk Hummel, *A Complete Theoretical and Practical Course of Instructions on the Art of Playing the Piano Forte Commencing with the Simplest Elementary Principles and Including Every Information Requisite to the Most Finished Style of Performance* (London: T. Boosey, 1828).

4. Carl Czerny, *Complete Theoretical and Practical Piano Forte School, from the First Rudiments of Playing to the Highest and Most Refined State of Cultivation: with the Requisite Numerous Examples, Newly and Expressly Composed for the Occasion,* 3 vols., Op. 500 (London: R. Cocks, 1839).

5. Friedrich Wilhelm Kalkbrenner, *Méthode pour apprendre le piano a l'aide du guide mains,* Op. 108 (Paris: J. Meissonnier Fils, 1830).

6. Adolph Kullak, *The Aesthetics of Pianoforte-Playing,* translated by Theodore Baker and edited by Hans Bischoff (New York: Da Capo Press, 1973).

7. Amy Fay, *Music-Study in Germany,* reprint, edited by Fay Pierce, (New York: Dover Publications, 1965).

8. Elisabeth Caland, *Die Ausnützung der Kraftquellen beim Klavierspiel, physiologisch-anatomische Betrachtungen* (Magdeburg, Germany: Heinrichshofen's Verlag, 1922).

9. C. A. Ehrenfechter, *Technical Study in the Art of Pianoforte-Playing (Deppe's Principles)* (London: William Reeves, 1891).

Chapter 19. Liszt and Leschetizky

1. Walter Beckett, *Liszt* (London: M. M. Dent & Sons, 1956), p. 4.

2. Elyse Mach, ed., *The Liszt Studies* (Milwaukee, WI: Associated Music/Hal Leonard, 1973). Quoted from "A Diary of Franz Liszt as Teacher," p. xiii, translated by Elyse Mach from Madame Auguste Boissier, *Liszt als Lehrer* (Berlin: Zsolnay, 1930).

3. William Mason, *Memories of a Musical Life,* reprint (New York: Da Capo Press, 1970), p. 81.

4. Arthur Friedheim, *Life and Liszt: The Recollections of a Concert Pianist* (New York: Taplinger, 1961), p. 48.

5. Amy Fay, *Music-Study in Germany,* reprint, edited by Fay Pierce (New York: Dover Publications, 1965), p. 31.

6. Mach, "A Diary of Franz Liszt," p. xv.

7. Ibid., p. xvii.

8. Ibid., p. xxiv.

9. Herbert Westerby, *Liszt, Composer, and His Piano Works* (London: William Reeves, 1936), p. 288.

10. Mach, "A Diary of Franz Liszt," p. xviii.

11. Ibid., p. xxiv.

12. Ibid., p. xix.

13. Julio Esteban, *Liszt Technical Exercises* (Van Nuys, CA: Alfred Music, 1971); Elyse Mach, ed., *The Liszt Studies,* ibid.; Imre Mezo, *Technical Studies for Piano,* Vols. 1–3 (Farmingdale, NY: Editio Musica Budapest/Boosey & Hawkes, 1983).

14. Ethel Newcomb, *Leschetizky as I Knew Him* (New York: Da Capo Press, 1967), p. 107.

15. Quoted by James Francis Cooke, *Great Pianists on Piano Playing* (Bryn Mawr: Theodore Presser, 1913), p. 83.

16. Ibid., p. 355.

17. Malwine Brée, *The Groundwork of the Leschetizky Method,* translated by Theodore Baker (New York: G. Schirmer, 1902).

18. Quoted by Countesse Angèle Potocka, *Theodor Leschetizky, an Intimate Study of the Man and the Musician,* translated by Geneviève Seymour Lincoln (New York: The Century Co., 1903), p. 89.

Chapter 20. Breithaupt and Matthay

1. Rudolf M. Breithaupt, *Die natürliche Klaviertechnik,* 2 vols. (Leipzig: C.F. Kahnt Nachfolger, 1905, 1907). Vol. 2 was translated into English by John Bernhoff, published by the same publisher in 1909.

2. Friedrich Adolf Steinhausen, *Die physiologischen Fehler und Umgestaltung der Klaviertechnik* (Leipzig: Breitkopf und Härtel, 1905).

3. William Townsend, *Balance of Arm in Piano Technique* (London: Bosworth and Co., 1890).

4. Maria Levinskaya, *The Levinskaya System of Pianoforte Technique and Tone-Colour Through Mental and Muscular Control* (London and Toronto: J.M. Dent and Sons, 1930).

5. Tobias Matthay, *The Act of Touch in All Its Diversity; An Analysis and Synthesis of Pianoforte Tone-Production* (London: Bosworth and Co., 1903).

6. Ambrose Coviello, *What Matthay Meant, His Musical and Technical Teachings Clearly Explained and Self-Indexed* (London; Bosworth and Co., n.d.).

7. Tobias Matthay, *Musical Interpretation, Its Laws and Principles, and Their Application in Teaching and Performing* (London: Joseph Williams, 1913). Perhaps the most accessible volume of Matthay's writings is *The Visible and Invisible in Pianoforte Technique, Being a Digest of the Author's Technical Teachings Up To Date* (London: Oxford University Press, 1932).

Chapter 21. Ortmann and Schultz

1. Thomas Fielden, *The Science of Pianoforte Technique* (London: MacMillan and Co., 1927).
2. James Ching, *Piano Technique: Foundation Principles* (London: Chappell, 1934).
3. Otto Ortmann, *The Physical Basis of Piano Touch and Tone: An Experimental Investigation of the Effect of the Player's Touch upon the Tone of the Piano* (London: Kegan Paul, Trench, Trubner, and Co., 1925).
4. Otto Ortmann, *The Physiological Mechanics of Piano Technique: An Experimental Study of the Nature of Muscular Action As Used in Piano Playing, and the Effects Thereof upon the Piano Key and Piano Tone* (London: Kegan Paul, Trench, Trubner and Co., 1929); reprint (New York: Dutton and Co., 1962).
5. Arnold Schultz, *The Riddle of the Pianist's Finger and Its Relationship to a Touch-Scheme* (New York: Carl Fischer, 1936).

Chapter 22. Other Twentieth-Century Pedagogy

1. Walter Gieseking and Karl Leimer, *Piano Technique* (New York: Dover Publications, 1972).
2. Abby Whiteside, *Indispensables of Piano Playing* (New York: Coleman-Ross Co., 1955).
3. Abby Whiteside, *Mastering the Chopin Etudes and Other Essays,* edited by Joseph Prostakoff and Sophia Rosoff (New York: Charles Scribner's Sons, 1969).
4. William S. Newman, *The Pianist's Problems: A Modern Approach to Efficient Practice and Musicianly Performance* (New York: Harper & Brothers, 1956).
5. Luigi Bonpensiere, *New Pathways to Piano Technique: A Study of the Relations Between Mind and Body with Special Reference to Piano Playing* (New York: Philosophical Library, 1952).
6. Heinrich Neuhaus, *The Art of Piano Playing,* translated by K.A. Leibovitch (London: Barrie and Jenkins, 1973).
7. József Gát, *The Technique of Piano Playing,* translated by István Kleszky, 2d ed. (London: Collet's Holding, 1965).
8. George Kochevitsky, *The Art of Piano Playing: A Scientific Approach* (Secaucus, NJ: Summy-Birchard/Warner Bros., 1967).
9. Gyorgy Sandor, *On Piano Playing* (New York: Schirmer Books, 1981).

Chapter 23. Great Pianists of Today

1. Elyse Mach, *Great Pianists Speak for Themselves,* 2 vols. (New York: Dodd, Mead, 1987, 1988).

Chapter 24. Keyboard Teaching and New Technology

1. For an informative introduction to synthesizing techniques, see Steven Powell, "The ABCs of Synthesizers," *Music Educators Journal* 73 (December 1987); 27–31.

2. See Craig Anderton, *MIDI For Musicians* (New York: Amsco Publications, 1986) for an in-depth discussion of technical and practical aspects of MIDI.

3. The intellectual debt to Seymour Papert, *Mindstorms* (New York: Basic Books, 1980), will be evident to readers familiar with this book.

4. Baroque contrapuntal works obviously lend themselves to contrasting voices, but an example of a Romantic piece that could be successfully "orchestrated" is the Mendelssohn *Song Without Words,* Op. 53, No. 1. The three distinct textures at the beginning all suggest contrasting colors. The addition of a fourth voice in measures 9–10 and the changes in texture in measures 23–24 and 28–29 both affect the choices of sounds for each part, and throw open to discussion the relationship of this fourth voice to the others.

5. *Musique Concrete* is the use of recorded natural or pre-existing sounds in musical compositions. Composers of *Musique Concrete* include Edgar Varèse, Luciano Berio, and Karlheinz Stockhausen.

6. Jon H. Appleton, quoted in "Computers are Giving Music Educators New Sounds and New Ways to Teach," *Chronicle of Higher Education* (October 21, 1987): 14–16.

7. *Con brio,* newsletter of the Music Teachers National Association (September, 1988).

8. Kenneth Rumery, "Bringing Your Classroom On-Line," *Music Educators Journal,* 71 (January 1985); 21–24).

9. *TESS: The Educational Software Selector* (New York : Columbia University, Teachers College Press, 1985) contains useful forms for helping keep track of courseware. The publisher has granted permission to reproduce these forms for personal or institutional use if the permission is requested.

10. For lists of hardware capability, see Fred T. Hofstetter, *Computer Literacy for Musicians* (Englewood Cliffs, NJ: Prentice-Hall, 1987), pp. 67–77.

INDEX